Holding Juno

HOLDING

MARK ZUEHLKE

JUNO

CANADA'S HEROIC DEFENCE
OF THE D-DAY BEACHES:
JUNE 7-12, 1944

Douglas & McIntyre
Vancouver/Toronto/Berkeley

Douglas & McIntyre
2323 Quebec Street, Suite 201
Vancouver, British Columbia
Canada v5t 4s7
www.douglas-mcintyre.com

National Library of Canada Cataloguing in Publication Data
Zuehlke, Mark
Holding Juno : Canada's heroic defence of the D-Day beaches,
June 7–12, 1944 / Mark Zuehlke.

Includes bibliographical references and index.
ISBN–13: 978-1-55365-102-4
ISBN–10: 1-55365-102-2

1. World War, 1939–1945—Campaigns—France—Normandy.
2. Canada. Canadian Army—History—World War, 1939–1945. I. Title.

D756.5.N6z825 2005 940.54'21422 c2005-901195-5

Library of Congress information is available upon request

Editing by Elizabeth McLean
Jacket and text design by Peter Cocking
Jacket photograph Private Hole, LAC PA-177100
Typesetting by Rhonda Ganz
Printed and bound in Canada by Friesens
Printed on acid-free paper
Distributed in the U.S. by Publishers Group West

We gratefully acknowledge the financial support of the
Canada Council for the Arts, the British Columbia Arts Council,
and the Government of Canada through the Book Publishing Industry
Development Program (BPIDP) for our publishing activities.

OTHER MILITARY HISTORY BY MARK ZUEHLKE

Juno Beach: Canada's D-Day Victory: June 6, 1944 *

*The Gothic Line: Canada's Month of Hell in World War 11 Italy**

The Liri Valley: Canada's World War 11 Breakthrough to Rome *

Ortona: Canada's Epic World War 11 Battle *

*The Canadian Military Atlas: The Nation's Battlefields from the
French and Indian Wars to Kosovo* (with C. Stuart Daniel)

The Gallant Cause: Canadians in the Spanish Civil War, 1936–1939

* Available from Douglas & McIntyre

When will the earth grow weary of the shock
Of this chaos? When, with impatient hands,
Will it obliterate the shame and mock
Of desolation glutton war demands?

BOMBARDIER W.S. BEIRNES,
3RD CANADIAN INFANTRY DIVISION

Valour is of no service, chance rules all,
And the bravest often fall by the hands of cowards.

TACITUS, *THE HISTORIES*

If I get out of this, I'm not going to take shit from anyone.

LIEUTENANT BILL MCCORMICK,
IST HUSSARS

[CONTENTS]

PREFACE

IN THE SPRING OF 2004, on the sixtieth anniversary of the Allied invasion of Normandy, my book *Juno Beach: Canada's D-Day Victory: June 6, 1944* was released. Detailing the Canadian experience in that momentous event, it spanned a single day. My original plan had been to carry the story beyond June 6 and include the bitter fighting that raged between June 7 and June 12 as the Germans attempted to cast the invasion forces back into the icy English Channel. But it had been with good reason that Cornelius Ryan entitled his book on the invasion *The Longest Day*. So much transpired to so many Canadians during the landings, their fierce battle to win the sand, and then the deadly advance inland towards final objectives that the book threatened to grow to Tolstoy-like thickness. Phone calls were made, e-mails exchanged, and on a chilly December day my publisher Scott McIntyre and I agreed to divide the story. We opted to focus the spotlight of the second book on a period of history normally compressed, as I had originally planned, onto the back end of books about D-Day, or barely mentioned in broader works that cover the Normandy campaign or the entire war. *Holding Juno* is the result—the second in a planned series of works covering the Normandy campaign.

To my knowledge, this is the first book purely dedicated to Canada's role in the six days dubbed the bridgehead battle by Colonel C.P. Stacey, the Department of National Defence official historian of

I

the World War II Northwest Europe campaign. I embarked on this idea with some trepidation. Did enough happen to the Canadians during those days to warrant lengthy treatment? Would there be enough historical documentation to unravel the ebb and flow of battle? Were these days a period that war veterans remembered with any clarity?

I soon determined the answer to all these questions was an unqualified yes. Many veterans described this fight as the toughest they ever lived through, worse than D-Day itself. Delving into the unit war diaries, after-action reports, and regimental histories unearthed a vast amount of material. As had been the case with my other books on Canada's experiences in World War II, the problem was not finding too little compelling material but rather discerning what must be set aside. It is especially difficult to decide that various accounts by veterans have to be excluded for simple want of space.

As in earlier books, I have sifted veteran accounts here through the filter of official records generated by the military at the time, in order to create a narrative that honours their remembrance while remaining historically accurate. This is not a purely oral history where the story is confined to the memory of participants without interpretation or expansion. Such works have their place and merit, but often lack context that would enable readers unfamiliar with the period to align the experiences into an understandable whole. As is often the case, particularly as veteran memory fades with the passage of years, few can recall in full detail what they and comrades endured. Like creating a patchwork quilt, it is necessary to stitch one recollected detail in front of, alongside, or behind incidents provided by other veterans, anchored together by historical record to create a fully realized account.

I leave it to the men who lived through those days when none knew if they would be able to hold Juno Beach and ensure the invasion's success to decide whether I came close to getting it right. They buried friends and brothers in the Norman soil and carried home with them countless images and emotions experienced during those terrible days of battle.

ACKNOWLEDGEMENTS

WITHOUT THE WILLINGNESS of veterans to delve into the past and relate often painful, long-buried memories, a book such as this would not be possible. My thanks to all who did, and they are listed in the bibliography. Once again, I am greatly indebted to John Gregory Thompson of Ingersoll, Ontario for his interviews of veterans scattered throughout the southern part of that province. Ken MacLeod of Langley, B.C. shared his large collection of video and audio interviews conducted over many years. John Bardsley of Victoria took on the task of interviewing other veterans. At Royal Military College, Major Michael Boire provided interviews with lieutenant colonels Don Mingay and Ernest Côté—key officers in 3rd Canadian Infantry Division. Michael also dug into the RMC records on my behalf and unearthed much material on the division's three infantry brigadiers.

David O'Keefe at the Black Watch Regimental Museum in Montreal provided essential information on Brigadier Ken Blackader that I would not otherwise have found. Staff and volunteers at other regimental museums and archives also generously assisted where they could. The Royal Canadian Military Institute in Toronto kindly opened their excellent library to my study. In Ottawa, staff at the Department of National Defence's Directorate of Heritage and History, the Canadian War Museum library and archives, and Library and

Archives Canada were as essential in helping me track down key documents. Carol Reid at the war museum's archives deserves special mention. As does Roger Sarty, for helping me lay hands on vital documents covering the Royal Canadian Navy's role in the bridgehead battles. In Victoria, staff of the University of Victoria's Special Collections were once again a pleasure to work with and Doctor Reginald Roy's collection is a treasure. A World War II veteran, the former Military History Chair at UVic used this position wisely, creating a notable library collection and vast oral and documentary archive.

My friend Alex McQuarrie helped out yet another time by translating various documents written in French. Before he passed away, Colonel Tony Poulin did likewise. Blessed with a keen memory and soldier's knowledge of strategy and tactics, he provided counsel in understanding how men acted and felt during World War II combat. Also generously contributing in this way was another friend, the late Colonel Strome Galloway. Readers will find some of the war experiences of these two brave soldiers in my three books detailing Canada's role in the Italian Campaign.

Professor Jack Granatstein permitted consultation of his files on Major General Rod Keller at York University.

Rosalie A. Hartigan permitted me to quote passages from her late husband Dan Hartigan's book, *A Rising of Courage*. Also used with permission from *Battle Diary: From D-Day and Normandy to the Zuider Zee*, by Charles Martin, are several passages by this former Queen's Own Rifles Company Sergeant Major. Jean Portugal's monumental seven-volume oral history *We Were There* was an incredible resource and it was a pleasure to meet this fine journalist and oral historian at the Royal Canadian Military Institute. The Royal Winnipeg Rifles Association (British Columbia Association) generously donated a copy of their compiled collection of veteran accounts entitled *Perspectives*. Similarly, the Regina Rifles provided *The Recollections of the Regina Rifles*.

K.O. Moore and his wife went to great effort to track down the negative of the photograph taken of Moore and his bomber crew in order to provide a print for use in this book.

Portions of this book were researched and developed in the fall of 2003 while I was writer-in-residence at Berton House in Dawson, Yukon. Thanks to Berton House Writer's Society, the late Pierre Berton, and the Canada Council for the Arts for this opportunity.

The dedication of my publisher Scott McIntyre at Douglas & McIntyre to supporting the production of books about Canada's role in World War II has been vitally important. Many thanks to everyone on the D&M team for making the books look so good.

Once again, Elizabeth McLean, my editor, agreed to tackle another book on battle. You're a gem. C. Stuart Daniel made the battlefield and movements of troops easier to visualize with his, as always, fine map work. Carolyn Swayze, agent extraordinaire, continues to deftly manage financial and contractual complexities, enabling me to concentrate on writing.

Last, but most importantly, I am blessed with the companionship of Frances Backhouse and look forward to having her by my side while we explore many more battlefields.

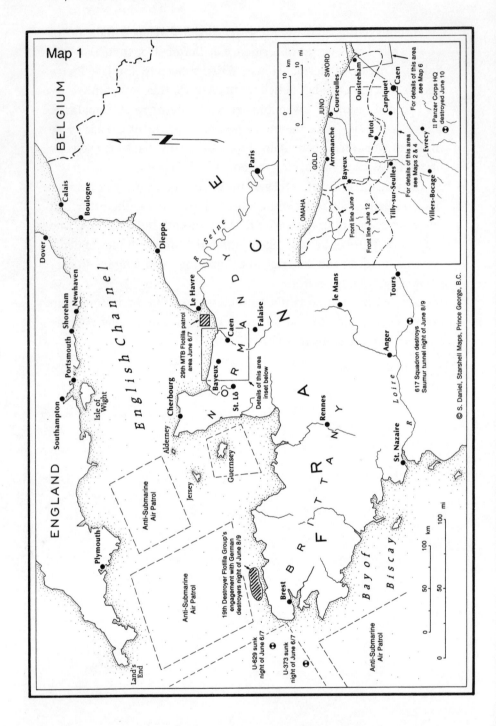

Map 1

BELGIUM

Calais

Boulogne

Dover

Dieppe

R Seine

Paris

ENGLAND

English Channel

Southampton

Plymouth

Portsmouth

Shoreham

Newhaven

Isle of
Wight

Land's
End

Le Havre

Caen

Falaise

Bayeux

St. Lô

Cherbourg

Alderney

Jersey

Guernsey

N O R M A N D Y

le Mans

Anger

Tours

R Loire

Rennes

St. Nazaire

B R I T T A N Y

Brest

Bay of Biscay

29th MTB Flotilla patrol
area June 6/7

Details of this area
inset below

Anti-Submarine
Air Patrol

Anti-Submarine
Air Patrol

Anti-Submarine
Air Patrol

19th Destroyer Flotilla Group's
engagement with German
destroyers night of June 8/9

U-629 sunk
night of June 6/7

U-373 sunk
night of June 6/7

617 Squadron destroys
Saumur tunnel night of June 8/9

0   50   100   km

0   50   100   mi

© S. Daniel, Starshell Maps, Prince George, B.C.

OMAHA

GOLD

JUNO

SWORD

Arromanche

Courseulles

Ouistreham

Bayeux

Putot

Carpiquet

Caen

Tilly-sur-Seulles

Evrecy

Villers-Bocage

II Panzer Corps HQ
destroyed June 10

For details of this area
see Map 6

For details of this area
see Maps 2 & 4

Front line June 7

Front line June 12

0   10   km

0   10   mi

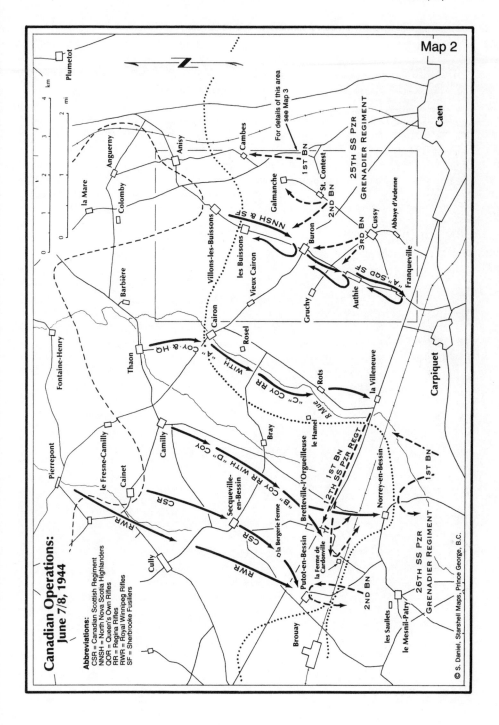

Map 2

Canadian Operations: June 7/8, 1944

Abbreviations:
CSR = Canadian Scottish Regiment
NNSH = North Nova Scotia Highlanders
QOR = Queen's Own Rifles
RR = Regina Rifles
RWR = Royal Winnipeg Rifles
SF = Sherbrooke Fusiliers

km
mi

0   1   2   3   4

Plumetot

la Mare
Colomby
Anguerny
Anisy
Cambes

For details of this area
see Map 3

St. Contest
1ST BN
25TH SS PZR GRENADIER REGIMENT
Caen

Galmanche
2ND BN
NNSH & SF
Villons-les-Buissons
les Buissons
Vieux Cairon
Buron
3RD BN
Cussy
Abbaye d'Ardenne
"A" SQD SF
Franqueville
Barbière
Gruchy
Authie

Cairon
Rosel

Fontaine-Henry
Thaon
"A" COY & HQ
WITH "A"
"C" COY RR
R MUE
Rots
la Villeneuve
Carpiquet

Bray
le Hamel

Pierrepont
le Fresne-Camilly
Cainet
Camilly
"B" COY RR WITH "D" COY
CSR
Secqueville-en-Bessin
la Bergerie Ferme
Bretteville-l'Orgueilleuse
1ST BN
12TH SS PZR REGT
Norrey-en-Bessin
1ST BN

RWR
CSR
Putot-en-Bessin
la Ferme de Cardonville
2ND BN
26TH SS PZR GRENADIER REGIMENT

Cully
RWR
Brouay
les Saullets
le Mesnil-Patry

© S. Daniel, Starshell Maps, Prince George, B.C.

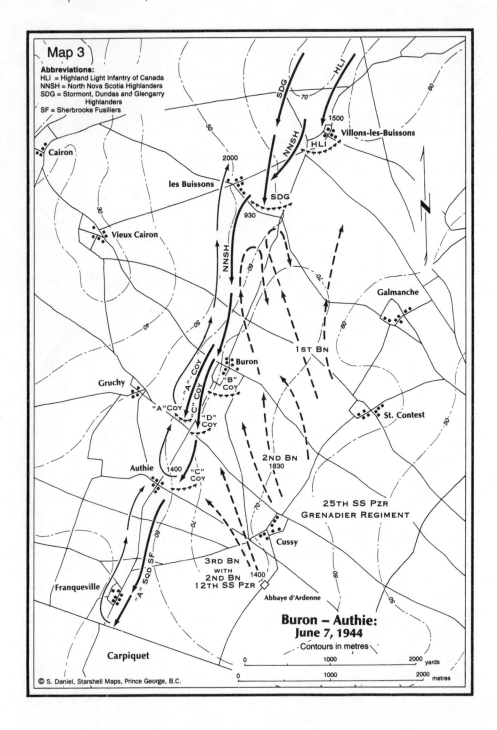

Map 3

Abbreviations:
HLI = Highland Light Infantry of Canada
NNSH = North Nova Scotia Highlanders
SDG = Stormont, Dundas and Glengarry
        Highlanders
SF = Sherbrooke Fusiliers

Cairon

Villons-les-Buissons

les Buissons

Vieux Cairon

Galmanche

1ST BN

Buron

Gruchy

"A" COY

"C" COY

"A" COY

"B" COY

"D" COY

St. Contest

2ND BN
1830

Authie

"C" COY

25TH SS PZR
GRENADIER REGIMENT

Cussy

Franqueville

"A" SQD SF

3RD BN
WITH
2ND BN
12TH SS PZR

Abbaye d'Ardenne

Buron – Authie:
June 7, 1944

Contours in metres

Carpiquet

0   1000   2000 yards

0   1000   2000 metres

© S. Daniel, Starshell Maps, Prince George, B.C.

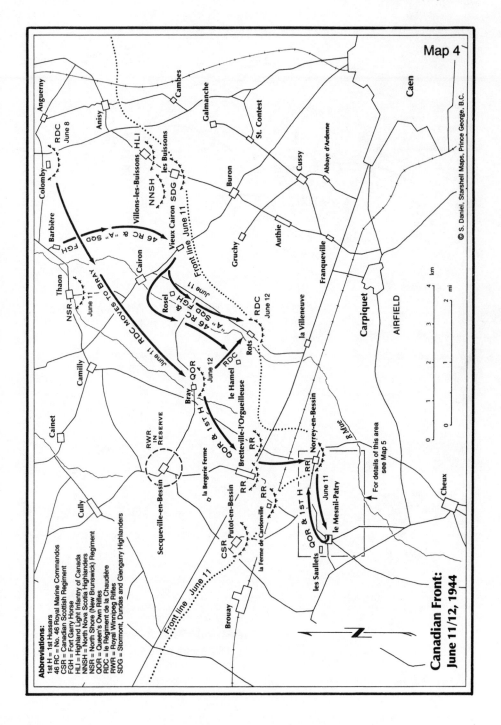

Map 4

Canadian Front:
June 11/12, 1944

Abbreviations:
1st H = 1st Hussars
46 RC = No. 46 Royal Marine Commandos
CSR = Canadian Scottish Regiment
FGH = Fort Garry Horse
HLI = Highland Light Infantry of Canada
NNSH = North Nova Scotia Highlanders
NSR = North Shore (New Brunswick) Regiment
QOR = Queen's Own Rifles
RDC = le Régiment de la Chaudière
RWR = Royal Winnipeg Rifles
SDG = Stormont, Dundas and Glengarry Highlanders

© S. Daniel, Starshell Maps, Prince George, B.C.

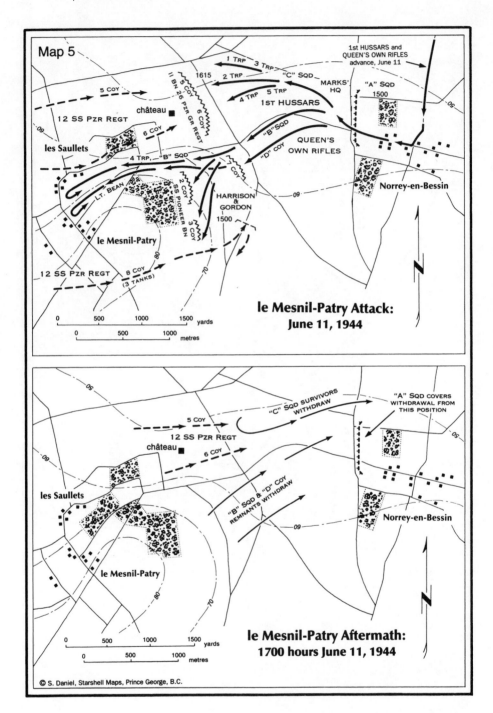

Map 5

1st HUSSARS and
QUEEN'S OWN RIFLES
advance, June 11

1 TRP   3 TRP
1615   2 TRP   "C" SQD   MARKS'   "A" SQD
                            HQ   1500
5 COY   4 TRP   5 TRP
                  1ST HUSSARS

château

12 SS PZR REGT   6 COY

                  "B"SQD
les Saullets   QUEEN'S
        4 TRP, "B" SQD   "D" COY   OWN RIFLES

                                          Norrey-en-Bessin

LT. BEAN   SS PIONEER BN   2 COY
                             3 COY
                             HARRISON
                             &
le Mesnil-Patry   GORDON
                             1500

12 SS PZR REGT   8 COY
                  (3 TANKS)

0   500   1000   1500
                                   yards
0   500   1000
                         metres

le Mesnil-Patry Attack:
June 11, 1944

"A" SQD COVERS
WITHDRAWAL FROM
THIS POSITION

"C" SQD SURVIVORS
WITHDRAW

5 COY

12 SS PZR REGT

château   6 COY

les Saullets
                  "B" SQD & "D" COY
                  REMNANTS WITHDRAW

                                          Norrey-en-Bessin

le Mesnil-Patry

0   500   1000   1500
                                   yards
0   500   1000
                         metres

le Mesnil-Patry Aftermath:
1700 hours June 11, 1944

© S. Daniel, Starshell Maps, Prince George, B.C.

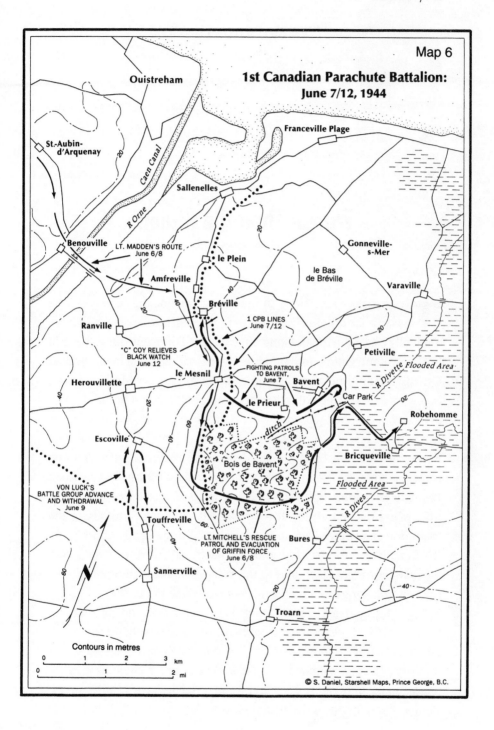

Map 6

1st Canadian Parachute Battalion: June 7/12, 1944

Ouistreham

Franceville Plage

St.-Aubin-d'Arquenay

Caen Canal

Sallenelles

R Orne

Gonneville-s-Mer

Benouville

LT. MADDEN'S ROUTE June 6/8

le Plein

le Bas de Bréville

Amfreville

Varaville

Bréville

Ranville

1 CPB LINES June 7/12

Petiville

"C" COY RELIEVES BLACK WATCH June 12

R Divette Flooded Area

le Mesnil

FIGHTING PATROLS TO BAVENT, June 7

Bavent

Herouvillette

le Prieur

Car Park

Robehomme

Escoville

ditch

Bricqueville

Bois de Bavent

Flooded Area

VON LUCK'S BATTLE GROUP ADVANCE AND WITHDRAWAL June 9

Touffreville

R Dives

LT. MITCHELL'S RESCUE PATROL AND EVACUATION OF GRIFFIN FORCE June 6/8

Bures

Sannerville

Troarn

Contours in metres

0   1   2   3   km

0   1   2   mi

© S. Daniel, Starshell Maps, Prince George, B.C.

Worse Than the Beach

THE STORM THAT LASHED Juno Beach during the early morning assault landings, churning the grey sea into an icy cauldron, gradually eased during the long afternoon of D-Day. By dusk, the thin line of infantrymen and tankers strung along the cloven-hoofed Canadian front line was digging in under a clear sky. A close to full moon washed the terrain in a gentle light, and a warm breeze helped dry saltwater-soaked wool and canvas uniforms. Here, some six miles from the beach, the number of soldiers was painfully few and they were scattered into battalion-sized strongpoints largely isolated one from the other. Of the nine infantry battalions forming 3rd Canadian Infantry Division's fighting teeth, six were on the immediate front line, while the remaining three provided a tenuous link along the main line of advance back to the supporting units busily building up the Canadian presence on the beach itself. All but one of the front-line battalions had taken part in the amphibious assault that had won the five-mile-long stretch of sand codenamed Juno Beach.

Landing against a prepared German defence force deeply dug into heavily fortified positions, the battle for the beach had cost these battalions dearly. Piling off their landing craft into chest-deep water, the infantry had been whipped by bullets and exploding shells as they entered a maze of offshore steel and wood obstacles strung with mines. Behind them, many of the amphibious tanks that were to have led the way and suppress the Germans with point-blank fire from main guns and machine guns had foundered in six- to eight-foot waves.

Amazingly, most of the soldiers, accompanied by a handful of Sherman tanks, had managed to struggle out of the icy water to cut a bloody path through the enemy pillboxes, gun pits, and firing positions, quickly winning toeholds inside the three towns forming the backbone of the German defensive line. Courseulles-sur-Mer on the western flank, Bernières-sur-Mer in the centre, and St. Aubin-sur-Mer to the east each fell in turn. By noon, the assault battalions were pressing inland—behind schedule, but on the move to reach the objectives the division had been assigned to win on this first day of the Allied invasion of Fortress Europe. Nine miles from Juno stood Carpiquet airport, a vital objective. Just to the north of the airport and fronting the Canadian line of advance was the Caen-Bayeux highway, which must be cut to deny its use by the enemy.

With grim determination, the Canadians had marched out from the coastal towns towards these objectives and had been met by a foe equally determined to block or at least delay their advance. Tankers slugged it out with well-camouflaged antitank guns, while the infantry were brought under fire by snipers and one machine-gun position after another. The fields of Normandy were generally fenced by hedgerows the farmers called *bocage*, which provided excellent concealment until the advancing soldiers moved into the Germans' pre-plotted kill zones. Almost as many men died or were wounded during the gruelling push inland as had fallen during the beach assault.

By day's end, despite having been the last of the five Allied divisions to land on D-Day, the Canadians were farther inland than any other. But they were still about three miles short of the assigned objectives. And the price paid by the assaulting battalions for the ground won on June 6 was staggering. Of the 914 total Canadian casualties on D-Day, 696 were men of these six battalions. They were the Queen's Own Rifles, North Shore (New Brunswick) Regiment, and Le Régiment de la Chaudière of the 8th Canadian Infantry Brigade and the Royal Winnipeg Rifles, Regina Rifles, and Canadian Scottish Regiment of the 7th Canadian Infantry Brigade. In support had been two tank regiments of the 2nd Canadian Armoured

Brigade—the 1st Hussars and the Fort Garry Horse. Landing on the heels of the leading brigades had been 9th Canadian Infantry Brigade's North Nova Scotia Highlanders, Highland Light Infantry, and Stormont, Dundas and Glengarry Highlanders supported by 2nd Canadian Armoured Brigade's Sherbrooke Fusiliers. Also coming ashore in the wake of the assault brigades were the gunners of the division's artillery field regiments—the 12th, 13th, 14th, and the seconded 19th Army Field Regiment. Late in the afternoon, the 3rd Anti-Tank Regiment and the 4th Light Anti-Aircraft Regiment arrived, the latter setting up its flak guns to help protect the beach from air attack.

The Canadians had not landed on Juno Beach entirely alone. To enhance the fighting strength of the division, two squadrons of the 2nd Royal Marine Armoured Support Regiment crewed powerful 95-millimetre fort-buster Centaur tanks, while other British soldiers from the 5th Assault Regiment, Royal Engineers brought their specialized assault tanks and armoured bulldozers into action.

Of all the units that landed on Juno Beach during this longest of days, none suffered greater casualties than the Queen's Own Rifles of Canada—61 men dead, another 82 wounded—from a starting strength of just 850 souls.[1]

QUEEN'S OWN Company Sergeant Major Charlie Martin was staggered by his beloved regiment's losses. His pain was heightened by the fact that most of the dead and wounded were men Martin had known personally for several years. The CSM had enlisted as a private in June 1940, just in time for the Toronto-based regiment's mobilization. A year later, the Queen's Own shipped out for Great Britain to add its numbers to the half-million Canadians concentrating there in anticipation of defending the country from a feared German invasion. When that failed to materialize, First Canadian Army began the slow process of preparing for an assault on German-occupied Europe.

It proved a long wait. The Canadians passed their time in seemingly endless training, engaged in the tedium typical of life in military camps, and enjoyed sporadic periods of welcome leave that most spent drinking or trying their luck at seducing English girls. Martin was a little different from most of his comrades. He proved not only to be a good soldier but was also possessed of a curious mind that led to his volunteering for countless special courses. He studied knife fighting, judo, marksmanship, advanced first aid, and—for no particular reason other than that it was offered—Russian.

His dedication to learning the skills of soldiering and the easy way he had of exerting authority over his section mates resulted in his being awarded corporal's stripes in early 1942 and then sewing on the third stripe of a sergeant in February 1943. A few months later, he asked for the hand of an English lass from a small mining town close to Newcastle-on-Tyne and married her on October 30 at Shoreham-by-the-Sea. The sergeant seldom saw his new bride, of course, for the Canadians were based in camps throughout southeast England, while Vi Martin served as an Auxiliary Territorial Service radio operator posted to the Royal Artillery in London.[2]

As the pace of training intensified in late 1943 and reached an almost feverish pitch in early 1944, leaves grew less frequent. By then, the Queen's Own, like every battalion of 3rd Canadian Infantry Division, and the three tank regiments of 2nd Canadian Armoured Brigade were concentrating on learning the ins and outs of amphibious landings and capturing a heavily defended beach. Although never told they were to be part of Operation Overlord—the long expected invasion of Germany's Fortress Europe—the nature of the training and its growing urgency served as warning that they just might play a starring role in the greatest amphibious operation in military history.

When the division was locked down in guarded camps close to Southampton and Portsmouth in the last week of May, it had become obvious to Martin and his comrades that they were bound for a momentous combat debut. For although the Canadians had by this time been training for years, few had faced battle. Scattered through the division were a handful who had survived the Dieppe debacle of August 19, 1942. Of the nearly 5,000 Canadians who had attempted the landing, fewer than half returned to Britain. Left behind were 807 dead and 1,946 prisoners. Also filtered thinly through the ranks were a number of soldiers who had seen service with 1 Canadian Corps in

Italy since that front opened with the invasion of Sicily on July 10, 1943. But the majority of the division's officers and other ranks had never fired a shot in battle nor been fired upon until the landing craft had carried them into the beaches.

NOW, APPROACHING MIDNIGHT of June 6, Martin thought it a miracle any of them had survived this terrible day of bloodshed. Martin's 'A' Company mustered only about half the number who had sailed towards the beach as dawn broke over Normandy. Martin had been assigned to the Landing Craft, Assault carrying the platoon that he had served in until being promoted to CSM. Almost to a man, everyone there had been together since enlisting four years earlier.

When the ramp of their LCA dropped, Martin had led the way into the water. Sergeant Jack Simpson, one of his best friends, was by his side as they sloshed out of the freezing water onto the beach. Then a bullet scythed Simpson down and Martin left him lying dead on the sand. The platoon had been cut to ribbons. Lieutenant Peter C. Rea was wounded, as were the two other section sergeants. Hugh "Rocky" Rocks, the regiment's prized lightweight boxer, was killed. Also dead were George Dalzell, Gil May, Hector J. Bruyère, Willie McBride, Tommy Pierce, Jamie McKechnie, Ernie Cunningham, and Sammy Hall. Iroquois Herman Stock died yelling his defiance at the invisible German gunners while standing in the open, firing his Bren gun from the hip in an attempt to suppress the enemy fire that was slaughtering his mates. With the platoon's leadership lost, Martin took over.

Finally, he and the company's two snipers, Bill Bettridge and Bert Shepherd, cut a way through the wire and mines blocking the advance. Martin led the way into the houses of Bernières-sur-Mer and shortly thereafter the platoon reached the company's initial objective, a road running through the southwest part of the town. There were just five of them, and Martin had no idea of the whereabouts of the rest of the company. Slowly, a few others from the platoon, including some wounded, filtered in. Then the remnants of the other two platoons and the company commander, Major Elliot Dalton, arrived. Martin, reverting back to his CSM role, conducted a quick head count and reported to Dalton that they had suffered more than 50 per cent casualties and that a good number of the men still on their feet were also carrying wounds.

Alongside were two Sherman tanks of the 1st Hussars. With orders to start pushing inland as quickly as possible, Dalton organized the survivors of 'A' Company into a two-section column. He positioned himself at the head of the platoon with the most men still standing, along with the remnants of his company headquarters section and one tank. Martin took charge of the second column formed from the other two platoons and the remaining tank. Any hopes the advancing soldiers had that the ferocity of fighting would slacken once they cleared the beach were quickly snuffed out by fire from snipers and hidden machine-gun positions the moment they emerged from the shelter of the town's houses. After a couple of hours of this nightmarish push up an open road flanked by flat farm fields backed by thick hedgerows, Martin decided that "this kind of advance was worse than the beach itself."[3]

Still, by nightfall, the regiment had reached the village of Anguerny and dug in, with outposts slung out onto a hill to the left and forward in the hamlet of Anisy. The men were exhausted, but despite being put on 50 per cent alert, where every second man stood guard while the man next to him supposedly slept, most remained awake and on edge. Each soldier knew that the Germans were still out there in the darkness and in all likelihood massing for a counterattack intended to throw the small number of invaders back into the sea. Suddenly, this was rammed home when the lines on one side of the battalion erupted in gunfire. Martin heard shouts in English and German intermixed with the staccato bark of Bren guns squaring off against shrieking Schmeisser submachine guns, and realized the Queen's Own lines had been infiltrated by a German patrol trying to test their strength. With men running this way and that, it was impossible to tell friend from foe. Then, as suddenly as it had begun, the firefight ended. Three Canadians lay wounded and four Germans were prisoners. The rest of the Germans, thought to be from the fanatical 12th ss (Hitlerjugend) Panzer Division, had skulked back into the darkness.[4]

As the rate of gunfire wound down, Martin realized it had been more than forty-eight hours since he had boarded ship in Southampton to sail across the English Channel to Normandy. During that time, he had not had a moment's sleep. He also knew there was no way he was going to get any shut-eye this night and that morning would see the battalion on the march again, driving towards the division's D-Day objectives. It struck him then that June 6, for all its horrors, was just the first day of what promised to be a long, hard battle to not only gain a solid footing in Normandy but to hold on to Juno and the other invasion beaches.

PART ONE

MEETING ENGAGEMENTS: D+1

Like Lions

THEIR PRECARIOUS TOEHOLD on the beaches of Normandy was certainly no guarantee the Allies would march rapidly across France, the lowland countries, and ultimately into the heart of Nazi Germany to bring the war to a triumphant end. Although the evening of June 6 had ended with 130,000 men ashore on the five invasion beaches and a further 23,000 airborne troops dropped on the invasion force's eastern and western flanks, this impressive number of men was confined to a narrow strip of ground. The deepest lodgement was the six-mile penetration won by 3rd Canadian Infantry Division and 2nd Canadian Armoured Brigade advancing out of Juno Beach. Just thirty miles lay between the extreme right flank of the Allied front, where the 4th American Infantry Division had landed on Utah Beach at the eastern base of the Cotentin Peninsula, and 3rd British Infantry Division's Sword Beach on the River Orne's western bank.[1]

At Utah, 4th Division had got ashore thanks to a navigational error compounded by the stronger than expected current of an incoming tide. The assault landing craft were swept two thousand yards southeast of the originally designated and heavily defended strip of sand. Landing on this wrong stretch of beach, the assault forces found it only lightly screened by German defenders they were able to quickly brush aside.[2] The reason for the lack of defensive positions soon became clear, however, as the Americans marched out past sand dunes into a quagmire of deliberately flooded farmland meant to dissuade any use of this beach for landing.[3]

Slogging out into this swampy mire, the assault forces easily linked up with elements of the 101st Airborne Division that had landed during the night. But the going remained so difficult that by day's end an advance of only four miles in width and depth was all that had been achieved. No linkage existed between 4th Division and the 82nd U.S. Airborne Division, which had dropped several miles to the west to screen the original landing beach. Both American paratroop divisions were in a bad way. Like their British and Canadian counterparts in the 6th Airborne Division, which had landed on the invasion's extreme eastern flank, they had been badly scattered during the jump. Thrown to the winds in sticks of a dozen or fewer, the paratroops had suffered terrible casualties. Men drowned in flooded fields, drifted into the tangling branches of trees, and shot it out with German reaction forces, while trying to regroup and carry out assigned missions. By the end of D-Day, the two American airborne divisions had suffered 2,499 casualties—about 15 per cent of their total strength.[4] By contrast, 4th Division counted only 197 men dead or wounded from a total of 23,000 who landed on Utah.[5]

Yet Utah remained anything but secure, with a fifteen-mile-wide gap between it and the rest of the invasion beaches to the east. Closest to Utah lay the other American beach, Omaha, midway between Pointe du Hoc and Port-en-Bessin. Here, 1st Infantry Division, reinforced by the 29th Infantry Division's 116th Regiment, had been chopped to pieces on the sand. The battle for the beach raged so long that American First Army commander Lieutenant General Omar N. Bradley seriously considered evacuating the perilous beachhead and having the follow-on units either land on the British beaches or at Utah.[6] After six hours, the beach finally fell, and by dusk the densely sown minefields girdling the inland advance routes still effectively choked forward movement. The price paid for taking Omaha was more than 2,000 casualties and the Americans managed to advance barely a mile on a three-mile-wide front. Omaha was declared a "slight and insecure" lodgement.[7]

Left of Omaha was another four-mile-wide gap between the Americans and the right flank of British Second Army's 50th Infantry Division at Gold Beach. Although this division had not achieved as deep a penetration as the neighbouring 3rd Canadian Infantry Division, by nightfall its most leftward battalion was brushing shoulders with its Canadian counterpart near the mediaeval fortress village of Creully—four miles inland from Gold. Overall, the British-Canadian front was more concentrated than that of the Americans, but there remained a worrisome three-mile separation between the Canadians and 3rd British Infantry Division, which had landed on Sword Beach about five miles east of Juno.

Closing this gap was assigned to 3rd British Division's 9th Brigade, which was to drive southwestwards from Sword to Cambes and then on to St.-Contest, linking up with the Canadian left flank. But the ferocity of German counterattacks directed against 6th Airborne Division's tenuous grip on the Orne River bridge crossings forced two of the brigades' three battalions to swing across Sword Beach to reinforce the paratroops. The remaining battalion was also diverted—sent to help Royal Marine No. 41 Commando gain control of the key coastal town of Lion-sur-Mer.[8] While nightfall found the battle for control of the town still raging, the paratroopers secured a firm grip on the Orne bridges.

Despite the wide dispersion of 6th Airborne during the drop, all its brigades and individual battalions succeeded in carrying out their most critical missions. This was as true for 1st Canadian Parachute Battalion—serving as part of the division's 3rd Brigade—as any of the others. The Canadian paratroops had managed to regroup in sufficient strength to seize and then dynamite two bridges on the River Dives and one of its tributaries. Meanwhile, the main body of the battalion had managed to capture the vital le Mesnil crossroads that stood in the centre of the 180-foot-high le Plein–Bois de Bavent ridge, which separated the Orne and Dives valleys. Despite some bitter fighting, paratroop casualties incurred accomplishing these missions proved surprisingly light—a testimony to their high level of training—19 killed and 10 wounded. But because the battalion had been so badly scattered in the jump, many men were captured trying to work their way through enemy-controlled territory to the assigned area of operations. Eighty-four of the 543 men who jumped on the night of June 5–6 were taken prisoner, a loss of almost 15 per cent of the unit.[9]

The primary task for 6th Airborne Division in the immediate days ahead was to block any German attempt to counterattack the invasion's eastern flank by breaking through the paratroops holding the Bavent ridge and capturing the major bridges on the Orne and Caen-Canal waterways near Ranville. If these bridges fell, they would provide easy passage for German armoured columns to slam into the left flank of the British at Sword Beach, raising the spectre that the beach would be quickly overwhelmed, with the other lodgements to the west easily rolled up in turn.

The dramatic alteration of 3rd British Division's operational plan when 9th Brigade was sent to these new missions left the Canadian division's eastern flank exposed at the deepest point of its six-mile-deep incursion. Here, the Queen's Own Rifles held the villages of Anisy and Anguerny and the North Nova Scotia Highlanders had occupied Villons-les-Buissons to the southwest. Back of these two battalions, Le Régiment de la Chaudière stood in reserve at Basly, the Highland Light Infantry and Stormont, Dundas and Glengarry Highlanders were concentrated around Bény-sur-Mer, and just two miles from the sand the North Shore (New Brunswick) Regiment had dug in at Tailleville. Each battalion was left on the night of June 6–7 warily eyeing its eastern flank in expectation of a German counterattack from that direction. The gap between the Canadians and the British thrust 3 CID into a long fingerlike salient that would only be more dangerously extended when the advance renewed at dawn. It would be up to the Canadians to protect their left flank while pressing on towards the objectives of Carpiquet airport and the Caen-Bayeux highway—a development that caused much anxiety at 3 CID's divisional headquarters.

Equally worrying to the Canadians was the inward bulge in the centre of the division's front line, which resulted in the two most forward infantry brigades being separated by almost three miles of no man's land. Unable to tie their flanks together, 9 CIB and 7th Canadian

Infantry Brigade, concentrated around Bretteville-l'Orgueilleuse, faced fending for themselves as night fell. This situation was particularly worrisome for 7 CIB because of the heavy casualties its battalions had suffered during the landing. Badly weakened, the brigade would be hard pressed to stave off a strong counterattack.

A concern for all the divisional commanders ashore on the night of June 6 was the fact that the landing of follow-on troops and vitally needed supplies was proceeding much more slowly than anticipated. By the close of landing operations that night, the buildup of each beach was between eight and twelve hours behind schedule. This was due to delays in landings because of continuing rough seas and problems constructing vehicle exits off the sand, which combined to cause traffic jams on the beaches. Equally worrying was the fickle nature of the weather. Although the storm that had initially delayed the invasion by a full day had abated by the afternoon, Allied meteorologists offered no assurances that the improved weather would hold.

Not only the divisional commanders and their staffs fretted over the unseasonable weather. Everyone up the chain of command to British Prime Minister Winston Churchill himself sought constant assurance, without success, that the weather would remain fine. The threat of renewed storms, Churchill later wrote, "was the element which certainly hung like a vulture poised in the sky over the thoughts of the most sanguine."[10] Churchill took heart, however, in the fact that the Allied invasion force had managed to get ashore at all. He had never assumed that "the most difficult and complicated operation that has ever taken place" would succeed.[11]

Like the Operation Overlord planners, the prime minister had feared the English Channel would run red with the blood of young British, Canadian, and American soldiers and that the war might drag on for years more before such a major offensive could again be staged. Supreme Headquarters Allied Expeditionary Force commander General Dwight G. Eisenhower had so worried the invasion might fail that he scribbled a draft press release addressing this eventuality and stuck it in his back pocket. "Our landings... have failed," it read. "I have withdrawn the troops... If there is any blame or fault attached to the attempt, it is mine alone."

By midday, when it became apparent the landings would succeed in at least winning a toehold on the continent, Eisenhower had handed the release to an aide and announced dryly to a group of journalists that the landings were underway.[12] At dusk, he learned that the British and Canadians had managed to put 75,215 soldiers ashore and another 7,900 paratroopers in by air while the Americans had 57,500 on the ground.[13]

But the victory had been hard won. Although far lower than the feared casualty rate of 15 per cent of the landing force, the price had been stiff enough—approximately 10,000 dead, wounded, or captured by day's end. Of these, a third were estimated to have been fatal.[14]

By midnight, the presses throughout the United Kingdom were rolling with massive front-page headlines that blared the news of the D-Day victory to a public long beleaguered by bad news and endless hardship. "Allied invasion troops, surging into France in non-stop waves, have fought their way into Caen, a town ten miles from the coast. Heavy street fighting is going on," proclaimed the *Daily Express*.[15] Caen, of course, remained firmly under the heel of many a German jackboot, but the pivotal importance of this city's capture to the Allied operation had obviously been hinted to British journalists. Indeed, Caen served as a vital arterial centre for the network of roads and railways radiating to the rest of northern Normandy and on to Paris.

To British General Bernard Law Montgomery, the mastermind behind Operation Overlord's strategic plan, the city had always been of "immense strategic importance." This was not so much for itself per se, but because "it was a vital road and rail centre through which passed the main routes leading to our lodgement area from the east and southeast. As the bulk of the German mobile reserves were located north of the Seine, they would have to approach our bridgehead from the east and would thus converge on Caen."[16]

Southeast of the city, the ground between Caen and Falaise flattened into a wide plain, ideally suited for the rapid development of airstrips from which Allied fighters and fighter-bombers could begin operations from French soil. The tactical importance of the Falaise plain and the funnelling of Normandy's transportation routes through Caen made it impossible for the Germans to allow the city to fall without a determined fight. Montgomery expected that by setting the British Second Army driving hard out of Sword, Juno, and Gold beaches in an arc towards Caen he would force the German divisions rushing south from encampments north of the Seine to concentrate on blocking this advance.[17] Failure to do so would not only result in their loss of transportation junctions, but would also leave the gate open by which the Allies could break out of Normandy towards the Seine and Germany itself.

But Montgomery did not intend to immediately achieve a breakout at Caen. Instead, this part of Overlord was an elaborately staged feint to distract German attention and "draw the main enemy reserves, particularly his armoured divisions, into that sector and to keep them there—using the British and Canadian forces under [General Miles] Dempsey for this purpose." While Dempsey's Second British Army met—and he hoped destroyed—the heavy German forces counter-attacking here, Montgomery planned that the American First Army under Bradley would attack "southwards, and then... proceed in a wide sweep up to the Seine about Paris. I hoped this gigantic wheel would pivot on Falaise. It aimed to cut off all the enemy forces south of the Seine, the bridges over the river below Paris having been destroyed by our air forces."[18]

Montgomery not only wanted to push the Germans out of Normandy, he expected to cut off the Seventh Army—defending the coastline south of the Seine—and then destroy it entirely. The plan was a bold one, and for it to succeed the Canadians and the British divisions of Dempsey's army must bear the brunt of the fight to come.

AT 0200 HOURS ON JUNE 7, 3rd Canadian Infantry Division's part in that fight started with an attack on the North Nova Scotia Highlanders while they were still in the midst of establishing a defensive line for the night. Having pushed farther inland than any other Allied troops, the lead column of the North Novas had only halted its advance along the highway running from Courseulles-sur-Mer to Caen when night fell. To speed this inland push, the infantry had been mounted aboard every available Bren carrier and had clung to the outside hulls of the supporting Shermans of the Sherbrooke Fusiliers. North Nova commander Lieutenant Colonel Charlie Petch finally ordered his battalion to hold up at a junction where the highway met a road running southwest from Villons-les-Buissons directly to Carpiquet airport. Intending to carry on by this road to the airport objective in the morning, Petch concentrated his companies around the intersection.

About a quarter mile to the left of this position, the Queen's Own Rifles had a company dug in at the village of Anisy. The Queen's Own, however, were not in control of a road running directly past the southern edge of the village to Petch's intersection. Worried that this route provided a perfect line of approach from the southeast for elements of the 21st Panzer Division believed to be lurking on this flank, Petch sent a section of pioneers to establish a roadblock midway between the intersection and Anisy. Accompanying the pioneers on this foray into no man's land was a detail from the battalion's Bren carrier platoon commanded by Sergeant Don Baillie.[19] Once they reached the mining position, Baillie ordered the carriers parked behind the cover of a hedge from which his men could cover the pioneer party as it strung antitank and anti-personnel mines across the road and along the verges.

It was a lovely moonlit night. Nowhere on the front lines could any sound of fighting be heard, so Baillie and his men were confident that the roadblock party was secure. Dismounting from their carriers, the soldiers ambled out onto the road to get a better view of the fireworks display back at the beach, which outmatched any peacetime celebration they had ever seen. Hovering over the great armada standing offshore from Juno, were the silhouettes of a handful of German bombers that had drawn the ire of hundreds of anti-aircraft gunners aboard the many ships. Thousands of tracers streamed into the night sky, which suddenly brightened with a false dawn whenever an enemy bomb exploded. This far from the beach, the exploding bombs and rattle of anti-aircraft guns sounded no louder than firecrackers igniting in long strings. But the noise did drown out the night sounds of crickets and the scraping of shovels and picks being wielded by the engineers.

The pioneers were working quickly, eyes down and focussed on the task of laying mines, while the carrier men gazed nonchalantly away from the front towards the beach. Squatting in the middle of the road, arms lazily resting on his knees, Private Ern Jollymore suddenly sensed the presence of something large looming close to his back and glanced over his shoulder. Just up the road, something dark and bulky bore down on the pioneers.

"It's a Jerry tank!" hissed the man at his shoulder. Jollymore followed him in a mad dash to the cover of a hedge just as the tank's machine gun spat out a long burst.

Cut off from their carriers by the streams of fire, Baillie's men were forced to abandon the vehicles. Seeing the shadowy figures of German infantry darting across an open field towards them, the Bren carrier men and pioneers started shooting with rifles and Sten guns while scrambling back to the battalion's main line on foot. This quick and apparently unexpected response to the German infiltration attempt served to deter the enemy from pressing the attack. After punching a few rounds from its main gun towards the North Nova lines, the tank swerved around and grumbled off into the night with the infantry following close behind.

Meanwhile, in 'D' Company's position, directly astride the intersection, Sergeant Jimmy McInnis spotted a German soldier with a knife clamped in his teeth crawling up on Sergeant Viril Bartlett's slit trench. Before McInnis could act, the German gripped the knife and dropped into the hole. Fearing he would be too late to save his friend from a slit throat, McInnis grabbed his Sten gun and ran. Seeing the German's head bob up out of the slit trench, the sergeant shoved the Sten's barrel practically into the man's face. The enemy dropped the knife and threw his hands up in surrender. McInnis was surprised and relieved to see that, apart from the German, the trench was empty. Casting about, he soon discovered that Bartlett had decided the night was too peaceful and pleasant to spend bedded down with the worms in a slit trench. He had constructed a soft mattress of wheat in the grain field next to their position and still slept soundly. Thinking it a shame to disturb the man, McInnis let him lie and escorted the prisoner to battalion headquarters.[20]

At battalion headquarters, the captured German was identified as a member of a Panzer Grenadier unit, most likely from the 192nd Panzer Grenadier Battalion of the 21st Panzer Division. Petch was just absorbing this information when 'B' Company out on the left flank reported being under attack by German infantry mounted on half-tracks—providing confirmation that the North Novas were squaring off against Panzer Grenadiers.

Highly mechanized infantry, Panzer Grenadier regiments were an integral component of Panzer divisions intended to operate either independently or alongside the division's armoured regiments. These units generally used heavy infantry carriers known as half-tracks because the vehicle's rear drive was mounted with dual tracks while the front was fitted with standard wheels. A common half-track used by Panzer divisions was the SdKfz251, which carried a crew of up to twelve men protected by armour ranging in thickness from six to fifteen millimetres. One variant of this half-track was armed with two 7.92-millimetre machine guns, but others mounted lighter machine guns or none at all. Powered by a six-cylinder gas engine, the half-track had an average top speed of thirty-three miles per hour.

One half-track well ahead of the rest rumbled directly towards Lieutenant Fraser Campbell's No. 10 Platoon. Not realizing that the Bren carrier troops out with the pioneers had abandoned their vehicles, Campbell's men first mistook the approaching vehicles for the returning roadblock detail. But when a sentry called out a password challenge, the shadowy figures aboard the blacked-out vehicle responded with guttural German shouts and gunfire.

No. 10 Platoon answered with such a heavy fusillade that the half-track swerved away from the line and began circling wildly around in the grain field, dodging behind one haystack after another, before swinging back towards 'B' Company's position. Lance Corporal J.E. Porter looked out of his slit trench only to see the front end of the half-track bearing down on him. Firing several shots from his bayonet-mounted rifle, he ducked deep into the hole just in time to avoid being crushed as the front wheels ground right over the trench. Lying on his back with the rifle pressed against his body, Porter was unable to get the bayonet all the way into the trench and the rear tracks of the half-track snapped the blade like a twig. Then abruptly, the half-track stalled with the track suspended directly overhead, leaving Porter trapped.

With a sitting target to aim at, all of 'B' Company blazed away at the half-track with rifles, Stens, and Bren guns. The concentrated fire hammering the lightly armoured hull convinced the four Germans aboard to surrender. One had been wounded during the short firefight, as had two 'B' Company men. Porter was only able to escape from his hole when some of the men dug in from the side of one track to drag him out.[21]

'B' Company was just starting to recover from this first incursion into its lines when two more half-tracks roared out of the darkness with MG 42 machine guns mounted on pintles behind the driver compartments blazing. The company commander, Major J.W. Douglas, quickly ordered his men to mark their position with tracer rounds and then radioed for the Sherbrookes' Sherman tanks standing behind the company to rake the ground in front. Lieutenant S.W. Wood's No. 4 Troop of 'B' Squadron responded instantly with fire that ripped not only into the two half-tracks closing on the position but also the disabled one, setting all three ablaze. Wood's personal Sherman was the new British-designed Firefly, equipped with a powerful 17-pound main gun in place of the standard 75-millimetre. A shell from the lieutenant's tank tore one of the half-tracks apart, while another round blew a cow wandering about the field into gore.[22] The combined effect of No. 4 Troop's fire, noted the North Nova Scotia's war diarist, "apparently discouraged the [Germans], as they withdrew."[23]

NO SOONER had this force been repelled than what appeared to be a full company of Panzer Grenadiers mounted aboard more than twenty vehicles plowed into 'A' Company of Le Régiment de la Chaudière just outside Colomby-sur-Thaon, a little over a mile back of the North Novas. The attack's main force fell upon the company's No. 9 Platoon, commanded by Lieutenant A.P. Ladas. Caught by surprise, the platoon was overrun before it could respond and most of its men were left no choice but to surrender or die, even as Ladas attempted to rally them with the cry, "À l'assaut les boys." With a grenade in each hand, Ladas charged the approaching half-tracks and was instantly cut down by machine-gun fire along with two of his men.[24] The Germans quickly whisked off forty-one other men from the platoon as prisoners, along with 'A' Company's second-in-command, Captain Pierre Vallée.*

The remaining two platoons of 'A' Company and two of the battalion's six-pound antitank gun crews were quickly entangled in a fierce melee with the attacking Germans. "My men were exhausted but they fought like lions," Major Hugues Lapointe wrote later of his company's desperate fight. "There was no defensive line as such, our being entirely surrounded. There followed close-combat action with grenades and point-blank firing of weapons. POWs occurred on both sides. Four half-tracks were knocked out and were aflame, their ammunition exploding and whizzing over our heads. It was like daylight as the vehicles burned!"[25]

The bravery of one antitank gunner ultimately prevented 'A' Company's slaughter. One of the six-pounders had been knocked out of action in the opening minutes of the German attack, and soon all but a single crew member manning the second six-pounder were dead or wounded. The lone survivor, Private L.V. Roy, continued to load and fire the gun single-handed with deadly effect even as the Germans subjected his position to withering small-arms fire. Virtually every well-aimed shot from Roy's gun sent another half-track up in flames until finally the attack crumbled. When the Germans withdrew, seventeen destroyed vehicles remained scattered throughout 'A' Company's position along with an undetermined number of dead Germans. The Chaudières had been equally battered, due primarily to the capture of most of No. 9 Platoon and the death of Lieutenant Ladas and two of his men, along with the losses suffered by the antitank gunners.

---

* The Canadian official history by Col. C.P. Stacey lists these Chaudière POWs as casualties suffered by 3rd Canadian Infantry Division on D-Day itself, but they were lost during this engagement in the early morning of June 7. (Stacey, *The Victory Campaign*, 650)

Not until dawn, however, did other Chaudières check Roy's gun position. The private's lifeless body was found draped over the breech of the gun he had served so bravely.*

WHILE HALF-TRACK–MOUNTED Panzer Grenadiers struck the North Novas and Chaudières throughout the length of the long finger of the Canadian left flank, other enemy troops skulked on foot. Some were 192nd Panzer Grenadier Battalion patrols probing for weaknesses or gaps in the lines, and seeking prisoners. Others were 716th Infantry Division stragglers. This coastal defence division had been largely destroyed attempting to defend the beaches on which Second British Army had landed on D-Day. While the survivors from the 716th tended to avoid combat, the Panzer Grenadier patrols posed a significant hazard to Canadians moving along the main road that ran from the front lines back to the beachhead at Bernières-sur-Mer.

Lieutenant Colonel Petch's jeep driver Private Lloyd MacPhee learned the dangers inherent in such travel during one of the many errands that saw him motoring back to the beach from the junction at Villons-les-Buissons early in the night. His first trip to fetch the battalion's medical officer from the beach had proved uneventful. Then he returned to Bernières to guide three tanks up to the Sherbrookes. While at the beach, another jeep driver warned MacPhee he had seen some Germans lurking around the road who had fired on several vehicles from the cover of thickets. Shrugging the danger off, MacPhee drove back to the North Novas at the head of the tank convoy without triggering any enemy reaction. Figuring that this should be enough running about for the night, the private had just set to digging a slit trench when summoned again by the colonel.

---

* As the only Commonwealth decoration that can be issued posthumously is the politically charged and rarely awarded Victoria Cross, L.V. Roy's heroism went officially unrecognized, but to the Chaudières in Normandy his sacrifice was viewed as a symbol of devotion to duty, courage, and sacrifice for the whole unit. Today, the Chaudières award the L.V. Roy Trophy annually to the Regiment's company that obtains the best results in the unit's military and sports competition.

Petch had four Germans, one of whom was wounded, on his hands and standing orders from 9th Brigade headquarters that all prisoners should be sent there for interrogation. He also had two wounded North Nova stretcher cases. One of the stretchers was laid across the jeep's hood and the other sideways behind the driver's seat, while the wounded German was ordered to sit in the back corner. The remaining three prisoners were to walk behind the jeep under the watchful eye of a Sten-toting Lance Corporal Wheaton.

MacPhee crawled out of the North Nova Scotia position at an irritating snail's pace necessitated by having to match the pace of the Germans on foot. Soon realizing that the party would be lucky to reach the beach before dawn, MacPhee suggested to Wheaton that everyone crowd onto the jeep somehow. Putting one German on the back of the jeep opposite the wounded man, another in the front seat next to MacPhee with the remaining German on his lap, and Wheaton standing on the hood next to the stretcher so he could watch over them all seemed to work well enough.[26]

Just as MacPhee was preparing to roll off again, another jeep came up behind him, bearing Sherbrooke Fusiliers Adjutant Captain G.W. Cote and Signals Officer Lieutenant T.C. Stevens bound for 2nd Canadian Armoured Brigade headquarters. At the wheel of this jeep was Sergeant N.H. Barter.[27]

As MacPhee started up a slow grade in second gear, a group of soldiers appeared, marching in the opposite direction. Only as he pulled over to let them pass did MacPhee make out the coal scuttle profile of their helmets. Before any of the men in the jeeps could react, they were surrounded and yanked out of the vehicles. In the tense first moments of their capture, Lieutenant Stevens was killed.[28]

The Germans left the two wounded North Novas lying on their stretchers next to a hedge on the roadside and fortified with a captured bottle of rum. One, Private G.L. Harvie, would be safely recovered in the morning, while the other man succumbed to his wounds during the long night.[29]

MacPhee and the other Canadians were escorted off into the night. The German patrol had unwittingly pulled off an intelligence coup, for the two Sherbrooke officers had in their possession a full set of Second British Army's radio procedures, code signs, and orders for operations. German intelligence officers quickly matched this lucrative haul of documents to a set of Canadian operational maps retrieved during the night from a disabled vehicle. Place names on the maps were marked with nicknames, such as Orinoco for the Orne River. "Taken together with the wireless codes," a German officer later wrote, "we were able to understand much of the enemy's radio traffic... all that was left was to form special recce units to do radio listening work and so on; and in this way we were repeatedly successful. In effect it was espionage by radio."[30]

Throw Them into the Sea

T HE GERMANS attempting to meet the invasion needed every possible intelligence advantage because they were seriously handicapped by both Allied action and a cumbersome, inherently chaotic command structure. Consequently, while local German divisions and commands, by late evening of June 6, had begun moving to counter the invasion at a tactical level, their actions were not guided by any comprehensive strategic plan. Believing that the inevitable invasion was not yet due and would occur in the Pas de Calais or even farther up the northern coast, Hitler and his staff officers at Oberkommando der Wehrmacht (Armed Forces High Command) refused to accept that this was *the* invasion. Rather, they remained convinced that the landings in Normandy were a feint made in force to draw divisions—particularly armoured ones—away from Pas de Calais. Once this soaking off of strength had weakened Fifteenth Army's defences, the Germans believed the Allies planned to land in force, cut off all the troops attempting to throw back the decoy invasion, and destroy them. In one bold stroke, the Allies would assure themselves of ultimate victory by imposing a defeat far exceeding the disaster of Stalingrad.

Although on May 2, 1944, Hitler had intuited from intelligence reports of a major buildup of Allied divisions in southeast England and Wales that an invasion of Normandy and Brittany was possible, oкw staff had remained skeptical. Only the fact that Hitler "kept harping on it and demanded more and more reinforcements for that sector" led to the strengthening of woefully inadequate defences along the Normandy coast.[1]

Generalfeldmarschall Erwin Rommel, heading Army Group B, was responsible for defending Europe's northwest coast from Holland to the Loire under Commander-in-Chief, West, Generalfeldmarschall Gerd von Rundstedt. The sixty-eight-year-old von Rundstedt's position had been reduced to titular status by Rommel's appointment to command of the newly formed Army Group B in January 1944. While Rommel was to keep him informed of his orders for strengthening coastal defences, the old Prussian was under no illusions that he could countermand the younger man. Rommel had Hitler's ear and reported directly to him through oкw, while von Rundstedt so disdained "that Bohemian corporal" and his toadies at oкw that he refused to talk directly with them. He left this distasteful task to his Chief of Staff, General der Infantrie Günther Blumentritt.[2]

The most popular war hero in Germany, Rommel was also greatly respected by his Allied adversaries for his leadership during the German Northwest African campaigns. Within the Wehrmacht, however, Rommel was less popular. Although he had won Germany's highest decoration, the Pour le Mérite, for heroism during the Caporetto offensive in World War I, he spent the majority of the interwar years in obscure postings after being judged lacking in General Staff ability. His outspoken nature and unorthodox military theories, however, served to bring him to Hitler's attention. Although he refused to join the Nazi Party, Rommel initially respected the ever more popular fascist leader and benefited from the relationship with a reinvigorated career when he was appointed to command the Führer's personal headquarters.

Following the successful invasion of Poland, Rommel asked Hitler for a Panzer command and was given the 7th Panzer Division, which he commanded during the blitzkreig across France in 1940. Rommel led the division from the front, seeming to instinctively recognize how to exploit enemy weaknesses through rapid and flexible mobile offensive action. In Africa, when he showed the same capability,

Hitler and the Nazi propaganda machine lionized him to the point where he became a living symbol of German military prowess. As his stature grew, many Wehrmacht generals dismissed Rommel as a political general, who would have remained in the bottom drawer if not for his Nazi connections. Rommel's reliance on instinct over military doctrine was a character trait that he and Hitler shared. Both had triumphed at times when the conservative generals on OKW's staff had predicted failure and this served to draw the two more closely together.[3]

If Rommel enjoyed a unique relationship with Hitler, he still had no illusions that he enjoyed a free hand in preparing for the invasion. Hitler and OKW insisted on being consulted at every turn, constantly meddling in the disposition of divisions and allocation of resources. As well, Rommel had no authority over Luftlotte 3—the Luftwaffe air arm in the region—nor the naval command, Marine-gruppe West. These reported to and received orders from their respective supreme commanders, who in turn were subordinate to OKW and Hitler. Even the coastal defence construction unit—Organization Todt—reported to Reichsminister for Armament and War Production Albert Speer, who took his direction from the Führer, rather than Rommel. Should Rommel want something from those outside his direct authority he generally had to go cap in hand to Hitler, the Führer's Chief of Staff, Generalfeldmarschall Wilhelm Keitel, or OKW Operations Chief, Generaloberst Alfred Jodl. Army Group B's Chief of Staff, Generalleutnant Hans Speidel, rightly declared that a system that effectively denied his superior decisive control over the theatre of operations "led not only to a confused chain of command, but to a command chaos."[4]

That chaotic structure had plagued Rommel as he prepared to meet the invasion. The compromises arising from a proliferation of views strongly advanced by high-ranking officers and Nazi politicians had frustrated his strategy. Believing the battle would be decided on the beach, Rommel had declared: "Never in history was there a defence of such an extent with such an obstacle as the sea. The enemy must be annihilated before he reaches our main battlefield... We must stop him in the water, not only delaying him but destroying all his equipment while it is still afloat... The high water line must be the main fighting line."[5]

Lacking sufficient manpower, Rommel had been forced to sacrifice a defence in depth in order to pack as many men as possible into fighting positions right up against the coastal beaches. He had also proposed deploying the Panzer divisions close enough to the shore that each could bring its guns and tanks to a specific section before the Allies broke through the largely immobile beach defences. "It is more important to have one Panzer division in the assaulted section on D-Day, than to have three there by D plus 3," he said.[6]

Rommel's plan had immediately drawn stiff opposition from Panzer Group West commander, General der Panzertruppen Leo Freiherr Geyr von Schweppenburg, another powerful player in the tortuous German command structure. Formed in late 1943, Panzer Group West was tasked with training Panzer forces in the western theatre and with advising von Rundstedt on Panzer tactics and operational requirements. By early 1944, all Panzer divisions and corps in Western Europe were effectively under von Schweppenburg's command. In stark contrast to Rommel, the general thought the "Atlantic Wall" was destined to collapse at the first major assault.

Born in 1886, von Schweppenburg was considered a leading tank expert by many Wehrmacht generals. He had commanded his first mobile unit regiment in 1933, led the 3rd Panzer Division into Poland in 1939, and in 1940 taken the helm of xxiv Corps for the invasion of Russia. After two years of fighting on the Eastern Front, he was transferred to command of the lxxxvi Corps in France before heading up Panzer Group West. Having years of Eastern Front combat experience, von Schweppenburg recognized the near impossibility of holding long, exposed front lines in the face of a determined attacker. He also had the unique background of having served from 1933 to 1937 as a military attaché in London and so had a good sense of British army tactics and the psychology of its generals.

The repulse of the Dieppe raid, von Schweppenburg believed, had lulled Germany's high command into believing an invasion could be met on the beaches and destroyed before it got established ashore. This theory was partially based on an assumption that the German martial spirit was greater than that of the British, Americans, or Canadians who would have to win the beach. Had not Dieppe proven this superiority? its proponents asked disingenuously. But von Schweppenburg countered that Dieppe had not been an invasion, so such an assumption was "irresponsible." Taken "together with Rommel's misguided doctrine on coastal defence," the Panzer general said, "this idea was fundamentally responsible for the grotesque defense situation, which was contrary to all experiences of strategy and recent war developments."

Von Schweppenburg grudgingly conceded that "Rommel was an able and experienced tactician, although entirely lacking in strategic conceptions." This inability to think strategically, von Schweppenburg maintained, had led Rommel to the ludicrous conclusion that his only option was to defend the entire coastline. But how could eight hundred miles of coast be defended? Given "the formidable enemy air superiority and the number, caliber, and effectiveness of the naval guns of the combined Anglo-American battle fleets, a landing... could not be prevented and would succeed in any case. The only solution," von Schweppenburg concluded, "would be to utilize the only German superiority—that of speedier and more flexible leadership which employed mobile reserves. High-quality Panzer units should be held in reserve to crush an enemy penetration inland."[7]

The Panzer Group West commander easily won the support of Generaloberst Heinz Guderian, the old Panzer master strategist who was Hitler's advisor on Panzer tactics, but neither man could convince either the Führer or Rommel that the "Atlantic Wall" strategy was doomed to failure. Hitler was determined that not a yard of European territory should be yielded, so Rommel's plan found the sympathetic ear of the man who ultimately mattered most in the German command chain. After hearing the arguments of Rommel and the Panzer generals, Hitler offered a compromise that satisfied nobody. He split control of the Panzers between Rommel and von Schweppenburg, giving the latter his mobile armoured reserve in the form of just four divisions—1st ss Panzer, 12th ss (Hitlerjugend) Panzer,

Panzer Lehr, and 17th ss Panzer Grenadier. Except for these units, "one Panzer division after another was marched to the front and required to dig in 10 to 20 kilometres behind the coastline."[8]

CONSEQUENTLY, ON JUNE 6 the Germans had in place neither a strong tactical nor strategic reserve.[9] In Normandy, the armoured unit dug in closest to the beaches was the 21st Panzer Division, which found itself facing a night drop by 6th British Airborne Division on the eastern shore of the River Orne and the westerly British-Canadian landings. Its commander, Generalleutnant Edgar Feuchtinger, had dithered between moving on his own authority to stamp out the airborne troops or seeking instruction from up the chain of command. This was partly due to his own lack of resolve, but also a standing order that no offensive action by Panzers was to be taken without Army Group B authorization, to avoid such divisions becoming engaged in a piecemeal fashion. The command chaos Generalleutnant Speidel had warned of proved itself, as hour after hour passed with nobody at either Army Group B or Seventh Army headquarters assuming overall control of the German response.

"If Rommel had been with us instead of in Germany, he would have disregarded all orders and taken action—of that we were convinced," Major Hans von Luck, commander of the 21st Panzer Division's 125th Panzer Grenadier Regiment, later wrote.[10] With the Germans firmly believing that the invasion was still sometime off, however, Rommel had departed on June 5 to celebrate his wife's birthday at their home near Ulm and then to try convincing Hitler to bolster the number of Panzer divisions in Normandy.[11]

From their respective headquarters, Speidel and Blumentritt sought authorization from okw to release the Panzers, only to be told that such an order must come personally from Hitler. But Hitler slept until 0900 hours on June 6 and nobody had the temerity to interrupt his slumber, so it was not until 1030 that orders from okw placed the 21st Panzer Division under area commander General der Artillerie Erich Marcks of the LXXXIV Corps. Marcks, who had worked with Guderian during the interwar years developing blitzkrieg tactics, immediately ordered the division to attack west of the Orne in an attempt to break through to either Sword or Juno beaches and roll the invasion up by destroying the beachheads.[12]

Hours passed as the division's officers struggled to manoeuvre their units into position for the planned counterattack. Once it got underway, the division did succeed in driving into the gap between 3rd British Infantry Division and the Canadians, but too small a force had been committed and the attack crumbled.

At the same time as 21st Panzer Division's counterattack was falling apart, help in the form of leading elements of the 12th ss (Hitlerjugend) Panzer Division began arriving. Also ordered to concentrate against the Normandy beaches was the Panzer Lehr Division and the general command of 1 ss Panzer Corps with its inherent corps troops—all to come under direct authority of Seventh Army Commander Generaloberst Friedrich Dollman.[13] Once this force massed around Caen, Dollman intended to attack the enemy by driving a three-division-strong wedge into the gap between the forces advancing out of Sword and Juno beaches. The attack would be directed at the section of coastline directly west of Lion-sur-Mer, where the last truly organized elements of 716th Infantry Division were isolated but still holding the ground between this village and Luc-sur-Mer on the Canadian left flank. Operational command for the attack would rest with Obergruppenführer Josef (Sepp) Dietrich, who headed up 1 ss Panzer Corps.[14]*

Dietrich's corps was comprised of two ss divisions, the 12th and the 1st ss Panzer Division. As the latter division was encamped in Belgium east of Antwerp, it was too far away to join the planned counteroffensive. Dietrich would have to rely on the three Panzer divisions in the vicinity, two of which had never previously served under his command and were regular army rather than ss formations.

Born in 1892, this illegitimate son of a peasant girl had won the Iron Cross, 1st Class during World War 1 while serving as a sergeant major. He likely would have led an obscure working-class life except

* Canadian Army, German Army, and ss rank equivalencies are explained and compared in Appendix C.

for memberships during the interwar years in Germany's burgeon-
ing Fascist movements. First he served in the SA—the Brown
Shirts—under Ernst Röhm, before switching allegiance to Hitler's
Nazi Party after the two organizations broke apart in 1933. Hitler
rewarded Dietrich's loyalty by putting him in charge of recruiting the
leader's SS bodyguard unit. When the rift between the SA and the
Nazis deepened the following year, Dietrich was a pivotal figure in
the June 30, 1934 Night of the Long Knives, during which Röhm, the
SA leadership, and many others who opposed Hitler's ascendancy
were brutally slaughtered.

Impressed by Dietrich's "cunning, energetic, and brutal" nature,
Hitler continued to promote the man as the SS matured from a paramilitary organization into one with a formal military arm. In 1938,
the bodyguard force, known as the Leibstandarte, was transformed
into motorized infantry and later expanded into a Panzer division.
Both formations were under his command. One of his principal staff
officers, Rudolf Lehmann, recognized that Dietrich "was no strategic
genius... His forte did not lie in formulating a complete tactical evalu-
ation. But he had an extraordinary sense of growing crisis and for
finding the favourable moment for action."[15]

Finding that kind of opportunity for the planned counterattack
would prove difficult. Dietrich wanted to await the arrival of Panzer
Lehr—still moving towards the Normandy coast from its assembly
point at Nogent le Rotrou, ninety-five miles southwest of Caen. He
also wanted to tee up as much air support as possible, both to strike
against the enemy troops and to protect his advancing units from the
punishing fighter-bomber and strafing attacks they had endured
throughout the march to the coast.

By 0400 hours on June 7, having hurried back from Germany,
Rommel was briefed by Seventh Army's Chief of Staff Generalleutnant Max Pemsel on the status of the three I SS Corps Panzer divisions. They had, he learned, "been brought into the assembly areas
and had been ordered to begin the counterattack without any other
considerations and with all available forces."[16] With Panzer Lehr still
far off in the distance and its commander reporting that his first
fighting units could not possibly reach Caen until the morning of

June 8, this was clearly not the case. For its part, 21st Panzer Division was badly scattered and disorganized after its botched solo counterattack into the gap between Juno and Sword. Various elements of this division were still tangling with the paratroops west of the Orne and its 192nd Panzer Grenadier Battalion had become entangled in running night battles with the Canadian battalions on 3 CID's left flank. Whether significant elements of this division would be able to reorganize by morning to participate in the counterattack was unclear.

As for 12th SS Panzer Division, many of its units were also still on the march and expected to filter into the area by fits and starts throughout June 7. At the head of this mechanized juggernaut grinding into Normandy was Standartenführer Kurt Meyer, commander of the 25th SS Panzer Grenadier Regiment. As darkness fell, Meyer received instructions from his divisional commander, Brigadeführer Fritz Witt, to prevent the Allies capturing Carpiquet airport and entering Caen. The 12th SS would form up alongside the 21st Panzer Division through the night and then attack during the day with their armoured shoulders brushing. This was not just a spoiling attack intended to stop the British-Canadian advance. Witt told Meyer, "The division is to attack the enemy along with the 21st Panzer Division and throw them into the sea. H-Hour for the attack is 7th June at midday."[17] That the 21st Panzer Division was in a shambles and much of the 12th SS still well short of the assembly point for the attack was disregarded. Witt wanted action and Meyer was equally determined to take the fight to the Allies.

A tactical headquarters was set up at the side of the Caen-Bayeux highway in a small country house surrounded by tall trees that provided necessary camouflage from detection by Allied aircraft. There, Meyer anxiously awaited the arrival of his regiment's various battalions. As the commander of each unit pulled in, Meyer gave a quick personal briefing before hurrying the officer on to an advanced forming-up position in the area of Cussy and the Abbaye d'Ardenne.

The Abbaye was a ruined monastery about two miles northwest of Caen in which the 12th SS had established a forward command post. A thick stone wall surrounded the abbey, separating the buildings and internal compound from a small orchard protected by a second, equally stout wall.[18] Two square-shaped towers attached to the abbey's church provided a panoramic view over the "gently undulating plateau" stretching almost ten miles to the beaches. "As if on a theater stage, villages with their orchards, stands of trees and small wooded areas, were staggered into the distance, scattered among the corn and beet fields, and the livestock pastures. Tethered balloons were visible in the sky on the horizon. They were meant to secure the landing fleet from low-level air attacks. The objective, the coast, seemed within reach," one 12th ss officer observed.[19]

THROUGHOUT THE NIGHT, that objective—Juno Beach—had been randomly pounded by German bombers as Luftlotte 3, virtually absent during the day, fitfully attempted to disrupt the Allied buildup of supplies and personnel. By nightfall, the entire five-mile stretch of beach was "a maze of commodity stacks with thousands of personnel employed around them" that presented a tempting target to the Germans. Royal Canadian Army Service Corps Captain "Pat" Patrick was assigned as the Beach Ammunition Officer for the RCASC unit attached to the 9th Canadian Infantry Brigade. His job on D-Day had been to oversee the landing of 330 tons of ammunition from two Landing Craft, Tanks. This great stack of munitions was piled up in a huge dump on the beach near Bernières-sur-Mer awaiting allocation as needed to 9 CIB's battalions.

With Captain Dave Morwood, Patrick was busy digging a two-man slit trench when a lone German plane "flew toward us along the beach, dropping anti-personnel bombs. We watched the flashes coming closer and, at the same moment, decided we should dive for cover." Patrick plunged into the hole and Morwood piled in on top as a bomb went off practically on their position.[20] While neither man was injured, elsewhere on the beach it was a different story as the planes "bombed the beaches—killing, wounding, blowing up ammunition and destroying equipment."[21]

Standing off the beach aboard Landing Ship, Tank 402, 'D' Company's No. 12 and No. 15 Platoons of the Cameron Highlanders of Ottawa had been delayed by the congestion on the beach from landing their heavy mortars on D-Day. During the night, the mortar teams witnessed four separate German air attacks "during the early hours and before dawn." The company's war diarist reported "many bombs landing on the beaches" with "two bombs [striking] very close to [the] ship, about three to five hundred feet away. Mostly low-level attacks."[22]

Also stuck offshore aboard another LST was the Camerons' commander, Lieutenant Colonel Percy Carl Klaehn. He and the Camerons' command group had been stranded when the Rhino Ferry shuttling personnel from the LST to shore was disabled during its first trip to the beach. A frustrated Klaehn learned that a replacement Rhino would not be available until D+1. "There were five air raids during the night," he confided to his diary, "which were met with intense flak. No damage to ships, but beaches got quite a pasting."[23]

Relatively few German planes managed to penetrate the screen of shipboard and beach-based anti-aircraft guns and hovering Allied fighters waiting to pounce on them. Dodging wildly through walls of flak while also trying to duck fighter planes, the German bombardiers seldom managed to zero in accurately on the wealth of targets packed into the small space. When a patrol by Royal Canadian Air Force 401 Squadron arrived over Juno Beach at 0810 hours on June 7, the pilots watched a twin-engine Junkers-88 slam into the cable of a barrage balloon and plunge to the ground. Then one of the flyers spotted "at least a dozen" JU-88s descend out of the cloud cover. Squadron Leader Lorne Maxwell Cameron of Roland, Manitoba "called for everyone to pick his own target and the squadron broke up" with Spitfires swooping towards the bombers. Some of the German pilots threw their planes into dives towards the beach, while others turned away in a desperate attempt to lumber back to the covering protection of the cloud, the rear gunners blasting at the closing fighters with their machine guns.

"A melee ensued," the squadron's war diarist reported, that resulted in Cameron shooting down two bombers, two pilots sharing another kill, two others gaining a kill apiece, and another being awarded a probable kill. During Cameron's pursuit of the Junkers, he passed over Caen and Carpiquet airport. The intensity of flak coming up from the latter told him that it was obviously still in enemy hands. The Spitfire pilots were elated, the patrol having frustrated the German attack at no cost other than a bullet that harmlessly pierced Flight Lieutenant Alexander Foch Halcrow's perspex canopy just behind his head.[24]

Also over Juno Beach on several sorties during the day was Flying Officer Gordon F. Ockenden of 443 Squadron. Each approach to Normandy "saw us dodging our own barrage balloons. We watched the [sixteen-inch] shells from the battleship... drift by like small balloons as they headed inland, and we were fired on by the navy at least once each day as we got too close to the ships and they got twitchy (also poor aircraft recognition) as we had the big invasion stripes right from Day One [on the spitfires]."

During an afternoon patrol, Flight Lieutenant William Arnold Prest spotted four ME-109 fighters. The Canadians bounced the Germans, with Prest damaging one plane and Ockenden and another pilot combining their firepower "to blow up another." Squadron Leader Hall's Spitfire was struck by several bullets, but not seriously damaged, while Flying Officer Henderson "was lucky to walk away, after engine failure forced him down."[25]

Pilot Officer N. Marshall and Flying Sergeant R.D. Davidson of Squadron 401 were less fortunate. In the late afternoon, the squadron tangled with about six FW-190 fighters that had just finished strafing and bombing the beach when the Canadians attacked. A whirling dogfight ensued. When the guns stopped firing, one German fighter and two Spitfires had been downed. Marshall's plane was shot out of the sky by flak and he was listed as missing. Nobody saw Davidson, who had only joined the squadron two days before, go down. When he failed to return to base, the war diarist noted that Davidson was one of the pilots lost "of whom nothing is known." The squadron's tally for the end of the day was seven JU-88s and the single FW-190—"the highest one-day toll since the Battle of Britain four years earlier."[26]

WHILE THE LUFTWAFFE tried frantically to raid the beaches, but achieved little success in exchange for significant loss in aircraft and crews, the Kriegsmarine was better positioned to attack the Allied fleet. And, while it was true that the Luftwaffe had failed to develop any coherent strategy for meeting the invasion, Grossadmiral Karl

Dönitz had been feverishly working out a battle plan. Caught by surprise by the invasion itself, Headquarters Naval Group West had been unable to respond in any viable form on D-Day itself. When night fell, however, Dönitz ordered an array of boats to slip their berths and sail out to sea. With thousands of Allied ships squished into a narrow corridor extending from southern England across the Channel to Normandy, there was no shortage of viable targets. Should even a single German warship get in amid the Allied fleet, it could wreak havoc, as it would be nearly impossible for the Allies to determine who was friend or foe. But before such destruction could be wrought, the German raiders had to sneak or fight their way through the combat ships and aircraft tasked with screening the armada's flanks.

Dönitz's plan called for the motor torpedo boat flotillas based in Cherbourg, Boulogne, and Ostend to move immediately against the Allied ships. The 5th and 9th MTB flotillas in Cherbourg would lay mines and launch torpedo attacks against the ships operating in the area of the American beaches, while the 2nd and 4th MTB flotillas out of Boulogne carried out similar operations in the waters near Ouistreham. The 8th Flotilla would patrol the eastern part of the Channel, picking off any ships encountered.

The admiral was under no illusions that he could destroy the armada or even inflict enough losses to cripple its ability to support the invasion, for the German navy was simply not strong enough to go head to head against the protecting Allied ships. But he hoped, by harrying the armada's flanks and gaining the occasional breakthrough into its midst, to slow the rate of supplies being carried across the Channel from a steady stream to fitful spurts.

German MTB operations were seriously hampered, however, by a critical shortage of torpedoes for resupplying the boats. Dönitz hoped to compensate by sowing the Allied invasion shipping routes with a new type of mine—called the Oyster or Pressure mine. These mines settled to the sea bottom and were triggered by the hydrostatic pressure created when a ship passed over them at speed. They were next to impossible for minesweepers to catch in their nets and could be programmed to explode after the first ship passed over or to lie quietly until a specified number of ships had passed before detonating. This meant that once an area had been mined, there was no guarantee it could ever be crossed safely. Interspersed among this type of mine, Dönitz ordered acoustic and magnetic pistol-type mines to be sown as well. Both were fitted with delayed-action mechanisms and sometimes anti-sweeping devices that would destroy the minesweeper nets.

Again, Dönitz was not thinking the mines would sink hundreds of ships. His intention was to slow the ferrying of supplies to a crawl by forcing the Allies to embark on lengthy minesweeping operations to ensure that shipping routes were safe.

The final and highest stake cards up Dönitz's sleeve were the U-boats massed on the northwest European coast prior to the invasion. About seventy U-boats had been held back from operations in the Atlantic or Mediterranean theatres and kept in a high state of readiness in order to immediately attack the Allied invasion fleet. More than half of these were positioned in ports in the Bay of Biscay, with the remainder stationed in Norway. Counting among those in the Biscay ports was a special unit operating out of Brest—called the Landwirte Group—that comprised thirty-six U-boats.[27] Nine of these boats were fitted with Schnorkels, an air induction trunk and exhaust pipe that enabled them to use their diesel engines while submerged at periscope depth. This allowed the subs to operate for days at a time without taking the risk of surfacing to recharge their auxiliary battery-powered electrical engines. On D-Day, the Schnorkel boats were already at sea, and by noon all conventional boats stationed in pens at Lorient, St. Nazaire, and La Pallice were unleashed in force.[28]

The threat posed by the U-boats had long been anticipated by Allied naval commander Royal Navy Admiral Sir Bertram Ramsay. To block any attempt by the submariners to break into the Channel waters, Royal Air Force's Coastal Command had been instructed to create "a solid wall of air patrols over the southwestern approaches."[29]

[3]

Going into the Attack

A MONG THOSE FLYING an anti-submarine patrol in the early hours of June 7 was Royal Canadian Air Force Flying Officer Kenneth Owen Moore at the controls of a Liberator bomber. The twenty-one-year-old Rockhaven, Saskatchewan native commanded a mostly Canadian crew assigned to Royal Air Force No. 224 Squadron of Coastal Command. Nicknamed "K.O.," Moore had enlisted shortly after his nineteenth birthday in August 1941, quitting a 95-cent-a-day job at the Woodward's Department Store in downtown Vancouver to do so. He had decided to enlist after ending up in a smoky Eastside pub one night with several young Americans who had crossed the border to join the RCAF and get into a war the United States seemed determined to stay out of. "Damn, if they're prepared to do this, then what am I doing?" Moore thought. In the morning he and the ten Americans filled out enlistment papers at the RCAF's Vancouver recruitment post and received immediate orders to report to the manning depot in Edmonton for processing.

"This will come as a little surprise to you," he scribbled in a letter to his mother while sitting in a train car clattering through the Rockies, "but I'm now in the air force on my way to start training."[1] With just a high school education, Moore never dreamed of being selected for aircrew training. Instead, his ambition had been to become an

50

aircraft mechanic and he only took the aircrew qualification tests at the urging of the depot's staff officers, who sensed a young man with potential. Breezing through the tests, Moore was soon flying planes and loving every minute.

After initial training in Canada through the British Commonwealth Air Training Program, Moore reported to an Operational Training Unit in Nassau, Bahamas to learn the trade of flying Liberator bombers in an anti-submarine role. Originally designed as a long-range bomber for conventional raids against targets deep in Germany's heart, the Liberator had been identified in 1942 as better suited for closing the air coverage gap that existed in the mid-Atlantic along the vital maritime convoy routes. Powered by four Pratt and Whitney 1,200-horsepower radial piston engines, the B-24 Liberator boasted a 5,000-pound weapons load and a range capability of 3,300 miles. Swapping the retractable belly turret for an air-to-surface radar unit enabled the Liberator to hunt U-boats, which had previously been free to roam the mid-Atlantic without fear of attack by aircraft.[2] Carrying a normal munitions load of six depth charges, a Liberator had a patrol time of 16.5 hours—more than sufficient to reach the mid-Atlantic from bases in the United Kingdom and Iceland and then to linger for lengthy periods.

In Nassau, then-Sergeant Moore was assigned as a co-pilot in a crew commanded by a pilot officer. Once training was completed, the pilot, Moore, and the navigator expected to be assigned to an active squadron where they would form the nucleus for a complete crew. To Moore's dismay, however, the pilot washed out during training and he and the navigator were left high and dry with no prospect for posting to a squadron until after the next training course was completed. The two men spent a lot of time downtown bemoaning their fate over pints of beer and were joined in this task by others also awaiting the next course. One afternoon, four Wireless Operator Air Gunners (WAGS) wandered into the bar with a story of how they had been kicked back from a planned deployment because they made a fuss when it was announced they would be split up and scattered to other crews. Looking at the assembled beer-quaffing host before him, Moore said, "You know what's sitting around this table—a crew.

We've got four WAGS, two pilots, and a navigator. They're supposed to want crews. What the hell are we sitting here for? We should be a crew."

"Yeah, well, you go and convince them then," one WAG snorted.

Arranging a meeting with the chief flight instructor, Moore said, "Understand your business is to train crews. We got a bunch of guys drinking beer every afternoon and I'm one of them, but we think we should be a crew." Moore expected a curt dismissal and reprimand for his temerity. After checking the personnel files, however, the officer calmly agreed.[3]

With Moore in charge, the seven Canadians were assigned to No. 224 Squadron in St. Eval, Cornwall. They reported for duty in July 1943, almost two years after Moore's enlistment, and added three more non-Canadian air crew to form the full ten-man complement required to man a coastal command Liberator. After flying several missions into the Atlantic, the squadron shifted to regular patrols of the Bay of Biscay and into the Mediterranean in support of the Allied invasion of Italy. By D-Day, Moore had about thirty missions under his belt and credit for crippling a U-boat during an action in March 1944.

Because of the invasion, St. Eval was bursting at the seams with planes and crews. Whereas, prior to the buildup for Operation Overlord, the base had supported two coastal command squadrons, five squadrons now used it. Shortly after midnight on June 7, Moore lifted off the runway and joined a formation of No. 224 Squadron Liberators carrying out a "Cork" patrol intended to close the English Channel's southern approaches to U-boats coming up through the Bay of Biscay. Moore and his crew were jumpier than normal, still shocked by the events of an operation carried out two weeks earlier. On that night patrol, they had been one of four crews assigned to fly close to St. Nazaire, drop flares over the coast to simulate an invasion, and stir up a false alarm response by the enemy. Each plane operated alone and Moore's flight proved uneventful. The crew had dropped their flares and returned home, but then learned that none of the other three planes had come back. Their disappearance remained a mystery on June 7, and Moore worried the Germans had developed a secret weapon that enabled night fighters to track down the Liberators and outfight them. Or perhaps it was some new form of anti-aircraft gun. Or perhaps the crews had simply run out of luck.

Luck was something most flyers believed in. Moore didn't have a lucky charm as such, but the crew did have a mascot that accompanied them on every flight. Moore and his gang had purchased Dinty—a big teddy bear—in a Montreal bar shortly before they flew a Liberator out from Canada to England. In the morning, Moore and a couple of the other men had shrugged off hangovers and took the bear to a tailor so he could be readied for aircrew service, complete in a proper uniform. Dinty had been at their side ever since, always being positioned front and centre in crew photographs.

The Liberators spread out so that every fifteen minutes one passed over any given spot along the part of the Channel approaches they were corking shut near the French coast. Each plane had twelve depth charges aboard that would be dropped in sticks of six during an attack. It was a fine night with a full moon shining and only a two-tenths cloud cover concentrated along the French coast. Ukrainian-Canadian WAG Mike Werbiski was manning the air-to-surface radar, scanning for targets. "Got something," he announced tersely on the intercom.

Moore quickly told him to shut the radar down to prevent detection by the enemy, if in fact the signal was that of an enemy ship rather than radar clutter. At the same time, he shoved the Liberator down to two hundred feet and roared at top speed past the position Werbiski had identified. Off to the flank, Moore clearly saw the silhouette of a U-boat running on the surface and started a slow turn that would bring the Liberator back in a complete 360-degree circle by holding a rate of three degrees turn per second. This rate of turn was standard procedure for coastal command during night operations, enabling a plane to hack back with precision onto a point passed over earlier on even the darkest of nights. Tonight, however, Moore could clearly see the U-boat pinned by the harsh moonlight as if by a wide searchlight. Standard operating procedure established by coastal command called for attacks to be brought in against surface craft at an altitude of three hundred feet. Moore believed that if something was SOP, then the enemy probably knew about it.

"Why attack at an altitude they know they're going to be attacked at?" Moore had asked his crew previously. They agreed with the proposition and so Moore started attacking at a mere fifty feet or even less from the ocean, so low the four big props would lift a thick wake as the plane roared over the water. "There weren't any steep turns involved," Moore later said, "so you were pretty well set up and my little rule of thumb was that I kept the stuff going over the cockpit. If the enemy shellfire was going over top of it, you knew you were all right."[4] At just under fifty feet of elevation, Moore bore in on the target at 190 miles per hour while the crew got ready to execute the attack.

From his position in the front turret, navigator Warrant Officer Alex Gibb thought the submarine looked "as if it were painted on white paper." He could see the conning tower quite clearly and the anti-aircraft gun bristling on its extended bridge. In early 1944, the Type VIIC U-boat—the workhorse of the German submarine fleet—had been up-gunned. As the Liberator roared down on the ship, its anti-aircraft gunners started running towards the ship's 37-millimetre M42 automatic gun and the two double-barrelled 20-millimetre 38 II guns.

The gunner in the Liberator's front turret opened fire with his dual 12.7-millimetre Browning machine guns before the Germans could bring their own guns into action. Gibb saw one German sailor clutch his stomach and pitch forward, while the others dived for cover. Then the Liberator was flashing over the conning tower. The second navigator, Warrant Officer J. "Scotty" McDowell, peering through the Mark 3, Low Level bomb sight, punched the release button and six depth charges plunged down on the U-boat in a perfect straddle of three to each side.

"Oh, God, we've blown her clean out of the water!" the rear gunner yelled as the plane passed over the stricken U-boat. Moore hauled the bomber around for another pass and saw water still heaving up from the explosions and "distinct patches of black oil in the dark green sea. In the patches were dark objects; almost certainly bodies."[5] RAF intelligence analysts would later determine that the submarine sunk was U-629. All fifty-one hands aboard were lost.*

After carrying out the single pass that Coastal Command allowed for confirmation of a kill, Moore jumped the Liberator back into its assigned slot in the cork patrol. Little more than a minute later, just off the tiny island of Ushant, Werbiski reported the bearings of another contact dead ahead. As the radar operator shut down his set, Moore lost elevation and slipped to port in order to put the potential U-boat on the Liberator's starboard side. McDowell was first to sight the German sub, up-moon of them and slightly to port. Moore dropped the bomber down to his preferred attack height of a little under fifty feet. When the nose gunner opened fire from a range of a mile, the German anti-aircraft gunners immediately answered back with fire from all their anti-aircraft guns. Navigator Gibb watched with horrid fascination as "a perfect fan of tracer from the conning tower" darted towards them and streamed overhead. The Liberator passed over the submarine seconds later, and he toggled the bomb release. Two depth charges struck on one side and four on the other in what was the crew's second perfect straddle of the night.

When the depth charges exploded after such a well-placed straddle, a submarine normally broke apart. This time, however, the U-boat seemed to only drop a little at the stern and list slightly to

---

* Recently, there have been reports from various German sources that the identification of this U-boat as U-629 was incorrect and that it was instead U-441. Also a Type VIIC U-boat, 441 had been converted in late 1943 into an experimental boat called U-Flak 1. Fitted with a four-barrelled 22-millimetre fast-firing anti-aircraft gun on an extended front bridge, the boat was designed to lure Allied anti-submarine aircraft into attacking it so they could be destroyed by its deadlier firepower. The experiment proved largely a failure and by June 6 the boat and its three sister ships had been converted back to standard U-boats. Both U-boats had a crew of fifty-one and it is agreed by all sources that all perished when each of the two boats was sunk by Coastal Command aircraft in the early morning hours of June 7.

starboard. It then chugged slowly onward, trailing oil in its wake. With no depth charges remaining to renew the attack, Moore was just going to issue a call for a reinforcement bomber when mid-upper gunner WAG Don Griese shouted: "She's going down! It's like a Hollywood picture!" As Moore banked for another pass, he could see the U-boat's bow sticking almost straight out of the sea. Then, surprisingly slowly, U-373 slid back into the sea and was gone. Flying over the spot where the U-boat had gone down, the bomber's spotlight illuminated three dinghies crowded with sailors floating amid a cluster of debris and a thick oil slick.[6]

"Sighted two subs, sank same," Moore had radioed back to base.[7] Despite the laconic nature of the message, Moore and his crew knew they had carried out a stunning feat. Everyone was slapping each other on the back and laughing. What they had feared would prove a night of ill luck had proved to be filled with good fortune.

When the bomber touched down several hours later at St. Eval and the kills were confirmed by RAF intelligence, Moore learned that he had made aviation history—the war's only double submarine kill by a single bomber during one patrol. The next day, Moore was given an immediate award of the Distinguished Service Order. A United States Silver Star soon followed. For their part in the attack, radio operator Warrant Officer William P. Foster and navigator McDowell received Distinguished Flying Crosses, while flight engineer Sergeant J. Hamer won a Distinguished Flying Medal. The Canadian government's response to Moore's achievement was bizarre. As he was seconded to the RAF, Moore's DSO was considered an award granted by Britain rather than Canada. The DSO was only rarely awarded to air force officers, being generally reserved for the army, and a DFC would have been a logical Canadian decoration. Instead, Moore initially heard nothing at all from RCAF headquarters or the Canadian government. Several weeks later, however, he received a letter of appreciation from the government accompanied by the offer of one thousand complimentary cigarettes. He could either accept the cigarettes now or have them held in trust by the government until his return to Canada. A nonsmoker, Moore declined the offer by letter.[8]

WHILE MOORE AND HIS CREW were making military aviation history over the southern approaches to the English Channel, another dramatic event played out to the north of the Normandy beaches near the mouth of the Seine estuary. Here, four motor torpedo boats of the Royal Canadian Navy's 29th MTB Flotilla patrolled about thirteen miles southwest of Le Havre. Although the sky was clear, a hard wind churned up the water and made it "a bad night for coastal craft" such as MTBS 459, 460, 465, and 466. Commanding the four-boat patrol was the 29th's senior officer Lieutenant Commander C.A. "Tony" Law, aboard MTB 459.[9]

"In spite of the rough seas we maintained 20 knots," Law later wrote, "the saucy MTBS creating plumes like the spread tails of haughty peacocks and leaving wakes like the powerful wings of seagulls... On we went, threading our way through the thickening flotillas of landing craft which made it impossible to steer a straight course... Our unit was to patrol three miles northeast of the Assault Area, adjusting our position every hour because of the strong tides."[10]

Until the spectre of Nazism had touched his consciousness in 1937, Law had been basking in the limelight as one of Canada's most promising young painters. In the early 1930s, he studied under Group of Seven artist Fred Varley and also with Franklin Brownell before going on to win the Jessie Dow Prize. His ability to harmonize colour and form, combined with an apparently instinctive grasp of natural subjects, gave his work a beguiling sense of effortlessness. Some said that Law's artistic talent was inherited from his grandfather, who had also been a gifted painter. Had it not been for the rise of Hitler in a resurgent Germany, Law probably would have stayed unwaveringly on the artistic track to which he seemed ideally suited. But if his grandfather had provided him with a painter's gift, he had inherited from his father an interest in things military. In World War I, Law's father had served as a major in the Royal Canadian Regiment, and the young Law had in fact been born overseas in England in 1916 while his father was serving in the Canadian Expeditionary Force there. Although both his parents were Canadians, his mother had been living in England when she met her husband-to-be. In 1917, the Laws had returned to Canada and settled in Quebec City.

By 1937, Law was convinced that war was inevitable and so attempted to join the Royal Canadian Navy Volunteer Reserve. Learning that there were no openings, he applied instead to the army and
was accepted into the Royal Canadian Ordnance Corps on April 20,
1937 as a second lieutenant. When war broke out, he was quickly promoted to captain, but still itched to get into the navy. Hearing that the
RCN was actively seeking young officers to loan to the Royal Navy for
service in Motor Torpedo Boats, Law finagled a transfer in January
1940. That spring, the young Acting Temporary Probationary Sub-
Lieutenant, RCNVR arrived with a batch of other Canadian officers in
England and passed through various courses relevant to MTB operations. A year later, he was appointed to a Motor Gun Boat Flotilla (pre-
cursor of MTBS) as a first lieutenant and boat navigator. In early 1944,
Law and Lieutenant J.R.H. Kirkpatrick were selected to head up the
two MTB flotillas Canada was forming to take part in the invasion—
the 29th and 65th Motor Torpedo Boat Flotillas.

Law took command of the 29th. Each flotilla was equipped with
eight MTBS of a different class. Kirkpatrick's 65th was outfitted with
eight 'D' class Fairmiles. Measuring 115 feet from bow to stern and
powered by four 1,250-horsepower Packard engines, the Fairmiles
were capable of twenty-nine to thirty-one knots. To compensate
for this comparatively slow top end by torpedo boat standards, the
Fairmiles came heavily armed. Each boat carried four 18-inch torpedoes, two six-pounders, two twin .5-inch power-mounted guns, twin
Oerlikons, and twin Vickers hand-operated machine guns mounted
on either side of the bridge. They also carried two depth charge
launching rails and had an armour-plated bridge to protect the command and control centre. Each Fairmile had a crew of three officers
and twenty-six ratings. Their size enabled the Fairmiles to weather
severe seas and they were capable of staying out on operations for
long periods. Being so much larger than normal torpedo boats, the
Fairmiles were known as "Long Boats" or simply "Longs."

The G-Type motor torpedo boats with which the 29th Flotilla was
equipped stood at the opposite end of the MTB scale from the Fairmiles. They were only 71.5 feet long and could gallop along at forty-

one knots, a pace made possible by three American Packard–built Rolls Royce 1,250-horsepower engines (later replaced by 1,500-horsepower engines). Normal crew size was two officers and four ratings, but as Law was the flotilla's senior officer, his MTB 459 carried an extra officer and signalman.[11] Although not as heavily armed as the Fairmiles, the G-Types still packed a lot of fighting teeth that convinced the RCN staff who commissioned them that they were "formidable as gun boats."[12] Each boat was armed with a power-mounted two-pound pom-pom gun forward, a twin-barrelled 20-millimetre Oerlikon anti-aircraft gun aft, and a pair of twin Vickers .303 machine guns mounted on the port and starboard sides of the bridge. Normally, they also carried four 18-inch torpedo tubes, but these were stripped from the 29th's MTBs in April and replaced with two depth charge launching rails to enable the flotilla to perform a special anti-submarine role.

British intelligence had caught wind of the possibility that a "small very fast type of U-boat called a W-boat... might make its first appearance in the enemy's attempt to defeat the invasion."[13] So-called because it was believed powered by a Walter hydrogen peroxide–fuelled turbine, the W-boat was reportedly capable of forty knots on the surface and a remarkable thirty knots when submerged.

For the sailors of 29th Flotilla, the loss of their torpedo fighting capability was "a hard blow" that left them feeling virtually unarmed.[14] The prime offensive weapon that any MTB brought to bear against enemy surface ships was its torpedo firing capability. With torpedoes, the tiny boats that were normally sneered at by "big ship" men were "capable of sinking a battleship." Law was quick to point out that a pair of Italian torpedo boats had sunk the large modern battle cruiser HMS *Manchester* off Tunisia in August 1942 and that Allied MTBs had proven their worth by sinking thousands of tons of enemy shipping throughout the war.

So it was not surprising that he and his fellow torpedo boat sailors felt "the bottom had dropped out of everything, and our faces were long and sad as we watched our main armament and striking power being taken away."[15] To exchange the torpedoes for depth charges in order to undertake a job that "had the disadvantage of being purely hypothetical since there was no certain evidence of the existence of the W-boat" seemed the height of folly to the flotilla commander.

Within a matter of weeks, the foolishness of this decision was confirmed when the 29th was assigned not to chase phantom W-boats about the English Channel on D-Day, but to instead patrol the waters northwest of Juno and Sword beaches in order to protect the fleet from German surface craft. With no time to refit the boats with torpedo racks and tubes, the flotilla went into the operation still mounting depth charge racks and lugging forty-eight hundred-pound depth charges. Late on June 6, four of the MTBS departed Portsmouth for the French coast. In the lead was Law aboard MTB 459. Following in a closely grouped line behind was firstly Lieutenant Dave Killam's 460, then Lieutenant Charlie "Chuff-Chuff" Chaffey's 465, with Lieutenant Barney Marshall on 466 bringing up the tail. The first few hours of the patrol passed uneventfully, but at 0406 hours Law overheard a signal from Lieutenant Commander Don Bradford of the Royal Navy's 55th MTB Flotilla reporting that his three-boat patrol was investigating a radar contact north of his patrol area. Soon, Law saw star shells bursting high in the night sky and lines of tracer flashing back and forth at sea level as the British ships tangled with what seemed to be a larger force of German vessels. With his own patrol area tediously quiet, Law decided to go to Bradford's aid and ordered the MTBS to action stations.

Before Law's MTBS had gone very far, however, the battle abruptly fizzled out. A few minutes later, Law saw Bradford's boats approaching. When the 55th's MTBS passed about two hundred yards ahead of his boats on a southerly course, Law decided to track on astern of them. As his patrol was just coming about, Law made out the silhouettes of six enemy ships to the northeast. "I broke off and headed in that direction," Law wrote, "radioing to Dave, Chuff-Chuff, and Barney: 'Maximum speed; we're going in to attack.'"[16]

When Law had his pom-pom gunner fire star shells, the silhouettes were clearly illuminated in the harsh red glare and identified as six R-boats heading on an easterly course in line-ahead formation.

Law's boats quickly closed abeam of them. Designed for service as minesweepers, R-boats were also commonly used as attack vessels and for convoy protection. There were numerous classes of these vessels, but all were generally about 125 to 135 feet long and capable of twenty to twenty-four knots. Crewed by either thirty-four or thirty-eight men, the R-boats were far more heavily gunned than Law's MTBS. General armament consisted of one 37-millimetre gun and up to three two-barrelled 20-millimetre guns.[17] A RCN report on operations during the invasion stated dryly that the R-boats possessed a "marked superiority in firepower" over the small G-Type MTBS.[18]

Despite being outnumbered and outsized, Law never considered breaking off and running. Instead, he made the R-boats scurry for survival. "At 700 yards all four of our boats opened up with intense, concentrated fire, and we closed in to 150 yards. It was a furious battle. The tracer, thick and penetrating, hit 459 in several places, including the chart-house, thus putting the QH (electronic navigational aid) set out of action. [First Lieutenant] John Shand, shaken by the explosion, pulled aside the curtain and looked up to the bridge to see what was going on. He was confronted by three pairs of glassy, frightened eyes. [Third Officer] Footsie, the coxswain, and I had also been shaken by the force of that last resounding Oerlikon shell."[19]

Able Seaman W. Bushfield, the pom-pom gun loader, was badly wounded by shrapnel. Despite being in intense pain, he kept on loading ammunition into the continuously firing gun, an act that earned him a Distinguished Service Medal. Aboard MTB 466, another gunner, Able Seaman J. Wright, displayed the same courageous spirit. "When wounded in the back by Oerlikon splinters he nevertheless kept up rapid and continuous fire until action had broken off," read his subsequent DSM citation. Wright only stepped away from his gun when the boat's first lieutenant ordered him to seek first aid treatment.[20]

Able Seaman T. Howarth was also wounded on MTB 466, and aboard MTB 460 Able Seaman P. Durnford suffered injuries. All four of the craft sustained superficial hull damage in the fierce running gun battle.[21] Even though the German boats were more heavily gunned and numerous, they took the worst of the fight, with one bursting into flames and exploding. A fire that was quickly extinguished broke out aboard another.

Suddenly, mines started exploding all around the racing boats and Law realized that they had strayed into a "British minefield known as the Area Scollops a few miles off Le Havre. After our ten-minute engagement at close range, I was forced to disengage, making a smokescreen as we steamed northwards out of the dangerous minefield, which had doubtless frightened the wits out of the enemy as well as out of me."[22]

Realizing where he and the R-boats were now situated, Law decided that the Germans had been attempting to break off the action and escape into the city's heavily protected harbour. Le Havre was known to be a primary base for R-boats operating on this area of the European coast, with some fifty-five R-boats based in the city's port. The ones Law had engaged were almost certainly part of this formation.[23]

Given the small size of the MTBs, only rudimentary first aid was available for the wounded men, as the crew had no room for specialized medical personnel. On MTB 459, the third officer could only wrap Bushfield's wounds with field dressings, give him a shot of morphine, and then have him carefully moved down to the coxswain's cramped cabin, where he was made as comfortable as possible.

Returning to their original patrol area, the boats closed in together so that the officers could discuss damages and casualties. Then Law had "McAulley, the wireless operator, with a cigarette dangling from the corner of his mouth and his tin hat pushed far back on his head, bang out a coded message... giving... a brief outline of our engagement with the six R-boats."[24]

The MTBs resumed their patrol until relieved at 0500 hours just as a "cold dawn broke over a sea still capped with ruffled foam." Only then could Law turn the boats and carry his wounded homeward.[25]

[4]

A Picnic

As JUNE 7TH's pre-dawn light brushed the farm fields, country villages, and sandy beaches of Normandy in a delicate golden wash, Allied and German soldiers readied weapons, gulped rations, and prepared for another long day's fighting. The smoke of fires caused by shellfire and exploding bombs drifted up from ruined buildings, smouldering orchards, and the wreckage of military equipment. Several miles east of Juno Beach, a larger, darker cloud boiled out of bomb-battered Caen—grim testimony to the beginning of that city's tragic destruction. Six miles inland from the beach, the breezes were light under clear skies. Stretched across an eight-mile-wide front, the men of 3rd Canadian Infantry Division and 2nd Canadian Armoured Brigade moved forward, intent on finishing the business of reaching the objectives that were to have been in hand by the end of the previous day. Carpiquet airport, the Caen-Bayeux highway, and the parallelling railroad lay little more than three miles to the south, an easy morning's march away.

To 9th Canadian Infantry Brigade on the left flank fell the task of seizing the airport. The North Nova Scotia Highlanders supported by the Sherbrooke Fusiliers would kick off from Villons-les-Buissons and lead the way with the Stormont, Dundas and Glengarry Highlanders and the Highland Light Infantry in trail. Standing behind the so-called Highland Brigade would be two battalions from the

8th Canadian Infantry Brigade—the Queen's Own Rifles and Le Régiment de la Chaudière. On the division's extreme left flank, 8 CIB's other battalion, the North Shore (New Brunswick) Regiment, was marching a mile east of its June 6 end position in Tailleville to capture the Luftwaffe radar station situated on a hill next to the village of Douvres-la-Délivrande. This would also enable the Canadian division to tie in with 3rd British Infantry Division advancing inland from Sword Beach. On the division's right flank, meanwhile, 7th Canadian Infantry Brigade would bull southwards to take up positions astride the Caen-Bayeux railway at Bretteville-l'Orgueilleuse and Putot-en-Bessin.

Despite the heavy casualties suffered on D-Day, a mood of determined optimism prevailed. While the previous day's fighting left no illusion that this day would be a stroll in the French countryside, the expectation was that the Allied juggernaut unleashed in Normandy would crush the opposing Germans in its maw. During the night, from his forward headquarters in an orchard outside Bernières-sur-Mer, Major General Rod Keller had issued orders for the advance, set schedules for its completion, and the brigadiers had in turn passed instructions to the battalions under their command.

At forty-three, Keller was the youngest Canadian major general—having attained divisional command on September 8, 1942. Five-foot-eleven and weighing about 170 pounds, Keller had ramrod-straight posture that created the impression of greater height. A stickler for military protocol, Keller was a spit and polish officer who expected his division to be as meticulously turned out as his own battle dress. Although most of the time strict and grim, Keller could as easily be charming and jovial—particularly when in company of women. Although married, he had spent much time in England away from divisional headquarters dallying at the estate of his upper-class mistress.

That had been fine by his General Staff Officer, Lieutenant Colonel Don Mingay, for he considered Keller a dunderhead qualified to be little more than the division's figurehead, while he and the headquarters staff ran things. In a time and an army where hard drinking went hand in hand with hard-driving soldiering, Keller's excessive boozing worried subordinates and superiors alike. But, despite a rumoured scotch-bottle-a-day habit, Keller was seldom seen to behave worse for it. On D-Day, however, the general had proved increasingly excitable from the moment he waded ashore in the late morning and his anxiousness seemed only to increase on June 7.[1]

If Keller seemed to be holding a relatively unsteady hand on the division's reins, the same could not be said of his infantry brigadiers. Each was a solid, experienced commander, ready for the tough job ahead, despite the fact that the two officers who had attended Royal Military College had been less than exemplary students. The youngest, 9 CIB's Douglas Gordon "Ben" Cunningham, had graduated in the class of 1929 with marks hovering on the line separating the middle and bottom thirds of his class. During his four years at RMC, he had demonstrated consistent indifference to academic studies. Cunningham had arrived at RMC in 1925, a lanky red-haired youth weighing just 135 pounds, but quickly adapted to the strict regimen of athletics and military drill, to be transformed on graduation as a six-foot-two "wiry athlete with imposing presence." Hockey and soccer were his key sports. Although ending every semester with reports that scolded his academic failings, he inevitably garnered praise for his military bearing and motivation. RMC Commandant Archibald Cameron Macdonell, the strict World War I veteran who ran the school with a stern hand through the interwar years, described him upon graduation as showing "indications of developing considerable strength of character and leadership."[2]

From RMC, Cunningham proceeded directly to a short-lived career in the financial industry on Toronto's Bay Street that ended abruptly with the stock market crash. He then entered Osgoode Hall, following his father's footsteps to a law degree attained in 1933. Returning to hometown Kingston, Cunningham opened a legal practice, but his first interest was the army. He joined the local Princess of Wales Own Regiment militia and soon became its adjutant. Shortly before the war, when asked about his availability for full-time military service, he responded, "available at any time to serve anyplace."[3]

With war, Cunningham answered the call to duty and by 1942 was the brigade major of 4th Canadian Infantry Brigade on the ill-fated day its troops hit the beach at Dieppe. Circling offshore in a

LCT command ship, Cunningham handled the fire support provided by the naval ships. For eight hours, with the ship repeatedly raked by fire from the beach that wounded his brigadier and killed or wounded many others aboard, the major continued calmly performing his job and then was instrumental in ensuring the evacuation of many troops from the blood-soaked sand. For his bravery, Cunningham was awarded an immediate Distinguished Service Order and the next day promoted to lieutenant colonel in command of the Cameron Highlanders of Ottawa. Following a short stint on the general staff of 1 Canadian Corps, he was promoted to brigadier of 9 CIB in November 1943.

Cunningham's counterpart at the helm of 7 CIB was Brigadier Harry Foster, who had conducted himself even more poorly during less than three years at RMC even though his father, a retired Permanent Force officer, had used a personal friendship with Macdonell to gain the young man entrance. As Harry was enrolled in the first year of a science program at McGill University, Macdonell agreed to let him into RMC only if he achieved an 80 per cent average at the Montreal institution. But Foster managed only 67 per cent and failed one course entirely. Yet Macdonell relented and accepted him anyway in 1922.

Having entered the college via influence rather than competition, Foster continued to put in a lacklustre academic performance. Five months after enrolling, Macdonell declared his efforts "satisfactory, albeit uneven." That the commandant was being surprisingly lenient towards Foster was evidenced by the fact that he had failed physics, chemistry, and English. More damning was the verdict that Foster "is a fine type but must cultivate cheerfulness." Cadets at RMC were "expected to grin and bear the pressures of military life. Demeanour was the most obvious indication of character. It was considered an accurate reflection of a cadet's potential to inspire and lead soldiers once he earned the King's Commission. In a school where most of the military instructors had fought in the trenches of the Western Front, sad sacks were considered unsafe leaders; optimism remained the order of the day in the cadet wing."[4]

By the end of the first semester of Foster's second year, Macdonell's frustration with the young man was evident. "Conduct, fair," he wrote. "This cadet does not begin to do himself justice, tho[ugh] I think he is trying now. Hope so. He had been slacking and drifting through life, not getting anywhere when I spoke to him. Grade 'A' in Riding, 'C' in P.T., 'D' in Drill and Musketry. He could easily be 'A' in each one."[5]

Even his peers were disappointed in Foster. In the December 1923 yearbook, he was described as suffering "to some extent from taking things too easily. When he wants to he can play a good game." Faced with a series of failing grades in his third year, Foster decided to pack it in and, with his father's blessing, withdrew from RMC in July 1924 to receive the King's Commission. Such a commission in the Permanent Force was available to all cadets after two full years at RMC.[6] An excellent horseman, he was posted to the Lord Strathcona's Horse cavalry regiment.

No longer having to worry about academic studies, Foster flourished in the regular army. By war's outbreak, he had risen in rank to captain and was pegged early for a fast-track career. In late 1939, he attended Staff College—a major rung up the ladder leading to brigade or divisional command—and in 1941 reached the rank of lieutenant colonel, with command of the 4th Princess Louise Dragoon Guards. The following year he was assigned as General Staff Officer 1 of 1st Canadian Infantry Division, an important posting that provided officers identified as having brigade potential with critical staff management experience. In late 1942, Foster took command of the Highland Light Infantry, a move that served to broaden this cavalry-cum-tanker's expertise by giving him experience in infantry command. The following year, he was promoted to brigadier of 7 CIB. Within a few months of assuming this duty, Foster was seconded to temporary duty as the commanding officer of Canadian forces engaged in the Kiska Island invasion in the Aleutians. He returned from that assignment just weeks before D-Day. Forty-two years old in June 1944, Foster was now regarded as a tough, hard-charging career officer already earmarked by First Army commander Lieutenant General Harry Crerar for eventual divisional command.

At forty-six, 8 CIB's Brigadier Kenneth Gault Blackader was a World War 1 veteran, who had distinguished himself in a long career.

Having gone overseas in 1916 as a lieutenant in the 5th Regiment, Royal Canadian Highlanders, Blackader had been wounded on August 8, 1918 during the Battle of Amiens. His heroism in the course of that action garnered a Military Cross.[7] After the Armistice, Blackader joined the Black Watch Regiment of Montreal and earned rapid promotion up the reserve unit's command chain. At war's outbreak in September 1939, he was a full colonel and the regiment's commander. He immediately set to raising 1st Battalion Black Watch for active duty and, in order to take it overseas, reverted to the rank of lieutenant colonel. In January 1942, Blackader left the regiment after being promoted to brigadier and command of 8 CIB.

Although it was unusual for someone his age to command a combat brigade, Blackader's reputation was rock-solid. That he had not been promoted to even higher command likely resulted from the fact that he was a militia soldier rather than a Permanent Force officer, combined with a lack of divisional command openings. Within the Black Watch, Blackader held almost legendary standing because of his long service with the regiment during the interwar years and his combat service during the Great War. But in many regards, Blackader retained the mannerisms and temperament of the upper-class World War I officer, so that he often seemed deliberately aloof and formal in his dealings with subordinates and superiors alike. He was not a man to suffer fools quietly or to hesitate in strongly stating his opinions about divisional operations.[8]

AT 0130 HOURS, Brigadier Harry Foster convened an Orders Group for 7th Canadian Infantry Brigade at his headquarters in a farmhouse on the edge of Colombiers-sur-Seulles. Here, the commanders of the Royal Winnipeg Rifles, Regina Rifles, and Canadian Scottish Regiment gathered around a large table in the crude kitchen. By the yellow glare of a kerosene lamp, Foster gave the tired men their marching orders.[9]

Knowing he was blessed with excellent battalion commanders, Foster did not waste time covering every detail of what they were to accomplish in the morning. Beginning at 0600 hours, the Winnipeg

Rifles would advance on the right and the Regina Rifles on the left to sever the Caen-Bayeux highway and the parallelling railroad a short distance beyond. The Canadian Scottish would remain in reserve, providing a firm base to the advance in case the Germans countered this attack in strength with one of their own before the lead battalions reached the iron rails.[10] Backing up the brigade would be a machine gun and mortar platoon of the Cameron Highlanders of Ottawa, three troops of the 3rd Anti-Tank Regiment, Royal Canadian Artillery, and two batteries of 17-pounder antitank guns drawn from the 62nd British Anti-Tank Regiment.

Intrinsic to the division's operational plans in the aftermath of the landings was the assumption that the Germans would respond according to their standard doctrine, with an immediate counter-attack. Foster hoped his brigade could reach the railroad before the German onslaught. With its sunken bed, the line would serve well as an antitank barrier. Briefing over, the battalion commanders raced to ready their battalions for the morning.[11] They had less than four hours to not only set out their plan of advance, but also determine how to meet the likely German counterattack. Nobody expected any sleep this night.

Immediately on returning to his headquarters in the village of Pierrepont, Canadian Scottish commander Lieutenant Colonel Fred Cabeldu summoned his company commanders to a briefing. His battalion had ended June 6 well forward of the other two 7 CIB battalions, but with the companies widely dispersed. The thirty-seven-year-old former real estate agent from Victoria still regretted that Foster had insisted his companies dig in for the night short of their D-Day objective. Convinced nothing stood in his way but a few demoralized Germans, Cabeldu had begged permission to keep moving despite the onset of darkness until he reached the Caen-Bayeux highway. Foster, bowing to instructions from Keller's headquarters, refused and ordered him to "freeze" in place for fear of the possibility of an "enemy tank counterattack."[12]

Because his units were so spread out, the lieutenant colonel had yet to know for sure whether all his company commanders had survived the day unscathed. When 'C' Company's Major Desmond Crofton arrived, Cabeldu happily shook his hand. Crofton wrote later "how glad the C.O. was to see one of his company commanders coming in, and then another, and all of them arriving, as he never thought that he would see all his old group intact."[13]

The scene unfolding at Cabeldu's headquarters mirrored that played out at other battalion headquarters, although his had been the only D-Day assault unit fortunate to have had no company commanders killed or wounded. Elsewhere, the assault battalions scrambled during the early morning hours to bring up major drafts of reinforcements to replenish the ranks, while replacement company officers attempted to acquaint themselves with new commands.

Regina Rifles Lieutenant Colonel Foster Matheson noted a good number of 'B' Company survivors—first cut apart during the landing and then heavily engaged in fighting within Courseulles-sur-Mer—straggle into the battalion lines during the night. The majority of these men had barely survived drowning when the landing craft dumped them into deep water well out from the beach. In the struggle to get ashore, many had abandoned weapons and ammunition in order to swim to shallower water. They had then spent the afternoon and night wandering country lanes in an attempt to reconnect with the Reginas. Lacking replacement weaponry for those without arms, Matheson ordered them "supplied with enemy equipment." The Reginas also welcomed into their ranks about one hundred reinforcements. Having withdrawn the terribly mauled 'A' Company from the front lines back to battalion headquarters at Reviers, Matheson used these men to restore it to combat strength.[14]

Most of the reinforcements received by the Royal Winnipeg Rifles went to bring the devastated 'B' Company back to a semblance of combat readiness. This company had been shredded on the beach, its commander Captain Phil Gower counting only twenty-six men fit for duty and all its platoon commanders either dead or wounded after the German beach fortifications were cleared.

The battalion was in the midst of integrating the reinforcements at 0200 hours when a German patrol blundered into 'C' Company's perimeter and was lashed by rifle and machine-gun fire as the troops hit it from the protection of their slit trenches. Most of the Germans immediately surrendered, while a few managed to escape into the darkness. The Canadians rounded up nineteen men and one officer, who was quickly shot and killed when he attempted to make a break for it.[15]

The Winnipegs' other assault company had been Major Lockhart "Lochie" Ross Fulton's 'D' Company. Although his men had suffered fewer casualties than 'B' Company, Fulton knew they were badly worn out from the hard fighting and undoubtedly had managed little rest during a night disrupted by the fireworks at the beach and 'C' Company's sharp fight with the German patrol. With dawn approaching, the thirty-seven-year-old officer from Birtle, Manitoba set out with his runner to check his company lines and ensure everyone was ready to begin the dawn move.[16]

The short firefight had left everyone in the battalion jumpy. Private Gordon Maxwell stared into the blackness beyond his slit trench and imagined anything moving out there must be Germans trying to creep up on him. His heart started pounding when two shadows slinked across his front. Maxwell drew a bead on the lead shadow, but eased off the trigger at the last moment. "I decided not to fire. If it was a German, we may have been able to take him prisoner. I finally figured out who the man creeping around in the darkness was. It had been a close call for Major Fulton."[17] Maxwell later confided that, although happy he hadn't fired, he was "such a poor shot I probably wouldn't have hit him anyway."[18]

UNAWARE OF HIS CLOSE brush with death, Fulton led his company out at 0615 hours towards the objective. Fulton's men trailed behind those of 'C' Company, which led the advance under the command of Major J.M.D. (Jimmy) Jones. Concerned by a gap between the Winnipegs and the 7th Green Howards of the 50th British Infantry Division advancing from Gold Beach, Lieutenant Colonel John Meldram assigned Captain D.B. Robertson to guard the battalion's right flank. He was given a platoon from 'A' Company, two sections of the carrier platoon, and one section of six-pounders from the anti-tank platoon for the task.

Hedgerows walled in the narrow lanes and it was difficult to locate any reference points to serve as guideposts. Consequently, 'C' Company soon took a wrong turn and wandered off into the blue.[19] When Fulton reported that the company he was supposed to be following was no longer out to the front, Meldram said, "Lead the battalion into Putot."[20] The lieutenant colonel, fretting that the Germans would soon counterattack, urged haste and left it to 'C' Company to find its own way back to the rest of the battalion.

'D' Company moved quickly, Fulton effectively using his map and compass to stay on a track that took the Winnipegs through the hamlet of Lantheuil and then a maze of grain fields, dairy cattle paddocks, and orchards that led unwaveringly towards Putot-en-Bessin. The only opposition was presented by a scattering of snipers who were either quickly wiped out or took to their heels after snapping off a shot or two. Occasionally, a German artillery shell shrieked down to explode nearby, but this seemed nothing more than undirected searching fire intended to harass the advancing troops. Neither the snipers nor the random shelling caused any casualties and little slowed the pace of the marching troops.[21]

So quickly did the Little Black Devils, as the Royal Winnipeg Rifles were known, and the Regina Rifles move in the early morning that Brigadier Foster decided at 0800 hours that the Canadian Scottish should join the advance by coming up in the centre between the two battalions. This battalion could then easily shift as needed to support the Winnipegs or the Reginas if either ran into stiff fighting, while also keeping the entire brigade in contact across a one-and-a-half-mile-wide front.

Despite the ease of the advance, Canadian Scottish Lieutenant Colonel Cabeldu was uneasy. "Rumours were running rampant through the ranks of the battalion that paratroopers were dropping. We were green troops in a strange land, therefore we believed everything that came our way."[22] Throughout the night, there had been numerous baseless reports over the Canadian wireless net that German paratroopers were being dropped to the rear of the forward battalions in an attempt to cut them off. At one point, the Sherbrooke Fusiliers came up on the net insisting that paratroops "had landed nearby but... were adequately handled by the infantry and our machine guns."[23] In the morning, no sign of phantom paratroops were found, but the reports of paratroop drops and fierce fights persisted.

The Canadian division's radio communications were badly confused by German signallers, in possession of the radio code books captured along with the two Sherbrooke Fusilier officers during the night, interjecting with regular disinformation. 9 CIB's Brigadier Ben Cunningham was so pestered by one German operator that he later commented on how "an interesting example of enemy ingenuity is afforded by the skill of a German wireless operator whose set was functioning on the brigade link to [the Sherbrooke Fusiliers.]" The German signaller "quickly adopted our wireless procedure, even to such details as: 'Report my signals' and 'Say again all after... ' His cleverness was annoying at the most, since it became difficult to know if wireless messages were being received, but his skill at mimicry was such that by the end of the day he could imitate the voice of Colonel [Mel] Gordon, OC [Sherbrooke Fusiliers.]"[24]

The sun soon rose high overhead and the heat became stifling as the Canadian Scottish, for want of a road running in the right direction, cut through grain fields. Captain P.F. Ramsay, second-in-command of 'B' Company, noted that "the yellow grain was almost waist high and the ground beneath dusty so that movement had to be cautious to prevent clouds of dust. Water discipline had to be maintained at a high level." The wisdom of not raising dust that could betray their positions was rammed home when a German ME-109 fighter plane roared overhead, only to be pounced upon by a Spitfire. "We witnessed the first daylight air skirmish above us and an ME came hurtling down in flames and a parachute blossomed out above us. A cocky young German pilot landed in the middle of the company," Ramsay wrote.[25] He was shunted off to battalion headquarters.

Although 7 CIB was moving forward quickly, the lead companies also anxiously expected at any moment to meet heavy resistance. As the men passed through small hamlets, local farmers generally offered up dire warnings along with copious helpings of calvados, a French apple brandy, and wine. At 0950 hours, Brigadier Foster radioed a report to Keller's headquarters that the Winnipegs had just been advised by "local inhabitants" that "150 enemy" were massed in St. Croix Grand Tonne and were "in goodly number" at Bretteville-l'Orgueilleuse.[26] Both these villages were byways on the Caen-Bayeux highway, situated directly in front of the brigade's line of advance.

Despite the grim cautions from locals, the Germans failed to materialize in any strength. 'D' Company continued brushing aside snipers that were more nuisances than effective opposition. At 1010 hours, Lieutenant Colonel John Meldram reported to Foster that Fulton's men, having found St. Croix empty of enemy, were crossing the highway and pushing on to Putot-en-Bessin. He expected to have an advance platoon in the village within ten minutes. For the Winnipeg Rifles, Putot was their final objective—codenamed Oak—for D-Day. Exactly at 1020, Foster reported that this battalion had reached Oak and was concentrating there.[27]

Instead of trading bullets with a determined enemy, Fulton and his men were met by a mayor bent on celebrating the village's liberation with "calvados he had saved for three or four years. So we drank to the victory." Then Fulton said, "I've got to move now. I've got to take up a position just to the side of the village." When the mayor asked if there was anything further he could do for Fulton's Canadians, the officer replied, "Well, we haven't been eating that well. We've been aboard that ship for three or four days and eating British compo rations and we've always been short of eggs in England."

"Do not worry," the mayor declared. "There's no shortage of eggs here."

"Well, that's nice if you want to deliver some eggs to us. But I need to move my company to our position now." Breaking up the party, Fulton marched his men out to the left of Putot and ordered them to dig in. Within a couple of hours, the mayor and several villagers showed up with "a big washbasin filled with a thousand or so eggs that were hard-boiled. It was rather pleasant."[28]

By this time, the rest of the battalion had arrived and Meldram deployed three companies forward and 'B' Company in reserve within the village. Guarding the left flank was Fulton's 'D' Company, with 'C' Company to the immediate front of the village just back of the railroad, and 'A' Company to the right of Putot where a white lime-stone-coloured bridge provided a road crossing over the railway.[29]

Out on 7 CIB's left flank, the Reginas had been neck and neck in the advance with the Winnipeg Rifles and each regiment would claim to be the winner. Foster credited the Manitoban regiment with this honour, while divisional headquarters diplomatically declared a tie.[30] Unlike the Little Black Devils, the Reginas had advanced in two columns, with 'C' Company leading 'A' Company and battalion head-quarters along a road running south from Camilly to Bretteville and from there across the highway and railroad tracks to seize Norrey-en-Bessin. 'B' Company, meanwhile, moved with 'D' Company in trail via Thaon to Vieux Cairon and then along the western bank of the River Mue through Rots to take up positions behind the railroad to the right of la Villeneuve. Matheson had split his battalion into two columns in order to sweep as much of the three-mile-wide gap between 7 CIB's eastern flank and 9 CIB's westernmost battalion as possible. Along the way, 'D' Company was to drop off and "occupy the road, rail and river crossing just south of Rots" in order to provide some semblance of flank protection. Even then, 7 CIB would be out on a salient with its left flank dangerously exposed.[31]

Because of this open flank, the Reginas had originally been expect-ing support from 'C' Squadron of the 1st Hussars Armoured Regi-ment. Needing first to resupply with ammunition and fuel, the tankers were unable to get on the road until mid-morning and then failed to link up with the fast-marching infantry. Unable to establish radio contact with the Saskatchewan battalion and unsure where in the open country it might be, 'C' Squadron's commander finally or-dered an about-face and rolled off towards the regimental harbour. He had only just turned the Shermans around when up came the nine tanks of 'A' Squadron and four tanks of 'B' Squadron that had man-aged to survive D-Day and had been pooled together into a composite unit, under command of Major Dudley Brooks. Determined to estab-lish contact with the infantry, Brooks turned 'C' Squadron around and the entire force pressed on towards Bretteville.[32] The tankers rolled up on the heels of 'C' Company just as it pushed into the village.

Matheson's wisdom in having 'B' and 'D' companies guard the left flank was confirmed when they met fairly stiff opposition. While the rest of the battalion enjoyed "a very friendly reception" from the villagers of Bretteville, 'B' Company had to call upon the mortars of the Cameron Highlanders to convince a group of heavily entrenched Germans to fall back. Intermittent small firefights continued throughout the morning until the two companies reached their assigned positions at about noon.[33]

This was much later than 'C' Company's arrival time at Norrey-en-Bessin, a village that "consisted of a score of houses which straggled along a main street for 500 yards." The street was actually a section of paved secondary road running through the village that linked it to St. Mauvieu, a mile to the south, and to le Mesnil-Patry, which lay just over a mile to the west. The road from Bretteville linked up to the street at Norrey's old church, around which were three or four shops."[34] From the bell tower of this four-hundred-year-old church, a German sniper started snapping off rounds at the lead platoon as it moved into the village along the Bretteville road. 'C' Company responded and it seemed to Rifleman John Swityk that "everything available was shot at the tower until Major [Stu] Tubb told us to stop since we were only giving away our position. I think F.H. (Froze and Hungry) Smith got the sniper. We were assigned to clearing houses; then some of us found some wine... we drank beside our [antitank] gun, which was sighted to cover the open field beyond the hedge. We all really thought it was a picnic."[35]

"Having been the first battalion in 21st Army Group to reach the final objective," Matheson declared, "[the] Regina Rifles were determined to hold it." Whichever 7 CIB battalion was first on the objective, the fact remained that this brigade was ahead of any other brigade in the Allied invasion force. Second British Army commander General Miles Dempsey acknowledged this fact in a message to Keller that read: "A battalion of 3 Canadian Division was the first unit in the Second Army to reach the final objective. That is something which you will always remember with pride."[36]

Sandwiched between these two battalions, the Canadian Scottish moved into Secqueville-en-Bessin and Cabeldu quickly got his four companies fanned out in a defensive arc south of it, which extended from immediately south of the village eastwards to where a low ridge bordered the River Chiromme opposite Bray. Orders issued, the lieutenant colonel then happily sat down in a farmhouse at 1330 hours and dug into a late breakfast prepared for him by the battalion quartermaster that consisted of "eggs and calvados (straight) to drink. I didn't know whether I liked it or not."[37]

From his position on the battalion's left flank, 'B' Company's Captain Ramsay thought Bray was "an insignificant conglomeration of barns and stone buildings with stone walls around some of them." On the opposite side of the village, just beyond a dense wood, Ramsay could hear the growl of engines and squeal of steel tracks that told him some of the 105-millimetre self-propelled Priests being used by the division's artillery regiments were moving into their assigned position, codenamed "Norah."[38]

The 13th Canadian Field Regiment's war diarist noted that "the gun position at Bray was most satisfactory and defensively ideal with a good tank killing ground forward." All would have been well, he figured, had the regiment been occupying the position alone and able to develop an all-round defensive perimeter. Unfortunately, good artillery positions were in short supply amid the broken farm country and small woods dominating the area near the Caen-Bayeux highway, so divisional headquarters had also ordered 12th Field Regiment and two batteries of Centaurs seconded to it from the Royal Marines to crowd into the same space. "The result," wrote the war diarist, "being a dangerously cramped group position without any advantage of perimeter fire!"[39]

There was good reason to be concerned about this, he thought, for as the afternoon progressed, many German troops that had been passed undetected by the infantry during their rapid advance began to emerge from hiding. Most were scattered remnants from the 716th Infantry Division, who could do little more than snipe at the gunners with rifles and light machine guns. But there was also a worrisome increase in the rate of German mortar and artillery fire falling on the gun position and beginning to harry 7 CIB's infantry battalions. "The regiment is being constantly annoyed by snipers, mortars, 88-millimetre airbursts, and machine guns," the 13th's war diarist wrote. Combined with news that 8 CIB's North Shore (New Brunswick) Regiment was locked in a bloody slugfest in front of Douvres-la-Délivrande radar station and confused reports that 9 CIB had stepped into the middle of a major German counterattack, a grim fight seemed imminent. But he was reassured by the fact that "an absolute determination to stand on the line come 'Hell or high water' was evident in all ranks."[40]

[5]

Performance Most Creditable

WHILE 7TH CANADIAN INFANTRY BRIGADE enjoyed relatively easy passage to its objectives on June 7, the 8th Canadian Infantry Brigade's North Shore (New Brunswick) Regiment stepped into a hornet's nest minutes after moving out from Tailleville towards the radar station. Situated just west of Douvres-la-Délivrande, the radar station was heavily fortified with two strongpoints surrounded by minefields and barbed wire. Six 50-millimetre guns, sixteen machine guns, and three heavy mortars gave the position formidable firepower, and its Luftwaffe operating and defence force of about 230 men had been greatly strengthened the night before by most of 1st Company of the 192nd Panzer Grenadier Regiment and several self-propelled guns.[1] This element of the 21st Panzer Division had participated in the desperate counterattack launched on the evening of June 6 into the wide gap between the Canadians at Juno and the British at Sword. When the attack collapsed in disarray, this company and its supporting armour had become separated, eventually taking refuge within the radar station's defensive network. The presence of the crack Panzer Grenadiers stiffened the backbone of the Luftwaffe garrison, which was trained more to provide security to prevent sabotage by the French underground than to fight Allied troops.

At 0700 hours, Lieutenant Colonel Donald Buell ordered 'A' Company to lead the way towards the radar station by first clearing the woods immediately to the south of Tailleville that bordered the road to Douvres-la Délivrande. For support, the North Shores had Major William Roy Bray's 'C' Squadron of the Fort Garry Horse Armoured Regiment and could call upon the guns of 19th Army Field Regiment.[2] Also moving up alongside the infantry were the Bren carriers of No. 7 Platoon of the Cameron Highlanders of Ottawa, equipped with 50-calibre Vickers heavy machine guns, under the command of Lieutenant Sharp.[3]

Casualties on D-Day had whittled 'A' Company down by about 25 per cent and the survivors were still badly shaken by the loss of their popular commander. Considered the elder statesman of the North Shores, Major Archibald McNaughton had almost been rejected as too old to lead his men into the invasion. The forty-seven-year-old from New Brunswick's Black River Bridge refused to be shunted off to a reserve command and waded ashore at the head of the company he had commanded since before the war. But McNaughton had been killed by a machine-gun burst during the fierce battle for control of Tailleville and now Captain J.L. Belliveau led the company towards the woods. Belliveau was a competent officer, but had not yet had the chance to win the confidence of the troops.[4]

Thirty minutes out of Tailleville, 'A' Company ran into opposition from Germans, who had reinfiltrated into the woods during the night.[5] At the same time, a number of German snipers popped up inside Tailleville itself, bringing the rest of the battalion under fire in the middle of forming up for the attack. A stray round or mortar shell fired from the radar station scored a jackpot when the battalion's ammunition dump, set up during the night inside the village, was detonated. This caused a brief but complete stall of the advance while the battalion reorganized its rear area and cleared the snipers out of the village.[6]

Belliveau and his men, meanwhile, continued working slowly through the woods in the face of strong German resistance. Before its capture the previous day, Tailleville had been a regimental headquarters for the 716th Infantry Division and the entire town was riddled with underground bunkers connected by a maze of tunnels. This system extended well out into the woods that 'A' Company was trying to clear, so it was easy for German snipers and light machine-gunners to use the tunnels to get in behind the advancing Canadians. Lacking "the confident touch Archie [McNaughton] would have provided," Belliveau was unable to prevent his men from going to ground when they came under persistent fire from all sides.

Finally, Buell "became irked at the slow progress, and prompting on my part did not seem to produce any faster results." Badgered by his own commander, Brigadier Ken Blackader, to get going, Buell dispatched Lieutenant Blake Oulton of the headquarters section "to find out what was causing the slowness."[7]

Running alongside the road, Oulton met up with Lieutenant Cyril Mersereau, whose platoon had just finished clearing a section of wood and was now forming a reserve for the other two platoons of Belliveau's company. Wishing his friend luck, Oulton pressed on into woods that proved "honeycombed with trenches, shelters, and tunnels." When he caught up with the other two platoons, Belliveau told him the woods were pretty well cleared, opening the way for the battalion's attack on the radar station. On his return trip, Oulton was dismayed to see that "Mersereau had been badly wounded during the few minutes that I had been forward."[8]

The moment Buell received Oulton's report, he sent 'C' and 'D' companies forward. As Major Ralph Daughney's 'C' Company pushed past the woods, small-arms fire from another line of scrub brush and straggly trees to the left of the road ripped into the leading platoons, joined by heavy mortar and artillery fire from the radar station. Shrapnel and high-explosive rounds plastered several of the Camerons' carriers that were moving beside the infantry.

The intense fire knocked out two carriers, including Lieutenant Sharp's command vehicle. Among those wounded were Sharp's batman Private Ladouceur, who was hit in the rear and legs by shrapnel. Another Cameron, Private Boucher, was critically wounded and only saved from death when Sergeant Gravelle slung the man over his shoulder and sprinted back to the North Shores' Regimental Aid Post. Sharp was chagrined to see his bedroll and dress kilt, both carefully packed into a box strapped to the back of the carrier, burned to a crisp.⁹

For protection from the intense gunfire ripping into his company, Daughney moved up the line by darting along the right side of the carriers, from one to the next. Following on his heels was Private Joe Ryan, his radio signaller. It seemed to Ryan that while the gunfire was primarily originating from the left side of the road, the mortar and artillery shells were shrieking in from both flanks. Suddenly a hail of shrapnel and ricocheting bullets scythed the air around the two men, who both jumped over the bushes bordering the road in a desperate search for cover. Losing hold of the stock of his Lee Enfield, Ryan hugged the ground and recoiled in shock as a chunk of shrapnel sliced the rifle in two at the point where the stock joined the breech. A second later, another shrapnel shard deeply slashed his right forearm while a piece of metal, possibly from a bullet shattering against the Bren carrier, pierced his right hand at the base of the index finger. "It hurt right away," he said later. "I knew I was hit. Bleeding very badly. Yelled out that I had been hit. There were guys on that side of the bush, but no medic at that time. Blood was running down my arm and off my hand. Someone put a bandage on and told me to get back to the beach."

Having lost track of Daughney during those terrifying seconds, Ryan was unable to tell him he was leaving. Setting off alone, the twenty-one-year-old from Kingston, Nova Scotia started working his way back to the rear. Staggering across an open field, he "stumbled and fell and just as I did a MG opened up and bullets went across the field. Could hear them snapping over me." Measuring the timing of the bursts, Ryan would leap up and run a few strides, then throw himself flat again just before the next rounds rent the air. Finally, he gained the protection of a wood and eventually found a dressing station where the medical staff treated his wounds and assigned him to a cot inside a bell tent.¹⁰

Frantic to get the attack moving, Buell jumped onto Major Roy Bray's Sherman and suggested that he join the tanker inside the turret. He quickly outlined a plan for the tank to carry out a reconnaissance ahead of the infantry in an attempt to find some weak point in the German lines. Bray told his driver to get rolling, and with a troop of three Fort Garry tanks in trail moved out towards the radar station. "We made a trip around the western edge of the wood, to the southern extremity, the German end," Buell later wrote. "There we halted and Roy and I dismounted, got into bushes on the east corner and had a good look with our glasses at both the radar station and the adjoining countryside. To my amazement there seemed to be a steady stream of troops moving from Douvres-la-Délivrande into the radar station. There appeared to be a certain amount of movement in the wood itself and there was undoubtedly movement south of the wood. We remounted in the tanks, wheeled around and went back to our side of the wood."[11]

Directing 'A' Company to concentrate its efforts on the east side of the wood, while 'C' Company pushed into the west side, Buell watched fretfully as the North Shores made extremely slow progress forward. It didn't help, as morning passed into a grim afternoon with gains measured in mere yards, that his supporting arms were being steadily siphoned off. First, the Fort Garry Horse tanks were called to race towards Anguerny because of reports that a major counterattack was slamming into the leading elements of 9th Canadian Infantry Brigade. Not that the tankers had been of much use, with the German artillery at the radar station positioned in heavy fortifications, enjoying an ideal field of fire from a dominating height that rendered any armoured approach suicidal.

Finally, the woods were cleared and at 1600 hours the radar station lay before them, surrounded by a 100-foot-deep stretch of open ground. Behind it stood "a labyrinth of concrete works and tunnels" and the bristling guns of the Germans. The moment the North Shores emerged from the woods, a wall of fire lashed them. Lieutenant Charles Richardson, in command of a 'B' Company platoon, found himself lying shoulder to shoulder in a ditch with Major J. Ernest Anderson, who commanded 'D' Company. "We were helpless," Richardson said later, "we couldn't do anything."[12]

With Lieutenant Colonel L.G. Clarke of the 19th Artillery, who had just dashed up to his position, Buell managed to gather a couple of his company commanders together for a huddle. The North Shore commander was intent on saturating the German position with artillery fire, but Clarke quickly disabused him of that notion when he apologetically reported that he had just been ordered to swing the guns away from the North Shores. All four of the division's artillery regiments and every available naval gun were being directed towards driving off the German counterattack developing on 9 CIB's front, the artillery officer said. That was the last straw for Buell. He radioed Blackader and stated flatly that "he had insufficient troops to do the job."[13]

While Buell started arguing with Blackader over whether he would be reinforced or permitted to withdraw the battalion from its exposed positions, many North Novas were realizing they were caught in more than German crossfire. Shortly after dawn on June 7, the British 51st (Highland) Infantry Division had begun landing on Sword Beach to increase the strength of Second British Army. Because the 3rd British Infantry Division's 9th Brigade had been tasked away from its original duty of anchoring alongside the Canadians, the 51st's Black Watch, 5th Battalion was dispatched with instructions to clear the radar station. Somehow communications between the divisional commanders had broken down, so that none of the British generals at Sword had the slightest idea that the North Shores were attempting to seize the same objective.[14]

Major Anderson was attempting to get 'D' Company extended into a proper fighting line within the woods when a flurry of tank shells coming from the left flank screamed overhead, causing several tree-splintering explosions that immediately drove his men to ground under a rain of wood and steel shrapnel. Out of a fogbank of smoke, Anderson saw the leading elements of the Black Watch supported by tanks emerge, both infantry and tankers "firing on our troops in the woods. I ran across the field to one of the tanks and got the tank fire stopped but the infantry carried merrily on through the woods. I fully expected to find few of our men alive, but casualties were surprisingly light."[15]

Hunkered down in the cover of two knocked-out Cameron Highlander carriers, Lieutenant Charles Richardson, Lieutenant George Fawcett, and Major Bob Forbes were discussing how 'B' Company was to be relieved by 'C' Company when "a jaunty English major arrived and asked who was in charge." Forbes said he was.

"'What's holding you up?' demanded the British officer, and he was told and shown the casualties.

"'Well, well, we'll soon fix that. Bring up a Petard,' he said."

Soon a turretless Churchill tank fitted with a short-barrelled twelve-inch demolition gun called a petard clattered up. It fired a forty-pound, square-shaped shell nicknamed a "flying dustbin," intended for destroying fortifications or breaching obstacles such as concrete walls. Forbes and Richardson both cautioned the major that there was no way they could cross the open ground, "but the major got into the tank... and away the Churchill rolled across the wheatfield."

"It was one of the most unrealistic scenes of the war," Richardson said. "In one moment that huge Churchill tank was chugging across the field. The next instant there was a terrific blast and when the dust settled, the grain was blowing gently in the breeze and there was absolutely no sign of the tank. A shell... had hit the Petard fairly and the double explosion wiped out the tank completely. Afterward, a classic remark among us was, 'Bring up a Petard.'"[16]

By the time this tragic farce concluded, Buell had received orders to extricate his battalion from the area of the radar station and move to a covering position immediately north of Anguerny. Although the North Shores were more than happy to hand off the radar station attack to the British battalion, they found the condescending manner of the troops and officers of the Highland regiment irksome, for they seemed to think that taking the position would be a simple task. In the end, however, the Germans besieged there would hold out for ten more days before surrendering.[17]

North Shore Padre R. Miles Hickey thought the ill-supported attack on the radar station had been "like blowing bubbles against Gibraltar. The huge construction was three stories underground, and there three hundred Germans sat, laughing at us no doubt."[18] It was a bitter setback for the New Brunswick regiment, but one with which Blackader sympathized even as he called them away to their new position.

"It should be stated," he wrote after, "that the widespread operations of North Shore Regiment, which included forming a wide flank
for the [No. 48 Royal Marine] Commandos, maintaining a firm left
flank for the [brigade] and continuing to move forward at the same
time... made matters very difficult for them, so that their performance under the circumstances was most creditable."[19]

THE NORTH SHORES were not the only Canadian battalion putting in
a creditable performance in the face of grave adversity this day. To the
south, out on the far left flank, the North Nova Scotia Highlanders
with the Sherbrooke Fusiliers in support had advanced directly into
the maw of a major ambush tripped by the 12th ss (Hitlerjugend)
Panzer Division in the late afternoon. For these battalions, June 7
would forever be a day of infamy.

On the evening of June 6, the North Novas spearheaded 9th
Canadian Infantry Brigade's advance towards Carpiquet airport with
a flying column of tanks and Bren carriers. This had enabled the
battalion to rapidly move inland despite being much delayed in
departing the beach for its D-Day objectives. Darkness had forced the
column to hold up on the northern outskirts of Villons-les-Buissons,
and it was from this point that the advance was renewed at 0745
hours on June 7.

Having enjoyed such success with the flying column on June 6,
Lieutenant Colonel Charles Petch decided to implement the same
technique to break through to Carpiquet airport. North Novas' 'C'
Company commander, Major Don Learment, was temporarily
detached from his command so that he could direct the column's
advance as he had the previous day. In the column's van were the
Sherbrooke Fusiliers Reconnaissance Troop's Honey tanks under
Lieutenant G.A. Kraus. Immediately behind, the North Novas' Bren
carrier platoon had loaded 'C' Company up on its eighteen vehicles.
Then came No. 11 Platoon of the Cameron Highlanders, with its
Vickers heavy machine guns mounted on carriers. Following closely
behind was a troop of M10 tank destroyers from the 3rd Anti-Tank
Regiment, two assault sections of the North Novas' pioneer platoon,
one section of its mortar platoon, and four of the battalion's anti-

tank guns. Temporarily in charge of 'C' Company was second-in-command Captain Frederic Charles "Hank" Fraser. Heading up the carrier platoon was Captain E.S. Gray.[20]

Learment's column was out on the tip of a wedge created by the North Novas and Fusiliers. While it moved directly along a country lane denoted on maps as GC220 that ran in an almost straight line from Villons-les-Buissons via les Buissons, Buron, Authie, and Franqueville to Carpiquet airport, the rest of the infantry and tanks spread out close behind but well out on the flanks. To the right, 'A' Squadron of the Fusiliers had 'A' Company riding on its Shermans, while on the left, 'B' Company was aboard 'B' Squadron. Coming up behind Learment's column, 'C' Squadron carried the infantry of 'D' Company.

At only twenty-five, Learment had enjoyed a path of rapid advancement since enlisting in the spring of 1940. In his third year at Acadia University, the native of Truro, Nova Scotia had been studying economics and was enrolled in the Canadian Officer Training Corps when he heard the news that Germany had invaded Belgium, Holland, and France. Realizing that the "Phony War" that had followed Poland's invasion in September 1939 was now over and not wanting to face probable conscription, Learment went to Amherst and enlisted at the North Novas' headquarters there.

Learment had gone to England as a lieutenant commanding a platoon in 'A' Company, but in late 1942 was assigned to headquarters as the intelligence officer and then adjutant before going to brigade for a stint as brigade adjutant. Returning to the battalion as a captain, he was appointed second-in-command of 'A' Company and then 'C' Company before being promoted to major in December 1943 and becoming the latter company's commander.

Learment never felt the weight of command lay too heavily on his shoulders because he "had the support of everyone else." The North Novas were a tightly knit regiment and the officers worked well together. Even Lieutenant Colonel Petch, who came to the regiment from a non-Highland unit and had been initially viewed with some suspicion because he wore "a flat cap instead of a Glengarry," had soon won their trust. This was helped in no little part by his quickly acquiring a kilt and other requisite Highlander kit.

The North Novas were also used to working with their Fusilier tankers, for they had started training together in late 1943 and been bivouacked in the same camp. Learment noted that "there was good camaraderie between us. We messed together and were very close."

Within 'C' Company, Learment was blessed to have a stable of competent, solid officers, with Fraser as his second-in-command and lieutenants Herb Langley, Jack Veness, and Bob Graves running the three platoons. Company Sergeant Major James Mackie was a rock upon which Learment and his officers knew they could always lean. Consequently, he was entirely comfortable having Fraser handle 'C' Company while he guided the flying column's advance.[21]

Learment's real "concern was to drive straight ahead while keeping in touch with battalion [headquarters] and brigade as well. The flank companies were in charge of protecting the axis of advance." The major assumed that the artillery regiment that was to support the brigade would be "keeping apace of the advance," so its guns would be able to range on any heavy enemy resistance encountered. Learment considered that aspect a "big picture" detail, though, and therefore not his worry. "What I was concerned about was getting to Carpiquet."[22]

Villons-les-Buissons was cleared easily, with the Sherbrooke Honey tanks shooting up several German light trucks that attempted to take flight.[23] Outdated American-made Stuart tanks that were lightly armoured and mounted only a 37-millimetre main gun, the Honeys depended on speed and agility to keep out of the range of German tanks, but could wreak havoc on regular transport vehicles.

Beyond the village, the "country was gently rolling plain with occasional clumps of trees, farm hedges and hay stacks. The only feature was the small villages where the farmers lived in groups of small houses, barns and outbuildings surrounding a church, some shops and [a public house.] The inevitable horse pond and a few fruit trees plus stretches of stone wall completed each community."[24]

The force had just departed Villons-les-Buissons when 'A' Company brushed up against the side of a wood bristling with snipers and machine-gun positions. Major Leon M. Rhodenizer ordered his men to unhorse from the Shermans and set about rooting these diehards of the 716th Infantry Division out of the woods. Among the trees, the major found a network of freshly dug slit trenches and an abandoned self-propelled gun. Then a German, who emerged from some bushes to surrender, led Rhodenizer and his men to a farmyard where four wounded comrades lay on the ground. 'A' Company's stretcher-bearers had just started treating the Germans when two more soldiers walked into the farmyard with arms raised. As the company continued sweeping through the wood, more Germans were flushed and taken prisoner. By the time this process was completed, the rest of the advancing force was almost out of sight.[25] 'A' Company clambered back onto the Shermans and dashed off in pursuit.

By this time, the Sherbrooke reconnaissance troop was closing on les Buissons. Suddenly, a great cloud of dust was kicked up to the right of the village and a second later one of the Honeys was knocked out. The crew managed to escape unscathed from the wrecked Stuart.[26]

With a well-entrenched gun covering the road into les Buissons, Learment ordered 'C' Company out of its vehicles and into a hasty attack while the rest of the force swung to the left to bypass the enemy position. While Captain Fraser teed up the attack with Bren carrier platoon commander Captain Gray, Learment had the mortar platoon hammer the gun position with a dozen rounds. Then Fraser took 'C' Company out on one flank of the gun to distract attention away from Captain Gray and his carrier platoon, which dashed in from the opposite flank to destroy the gun with a shower of grenades.[27] Gray personally led the grenade attack, an action that won him a Military Cross.[28] Gun silenced, the infantry quickly overran the village and captured a sixteen-barrelled mortar and three half-tracks that had been abandoned during the hasty retreat of what appeared to be an element of the 21st Panzer Division.

While this action was underway, 'B' Company and 'B' Squadron, out on the left flank, were suddenly smothered by heavy artillery and mortar fire coming from St.-Contest. Set on slightly higher ground than that between les Buissons and Buron, the village provided an ideal German observation and firing position. Until now, the North Novas and Sherbrookes had been under the impression that 3rd British Infantry Division was coming up on that flank in support.

Now they realized that they "were far in front with no force visible to support them on either flank. The Seventh Brigade was keeping pace but was so far over on the right that none of its units could be seen."[29]

With mortar rounds raining down around 'B' Squadron's Shermans, Major J.W. Douglas ordered his infantry to dismount and take cover. Having never been under heavy fire, many of the men panicked and scattered every which way. While Lieutenant Fraser Campbell managed to keep No. 10 Platoon together, the other two platoons proved difficult to round up when the enemy fire abated and Douglas ordered his men back onto the tanks. Once accomplished, the Germans—patiently waiting for the return of such nicely clustered infantry targets—opened up with another series of salvos.[30] Shrapnel wounded several men, including company second-in-command Captain D.L. Clarke, who was hit while talking on the wireless with Lieutenant Colonel Petch about the possibility of getting artillery counter-battery fire directed down on St.-Contest. The captain was the battalion's first officer casualty.[31]

Lieutenant Jock Grieve took over as second-in-command, handing his No. 12 Platoon off to Sergeant S.S. Hughes. The German fire was so intense that Douglas ordered his platoons to forget about riding the tanks and to make their way by foot to Buron. When he radioed Petch with a request for artillery support, the North Nova commander said none was available. All he could do was have the troop of self-propelled antitank guns open fire on the village, using the church steeple as an aiming point. This was quickly knocked down by a direct hit, but the German fire continued unabated. Finally, 'B' Company managed to gain Buron by carrying out a series of bounding dashes from one cluster of cover to another. Inside the village, it huddled behind the protection of a long stone wall.[32]

Learment's force had meanwhile managed to drive into Buron, seizing the village "in a short sharp skirmish." The major anxiously noted that "the enemy... were showing a growing tendency to fight to the last man rather than choosing to either surrender or run."[33] Although Buron still seemed infested with Germans hiding out in cellars and attics with the intention of sniping at the Canadians, Learment decided the column must push on towards Authie and leave the mopping up to the trailing 'D' Company and the Sherbrookes' 'C' Squadron. He was just issuing orders to this effect when a Bren carrier rattled up with Petch and Brigadier Ben Cunningham aboard, seeking a report on what was delaying the advance. Just as Petch dismounted, a shell exploded beside the carrier and the blast knocked the lieutenant colonel flat. Unhurt, Petch heard out Learment's report and then sanctioned the decision to press on to Authie and secure Carpiquet airport.

With the Honeys still leading, the flying column dashed across a mile of open country, chased by shellfire from St.-Contest the entire way. On the outskirts of Authie, several Honeys were knocked out by antitank fire from the buildings. Learment radioed Petch to report that his leading elements were taking "mortar and shell fire from both flanks and the front." He "asked for a troop of tanks and some artillery to take it on."

Petch, who had by now set up headquarters on the edge of Buron, whirled around to his artillery forward observation officer, who said "the artillery was out of range and it would be some time before it could be moved up. The only fire available was a cruiser, which the naval forward observation officer [also travelling with Petch's head-quarters] said could engage St. Contest for twenty minutes."[34] Petch urged the navy's FOO to get the guns firing and dispatched a troop of Shermans from 'B' Squadron under command of Lieutenant Ian MacLean to Learment's support. While the tanks rolled forward, the navy FOO attempted to establish radio contact with the cruiser. "This fire would have wiped St. Contest out," the North Novas' war diarist ruefully noted, "but faulty communications made it impossible to obtain it in time."[35]

As 'C' Company closed on Authie, the situation became increasingly confused because of the heavy fire being directed at it. Several times, the platoons were forced to bail off the carriers and take cover, so that the advance continued fitfully. When Fraser finally got his men up to the edge of the village, he discovered that one platoon had become completely disorganized during the advance because of the shelling and that it and its supporting carrier section were scattered back along the road between Authie and Buron.[36] A little while later, that platoon's commander, Lieutenant Bob Graves, arrived hoping to find his missing men. He told Fraser that the other companies were also being heavily shelled.[37]

'C' Company's two lead platoons under command of lieutenants Herb Langley and Jack Veness pushed into the village. Captain Gray sent one section of carriers around the left and then had the second section hopscotch the first to reconnoitre Franqueville, about a half mile away. When light mortar fire bracketed both sections as they were attempting the hopscotch move on the southeast corner of the village, Gray ordered a withdrawal back to a sheltered field on the northeast flank of Authie.[38]

Authie was finally cleared in another bitter fight as 'C' Company winkled snipers and machine-gunners out of basements and off rooftops. When the tanks arrived and wiped out six machine-gun positions that formed the crux of the German defensive network, Fraser reported the village in his hands. But the mortar and artillery fire kept intensifying, finally becoming so heavy that Lieutenant MacLean's tanks and the surviving Honeys were forced to hunt for covered positions, while the Bren carriers were moved to the shelter of a hedge before being sent back to Buron at about 1330 hours.[39] With the carriers went the separated platoon, which was unable to cross the open ground in the face of heavy fire to link up with the rest of the company. Gray remained in the village with his command carrier "to learn what was happening."[40]

Less than a mile off to the east, in the vicinity of the village of Cussy and the Abbaye d'Ardenne, reconnaissance troop commander Lieutenant G.A. Kraus detected the movement of a large number of tanks massing for a counterattack. Back at Buron, Petch, too, was receiving reports that a large enemy force was mustering on his left flank and decided "it was impossible to go on. There was no one within miles of us on either flank or in the rear," the regiment's war diarist wrote, "so the flanking companies were ordered to close up on 'C' Company and form a fortress."

The infantry were to dig in and prepare to defend their positions, while the Sherbrooke Fusiliers moved to take the German tanks on head to head, with several troops of 'A' Squadron driving on towards

Franqueville and Carpiquet airport in an attempt to turn the German flank.[41] Acting Major Fraser moved his two platoons slightly south of Authie, with the Cameron Highlanders machine-gun platoon positioned to their rear.[42] The tanks carrying 'A' Company, meanwhile, had unloaded "in a position slightly south of Buron and to the right of the main axis [the road]. 'B' Company was on the outskirts of Buron and almost on the axis, having been mortared off their tanks a short time previous to the report of enemy tanks being received. Both the company commander and second-in-command were wounded and evacuated. Captain A.J. Wilson, the support company commander, came up and took over. 'D' Company was dug in astride the axis just outside Authie, about 200 yards behind 'C' Company Headquarters position."[43]

Realizing there was nothing he could do to further aid Fraser's almost isolated pocket of troops, Gray mounted his carrier and dashed back to Buron to join Learment and Petch at the battalion's tactical headquarters.[44]

None of this ground, overlooked as it was from St.-Contest and the slight rise that ran across in front of Cussy and the Abbaye, was ideal for defence. But the North Novas and the Sherbrooke Fusiliers had no choice. They were now about eight miles from Juno Beach and to their left the British 9th Infantry Brigade was finally marching their way, but still more than three miles distant, with a large force of Germans visible between. The Canadians concentrated around Authie and back to Buron numbered about 1,500, including the tankers and their roughly forty still-operational tanks. No artillery, naval, or air support was available because the guns were either out of range or unable to establish proper radio communications, despite being drawn away from the other battalions of the division, so the immediate fight would be lost or won by these men.

As the North Novas started hacking slit trenches out of the Norman soil with shovels and picks and the tanks growled towards the advancing Panzers, the 12th ss (Hitlerjugend) Panzer Division thundered down the slope with torrential force and the two regiments fought their most desperate of battles.

[6]

Baptism at Authie

F ROM ONE OF Abbaye d'Ardenne's towers, Standartenführer
Kurt Meyer monitored the advance of the North Novas and
Sherbrooke Fusiliers through the morning while he organized the
12th ss (Hitlerjugend) Panzer Division's counterstrike. The 25th ss
Panzer Grenadier Regiment commander was grimly confident his
young soldiers, most as untried as the Canadians they faced, would
"throw the little fish back into the sea."[1]

Arriving at the Abbaye at about 0900 hours, Meyer only hoped
to perhaps see the coast from its height. Instead, "the country as far
as the coast lies before me like a sandtable model... The whole terrain
looks like an ant hill."[2] The North Shore (New Brunswick) Regiment
could be seen attacking the Douvres-la-Délivrande radar station,
along the length of Juno Beach stood hundreds of ships protected by
countless barrage balloons, and, more importantly, all the dispositions of the Canadian brigades moving towards the Caen-Bayeux
highway—"the swarming ants"—lay before him.

Thirty-four-year-old Meyer was the classic embodiment of the
young commanders who had made the Waffen-ss both feared and
respected by every Allied army they engaged. A fanatical Nazi, his
loyalty to the Führer was absolute, his belief in the superiority of
the Aryan race unquestioned. The illegitimate son of a World War I
sergeant major who died of his wounds while Kurt was still young,

Meyer had become a municipal policeman in 1929. In 1931, he joined the ss and was accepted into its premier division, the Leibstandarte Adolf Hitler, in the spring of 1934, after which he resigned from the police. By 1937, he had risen to the rank of an ss captain. During the invasion of Poland, he commanded a motorcycle company and quickly gained a reputation for his impetuous, daredevil style both in handling his men and riding motorcycles.

Bravely reckless, Meyer also possessed a keen tactical mind that convinced colleagues that he had an instinctive grasp of modern mobile warfare. Out on the leading edge of the Leibstandarte division's reconnaissance unit, Meyer slashed through France, Greece, and into Russia right up to the Caucasus—almost the deepest penetration achieved by German forces. Thrice cut off and surrounded, Meyer fought his way out each time with only a handful of survivors at his side. His battlefield exploits were rewarded with one decoration after another. By June 1944, Meyer wore the Iron Cross, 1st Class, and the Knight's Cross with Oak Leaves. He carried, too, the sobriquets "Schnelle [Speedy] Meyer" and "Panzermeyer," in recognition of his abilities and temperament.[3]

Obergruppenführer Sepp Dietrich, commander of 1st ss Panzer Corps, considered him a passionate soldier, completely dedicated to the practice of arms. For his part, Meyer increasingly saw battle as "magnificent in the best Wagnerian tradition," with himself in the role of Siegfried "leading his warriors to their death" and eternal glory.[4]

That the soldiers he led towards glorious battle were mostly teenagers fazed Meyer not a bit, for these were no ordinary young soldiers. Most had been instilled with Nazi ideology throughout the course of their short lives under the tutelage of the Hitler Youth movement—an organization intended to ensure that National Socialism controlled every segment of life within the German state. Youth movements, particularly those that promoted athleticism and outdoor sports, had always been popular in Germany—perceived as the best means for building good character—and Hitler Youth was just one of many when it first formed. But the Nazis transformed the concept into an ideological one, and in 1933 ensured theirs remained the only viable movement by forcibly seizing millions of dollars' worth of property from the other movements in an effort to drive them into financial ruin. In 1936, they extended Nazi control by outlawing all but the Hitler Youth and in 1939 conscription of children into the movement became mandatory.

Organized into cadres based on age, German children by 1942 received 160 hours of pre-military training a year, including small-bore rifle shooting and fieldcraft. While this differed little from the cadet corps training offered in Canada and Britain at the time, the Hitler Youth leaders also worked assiduously to indoctrinate their young charges in Nazi thinking and ethnic philosophies.

As the war turned against Germany and manpower shortages became acute, Hitler and Reichsführer Heinrich Himmler decided to form a new division that would "be a symbol of the willingness of German youth to sacrifice itself to the achievement of final victory."[5] Its ranks were to be filled entirely by volunteers who had mostly been born in the first half of 1926. This meant that the youngest of ten thousand who reported in Berlin for the division's formation in July 1943 were seventeen. At first glance, it would seem that the 12th ss was not all that different from many other divisions formed by either the Allied or Axis powers, where many recruits were aged between seventeen and nineteen years of age. But what made the division unique was that its enlisted ranks were made up almost entirely of eighteen- and nineteen-year-olds. The 1st ss Panzer Grenadier Battalion of Meyer's 25th Regiment was typical: within its ranks, 65 per cent were eighteen, 17 per cent nineteen, and only 18 per cent twenty or older.[6]

While the enlisted ranks were overwhelmingly teenagers with no previous combat experience, their ncos and officers were usually veterans of ss divisions that had seen hard service in Russia, with a sprinkling of personnel from the Wehrmacht added to make up deficiencies in numbers. At the battalion, regimental, and divisional headquarters level, all the officers were battle-hardened ss veterans. The 12th ss Panzer Regiment commander was Obersturmbann-führer Max Wünsche, who in the prewar years had been Hitler's adjutant. Winner of two Iron Crosses, the German Cross in Gold, and a Knight's Cross, he was considered an outstanding leader and mastermind in handling tanks on the battlefield. Commanding the 26th Panzer Grenadier Regiment was Wilhelm Mohnke, another stalwart member of Hitler's personal bodyguard, who had commanded an infantry company in the 1940 campaign in France. Although he lost a foot in Yugoslavia and was relegated to command of a replacement battalion, Mohnke was able to parlay his way to a new combat command with the formation of the 12th ss and the shortages of officers that resulted in the ss ranks. Major Gerhard Bremer led the division's reconnaissance battalion. All these men served under Brigadeführer Fritz Witt, who, like most of his senior officers, was a highly decorated veteran of the early campaigns fought by the ss in France and Russia. Only thirty-six years old, Witt had deep roots in the National Socialist machine and was recognized as a highly capable divisional commander.[7] Wehrmacht General der Panzertruppen Heinrich Eberbach, who saw service in close proximity to the 12th ss and came to know its officers well, considered "Witt, Meyer and Wünsche as Waffen-ss idealists but Mohnke and Bremer [were] bullies and brawlers."[8]

The grave manpower shortages plaguing the German army by 1944 had no effect on the 12th ss Division's total numbers, which on June 1 were actually larger than its mandated strength, with 20,540 officers, ncos, and men.[9] Where the shortages seriously compromised combat effectiveness was in leadership, for the division was short 144 officers and 2,192 ncos. This meant that inexperienced young soldiers would go into combat without a sufficient balance of veteran leaders to curb rash behaviour under fire.

About 12,000 troops served directly in the division's combat elements, while the rest provided support services. Each of the division's Panzer Grenadier regiments numbered 3,500 men, with roughly 500 of the men allocated to the four regimental support companies. These consisted of an infantry gun company armed with six 150-millimetre self-propelled guns, a flak company equipped with twelve 20-millimetre towed anti-aircraft guns, a reconnaissance company mounted on motorcycles, and a pioneer company to carry out engineering task. The remaining 3,000 were divided equally into three battalions.

Most of the division's remaining manpower was concentrated in the ranks of the 12th ss Panzer Regiment, which was divided into two battalions. I Battalion was equipped with the division's Panthers and II Battalion with Mark IVs. Rounding out the division's ranks was the 12th ss Panzer Reconnaissance Battalion, the 126th ss Panzer Artillery Regiment, and the division's inherent support companies that provided additional artillery and engineering ability, as well as medical, vehicle repair, supply, and administrative capability.[10]

Compared to 3rd Canadian Infantry Division, the 12th ss fielded much more overall fighting power. While the Canadian division's full strength was 18,000 men, fewer than 8,000 actually served in the nine rifle battalions, divided equally into three brigades. Another 2,400 manned the artillery and antitank guns of the four artillery regiments and single antitank regiment. Each infantry battalion had four rifle companies divided into three platoons and one 200-man support company. The support company was broken into an antitank platoon, armed with six carrier-towed six-pounders, a platoon outfitted with six three-inch mortars, and a carrier platoon fielding thirteen Bren carriers that could provide fire support by moving quickly to wherever the battalion was hotly engaged.[11]

Lacking tanks of its own, the division was augmented by 2nd Canadian Armoured Brigade, which consisted of about 3,400 men of all ranks equipped with 190 tanks and 33 light tanks (Honeys). The fighting teeth of this armoured formation was provided by three regiments, each mustering about 800 men and 60 tanks, of which 10 were Honeys and the rest Shermans.[12]

Like all Panzer divisions, the 12th ss was powerfully equipped with weaponry, including 175 tanks. Seventy-nine of these were Panther vs and ninety-six Mark IVs. The division had none of the monstrous fifty-seven-ton Tiger I models that were equipped with an 88-millimetre gun and 100-millimetre frontal armour. Only I ss Panzer Corps's 101st ss Heavy Panzer Battalion was equipped with Tigers, and this battalion was still grinding slowly towards the fighting on June 7. The Panther vs, however, posed a deadly threat to the Sherman M4s of the 2nd Canadian Armoured Brigade. Mounting a high-velocity 75-millimetre main gun and three 7.92-millimetre machine guns, the Panther weighed forty-five tons and boasted 120-millimetre-thick frontal armour that made it almost impervious to fire from Shermans. While the Tiger could easily punch a hole in a Sherman's comparatively thin 75-millimetre-thick armoured front at a range of three thousand yards, the Panther's lighter gun could still penetrate a Sherman at one thousand yards. A Sherman gunner might get lucky and pierce either German tank's armour at five hundred yards, if he lived long enough to close to that range. Despite the Panther's greater weight, at thirty-four miles per hour, it could outpace the Sherman's twenty-nine miles per hour top speed.

Fortunately, on June 7 most of the German tanks the Canadians saw forming up on their left flank were Mark IVs, although the Canadian tankers were quick to imagine they were seeing Panthers and to the infantry every tank looked to be a Tiger on the loose. Weighing twenty-four tons, mounting a 75-millimetre high-velocity gun and two 7.92-millimetre machine guns with 50-millimetre-thick armour, the Mark IV had a top speed of twenty-four miles per hour. Although lighter skinned than the Sherman, its main gun was superior to the Allied tank's standard short-barrelled 75-millimetre. Recognizing this deficiency, however, the British had introduced a variation to the Sherman for the D-Day invasion, dubbed the Firefly. This tank was fitted with a 17-pounder that gave it superior firepower to the Mark IV and was a close match to the Panther V, but only four tanks in each squadron were so armed. The rest were standard-issue Shermans.

While 2 CAB enjoyed slight supremacy in the number of tanks it brought to the field, the Panzer Grenadiers grossly outgunned the Canadian infantry in terms of heavy and light machine guns—859 compared to just 305. There was also no questioning that the most common of the German guns, the 7.92-millimetre MG 42, with its shrieking 1,200-round-a-minute rate of fire, was a superior weapon to the methodical Bren gun that chugged out only 500 rounds per minute of .303-calibre ammunition. In addition to their greater numbers of light and heavy machine guns, the Hitler Youth carried a huge number of submachine guns—two variants of Schmeissers that fired

9-millimetre bullets from a 32-shot detachable magazine. While the Canadians were also equipped with a 9-millimetre submachine gun, the Sten was less reliable than the Schmeisser and generally issued only to officers and NCOS.[13]

ON JUNE 7, the SS officer responsible for masterminding the counterattack on the Canadian flank was Kurt Meyer. His 25th Panzer Grenadier Regiment was in position to strike the 9th Canadian Infantry Brigade's advance column on its badly exposed left flank. Witt trusted Meyer completely, considering him a de facto divisional second-in-command who could be entirely relied upon. With some of his units still just arriving in the area, Meyer worked frantically to tee up a coherent counterattack that would be strong enough to rout the Canadians and ready to strike at the scheduled divisional jumping off time of 1600 hours. Meyer ordered two of his three Panzer Grenadier battalions to attack on line, with the third staggered to the left rear. Advancing on the left would be I Battalion, which assembled between Epron and la Folie, while the right flank of the attack would be carried out by II Battalion from a position near Bitot. III Battalion, meanwhile, would form up southeast of Franqueville, concealed from view of the enemy by a low ridge south of the Caen-Bayeux highway. Each battalion had a platoon of heavy infantry guns and a platoon of light anti-aircraft guns. The entire Pionier Kompanie was assigned to supporting I Battalion, which Meyer anticipated faced the hardest fighting. A battery of heavy field howitzers was also dedicated to each battalion and Wünsche's Panzers were to be heavily committed to supporting the infantry.[14]

No sooner had Meyer manoeuvred his battalions into their forward positions than the North Novas and Sherbrooke Fusiliers appeared on the march from Buron to Authie. From his vantage in the tower, Meyer could barely believe the catch being passed his way: "My God! What an opportunity! The tanks are driving right across II Battalion's front! The unit is showing its unprotected flank. I give orders to all battalions, the artillery and the available tanks. 'Do not shoot! Open fire on my orders only!'"[15]

To Meyer, it seemed the Canadian tankers were oblivious to the presence of his Panzers and grenadiers, not attempting to break past them to the airport. He was momentarily nonplussed by the boldness or foolishness of the action, whatever the case might be, aware also that the Canadians were throwing his entire divisional attack schedule into disarray. There was no way he could wait until 1600 hours to strike. The time for action was now, despite the fact that the entire 12th ss was not ready. The 26th Panzer Regiment was still east of the River Orne, moving towards its positions to the west of the River Mue, and the Panzer regiment equipped with Panthers was stalled nineteen miles east of the Orne awaiting fuel to fill its dry tanks.

Meyer decided that when the leading Canadian tanks passed by Franqueville, II Battalion would strike, with the available Panzers holding on the reverse slope south of the Caen-Bayeux highway in support. Once this battalion rolled the Canadians back and reached Authie, he would unleash his other battalions. "The objective: The coast."[16]

Minutes later, the first Sherbrooke tanks of 'A' Squadron went past Franqueville and started crawling up onto the highway. Meyer signalled for the attack to begin, calling for Wünsche to get his Panzers moving. With satisfaction, he heard the Panzer commander instantly shout into his radio, "Achtung! Panzer marsch!"[17]

The response was immediate, and at 1410 hours, Meyer saw "cracks and flashes near Franqueville. The enemy tank at the head of the spearhead smokes and I watch the crew bailing out. More tanks are torn to pieces with loud explosions. Suddenly, one Panzer [Mark] IV starts to burn, a blast of flame shoots out of the hatches."[18] While the German and Canadian tanks engaged in a fierce brawl near Franqueville, all the way back along the left flank to Buron and St.-Contest, the Panzer Grenadier battalions launched an assault towards Authie. A bloody melee ensued that left tankers and infantry on both sides dazed by its intensity.

At the same time as 'A' Squadron was ambushed, wrote the Sherbrookes' regimental historian, "the Panzer force on the left rushed forward and entered the engagement. Most of the Regiment was thus involved at once in the pitched battle, metal monsters lurking in the orchards, shouldering through hedgerows or lurching across the fields of grain, dodging [while] at the same time seeking out their opponents. Suddenly ribbons of tracer fire would lance forward across the open spaces as the monsters barked and sometimes in the shadows or in the open, stationary tanks would burst into flames. Meanwhile the chatter and rip of the enemy machine guns were answered by the drumming of our own gunfire as a group of infantry ran at the crouch from one hedgerow to the next."[19]

Captain Merritt Hayes Bateman, the second-in-command of 'B' Squadron, could see the hangars and runway of Carpiquet airport to the south of the Caen-Bayeux highway and railway. Barely a mile away, the D-Day objective was enticingly close. Then he glanced to his left towards the rising ground there and saw "what looked to be one hundred bloody German tanks and they were flanking us."[20]

Major George Mahon had been leading the squadron towards the very height of ground from which the Panzers started descending because he "couldn't see how we could ignore going for the commanding ground with or without infantry."[21] Sergeant A.J. Parsons was a passenger inside Mahon's Sherman, along for the ride to provide a wireless liaison link between the tankers and the infantry in order to leave the major free to run his squadron. He was squeezed into a cramped space beside the driver, next to the wireless set.

Mahon was champing at the bit to get 'B' Squadron through to the airport once he cleared this ridge and was pressing the driver, Trooper "Dusty" Rhodes, "to forge ahead." As the tank pulled ahead of the rest of the Shermans, an armour-piercing shell belted into its side. The round scored a direct hit on a useless pistol port welded shut to prevent its being forced open by enemy infantry and knocked the lid off. Parsons "looked up and saw a square hole and my first thought was that we were goners. It had smashed the CO's [Mahon's] arm between the elbow and shoulder and killed Lance Corporal John Kachor and slightly wounded the radio operator Corporal Gordon Drodge in the back. It took the major's arm out from the elbow to the shoulder. I got a piece of shrapnel in the left hand that was not serious.

"We hauled the major out of the tank and put him on the back. I applied a tourniquet on the arm to keep the bones from breaking out. We buried Corporal John Kachor."[22] Mahon handed command of the

squadron to Bateman, then he and the other four men who had survived the destruction of the Sherman headed off on foot towards the
rear. As he walked away, the major thought "it was hell to have committed them there and then not be able to finish the job." It would take
Mahon's badly mangled left arm almost two years to mend properly.[23]

With the situation becoming more chaotic by the moment, Bateman tried desperately to restore order to his badly shot-up squadron.
Suddenly, there "was a hell of an explosion. First thing I knew I found
myself on the ground. Whether I was blown out of the tank or
jumped or whatever I just sort of realized I was on the ground and
my tank was an inferno." His driver and co-driver had escaped, but
the loader and gunner perished inside the fiery tomb.[24]

Racing to a nearby tank, Bateman ordered its crew commander
out and got back to trying to extract the battered squadron from the
trap. He also wanted to support the North Novas in Authie, who were
visibly taking a beating from massed infantry attacks. Withdrawing
to a low rise, Bateman discovered that the squadron was down to
ten tanks. He quickly reorganized these into two troops, with the
remnants of No. 2 and No. 3 Troops under command of Lieutenant
Norman Davies and No. 1 and No. 4 Troops under Lieutenant K.L.
Steeves. Davies, with six tanks, was to lead the advance while Steeves
covered his left flank with the remainder.

Davies had gone only a short distance under intense antitank and
artillery fire when, looking over his shoulder, he realized his tank was
all alone "with about seven or eight enemy tanks at 1,000 yards on
my left. I halted, stopped two of them with the 17 [pounder gun], advanced, halted and fired again scoring another hit, then all hell
seemed to break loose. There were tanks coming up at full speed to
my rear (our own), tanks to my left firing at us, antitank blazing away
from our left and rear, and tracer and 75-[millimetre] gun flashes all
over the place. I moved forward again, apparently to a hull down [po-
sition] which turned out to be a bottleneck, as it was practically a tank
trap in an orchard, huge logs barred our way. Tanks were hit and
burning all around us by then, and it was impossible to keep track of
who was who. One was hit directly in front of me, one right beside
me, tracer was cutting down trees all over the place, so I decided to

withdraw with what was left of 2nd and 3rd Troops. 1st Troop had meanwhile stood to and covered our flank but had left themselves open by doing so and Lieutenant Steeves' tank went up in flames a couple of hundred yards away."[25]

With his wireless knocked out, Davies threw open his turret cover and waved frantically to three other Shermans in view, signalling them to withdraw to high ground to the immediate rear of the North Novas to await orders from brigade. Finally reaching a safe position, he held up, counted noses, and found only five of 'B' Squadron's tanks present.[26]

Sergeant T.C. Reid of 'C' Squadron's No. 2 Troop had been work-ing over German infantry fleeing Authie and thinking everything was "a breeze" when "suddenly out of the blue we got it. I... felt a jolt in my tank, looked back and found my blanket box shot through. The next shot unseated [loader/operator] Trooper Gailey, and then I saw what was hitting me. There were 18 hornets [Panzers] lined up in hull down about 2,500 yards away and they had us cold; their third round went through my engine and quickly after that they struck Lieutenant MacLean's and Lieutenant Steeves' almost simultaneously. They both burned up and then I saw Mr. Steeves and his gunner both frantically struggling to get out of the turret. Mr. Steeves fell back in and the gunner fell out. Mr. Steeves then reappeared and he was pretty badly burnt, also his co-driver whose hatch was caught by the gun being traversed over it."[27]

The tank battle was no less confusing or terrible for the ss tankers. Gunner Sturmann Hans Fenn was in Oberscharführer Helmut Esser's Panzer, which was at the rear of a five-tank platoon commanded by Obersturmführer Albert Gasch, advancing through gently rolling terrain. In a matter of seconds, the four Mark IVs ahead of Esser's tank erupted in flames. Attempting to escape the kill zone, Esser swung the tank around, only to have an armour-piercing shell penetrate the hull. One of Esser's legs was sliced clean off, but the crew commander managed to lever himself out of the turret as the tank brewed up. When Fenn tried to shove the gunner's hatch open, he found the rubber cover charred, jamming the lid closed.

Barely conscious due to smoke inhalation and burns, Fenn managed to crawl through the flaming chamber of the tank and escape from the loader's hatch. Suffering third-degree burns, Fenn stumbled back to the rear. Passing some grenadiers, he noticed that they "stared at me as if I was a ghost."[28]

BACK IN BURON, Major Learment was trying to organize carriers to race out to Authie and extract 'C' Company and the other elements dug in there before the Germans cut them off from the rest of the battalion and supporting units. As he was talking to Captain Fraser, who was preparing to make a last stand if the transport failed to get through, Learment saw a Cameron Highlander Bren carrier approaching. Standing in the middle of the carrier, as if at attention, was a badly wounded Sherbrooke officer. Every stitch of clothing had been burned off the man and his skin was black "from head to toe. His tank had gone off like a lighter."[29]

Despite their losses, the surviving Sherbrooke tanks were still in the fight, being reorganized by Lieutenant Colonel Mel Gordon to the rear of Buron in order to cover the infantry dug in there and at Authie. Born in Dixie, Ontario in 1905, Melville Kennedy Burgoyne Gordon had combined a career in law with a simultaneous one in the militia during the interwar years. Posted to command of 'B' Squadron of the Three Rivers Regiment in May 1941, he went overseas to England as a major. In January 1943, Gordon was promoted to lieutenant colonel and given command of the Sherbrooke Fusiliers.[30] A popular officer, he was proving remarkably unflappable in the face of battle. Even as his beloved regiment was shredded, Gordon focussed on how he could either blunt or stop the German armoured juggernaut and screen the North Novas should a retreat from Authie and Buron become necessary.

There was no question in Learment's mind that 'C' Company had to be rescued from its precarious position in Authie. Hoping to break through with a relief force, the major ordered 'B' Company and remnants of the scattered No. 15 Platoon of 'C' Company that had returned to Buron onto carriers, which attempted to dash through the

German fire. "As soon as the vehicles pulled clear of Buron they came under heavy shell and mortar fire and it soon became obvious," he wrote later, "that Authie could not be reached." The infantry were ordered back into their previously dug slit trenches and Learment ordered Captain E.S. Gray to take his dangerously exposed carriers back to the battalion's headquarters at les Buissons. By now he was gloomily assuming that the troops in Authie had been overrun, as all radio communication with them had ceased.[31]

IN FACT, THE NORTH NOVAS in Authie were still fighting, but were aware that their situation was desperate. A civilian had just guided Lieutenant Jack Veness to a gravel pit on the south side of the village, where about fifteen wounded Sherbrookes and Cameron Highlanders had managed to find shelter from the shelling. Several of the men were obviously dying, but he ordered the platoon stretcher-bearer to do what he could for the rest. Next to the gravel pit was one of the Camerons' carriers, with a mounted Vickers machine gun that was undamaged. The carrier was in perfect running order, but its crew lay dead beside it. Veness started the carrier up and drove it back to 'C' Company's defensive lines, which were concentrated on the edge of an orchard behind a thick hedge. The lieutenant was pleased with the addition of the Vickers, which augmented the machine guns stripped from two destroyed Sherbrooke tanks.

Looking about for Fraser, he discovered the captain aboard one of the wrecked Shermans, trying to use its radio to contact Learment. Fraser shouted that he wasn't having any luck. A couple of tankers, who had survived the destruction of the Firefly tank Fraser was standing on, were inside trying without apparent success to repair the damaged main gun's traverse system to bring it back into action. But Veness, with optimism born of combat naïveté, remained confident that they could hold, his belief bolstered even more when Lieutenant Lou Sutherland of 'A' Company marched out of Authie into the orchard with his entire platoon behind. But rather than being a relief force, Sutherland reported, he and his men had become separated from the rest of 'A' Company and were only in Authie by mistake.

Stiffened by this sudden infusion of almost forty men, however, the officers set about reorganizing their defence. Shaped in a rectangle, the orchard had "one long side bordering the main street of the town and a shoulder-high hedge all around it. Sutherland's platoon was placed along the street side. Veness had the end towards the enemy and half the other side. Langley had the rest. The extra Brownings from the tanks and the Vickers were mounted in the hedge on the side away from the town."[32]

Looking southwards, Veness saw about a dozen men in single file approaching the orchard through an open field that stretched out on the other side of the hedge. Knowing that Lieutenant Bob Graves had gone off in that direction in search of his missing platoon, Veness figured he had found the men and was coming back in. Wanting to avert any chance of a friendly fire accident, Veness ran out into the open, "shouting and waving his arms. He was out about one hundred yards when he suddenly saw there were more than a section, more than a platoon. And they were wearing green uniforms. Germans!"[33] Germans who immediately opened up on him with a hail of fire through which Veness somehow managed to zigzag safely back to the hedge.

Back under cover, Veness saw that the Germans had broken out of their single-file formation to form an assault arrowhead and were coming on in a wave that seemed to him as large as a battalion. Suddenly the 17-pounder gun on the disabled Sherman belched a shell towards the Germans, the turret traversed slightly to acquire a new target, and the gunner began blasting off rounds of high explosive. Just as the Firefly went into action, the orchard erupted under a heavy enemy artillery barrage filling the air "with flying earth, shrapnel and splinters of wood. Orchard trees seemed to bounce from their stumps and float in the air... The tank gun was firing as fast as it could be reloaded. The Vickers and Brownings took tremendous toll. But the Germans came on like fanatics. Soon they were within one hundred yards. Every Nova was shooting and the Germans were dropping so fast it did not seem that any could get through. But shells were blasting gaps in the hedge and Veness suddenly heard new firing. He swung around to see a green wave of massed Germans flooding into Sutherland's position. Sutherland and a few survivors were falling back, fighting as they went."[34]

Realizing the only way to safety was to fight their way back to the battalion, Veness gathered the twelve men left in his platoon and "led a dash at the ring of green uniforms," blasting a path "through with grenade and pistol and rifle butt."[35] Behind him, twenty North Novas, now completely surrounded by Hitler Youth, fought on. Langley was shot down when only three of his men were still standing. These were cut down a moment later. Locked in a point-blank shootout with several German tanks, the Firefly gunner smashed three opponents before his own tank exploded into flame. Nobody escaped. Captain Fraser, a handful of North Novas, and a couple of Cameron Highlanders still manning a Vickers kept firing until each in turn was killed.[36]

Lieutenant Sutherland saw Fraser fall as he and the remnants of his platoon scrambled into the cover of a house on the edge of Authie. German tanks were careering into the village, some smashing through stone buildings and walls to gain the main street. Leapfrogging his men across the same street under the nose of one tank's gun by using the smoke from an exploding shell to conceal them, Sutherland snaked through houses and backyards to gain the northwest corner of the village. From here, they slipped into the tall fields of wheat and crept off on a wide circuit that took them almost to the village of Gruchy before looping back to the safety of Villons-les-Buissons.[37]

Behind them, Authie was a cauldron of smoke and fire. Seemingly dazed young German soldiers in green camouflage smocks wandered about. Veness and his men were still in their midst, shooting a bloody path that carried them to the northeast side of the village without loss. In the distance, they saw 'A' Company dug in behind a hedge two hundred yards distant, but the ground between consisted of two pastures broken by a hundred-yard-wide field of high grain. Their only hope was to try sprinting to safety, but they immediately came under fire from a German tank that had moved up on the east flank of the village. Only Veness and four of his men made it to 'A' Company.[38]

Other small groups of North Novas were fighting their way back through Authie. A section of Sutherland's platoon under Sergeant Bill Gammon had been cut off while covering the escape of the rest. They kept firing until the Germans were only ten yards away and every weapon but Gammon's Sten was out of ammunition. As his men lowered their rifles to surrender, the sergeant used "the clouds and smoke hanging over the main road" to slip away. Dodging into a side lane, Gammon came face to face with two Germans. Quickly killing one with a burst of his Sten, he swung the gun barrel towards the other, only to have the weapon jam. Before the still startled German could bring his rifle to bear on Gammon, the sergeant smashed him in the face with the butt of the Sten and escaped into the wheat.[39]

In ones and twos, some North Novas fought on, while others surrendered after being surrounded or overrun. Two brothers—Sergeant Earl McKillop and Corporal Walter McKillop—were among a section of five men under the sergeant's command when their position in the orchard was overrun and they gave up. Then a great burst of fire from an unidentified machine gun in the hedge caused their captors to dive for cover. The McKillops and two others broke for it and made their way through the wheat back to safety.

Private Arthur Gould, who had been captured near Sergeant McKillop's overrun position, watched the successful escape. His captors coolly kept their guns on him, offering no such opportunity. Lance Corporal W.L. MacKay, bleeding badly from a bullet wound to his face, and two other men were also forced to surrender. Their young captors were in a rage, screaming with hate at the Canadians, for they had expected their baptism of fire to result in an easy victory and instead had been badly blooded.[40]

Despite the delay that Meyer's III Battalion had faced in driving the Canadians out of Authie, he remained confident that the regiment could fight its way to the coast as ordered. From his vantage in the abbey tower, it seemed the North Novas were "totally surprised." And now his other two battalions, heavily supported by tanks, swept towards Buron to wipe out that pocket of resistance. Victory seemed within his grasp.[41]

[7]

Don't Do Anything Crazy

O N THE SOUTHERN EDGE of the thin line of North Nova Scotia Highlanders gathered in front of Buron, Lieutenant Jack Veness brought 'A' Company's Major Leon Rhodenizer the grim news that 'C' Company had been destroyed in Authie and the Germans were likely to strike his lines in "overwhelming strength." Artillery and mortar fire was already bracketing the company line, and Rhodenizer's men were huddled deep into slit trenches positioned behind the cover of a hedge. The carrier Rhodenizer had used for a command vehicle lay in a wrecked pile nearby. Beside it, the company's wireless signaller sprawled dead on the ground. The major thought on Veness's news for a moment, but there was nothing he could do to better prepare for the imminent assault. "Okay," he said. "Grab a rifle and start shooting."[1]

Having learned from Veness that Lieutenant Lou Sutherland's platoon had been wiped out in Authie, Rhodenizer knew he had only two platoons left for the fight. After deducting the men who had been badly wounded by the incessant shelling, that meant fifty to sixty soldiers. To his front, the ground crawled with German infantry, but the more immediate threat came from a clutch of tanks closing in on 'A' Company's position. Still well outside the range of the Canadians' PIAT, the tanks halted and began taking potshots at the North Novas. Lieutenant Percy Smith's platoon, holding the flank reaching out towards Authie, took the brunt of this fire. Nine of his men died.

When the tanks momentarily ceased firing, the Panzer Grenadiers tried to swoop in, only to be driven off by the deadly accurate rifle and machine-gun fire the North Novas threw out. One assault after another was thrown back, as the Germans repeatedly tried the same tactic. Soon the ground in front of the Canadian position was scattered with twisted bodies clad in green camouflage, while the trenches behind the hedge filled with dead and wounded men dressed in bloodstained khaki.

Veness had taken a rifle and ammunition web belt off one of the wounded and was firing whenever he saw a target moving through the wheat. A glance at his watch showed that 'A' Company's fight had been going on for an hour. The men were looking increasingly desperate, counting the few bullets they had left.[2] They had gone into the day with fifty rounds apiece and twenty-five magazines for each Bren gun spread amongst them.[3] Too little for the intensity and duration of this fight.

Captain Joe Trainor, 'A' Company's second-in-command, came up behind Veness and shouted over to Smith, "Percy, how many men have you?"

"Six that are all right," Smith replied.

Out on the other flank, one of Lieutenant Jack Fairweather's Bren gunners stopped firing. The twenty-one-year-old lieutenant from Rothesay, New Brunswick crawled over and discovered the gunner had taken a bullet through his skull. The gun was also broken. He scavenged the few remaining magazines from the dead man and distributed them to the platoon's other two Bren gunners.

With so many men down and ammunition running out, the rate of fire the soldiers could put out was slacking off alarmingly, allowing the Panzer Grenadiers to crawl in on them through the cover of the tall wheat. German bullets were whipping through the air and the occasional grenade arced over the hedge to spray shrapnel down its length. All the time, the Panzers kept pounding them with high-explosive rounds and raking the hedge with machine-gun fire.

Rhodenizer's wireless set had stopped working, so he couldn't call for artillery. Not that there had been any available earlier. The company kept shrinking its lines in from the flanks, dragging the wounded into the centre of their little nest, trying to hold together as a unit.

Fairweather was unloading a damaged Bren magazine and jamming the rounds into the magazine for his Lee Enfield when his batman shouted, "They're behind us, sir!" Over his shoulder, Fairweather saw a large number of ss soldiers rise out of the wheat. The lieutenant rammed the magazine into the rifle and aimed it at the approaching Germans just as Captain Trainor called out, "Come out. It's all over."

"It was strange that the end of the road should be reached so suddenly," Fairweather later recounted, and he "wondered what his folks would think." During the prolonged firefight he had felt no fear, but now Fairweather suffered a flash of panic before he raised his hands high. "An ss gunner glanced at him and shifted his weapon as if to kill, then leered horribly and gave his attention to others. Cold fear returned to Fairweather."[4]

Veness had been looking to his front when Trainor ordered the surrender. The baffled lieutenant spun around and saw about twenty Germans all armed with Schmeissers covering his position. To his right, Fairweather and his men were standing with their hands up. Despite feeling suddenly sick to his stomach, Veness forced himself to calmly drop the rifle and raise his arms.

As he did so, Rhodenizer also rose from his slit trench and with visible anguish etching his face cried, "No! No! What's going on here?"

Trainor responded sharply, "Don't do anything crazy. We haven't a chance."

Grumbling under his breath, the major slowly lifted his hands. 'A' Company was finished.[5]

FROM HIS VANTAGE on the outskirts of Buron, Private Jack Byrne watched the German infantry and tanks coming across the fields towards 'B' Company's perimeter "and knew we were in trouble." Byrne had formerly spent more than a year as one of the crack sergeants running officers through the Canadian Combat School in England before wangling his way back to the regiment in time for the invasion by taking a voluntary demotion to private. Until this afternoon, Byrne had figured the training he and the officers of 3rd Canadian Infantry Division had gone through at the school gave them a fighting edge, but he now reckoned that the North Novas were doomed no matter how well prepared they were for combat.[6]

For sure, the troops in Authie had been wiped out. Now there were men in green uniforms swarming towards them from 'A' Company's lines, so those guys were probably gone. That left it to companies 'B' and 'D' to hold the line, or the whole invasion might be driven right back into the sea. The rate of fire coming at them was terrific—the air above No. 12 Platoon's fighting position was scythed by bullets and shrapnel from exploding artillery, mortar, and tank rounds.

A little way over from Byrne, Captain A.J. Wilson, 'B' Company's acting commander, thought the "situation appeared desperate" and consequently had "organized his defences for a last-man, last-round stand" based on holding a German antitank trench that cut across the road running through Buron from Franqueville to les Buissons. The ditch provided his men with a deep, continuous trench from which to fight rather than being isolated in shallow slit trenches hastily carved by soldiers operating in twos and threes. Wilson had two platoons of 'B' Company with him, the other having been left with Major Learment. The major was using that platoon to shore up the remnants of 'C' Company that had escaped Authie into some semblance of a fighting unit charged with holding the immediate front of Buron. 'D' Company was out to the southeast of Wilson's men, defending the badly exposed left flank. Behind the infantry, the few still operational Sherbrooke Fusiliers tanks were lined up in the cover of a large wood about a quarter-mile north of the village. Alongside Wilson's men stood two three-inch mortars and a six-pound antitank gun manned by men from the North Novas' support company, and several Cameron Highlander carriers mounted with Vickers machine guns.[7]

Back at his les Buissons headquarters, Lieutenant Colonel Charlie Petch turned to his Sherbrooke Fusiliers counterpart and said, "Mel, my boys are going to try to hold Buron and les Buissons." Gordon promised all the support he could muster and rushed back to his badly shot-up regiment. There was no longer any squadron integrity; the tankers had simply formed "into little groups... two tanks from this squadron, one from another till we had another troop and we were given an officer or NCO to command."[8]

Petch, meanwhile, continued attempting to bring up artillery support for his beleaguered battalion, but the 14th Field Regiment was having problems of its own. Having set off in its 105-millimetre self-propelled Priests at noon to gain a firing position that would bring Authie within range, the regiment had progressed in stages by troops to ensure continuous fire support to 9 CIB. But this made the advance ponderous. Authie remained out of range and Buron was also beyond the maximum shooting distance of 10,500 yards that the Priest could lob its heavy shot. Most of the gunners had welcomed being equipped with the American Priests for the D-Day invasion, but now they longed for the trusty old British 25-pounders that could range shot out to 13,400 yards and would have easily put them within firing range. When the regiment finally reached its new firing position in the late afternoon, the area was subjected to "continuous mortar fire" from the Germans still holding Douvres-la-Délivrande's radar station.[9]

Radio communication from the North Novas through brigade to the supporting regiments was badly fragmented throughout the afternoon by static interference, and disrupted even further by the English-speaking German signaller breaking into the net to sow confusion with a series of orders for various units to retreat.[10]

Major C.F. Kennedy and his men of 'D' Company were frantically trying to fend off the German infantry using the cover of a heavy mortar and artillery bombardment to crawl by the dozens towards them through the tall wheatfield fronting their position. Some of the Germans were shouting in English, "Surrender, Canada." Then Kennedy's No. 18 wireless set squawked with a message from someone speaking perfectly unaccented English instructing 'D' Company to immediately withdraw towards les Buissons. When Kennedy demanded to know the identity of the officer giving the order, the man just repeated that 'D' Company must retreat. Kennedy decided he was speaking to the enemy and shouted for his men to stand firm.[11]

At about 1830 hours, Learment suddenly saw Panzer Grenadiers moving around inside the village itself behind his position and realized his flank had been turned. "They were engaged with rifle and Bren gun and for a few minutes repulsed," he wrote. "However, they soon got an MG 42 into position from where it could fire from a flank right into the dug-in positions of the infantry. This had the desired effect of keeping our heads down, but not before most of our ammunition had been used.

"The first intimation I had of the enemy being close was when an SS trooper armed with a Schmeisser appeared over the rim of the trench and ordered us out. He was shot by someone in a trench behind us and rolled away in the wheat. In the meantime, I was able to get another magazine on the Bren gun and [to] fire it. As I went to fire the fourth and last magazine, the gun jammed and the same time another Hun put in his appearance. This time there was no alternative but to come out with our hands up."[12]

By now, casualties had reduced Learment's force to only about ten men. As the men wearily emerged from their slit trenches, Learment saw that the field around their position "was literally alive with camouflaged Germans."[13] They all seemed very young. While most of the Germans set off in the direction of 'D' Company's lines, a small escort party forced Learment and his men to run into Buron. Once inside the village, they were lined up against a wall in a small square and a MG 42 was positioned on either flank of the prisoners. Learment looked at the German soldiers manning the machine guns, considered the fact that none of the men had been searched for weapons, and decided they were about to be executed. "They were just raving crazy. You couldn't talk to those people."[14] Suddenly, a German NCO rushed into the square bellowing at the SS troopers.

As the machine-gunners stepped back from their weapons, the others rushed forward and started roughly searching the prisoners. "They were grabbing our wallets and had our wristwatches off before we could move. One grabbed my steel helmet and just shoved it off the back of my head." Learment and his men were repeatedly punched and kicked during the search. Then suddenly one of the Germans pointed to a grenade dangling forgotten from the web belt of Private Jack Metcalfe, who was standing alongside Learment. "The German raised his Schmeisser and as Metcalfe turned toward me he was shot three or four times in the back and fell screaming at my feet. The German then stepped over him and placing the machine-pistol at Metcalfe's head, shot him again. No notice of this was taken by the other Germans who continued their search as if nothing had happened."[15]

The Canadians were then marched out of Buron and along the road leading to Authie. A short distance out of the village, the small column came under shellfire and Learment realized the Canadian gunners had finally gotten within range. It was not propitious timing and several "were nicked by near bursts. Private Jeffrey Hargreaves was wounded in the legs and could not continue the march. We were not allowed to help him and he was shot as he lay on the ground. My batman, Private James MacNeil, was also slightly wounded but was able to continue, although we were not allowed to assist him in any way. As we neared Authie we saw some members of the two forward platoons of 'C' Company. They were all dead and three of them were laying close together in such a manner, with no weapons or equipment near them, as to suggest that they had been shot after capture, and this was later confirmed."[16]

Two Canadian corpses lay on the road and Learment saw Panzers deliberately grind over them.[17] One of the bodies was that of Corporal Thomas Davidson of Stellarton, Nova Scotia. Davidson had been among eight prisoners from 'C' Company executed in Authie by an impromptu firing squad comprised of three ss soldiers. After the killings, the Germans dragged the bodies of Davidson and another man out onto the road to ensure that passing traffic would run over them.[18]

Learment and the prisoners with him were hustled through Authie and marched to the ss regiment's headquarters at the Abbaye d'Ardenne. Along the way, there would be more killings as Panzer

Grenadiers of the 25th Regiment's III Battalion, which had captured most of the Canadians during the fighting at Authie and Buron, went berserk.

The 25th ss Panzer Grenadier Regiment's Standartenführer Kurt Meyer considered this unit shaky because its battalion commander's battle experience was limited and none of the company commanders had previously been in combat. Thirty-three-year-old Obersturm-führer Karl-Heinz Milius had won both the Iron Cross First Class and Second Class fighting as a sergeant in France in 1940, but had then been assigned to a series of instructional postings until his transfer to the 12th ss. Before the war, Milius had served in several Death's Head units guarding concentration camps. This included two years commanding a platoon of guards at Dachau. ss efficiency reports on Milius portrayed him as overly aloof, reluctant to heed advice, and overconfident. Three of his company commanders had been drawn from the Wehrmacht, but like all fifty of those officers assigned to the division they were devoted Nazis with past experience as Hitler Youth leaders. All, however, had seen service only in support units rather than combat companies. The same was true of the other company commander, ss Obersturmführer Georg-Walter Stahl.[19]

Under this uncertain leadership, III Battalion had faced its baptism of fire. Trained to believe they were elite troops in the finest traditions of the Waffen-ss, which considered itself the best fighting unit in the world, the young troops had faced a grim awakening. In the day's gruelling battle, the battalion lost twenty-eight soldiers killed, seventy wounded, and another twelve missing. Five of the wounded were officers.[20] Assured they were invincible, the teenagers had been forced to recognize their own precious mortality as they saw bullets and shrapnel cut down comrades by their side. Perhaps it was this cruel awakening to reality that whipped the soldiers of III Battalion into a killing frenzy.

In one incident after another, soldiers of III Battalion, often behaving like "maniacs," murdered small groups of Canadian prisoners. Lance Corporal W.L. MacKay of North Novas' 'A' Company had feigned death while watching in horror out of one slightly open eye as one trooper bayoneted Private Lorne Brown while he was trying to surrender. In Authie, a German officer had beaten in the brains of Private William Nichol, immobilized by wounds, with the butt of a rifle and then shot him for good measure.[21]

THE ELIMINATION OF Learment's force left companies 'D' and 'B' virtually surrounded and exposed to attack from Buron itself. At the antitank ditch, 'B' Company's acting commander Captain Wilson had been directing fire from his two mortars and one remaining operational six-pound antitank gun onto the Germans carrying out the frontal assault on 'D' Company. Now the weapons were swung to engage the enemy coming out of Buron on the road running to les Buissons. The Cameron Highlanders of No. 11 Platoon pitched in with fire from their heavy machine guns, but return fire killed their commander, Lieutenant J.S. Couper.[22] Cameron battalion second-in-command Major Roger Rowley, who had come forward to assess the situation at Buron, took over the platoon. The heavy-weapon fire from the antitank ditch sent the Germans scrambling back into the cover of the village, but when the guns fell silent, Wilson realized 'B' Company had shot its bolt. Rowley agreed, telling him that the Camerons were completely out of ammunition and the mortars also spent.

Wilson quickly lined the company Bren carriers up on the road, boarded all his men, and made "a break for it." Lance Corporal H.L. Fraser volunteered to stay behind and cover the withdrawal from the antitank ditch with his Bren gun. Once the carriers were well down the road to les Buissons, he followed them for a short way and then paused to burn off a magazine to keep the Germans buttoned in Buron. Fraser continued to dash a short way up the road, swivel, and fire off a magazine from his hip and then run again until he reached les Buissons. "His courageous act," Wilson wrote, "was a boost to the morale of everyone."[23]

Wilson had expected to find nothing at les Buissons but the tattered remnants of the North Novas, but instead the area was teeming with the entire Stormont, Dundas and Glengarry Highlander battalion. Mixed in amongst their ranks were pitifully few North Nova survivors who had escaped the overrunning of Authie and made their way back to the battalion's headquarters. The reinforcement battalion's Lieutenant Colonel G.H. Christiansen, noted as the 9th Brigade's most competent battalion commander, had established a defensive position to one side of the village, with 'D' Company "in front of a church, 'C' Company near some isolated houses, [and] 'B' and 'A' companies... astride the highway." That highway led straight to the one running from Villons-les-Buissons through Bény-sur-Mer to Courseulles-sur-Mer. If the Germans got past his battalion, Christiansen knew there was nothing to his rear to stop them from carrying right on to the beach but the Highland Light Infantry, which formed the brigade reserve at Villons-les-Buissons.

As his men worked feverishly to dig fighting positions, some damaged Sherbrooke Fusilier tanks limped by on their way to the repair unit in the rear. Christiansen watched them pass and then issued instructions for his men to "let tanks go through but that not one infantryman was to be allowed to pass." The lieutenant colonel was concerned that those North Novas making it back to les Buissons might understandably be of a mind to keep right on going, but he needed every available rifle on line to hold the Germans back.[24]

Christiansen need not have worried, for although the North Novas were badly shaken by the long day's battle and terrible losses, few were as yet broken of spirit. And out on the edge of Buron, 'D' Company was still locked in battle. Five times the Germans threw attacks at Kennedy's badly shredded company, and each time were thrown back.[25] There were Panzers in Buron now and others standing off to the east, all hammering the company perimeter with 75-millimetre guns. German mortar rounds spattered down like raindrops.

Trying to keep the Panzer Grenadiers at bay, Kennedy radioed a request for artillery to be fired directly to the front of his lines. Petch, who had just learned that the 14th Field Artillery now had its guns in range, agreed. A few minutes later, the first 105-millimetre rounds ranged in on the company and Kennedy reported the fire on target. The gun batteries then opened with a heavy, rapid concentration of shells. But the German attack continued. The battalion's war diarist wrote: "Under this fire enemy infantry advanced and penetrated the forward slit trenches... It was impossible to stop them as [the men] had to remain in their trenches to avoid our overhead fire and also the enemy's. They had no field of fire due to the high grain. Machine-gun fire and grenades were fired into the slits and... 16 Platoon, having run out of ammunition were forced to surrender and were rounded up. Under our heavy artillery fire... the captors went to ground and in the moment afforded by this break two sections of 16 Platoon escaped and returned to their company."[26]

It was about 2000 hours, the light fading from the day, when Kennedy heard the Panzers in the village clanking his way. From the wheatfield and town, Panzer Grenadiers rushed towards the Canadians. Those Germans armed with rifles had fixed their bayonets. Desperate, Kennedy pleaded for immediate tank support. Petch called Gordon, who turned to Captain Sydney Valpy Radley-Walter and told him to take the tanks under his command into the fray. The son of a small-town minister from the Gaspé Peninsula, Radley-Walter was normally 'C' Squadron's second-in-command, but now he led a Sherbrooke polyglot of just seven tanks out of the woods towards Buron. "I could see all the dead and dying [of both sides] where the Germans had come right across them," he later said.[27]

The Shermans rolled through Buron with their machine guns and 75-millimetre cannon blazing, barrelled right over 'D' Company's slit trenches, and punched into the Panzer Grenadiers coming through the wheatfield. Raked by the machine guns, the German infantry broke and fled for cover. Lieutenant C.F. Thompson wheeled his tank around to run back through Buron and saw a German tank "hiding behind a wall. We fired and hit it." The tank exploded in flames.[28]

Radley-Walter saw "one Canadian sergeant in the North Nova Scotia's group... in a trench. I waved to him as I passed and he pointed to a dead German hanging over the side of the trench with a bloody knife in his back from the close fight." Some of Kennedy's men followed the tanks back into Buron and managed to drive the remaining Panzer Grenadiers out. The Germans scattered towards Authie. A jubilant North Nova war diarist scribbled: "Many casualties were inflicted by the tanks' guns and in some instances, the enemy being so numerous, were run over by them."[29]

Watching the Sherbrooke Fusiliers attack from his position near les Buissons, the Stormont, Dundas and Glengarry war diarist was moved to write, "Attack magnificent! Words cannot express such courage and determination!"[30]

When Buron was cleared, the Panzers to the east pulled back, grumbling off towards St.-Contest. Thompson followed Radley-Walter's Sherman back to the woods and on to a field where the tanks lined up to shell St.-Contest. As soon as Thompson's tank halted, a mortar round hit it and a shrapnel splinter slightly wounded his co-driver. "The mortar fire was very heavy but we shelled till our ammunition was all gone" and then returned to the wood.[31] By now, virtually every Sherbrooke tank was out of ammunition. The regiment had lost twenty-one tanks during the day's fighting and had seven others badly damaged. Sixty tankers had been wounded, twenty-six fatally. But despite being outgunned, the Sherbrooke Fusiliers had knocked out at least thirty-one Panzers and prevented the German armour from driving through to the beach.[32] As well, noted the regiment's diarist, "many [self-propelled] guns, half-tracks, light transport, infantry and other weapons were knocked out or destroyed."[33]

'D' Company still defiantly clung to Buron, but Petch, with Brigadier Ben Cunningham's concurrence, had decided that the village must be given up. When darkness fell, he organized a small relief force in les Buissons and, accompanied by a single Sherman, went out to Buron to bring Kennedy and his men back. Putting the wounded onto the tank, the infantry marched briskly away from the smouldering ruin of the little village. The North Novas' long fight of June 7 was over, a pyrrhic victory won. At the cost of 84 dead, 128 taken prisoner, and 30 wounded, the North Novas had thwarted the 12th ss Panzer Division's intention to drive through to the coast.[34]

To a man, those who survived were badly shaken by the day's experience. Private Jack Byrne thought he and everyone else in the battalion was in shock. His own platoon of 'B' Company was down to eighteen men. Byrne looked into the eyes of many of his friends and saw the pupils were dilated. Men who were usually of a quiet nature jabbered on about nothing. There was a lot of patting each other on the back, as if the men needed to confirm physically that they still lived and breathed.[35]

The brave stand by the North Novas had given the Stormont, Dundas and Glengarry Highlanders time to organize their "fortress" next to les Buissons, so they could meet any enemy advance with a coherent defence. Until shortly before D-Day, the regiment had been known by the awkward moniker of the Glengarrians, but one night when Christiansen and Major Fred Lander were sitting over a pint in a pub, the barmaid had remarked, "There are a lot of you Glens around here." The two officers liked this new contraction so well they raised their mugs and shouted, "Up the Glens!" A rallying cry was born.

Peering out into the darkness, Christiansen calmly awaited the expected onslaught by the 12th ss once it reorganized around Buron. German artillery and mortar fire was already intensifying and casualties starting to be taken. One officer from an attached antitank unit supporting the Glens reported that his gun positions were so exposed that he was losing too many men wounded and must withdraw. Christiansen laughed softly and shook his head. "Hell no. We're staying right here, son," he said. The battalion's padre Captain Ted Brain echoed the lieutenant colonel more stridently. "To hell with withdrawal, we'll lick those bastards!" he growled.[36]

At 2115 hours, the Panzer Grenadiers sallied out of Buron towards les Buissons and Christiansen bellowed that there would be no withdrawal. From the slit trenches came a general shout of "Up the Glens!" Then rifles and machine guns spoke and a hail of small-arms fire combined with concentrated artillery ripped into the ranks of the advancing Germans. Several times, the ss troops attempted to renew the assault before finally pulling back beyond Buron to lick their wounds.[37]

From 3 CID's divisional headquarters in Bény-sur-Mer, Major General Rod Keller sent a wireless report to First Canadian Army commander Lieutenant General Harry Crerar that omitted mention of the reverses suffered at Authie and Buron. Instead, he played up the success of the 7th Canadian Infantry Brigade in gaining its D-Day objectives by 1030 hours and said his troops "continue to stake out our claims... Courage, dash and initiative of the Canadian soldier truly amazing."[38]

MEANWHILE, NOT FAR from Buron, Standartenführer Meyer watched with mounting agitation as his attack slowly petered out. Throughout the afternoon and long evening, he had dashed this way and that around the battlefield astride a motorcycle, trying to sustain the momentum of the assault. At one point, Meyer had been knocked from the motorbike by the blast of a shell. The motorcycle was mangled and he cowered in a hole beside a lost Canadian until the artillery concentration lifted. Then the two men went separate ways. Meyer found another motorcycle and continued dashing about. Even on the Eastern Front, where the Russians so loved their artillery, Meyer had never experienced such heavy and accurate artillery fire. Watching the shells smashing Buron "with enormous masses of steel," he was reminded of the legendary furor of artillery used by both sides at Verdun during the Great War.[39]

As the little village was reduced to rubble, Meyer admitted failure. But it was a failure that he felt justified in laying at the feet of the 21st Panzer Division, which had not come up in force on his right flank. Combined with the fact that the 12th ss 26th Panzer Grenadier Regiment had also been delayed in getting into position to his left, this meant that he ultimately had no choice but to order his regiment to cease its offensive. It would have been "irresponsible," he later claimed, "to continue the attack with open flanks and against the unbelievable field and naval artillery fire" because "the way is open deep into our flanks."[40] That his regiment had also been battered to a standstill by an outnumbered Canadian infantry regiment and equally outgunned tank regiment was something Meyer refused to concede. Total casualties suffered by the 25th ss Panzer Grenadier Regiment and the units supporting its attack were reported at 317, of which 79 were killed.[41]

Returning after dark to the Abbaye d'Ardenne, he found the courtyard filled with a large number of prisoners brought in by Milius's
III Battalion. But all too many other Canadians had been butchered
in Authie, Buron, or during the march to the abbey. The killings had
come randomly, with no apparent logic behind who was selected
to live or die. When one column from Buron was marching through
Authie, several grenadiers abruptly dragged six men out of the line
and into the kitchen of a farmhouse. Here, they were ordered to
face the wall and then shot one after the other in the back of the
head. Villager Louis Alaperrine was attempting to put a bandage on a
Canadian wounded by a shell when an ss officer stepped up and shot
the injured soldier twice in the head. A Sherbrooke Fusilier medic
wearing a Red Cross armband was gunned down while treating a
wounded North Nova by one of the NCOS guarding the column.[42]

Major Rhodenizer, who spoke perfect German and was one of the
column's prisoners, attempted to dissuade the Germans from further
killings in their native language. His intervention worked, for the
guards carried out no more murders.[43] But that didn't mean the column of prisoners was safe. Just past Authie, it was approached by a
line of ss troops marching towards the front. When the two groups
came alongside each other, an officer leading the German troops
began shouting angrily at the Canadians. Then he drew a pistol and
fired at them. As the prisoners desperately started running for cover,
his men opened fire as well. Seeing Private Douglas Orford cowering
helplessly nearby, the officer strode over and shot the young man
in the stomach. Then the officer bellowed more orders, formed his
men back together, and led them off into the darkness. On the road,
nine Canadians lay dead or dying. The survivors were again formed
up and route marched away from the scene.[44] In all, thirty-seven
Canadians were murdered in or close to Authie.[45]*

Elsewhere, III Battalion's bloodthirstiness continued. In the late
evening of June 7, Sherbrooke Fusiliers' chaplain Captain Walter

---

* The main intersection at the village's southern end is today named Place
des 37 Canadiens.

Brown, Lieutenant W.F. Grainger, and their jeep driver, Private J.H. Greenwood, took a wrong turn en route to les Buissons, strayed into no man's land, and were intercepted by a III Battalion patrol. A burst of fire killed Greenwood and badly wounded Grainger. Before losing consciousness, Grainger saw Brown walking towards the Germans with arms raised in surrender. Brown's fate would not be known until a unit of British tankers discovered his body several weeks later. Forensic investigators, attempting to determine the extent of the atrocities committed against Canadians by the 12th ss, determined that the chaplain had been killed by a single bayonet thrust through the front of his chest into his heart. The body was then abandoned in an empty field.[46]

At the Abbaye d'Ardenne, the officers were initially separated from the other ranks. Majors Rhodenizer and Learment were the senior officers, then lieutenants Jack Veness and Jack Fairweather. The two majors were bustled into a dank room and placed under guard until Meyer walked in with a translator in tow. "You're Major Learment and commander of Company 'C' of the North Nova Scotia Highlanders," Meyer said through the translator, and then correctly identified Rhodenizer's company. Learment was shaken. He had no idea how the steely-eyed ss officer could know the battalion's entire order of battle and yet there was no doubting that he did. Neither man gave Meyer any information besides name, rank, and serial number, answering most questions with silence. Finally, Meyer, bored of the proceedings, returned Learment's billfold, and had them taken back into the yard to join the rest of the prisoners.[47]

Before the Canadians left the abbey to march to a prison camp, ten prisoners were randomly singled out and led off by several military policemen. Only one of these men, Lieutenant Thomas Windsor of the Sherbrooke Fusiliers, was an officer. Five others were tankers and the remaining four North Novas. The column of a little more than a hundred prisoners was escorted towards Caen. "As we marched along I heard a shout from behind and turned to see a German lorry swerve into the marching column, pull out and continue on its way," Learment wrote.[48] There had been plenty of room for the truck, bearing Red Cross markings, to pass to one side, and several Canadians saw the Germans in the cab shake their fists and jeer loudly as it accelerated. North Nova privates Roderick MacRae and Douglas Tobin were fatally injured when struck by the truck, while Sergeant Major R. Adair was badly injured.[49] The column was not further molested during the rest of the journey to a school at Bretteville-sur-Odon, where the officers were put into an empty classroom and the men confined in a walled-in yard. Most of the men dropped wearily onto the ground and plunged into an exhausted sleep.[50]*

The ten prisoners picked out of the column by the military policemen had meanwhile been locked in a room with a badly wounded North Nova, Lance Corporal Hollis McKeil. These men were then interrogated one after the other and each executed in turn when their session of questioning was concluded. Six had their skulls smashed in by a cudgel; the other five were killed by a single gunshot to the head. McKeil, Lieutenant Windsor, privates Charles Doucette and Joseph MacIntyre, and Trooper Roger Lockhead were shot, while privates Ivan Crowe and James Moss and troopers James Bolt, George Gill, Thomas Henry, and Harold Philip were bludgeoned to death.[51]

While these murders were being committed, Meyer was in a nearby room consulting with his battalion commanders over what action the 12th ss and specifically his regiment should take to regain the battlefield initiative. It was obvious that both 9 CIB and the 25th Panzer Grenadiers, like two punch-drunk boxers, had battered each other to a blood-soaked draw. Meyer's men had thrown the Highlanders and Sherbrooke Fusiliers back almost two miles and denied them Carpiquet airport. This was a significant setback for the Canadians, who would now have to fight their way through his grenadiers

---

* On July 21, Major Learment and an American pilot escaped from a prison train bound for Germany. Thirty minutes later, lieutenants Jack Veness and Jack Fairweather also jumped off the train as it lumbered across France. In all, twenty-two Canadian and American prisoners succeeded in making a break for it. Most, including Learment, Veness, and Fairweather, linked up with a French resistance group commanded by Captain Georges Lecoz. They served alongside the partisans until the Allied advance reached them in late August.

and supporting Panzers to achieve their objective. Meyer was confident that he could repulse any such attack. But the Canadians had dealt a hammer blow to his attempt to drive through to the coast and now barred the way with a strong blocking position at les Buissons. Its left flank was covered by 8th Canadian Infantry Brigade, which was holding positions from Anisy back to Basly. It was impossible for him to break through the Canadian fortress at les Buissons or to turn its flank with the weakened forces at his disposal.

What Meyer needed was reinforcements. These only slowly trickled in during the late-night hours of June 7 and the following morning, as the 26th Panzer Grenadier Regiment made its way through his lines to take up position west of his left flank. Until Wilhelm Mohnke's 26th began moving into that portion of the line, a wide gap had existed between Meyer's grenadiers and the other 12th ss unit on the scene, the 12th Reconnaissance Battalion commanded by Major Gerhard Bremer. A highly mobile unit equipped with half-track armoured personnel carriers, the 12th Reconnaissance had spent June 7 engaging battalions of the 50th British Infantry Division advancing towards Bayeux from Gold Beach. The 26th soon filled this gap so that the 12th ss ended the day with a solid front facing the entire breadth of the Canadian lines.

Mohnke's men had been badly delayed by the constant need throughout the march to seek shelter from air attacks that intensified as the day progressed. Only by breaking into small, widely spaced groups did the regiment manage to avoid heavy losses to the British and Canadian fighter-bombers that dogged them with strafing machine-gun fire, rockets, and bombs. Mohnke's orders were to assemble his regiment at the village of Cheux and to wrest Putot-en-Bessin and Norrey-en-Bessin from the Canadian grip. To his left, the Panzer Lehr Division would join the attack in order to drive a wedge between the 50th British Infantry Division and 3 CID. This would enable both Panzer divisions to then shoulder northwards to the beaches. A serious hitch in the plan, however, was that Panzer Lehr was still far short of its start lines and would be in no position to attack alongside the 26th Panzer Grenadiers. As had been true with Meyer's assault on June 7, Mohnke's Grenadiers would have to fight alone.[52]

[8]

The Devil Danced

FIGHTING INDEPENDENTLY with exposed flanks and neither artillery nor tank support was common coin to the paratroops of 1st Canadian Parachute Battalion. They and the other battalions that comprised 6th British Airborne Division had managed to achieve every important D-Day mission assigned to them, and on June 7 set to consolidating the positions won. While some Canadian paratroops still wandered lost or purposefully navigated through no man's land to reach the battalion's objectives, most were engaged in setting up a strong defensive position astride the vital le Mesnil crossroads. Another smaller group remained dug in at the village of Robehomme, which overlooked a bridge crossing the River Dives that the paratroops had blown on D-Day. The force here, under command of Captain Peter Griffin, numbered about one hundred. But only thirty to forty men—mostly from 'B' Company—were Canadian. Lost British paratroopers, drawn towards Robehomme by the sounds of gunfire as Griffin's men had fended off several determined German counterattacks on June 6, made up the rest.[1]

From the bell tower of Robehomme's small church, Griffin watched German infantry slowly tighten a noose around his position throughout the daylight hours of June 7. Three miles separated Robehomme and le Mesnil crossroads, with the town of Bavent situated at roughly the midway point. From his vantage, Griffin could see

German troops gathered around Bavent, which stood astride the road they needed to take to get through to the battalion. A stretch of low country almost a mile wide had been flooded between Robehomme and Bavent when the Germans had breached the banks of the River Dives as a defensive measure, intended to prevent these open fields' use as airborne drop zones. The raised roadbed connecting the two communities via Bricqueville provided the only viable route across the flooded ground. Griffin was under no illusions that his paratroopers could hold Robehomme indefinitely. They were surrounded and would eventually be outgunned and outnumbered. It would be wise to be gone from the village before the Germans decided they were strong enough to overrun the position.

Hoping that the Germans at Bavent might still be disorganized, Griffin and Lieutenant Norm Toseland decided to try slipping a patrol through to le Mesnil. Private W.J. Brady was one of the men sent on this mission. They returned soon enough, having determined that the Germans had established a roadblock to prevent such an attempt. With water covering the ground on either side of the road, there was no way the blocking position could be outflanked, even in darkness.[2] The Canadians had learned during the night of June 5–6 the perils of trying to slosh about in the flooded zones. Some men had drowned in water that was over their heads, while others had become hopelessly mired in deep mud, and it was virtually impossible to move quietly enough to avoid detection, anyway. There seemed no alternative. Griffin's small force would just have to stay put. The paratroops were determined to protract the siege as long as possible, exacting a stiff price for their inevitable elimination.

AT THE CROSSROADS, Lieutenant Colonel G.F.P. Bradbrooke had problems of his own. The aloof commander of the parachute battalion, who had proven before the invasion to be more concerned with fussy administrative paperwork than preparing the men for combat, had gathered about four hundred Canadian paratroops around him by the morning of June 7. He had also surprised some of his officers and men during the long day's fighting on D-Day by leading them with steely resolve on a bitterly contested march from the drop zone to the crossroads. There had been those who had thought Bradbrooke would prove a poor combat officer, but his performance that day indicated otherwise.

Most of the men at the crossroads were armed with rifles or Sten guns. Only a few had Bren guns. Ammunition and grenades were in short supply. During the dispersed drop, the containers holding the heavier weapons had by and large gone astray. Those that were found had usually broken open and the equipment inside was either wrecked or damaged. The mortar platoon had lost its mortars this way, and the majority of the battalion's wireless sets had similarly been scattered to the winds or broken. Equipment lost in the drop tallied up to 50 per cent of the battalion's total.[3]

The crossroads formed the intersection point for five roads that ascended the ridge's gradually rising slopes from opposite compass points. Bavent ridge was only a significant feature because the country surrounding it was so low and flat. Running along a generally north-south line from Sallenelles near the coast almost to Troarn, which was east of and parallel to Caen, it formed the only viable defensive ground that the airborne division could use to advantage in securing its eastern flank. If the counterattacking Germans broke through the defensive line holding the ridge, they would likely succeed in pushing the division's lines back to the River Orne bridges. These bridges, captured by British glider troops on D-Day, were vital to Second British Army's plan to break out from the Normandy bridgehead and advance towards Paris.

Holding the ridge from Sallenelles to Bréville was the 1st Special Service Brigade, a commando force that had landed at Sword Beach and linked up with the airborne troops late on June 6. From Bréville, which stood atop the highest point, to where the ridge overlooked the southern extremity of a small forest known as the Bois de Bavent was the responsibility of 6th Division's 3rd Brigade. The 9th Parachute Battalion held the line from right of Bréville to just short of the crossroads, then the Canadians took over the defence from the crossroads to the forest's northern edge, where they handed off to the 8th Parachute Battalion.

The crossroads was easily identifiable on the ridge's skyline because rising above it was the smokestack of a nearby brick and pottery plant. Bradbrooke had been quick to establish his headquarters inside the building, whose stout walls provided good protection against the German artillery and mortar firing that was directed against the paratroopers with ever increasing intensity as June 7 wore on. A short distance to the right of the crossroads, Brigadier James Hill put his headquarters in a small château and the 224 Field Ambulance's aid post set up on the same property. Each of the 3rd Brigade's battalions was responsible for about a mile of line that numbers would not allow to be held by positioning men along its entire length.[4] Instead, Bradbrooke organized small strongpoints, with the strongest in front of the crossroads, and covered the flank positions with Vickers machine guns. These weapons had arrived mid-morning, having been landed at Sword and moved up to the battalion by jeep. A good stock of ammunition and a trio of mortars were also included in the resupply package. Happy to be back in business, the mortar crews established a firing position beside the brick factory from which they could bombard targets to the front of any point on the Canadian line.[5]

In addition to the vital supplies, Bradbrooke also received the cheering news that the battalion would be able to call on the British cruiser *Arethusa* and a destroyer for naval gun support. These two ships had been allotted specifically to fire missions assigned by 3rd Brigade, which was also given the dedicated support of the 302nd Field Battery of one of the 3rd British Infantry Division's artillery regiments.[6] The paratroops would not have to rely entirely on their own combat resources, after all.

The arrival of the mortars proved in the nick of time, for no sooner had they been dug into firing pits than a strong force of infantry supported by several self-propelled guns and Mark IV tanks struck the Canadian line. These were troops of the 346th Grenadier Division's 857th and 858th regiments. The 346th had just arrived in the area after marching through the day and night from Le Havre, the only division to be released from the Pas de Calais on June 6 to meet the Allied invasion in Normandy.[7] On D-Day, the Canadian paratroops had fought elements of the 716th Infantry Division. A coastal defence unit, the 716th had been comprised of soldiers generally considered unfit for service in active combat divisions. With its fighting teeth concentrated in bunkers directed towards the beach areas, the division had been ill-positioned to offer a coordinated defence against 6th Airborne Division's drop and was shredded by day's end. Brigadier Hill, however, reported that the 346th "was a first class German division," so the Canadians faced a tough, competent adversary.[8]

German infantry came out of the woods west of the Canadians and headed across the open ground. The paratroops cut into them with a deluge of small-arms fire that dropped several dozen of the grenadiers, but the rest charged doggedly onward. When they closed to within a hundred yards, 'B' Company fixed bayonets and rushed out to meet the enemy rather than being overrun in their holes. Stunned by the ferocity of this charge, the grenadiers took to their heels and several were taken prisoner. One of the captured soldiers warned that the "Germans were desperate to capture the brickyard and the crossroads." Having had the wind knocked out of them, however, the grenadiers opted against launching a second attack in favour of sniping at the Canadian lines and harassing them with mortar and artillery fire.[9]

The sudden appearance of the 346th Division on his front left Bradbrooke with two quandaries. First, there was obviously now a large, determined German force between the crossroads and Robehomme, where Captain Griffin and the hundred paratroops with him were besieged. The lieutenant colonel was anxious to find a way to extract those men before they were overrun. Second, the Germans were obviously well endowed with armoured support—something he totally lacked. Leaving the German commander free to attack the Canadian front at will guaranteed that the combined tank and infantry forces would eventually penetrate the line and possibly overwhelm his men.

Bradbrooke decided the solution to both his problems was to be found in aggressive patrolling. While sending fighting patrols towards Bavent to throw the Germans off balance and perhaps force them to assume a defensive posture, he would also send a small patrol through the Bois de Bavent to find an unblocked route to Robehomme that could be used to guide that unit home.

Lieutenant Bob Mitchell, who commanded 'A' Company's No. 2 Platoon, drew the job of trying to get through to Robehomme. Knowing he could only succeed by remaining undetected, the lieutenant decided to take just three men along. Private Ray Newman, who had proven his worth the night before as a scout for Mitchell, walked point.[10] The other two men were selected more for their language skills than fieldcraft. Private E. Schroeder spoke fluent German, while Private L.S. Jones was equally adept at French.[11]

In the early afternoon, Mitchell and his three men crept past the front lines towards the woods. Newman thought it a shame to be going on such a mission with an empty stomach, but there had been no alternative. No rations had come up with the ammunition and heavy weapons, so food was in desperately short supply. Of course, when the paratroops were in action they would always take bullets over food. Death by starvation was not as likely as being killed by the enemy.

It was still light when Newman spotted "a character skulking along the edge of the Bois de Bavent. He was wearing a black beret, a civilian coat and airforce blue pants. He didn't fool us for a minute. We lined him up in our sights and ordered him to advance. Sure enough, he turned out to be a Canadian Typhoon pilot who had been shot down on D-Day and who was now very relieved. We explained to him how to behave in the kind of territory we were in, and sent him on his way to le Mesnil."

The patrol pushed into the woods on a circuitous three-mile trek Mitchell had mapped out as the most likely route for reaching Robehomme undetected. Out on point, Newman kept expecting to sight enemy soldiers at any moment, or at least French civilians. But the forest remained eerily devoid of life. They had been briefed that Robehomme was surrounded, yet the four men passed through the woods without incident. Even more to Newman's surprise, they were then able to move up a soggy lane running through flooded pastures and fields to where it intersected the road running from Bricqueville to Bavent. It was now dark, and the Germans covering the road from a position east of Bavent failed to notice the patrol as it struck off on the raised roadbed running through the flooded ground that ended just short of Bricqueville. Skirting this settlement, which seemed deserted, Newman led the patrol into Robehomme by moving off to one side of a small road. That they made it through struck Newman as being nothing short of "miraculous."[12]

Of the forty or so Canadians at Robehomme, thirty-five hailed from 'B' Company, while only a handful of the British paratroops were from the same unit. This meant the Canadians had the most cohesion as a fighting force, so Griffin decided they would lead the way out, with Mitchell's little patrol on point as guides. Those wounded soldiers unable to walk were either put into a car volunteered by Robehomme's priest or a horse-drawn wagon provided by a local farmer. At 2330 hours, the entire force filed quietly out of Robehomme and headed into the darkness. Several times, the car, wagon, or both bogged down in mud, requiring a lot of pushing and pulling by the men on foot to wrest the stuck conveyance free.

Just past Bricqueville, a German sentry barked a challenge. The men at the head of the column immediately rushed the position, firing as they did so. In a matter of seconds, they killed seven of the eight Germans maintaining a guard post and captured the other. A few minutes later, "an automobile with headlights dimmed down to... narrow slits, and which therefore appeared ghostly, was perceived sliding along the Bavent road towards the column. When it was quite close it met a fierce volley of well aimed fire from our column," the battalion's war diarist later wrote. "It careened into a ditch and upon examination was found to contain the dead bodies of four German officers. The way was now clear to get on through the Bavent forest." At 0330 hours, the column reached le Mesnil crossroads. The Canadians were quickly integrated back into their units, which greatly bolstered the fighting strength of 'B' Company, and the British troops headed off to return to their various units.[13]

While Mitchell's patrol was engaged in rescuing Griffin's force, Bradbrooke had also sent out three 'C' Company patrols over the course of the day towards Bavent. Although the first patrol was to use stealth to reach the village, avoiding enemy contact was not in the plan. Rather, Sergeant Harvey Morgan was going to attack Bavent with six men, while Corporal Dan Hartigan and Private Colin "Wild Bill" Morrison of Innisfail, Alberta covered them from a low rise to the right of the village. For this job, Hartigan was packing his two-inch mortar, a rifle, two bandoliers of rifle ammunition, all the mortar rounds he could scrounge, several grenades, and a Gammon bomb.[14] The latter weapon, formally known as a Type 82 grenade, was a canvas bag stuffed with two pounds of plastic explosives fitted with a tumbler fuse covered by a plastic cap. Removing the cap exposed a detonator atop the fuse, which, when subjected to the slightest motion or impact, exploded the charge. The weapon had been invented by British paratrooper Lieutenant Jock Gammon to give airborne troops an ability to fight tanks without having to carry heavy conventional antitank mines.[15] Morrison, "a huge raw-boned farm lad of twenty-one," was equally heavily loaded down with bandoliers of magazines for his Bren gun.

The purpose of this nine-man attack on Bavent was "to make the enemy fire as many of their weapons as possible, and so give the Canadians an estimate of their strength in the village." During the pre-patrol briefing, Morgan had calmly told the men that while Hartigan and Morrison covered them, he and privates Gilbert Comeau, Bill Chaddock, Clifford Douglas, M.M. "Pop" Clark, Eddie Mallon, and Jack Church would charge up the main street until Morgan yelled, "Take up positions!" Then all but Morgan and Chaddock would take cover and start sniping at anything that moved. Morgan and Chaddock, meanwhile, would attack the nearest two-storey building—nobody cared which one—and sweep it clear in a standard enter and search manoeuvre in order to wipe out any snipers or machine-guns positioned in the upper storey or on the roof. It was expected that the audacity of this action would badly shake the Germans in the village and weaken their resolve to tackle the obviously fighting mad Canadian paratroops.

With superb training in fieldcraft, the patrol managed to gain the edge of Bavent without being detected. Hartigan and Morrison scrambled into their position just in time to get set up, as Morgan led the other men in the charge. As the men dashed up the street, they were met by heavy small-arms fire from the other end of the village. With Hartigan popping smoke rounds into the street to cover the running Canadians, Morrison started burning off one Bren magazine after another at the many live targets revealing themselves. Despite the covering smoke, a machine-gun burst stitched across Comeau's chest and he dropped dead on the cobblestones seconds before Morgan shouted, "Take up positions."

The sergeant and Chaddock burst through the entrance door of a house as per procedure almost side by side. One swept "the first room to the left, the other to the right, where they killed two German soldiers. Then, after exploding a hand grenade on the space above the hall stairway, up they went and cleared the upper floor. They did a rapid search and, within seconds, Morgan led Chaddock to another building, tossing grenades in as chunks of concrete and brick flew everywhere from enemy machine-gun fire. The bullets sprayed nearby as they stepped aside to let their lobbed-in grenades explode. Another standard-drill entry brought them face to face with a big German sergeant. He and Morgan must have fired at the same instant, for the German fell to the floor and Morgan was wounded. He had two Schmeisser rounds in his abdomen."

Hartigan and Morrison covered the fighting party's rapid retreat from the village, with the corporal throwing down a mix of smoke for cover and shrapnel bombs to keep the Germans ducking. The whole raid was concluded in minutes, and then the patrol scrambled back to the crossroads under heavy protective fire laid down by the men in the front lines. When Morgan "came tumbling over a low stone wall, which had marked our jumping off point to begin with," Hartigan noticed that "he was clasping his bleeding abdomen." The sergeant gave a terse report to 'C' Company's Lieutenant Sam McGowan and then, rejecting offers of assistance, walked straight to 224 Field Ambulance's surgery for treatment.[16]

Even as the patrol had scampered out of the southeastern corner of the village, the troops had noticed the Germans were also on the run—pulling back into Bavent's northwestern quadrant. A three-man follow-up patrol a couple of hours later, which managed to capture a slightly damaged German mortar on a rise overlooking the

Canadian troops take a break in the shelter of a hedgerow during the march inland on
June 7. R. Bell, LAC PA–140849.

The 29th Canadian MTB Flotilla (right) passes a convoy en route to its patrol area on June 7. Note the barrage balloons hovering over the convoy ships. Gilbert Alexander Milne, LAC PA–144576.

top · Infantry dig into open field on June 8. In the far distance, a squadron of Sherman tanks provides a defensive screen. R. Bell, LAC PA–131442.

above · This photo of Flying Officer Kenneth Moore and his crew was taken immediately after their return from the June 7–8 mission during which they sank two U-boats. Back row, left to right: Don Griese, Jack Hamer, Ernie Davidson, co-pilot (first name unknown) Catcheson, Alec Webb, J. "Scotty" McDowell. Front row, left to right: navigator Alex Gibb, Mike Werbiski, K.O. Moore, Dinty, Bill Foster. Courtesy of Kenneth Moore.

top left · Paratroopers of 1st Canadian Parachute Battalion dug in behind a hedgerow at le Mesnil crossroads on June 8. D.A. Reynolds, LAC PA–130154.

left · A 13th Field Regiment, RCA Priest self-propelled gun in action near Bray. Frank L. Dubervill, LAC PA–114577.

above · General Bernard Law Montgomery gives a press briefing shortly after coming ashore in Normandy to oversee the push in from the beaches. R. Bell, LAC PA–132475.

top left · Personnel of Le Régiment de la Chaudière manning a front-line position near Colomby-sur-Thaon on June 9. R. Bell, LAC PA-129043.

left · Men of the 9th Canadian Infantry Brigade digging a slit trench in an orchard on June 9. Picks and shovels were favoured over short-handled and small entrenching tools originally issued for this task. R. Bell, LAC PA-133955.

above · Men from the Regina Rifles support company man a three-inch mortar just outside Bretteville-l'Orgueilleuse. Front, left to right: Riflemen D.E. "Dan" Corturient, A.V. "Swede" Renwick, W.R. "Win" Powell. Background: Rifleman George Cooper, Sergeant Tom Holt, Rifleman Ben Wilson. Donald I. Grant, LAC PA-128794.

Private R.L. Randolf of the Canadian Scottish Regiment in his slit trench in front of Putot-en-Bessin with two-inch mortar at the ready. Note the use of branches for camouflage. Donald I. Grant, LAC PA–131431.

village and bombarded the enemy until all the munitions were expended, observed that the troops in Bavent had not yet reoccupied the abandoned area. Nor did they venture out to try and silence the mortar harassing them.

Hartigan noticed how this report substantially bolstered 'C' Company's morale. "They now knew their enemies were, like themselves, subject to human frailty. They [Morgan's platoon] had done it all, and the enemy though well armed and in good positions, had managed to kill only one of them... Knowing that they could shake up a much larger body of enemy soldiers boosted their confidence. Even so, everyone was happy to be well out of it and figured it would be some time before they'd have to do something as crack-brained again. Nine men with light but well-organized support from a firm firebase had assaulted a considerably greater enemy force, killed four to six of them and wounded others, and got away with it."[17]

But 'C' Company's patrolling work for June 7 was not yet over. To the amazement of all the section leaders, they were summoned to the company headquarters in an old house next to the crossroads and briefed by their commander, Major John Hanson, on another daylight mission towards Bavent that would be followed up by a patrol after dark. The sections of Sergeant Dick MacLean and Sergeant M.C. "Mosher" MacPhee would carry out both operations, while Morgan's section, now led by Hartigan, would be responsible for 'C' Company's defensive positions at the crossroads. The daylight task entailed escorting two Royal Engineers and a couple of British artillery Forward Observation Officers to where the earlier patrol had captured the mortar. From this height, the artillerymen would direct fire by the 302nd Field Battery on enemy targets, while the engineers plotted a route by which the night patrol could enter Bavent from the north. The purpose of this penetration was to plant booby traps and antipersonnel mines around an enemy vehicle park.

When Sergeant Dick MacLean briefed his men on the task, privates H.B. "Sinkor" Swim and Willard Minard looked at each other in consternation—realizing that this patrol and the night one would be using exactly the same route to approach Bavent as Morgan's fighting patrol had earlier traversed. The two privates muttered to each other that "taking the same route... was certain suicide."[18] Surely the Germans would twig to how the Canadians were getting into their front yard—much of which followed a tree-shadowed bank of le Prieur irrigation canal. All they had to do was set up a machine gun at their end of the canal and fire down its length to slaughter the advancing patrol.

Despite thinking the mission the height of lunacy, the fourteen paratroops walked out into the afternoon sun with their four charges in tow. A sharp breeze was blowing as they moved through several apple orchards and then ventured out on the narrow track that bordered the canal. The overhead branches rustled loudly, while the tall grass growing up around the trees shivered as if Germans were crawling around there. MacLean and Swim were on point, one watching forward and left and the other forward and right, while also furtively scanning the overhanging branches for enemy snipers. Finally, they reached a canal crossing, slipped over it, gained the rise, and hunkered down while the engineers discussed viable approaches for the night mission and the two artillery officers looked down upon an amazing target.

In a meadow beside Bavent, a large group of German soldiers had dug a series of slit trenches to form a fighting position and were now lying around on the grass enjoying the breeze and warm sunshine. One of the artillerymen spoke into the handset of the No. 18 wireless he carried. Soon a shell exploded to the east of the Germans. The FOO radioed a correction that brought a shell down this time west of the enemy. Both having landed well away from their position, neither round alerted the Germans to the closing threat, which struck a few minutes later when the artillery battery dropped a full concentration directly onto them. Although Swim knew the men below were the enemy, he found it "agonizing to watch their awful fate." When the smoke cleared, "dead bodies [lay] everywhere as the living squirmed along the ground, trying to reach their slit trenches."[19]

By 1530 hours, the patrol had returned unscathed to le Mesnil crossroads and the men were told to bed down in Hanson's house to get some rest before going out on the night patrol. It was the first sleep any of the men had managed since a dawn reveille on June 5 at Harwell Field in England. Yet the majority of the soldiers, including Swim, found rest elusive. After the early morning raid on Bavent and the shelling of the soldiers—obviously brought down on them by someone directing fire from nearby—the Germans would surely be lying in wait.

When one of the men began muttering darkly to the others that they should refuse the night mission, Swim slammed him against a wall, shouted into his face, and shook him roughly. But the soldier was undeterred, so Swim reported the man to MacLean, who in turn took the matter to Major Hanson. The major, a big, blustery, raw-boned man, called the entire section out of the house and lined them up. He dressed them all down, as if every one of them was attempting to shirk his duty. Then he grabbed the shirker, slapping him roughly several times, and left "him in no doubt about what would become of him if he ever showed signs of disloyalty again." As the major stormed off, the other paratroops looked at each other in dismay, feeling Hanson had tarred them with the same brush as the man who cracked. Sergeant MacPhee quickly called the men together and assured them this was untrue, but Hanson's fit of temper did little to improve chances of any managing some desperately needed sleep.

At 1900 hours, the patrol was formed up and given scant servings of food drawn from the twenty-four-hour ration packs of men who had either been evacuated with wounds or killed. Then the paratroops blackened their already filthy hands and faces with camouflage cream. The sergeants moved carefully down the line of soldiers, checking each man's combat knife, gun, grenade load, and ammunition for problems. As the light bled from the sky and a moderate evening gale blew in off the ocean, each man studied maps and aerial photographs of the ground that must be crossed in darkness, memorizing bearing markers vital for keeping oriented.

Thunder rolled in the distance and lightning flickered across the sky as the patrol of paratroopers and six Royal Engineers filtered through the front lines. Once again, the men crept through the orchards to the lane bordering the canal and ventured along it with mounting trepidation. Private Swim walked point, with Sergeant MacLean and the platoon's runner close behind. Then came Lieutenant Sam McGowan and his batman followed by Sergeant MacPhee, with the other Canadians and the engineers strung out behind. Bringing up the rear were privates Bill Chaddock, Ralph Mokelki, and Andy McNally.

Despite knowing the other men were there behind him, Swim felt as if he walked alone. All his senses were focussed out to his front, as he led the way up the "deadly straight section of the canal, breathlessly expecting an enemy magnesium flare and the violence of machine-gun fire [to come] lacing down the canal." Thankfully, the earlier lightning had ceased and the heavy storm clouds obscured the moon and stars. Finally, Swim estimated the patrol was almost up to the outskirts of Bavent and turned to pass the word for a halt to allow a brief pause before going into the assault. A soft rasping sound out front caused Swim to freeze. A rifle bolt easing home? Swim waited, listening. Behind him, the others froze in place, waiting for the man on point to move or act. It was his call.

Swim discreetly signalled for MacLean and the runner to come up and he whispered a report into the sergeant's ear. MacLean sent the runner creeping back down the line to fetch McGowan and caution everyone to maintain maximum silence. McGowan pondered Swim's description of the sound he had heard and decided that rather than a rifle bolt being prepared for firing, it was more likely a German emptying the weapon for some reason. He sent word for Mokelki, fluent in German, to join the point group.

Then they eased forward to find a German sentry, stupefied with terror, standing alone, leaning on an unloaded rifle, its butt braced against the ground. McGowan gently eased the rifle away from the shivering soldier and they left him standing there, sending word back along the line for the paratroops to just ignore the man as they passed. The lieutenant realized the German would be afraid to tell his comrades that he had seized up with terror at the approach of the paratroop patrol and had been disarmed. Had any resistance been offered, a knife would have been drawn and the man's life taken.

Swim guided the patrol past the enemy defences and into Bavent without incident. The paratroops slipped up darkened streets to the northeastern quadrant of the village, helping the engineers set booby traps in doorways and empty dugouts with explosives. On the edge of Bavent, the paratroops quickly established a firm all-around firebase among some of the buildings. While some of the men set up weapons here, the engineers and remaining paratroops ventured into the open ground towards the vehicle park. It seemed incredible that they remained undetected as the engineers opened truck doors to stuff bombs under seats, dropped charges down the barrels of unmanned heavy mortars, tucked other explosives into scattered buildings. Finished, the troops fell back to the firebase to rendezvous with the others.

It was about 0400 hours on June 8. Just as the men began to think an undiscovered extraction could be possible, a German shout broke the silence. The jig was up. "There was shouting from both sides. Tracers raced across the night through the apple orchards on the fringes of Bavent. Wild firing of hand-held weapons ripped the area as bullets snapped past and added to the ruckus. Soldiers and bullets careened through the dark streets of the village which neither side had known for long... Ricocheting steel whined, snapped and moaned on the night, feet scurried, men called for help, the devil danced to his own tune and blind combat in lovely Normandy took its toll."[20]

Bullets snicking all around him, Swim dived into a depression, only to realize it contained an open cesspool. Unable to claw his way out, drowning in the deep sludgy waste, Swim cried out for help. MacPhee dashed through the bullets to drag the man to safety and the two men zigged and zagged out of the village towards the canal. When they reached it, Swim dove into the water to wash as much of the sewage off his skin as possible. The patrol was scattered to the winds now, men making their way back to le Mesnil crossroads in ones and twos. It was 0700 hours when the last soldier walked into the front lines. Miraculously, not a single patrol member had suffered injury. From Bavent, the sounds of gunfire continued throughout the night as the Germans fought it out with phantoms, and the paratroops listened with satisfaction as the sound of random explosions carried on the morning breeze, testimony to the effectiveness of their booby-trapping operation.

The exhausted men of 'C' Company heard with relief, however, that they would not be expected to patrol back to Bavent again. Lieutenant Colonel Bradbrooke thought the patrols so far run had been sufficient to convince the Germans to keep their distance from the battalion's lines. Keeping the enemy at bay was critical, for if the Germans ever realized how few paratroops stood between them and the River Orne bridges, they would surely hit the battalion with overwhelming fury.

PART TWO

COUNTERSTRIKES: D+2 TO D+3

---

[9]

Green As Grass

I N THE EARLY MORNING HOURS of June 8, the invasion was more
than forty-eight hours old. Forced to face the failures of their
tactics on D+1, Allies and Germans alike had to modify ambitions
accordingly. Along the battlefront's entire length, the Germans,
meeting the invasion more fiercely than anticipated by the Allies, had
checked the divisions striking inland from the beaches. Yet General
Bernard Montgomery, who had arrived off the beaches aboard HMS
Faulknor just after dawn on June 7, considered this setback of minor
consequence. Boarding General Omar Bradley's command vessel,
the USS *Augusta,* at 0600 hours, Montgomery told the American general that his main concern regarding the First American Army operations was the gap between the 4th Division at Utah Beach and the
badly pummelled 1st Division on Omaha. Montgomery pressed
Bradley to secure his D-Day objectives, particularly by seizing
Carentan and Isigny in order to establish a link between the two
divisions. He then sailed eastwards to confer with General Miles
Dempsey, who assured Montgomery that "all was going according to
plan on the British beaches and there was no cause for anxiety."[1]

As the day progressed and *Faulknor* steamed back and forth in
front of the invasion beaches, Montgomery decided Operation Overlord was unfolding as it should. This perfectly fit his philosophy that
it was his duty to "conceive and execute a simple, workable plan

which could be easily understood by all concerned" and followed with clockwork precision.[2] At the outset of planning Operation Overlord, Montgomery had warned the staff of 21st Army Group that he would "not get bogged down in details... I will give orders to the next lower commanders. Nothing will be in writing either in the first place or for confirmation. I never read any papers. Half of all papers are not read and the other half are not worth reading." This was not an operational environment that encouraged subordinates to be bearers of bad tidings. So despite the growing crises many brigade and battalion leaders encountered on D+1, optimism prevailed from Montgomery's headquarters down the line to all the divisional commands. Everywhere objectives were failing to be won, casualties mounted, and the enemy responded with increasing tenaciousness, but all this went unacknowledged by the invasion command.

From *Faulknor*'s bridge, Montgomery saw "no enemy air action and few signs of battle on sea or land. It was difficult to imagine that on shore a battle was being fought which was deciding the fate of Europe."[3] Deciding he could only fully appreciate the situation beyond sight of the warship by getting onto the ground, Montgomery decided to go ashore next morning and establish his headquarters behind the 50th British Infantry Division's front lines.

Meanwhile, the invasion plan remained unaltered. Once Bradley established a link between his two divisions, the Americans would march on La Haye du Puits to cut off the Cherbourg Peninsula and then seize the vital port of Cherbourg. At the same time, Dempsey's Second British Army would maintain a flank-holding position along the west bank of the River Dives while simultaneously capturing Caen and Bayeux. Once this phase of the operation concluded, Dempsey would "pivot on Caen and swing his right forward" to break into the Caen-Falaise plain.[4] That had always been the plan and Montgomery saw neither need nor opportunity to justify its alteration.

Caen remained the primary objective for 3rd British Infantry Division and 3rd Canadian Infantry Division. Bypassing the city was not an option because its strategic position on the River Orne barred free access to the Falaise plain. One hundred miles long, the River Orne rose south of Argentan and flowed northwest to Thury-Harcourt, then north to Caen, and from there into the Channel. To gain the Falaise plain, British Second Army had to capture the bridges crossing the Orne in the city itself or the bridges southeast of it near Thury-Harcourt. To the southwest, the River Odon flowed in from the west to join the Orne on the city's southern perimeter. Leaving Caen in German hands would permit them to use it as a strong base from which to attack the rear of any bypassing force.[5] But the two divisions would have to fight their way to Caen through the mounting opposition offered by the German Panzer divisions beginning to arrive on the battlefield.

At the end of June 7, the 6th Airborne Division, with assistance from various units that marched to its aid from Sword Beach, had retained control of all the vital objectives it seized on D-Day east of the River Orne. For its part, 3rd British Division had been stymied in its attempts to seriously deepen the front west of the Orne that it had won on D-Day. Concentrating its attacks on the high ground in front of Lebisey, the division had been beaten back by thick automatic fire from heavily entrenched elements of 21st Panzer Division. Finally, in frustration, Major General T.G. Rennie broke off the head-on attacks in favour of trying to move battalions westwards to establish contact with the Canadians. This proved more successful, and by day's end his 8th Brigade was tied in opposite the North Shore (New Brunswick) Regiment near Douvres-la-Délivrande. But the Germans still clung tenaciously to the radar station set right between the divisional flanks. And although the British 9th Brigade had managed to get up beside 8th Canadian Infantry Brigade at Anisy, it was still well short of the forward position 9th Canadian Infantry Brigade held at les Buissons.[6]*

To the Canadian right, 50th British Infantry Division had enjoyed a more rewarding day. Unhindered by the presence of any Panzer divisions on its front, the leading battalions had easily swept aside the

---

* Coincidentally, both the Canadian and British 9th brigades were commanded by brigadiers named Cunningham—D.C. "Ben" Cunningham and J.C. Cunningham, respectively.

weak resistance offered by German infantry and were soon receiving a liberator's welcome in the streets of Bayeux. This city was the largest strategic objective as yet gained by the Allies.[7]

While the Canadians had reached their D-Day objective on the right flank when 7th Canadian Infantry Brigade cut the Caen-Bayeux highway and railway, the disaster that befell 9th Canadian Infantry Brigade's North Nova Scotia Highlanders had resulted in a withdrawal of two miles on the left. This left 9 CIB about three and a half miles shy of Carpiquet airport. Wrenching this ground back from the grasp of the 12th SS Panzer (Hitlerjugend) Division promised to be no easy affair. Major General Rod Keller's plan for the morning, however, was to do precisely that, with a renewed 9 CIB assault along the same route taken the day before. His other two brigades would, meanwhile, consolidate their positions to fend off expected counterattacks. Once 9 CIB punched through to the airport, the division would be "firmly entrenched in positions of great tactical value, prepared for further offensive operations" west of Caen. The city would be less than a mile to the left, and the moment 3rd British Division secured Caen, the drive into the Falaise plain could begin on a two-division front.[8]

Opposite the Allies, the German commanders charged with repulsing the invasion began to face the fact that no coherent strategy for defending Normandy had previously been developed. The tactical situation that had emerged on June 7 convinced Generalfeldmarschall Erwin Rommel that he must focus operations precisely on the same ground the Allies had selected as their primary objectives. To the west, he ordered Carentan "defended to the last man" to prevent the two American divisions making contact with each other. Then Rommel told I Panzer Corps Obergruppenführer Josef (Sepp) Dietrich that "a crippling blow should be delivered against the British before they became established" around Caen by hammering the full might of three Panzer divisions against the enemy standing between Caen and Bayeux. Rommel expected this attack on June 8, with primary emphasis and consequent artillery support given the 12th SS striking the Canadian front in the middle, while the 21st Panzer Division would come up on its right flank and Panzer Lehr Division the left.[9]

Despite thinking that Rommel's orders were absurdly grandiose given the straitened circumstances of these divisions, Dietrich hastened to comply with their general tenor. The 21st Panzer Division, tied down in holding actions against the 3rd British Infantry Division and 6th Airborne Division, was in no position to undertake more than modest local offensive attacks. Panzer Lehr was still grinding towards Normandy from a holding area near Seventh Army's headquarters in le Mans, dogged the entire way by Allied fighter-bombers. By late evening of June 7, the Panzer Grenadiers in the vanguard were only approaching Fontenay-le-Pesnel and Tilly-sur-Seulles, and still about six miles from the battlefront. The division's tanks were still far behind and hours away. Dietrich knew there was no way this division would be in position for a morning attack. That left 12th ss to fight alone, with only a portion of its strength yet in position.

Considering what he had available, Dietrich decided to hit the Canadian right flank in order to open a wedge between them and 50th British Infantry Division, through which the Germans could drive right to the coast. This tactic had failed on the opposite flank when 21st Panzer Division had been driven back during its attempted advance on the night of June 6–7 into the gap between the Canadians and 3rd British Infantry Division. Standartenführer Kurt Meyer's 25th Panzer Grenadier Regiment of the 12th ss, supported by elements of the 12th ss Panzer Regiment's 1 Battalion, had also failed to carry off virtually the same manoeuvre the following day. But Dietrich hoped to succeed this time by striking where the Allied divisions were only tenuously linked, unable to support each other or coordinate their response to meet the German onslaught.

It was a tall order for the 12th ss, as the entire division could not participate. Having battered 9 CIB back from Franqueville through Authie and Buron to les Buissons, Meyer's Panzer Grenadiers were now tied down keeping this brigade pinned in place. That left Wilhelm Mohnke's 26th Panzer Grenadier Regiment, which in the early morning hours of June 8 had passed behind Meyer's regiment to take up a position on its left, to carry out the attack. No tanks from 12th Panzer Regiment were yet available. The only armour Mohnke had were six 75-millimetre self-propelled guns from the 12th ss (Heavy)

Company allocated to III Battalion. Mohnke detailed I Battalion to capture Norrey-en-Bessin, II Battalion Putot-en-Bessin, and III Battalion to secure the left flank by advancing just behind and to the west of II Battalion. When Panzer Lehr finally arrived, it would broaden the German attack on this flank, accelerating the creation of what should be a rapidly widening gap between the Canadians and 50th British Infantry Division. Tactics decided, Mohnke set his men marching towards combat.[10]

DIRECTLY IN THE PATH of the advancing Panzer Grenadiers were two 7 CIB battalions—the Royal Winnipeg Rifles and Regina Rifles. Since arriving at their D-Day objectives in the mid-morning of June 7, the Canadian riflemen had been setting up defensive positions on ground little suited for defence. Brigadier Harry Foster was dismayed, noting that the terrain consisted of "gently rolling agricultural land, 75 [per cent] of which has standing grain. Villages are numerous, and generally speaking, stand in the low ground. Good observation is difficult due to the fact that from the beaches we have been continually fighting 'up hill' with the enemy [positions] on the next bit of higher ground. This very open ground tends to favour the defender as he can get long fields of fire with [antitank] guns, and good observation from the higher ground."[11]

Although reverting from the offensive to the defensive, the Germans would retain long fields of fire while 7 CIB's remained restricted. The four-to-five-foot-high wheat that stood unharvested in the fields only aggravated the problem.

Trusting his battalion commanders could make the best of a bad situation, Foster left the details of their defensive schemes up to them and concentrated on securing as many supporting arms as possible. Two platoons of the Cameron Highlanders of Ottawa, several batteries of the 3rd Anti-Tank Regiment, Royal Canadian Artillery, and two batteries of 17-pounder antitank guns from the 62nd British Anti-Tank Regiment soon moved into the brigade lines. Foster could not offer the infantry close tank support, however, because the remnants of the 1st Hussars were still reorganizing alongside the brigade's Canadian Scottish Regiment at Secqueville-en-Bessin after being mauled on D-Day.

Out on the brigade's left flank, Regina Rifles Lieutenant Colonel Foster Matheson established his headquarters in a large courtyard across from Bretteville-l'Orgueilleuse's towering thirteenth-century church, and decided to centre the battalion's defence on this village. He then pondered the problem posed by a two-mile-wide gap between his men and those of 9th Canadian Infantry Brigade to the east. If he kept the battalion tightly knitted around Bretteville, the Germans could easily turn his left flank to get behind the brigade's front lines. The only solution Matheson saw was to position his companies in four separate isolated locations "vital to the defence" in order to form a semi-circular defensive line arcing south from Rots to Norrey-en-Bessin through la Villeneuve.[12]

Responding to Matheson's orders, Major C.S.T. "Stu" Tubb's 'C' Company moved a mile south of Bretteville to occupy Norrey-en-Bessin. Matheson considered this village vitally important because it was situated on a low hill that provided a view of all possible approaches that could be used by the Germans. A towering Gothic church, considered one of the finest examples of such architecture in Normandy, dominated the place. 'B' Company occupied Rots a mile and a half east of Bretteville, while 'D' Company moved into la Villeneuve to cover the road and rail bridge crossings over the River Mue. Serving as the battalion reserve, 'A' Company remained in Bretteville with the Headquarters unit.[13]

A little to the west, Winnipeg Rifles Lieutenant Colonel John Meldram faced a different problem than Matheson. Putot-en-Bessin was less a village than a tight cluster of small farm plots, with houses, outbuildings, pocket orchards, pastures, vegetable gardens, and wheatfields all intermingled. Following Norman custom, most farms featured a rectangular or square courtyard surrounded by a stout six- to seven-foot-high limestone wall, the farmhouse, a barn, and other outbuildings. Establishing positions in this environment where platoons, let alone one company to another, were able to overlap their fields of fire proved impossible. But with the Caen-Bayeux highway at its back and the railway immediately ahead, holding the village was essential to preventing these lines of communication being used by the Germans. Meldram decided the only thing the Royal Winnipeg Rifles could do was to spread out in a scraggly line through the village as close to the railroad as possible. Where the tracks passed Putot-en-Bessin, they descended into a deep cutting that would be virtually impossible for tanks advancing from the south to cross.

Immediately west of the village, a north-south running road marked the assigned boundary line between 3rd Canadian and the 50th British divisions. This road crossed the railroad cutting via an overhead bridge. Meldram positioned two of Major Fred Hodge's 'A' Company platoons in front of the bridge and sent Lieutenant Frank Battershill's platoon three-quarters of a mile farther west to the hamlet of Brouay to establish a link with the British 7th Green Howards.[14] When Battershill got to Brouay, he discovered that the Green Howards were not to be seen nor were any other 69th British Infantry Brigade battalions coming up to anchor the Canadians' right flank.

Until the British infantry turned up, Meldram knew he had to strengthen his flank position to avoid having it turned. He therefore detailed 'F' Troop from the British 62nd Anti-Tank Regiment to join Battershill's platoon in order to cover the open ground west of him with its four towed 17-pounders.[15]

'C' Company, under Major Jimmy Jones, meanwhile established itself to the left of Hodge's company directly in front of Putot, with Major Lochie Fulton's 'D' Company extending the line a little to the east of the village. 'B' Company, commanded by Captain Phil Gower, stood in reserve in a position between 'C' Company's left flank and the battalion headquarters, which was situated in a stone-walled farmyard on the village's northern edge.[16] Stretching his meagre resources even thinner to link up with the Reginas, Meldram moved the Bren carrier platoon a thousand yards left of Fulton's position to la Ferme de Cardonville.[17]

Lieutenant Donald James had come onto Juno Beach at about 2300 hours on D-Day as a Winnipeg Rifles replacement officer, taking command of a 'B' Company platoon the next morning. This company had been shredded, losing most of its men and all platoon commanders and other officers except for Captain Gower. James recognized that he and his men "were pretty green troops" and wondered how they would do.[18] He was not the only one worried. Brigadier Foster had anxiously noted that because "one assault company had been practically wiped out on the beach... the gaps in its ranks had to be replaced by reinforcements of all sorts, some not even infantry."[19] A good number of these men were inadequately trained. Foster was particularly concerned that many were "not even familiar or well trained in our own grenades" or able to maintain, load, and fire the two-inch mortars.[20] Although in reserve, 'B' Company faced an open front merely set back somewhat more from the railway than the other companies. The men carved out their slit trenches on the edge of an orchard facing a wide grain field that lay between their position and the railway.

"The front at Putot was so fluid at the time," James later recalled. "There were people all over the place—Canadians, Germans and French. The French were in front of us going along the road on bicycles. And the wheat in the field in front of us was so high you couldn't see over it."[21]

'C' Company was in another orchard to the left of a farmyard enclosed by a high limestone wall and the farmhouse. No. 15 Platoon dug in alongside the wall, with No. 14 Platoon slightly behind and to the right, while No. 13 was also to the right, but out to the front in line with No. 15 Platoon, so that the company perimeter was roughly triangular-shaped. As No. 15 Platoon Rifleman Robert G. Smellie hacked out a slit trench that conformed to regulation dimensions of two feet by six feet with a three-foot depth, he was struck by what a "pleasant sight" the farm presented, with its old apple trees and the nearby wall. He spotted the farmer looking out a window "with dismay as we dug our slit trenches among his beloved trees." The men had been "instructed to have no communication that wasn't necessary with the French people. My buddy John Thompson and I collected the water bottles from the whole platoon and went into the farmyard to fill them. The farmer watched us filling the bottles at his well without comment and we did not speak to him. We were destroying his orchard, and our presence there would inevitably bring more conflict.

"That night we were treated to more fireworks. But we suffered less fear... because we were surrounded by the rest of our battalion."[22]

THE CRACKLING OF GUNFIRE, thump of explosions, and glare of flares lighting up the sky with blinding intensity to the east of Smellie's position erupted when 1 Battalion of the 26th Panzer Grenadiers slammed into the front lines of the Regina Rifles at 0330 hours. Without conducting any reconnaissance, Sturmbannführer Bernhard Krause threw his men into a pincer attack against Norrey, with two companies striking from the right and another the left. There was no attempt to achieve surprise as the troops moved forward noisily, their half-tracks grinding along in support. As they closed on Norrey, the Germans deployed mortars and began pounding the village.

Inside Norrey, Major Stu Tubb raced to where No. 13 Platoon on the right flank of the village was being hit. Hunkering down beside Lieutenant Ray Smith, Tubb saw what looked like a company-sized force coming up the open slope towards the village. Both sides were putting up flares that silhouetted the Germans in a white glare. Tubb, a tall, scholarly sort, who was noted for being soft-spoken and calm no matter the crisis, behaved true to form this night. Earlier, he and the artillery Forward Observation Officer from the 13th Field Regiment had pre-plotted defensive fire targets that precisely intersected the areas through which the Germans now advanced. Tubb called for artillery, and the 105-millimetre Priests of 'C' Company in its gun positions near Bray loosed off a deadly barrage of shells fused to explode over the heads of the Panzer Grenadiers.[23]

At the same time, Smith's platoon ripped into the advancing Germans with small-arms fire, while the Reginas at la Villeneuve and Rots hit the second Hitler Youth pincer that was approaching Norrey from the left with flanking fire. Tubb watched with satisfaction as the artillery shells thundered in, exploded "virtually over our heads [and] sprayed shrapnel forward into the intruders."[24]

When the first artillery concentration failed to stop the attack and the Germans kept pressing in on No. 13 Platoon, Tubb considered calling up his reserve platoon to thicken the line. Just as he moved to do so, "the Germans decided to call it quits for the time being. Later we recovered a couple dozen bodies we stacked like cordwood along a garden wall behind 13 Platoon. Several days elapsed before burial could be made in a small cemetery between Norrey and Bretteville. By that time the odour was pretty offensive."[25]

Tubb's No. 13 Platoon and the supporting artillery fire had caught I Battalion's No. 3 Company in the open, forcing it "to stop halfway up the slope in front of Norrey." When No. 1 Company attempted to come up on the right flank of No. 3 Company, it too was pinned down by the artillery concentrations. Meanwhile, No. 2 Company had one platoon trapped in a clover pasture, while the other two platoons had managed to secure a position among some houses by the railroad tracks. Realizing that his men were incapable of pressing home the attack without being slaughtered, Krause ordered them to break off. No. 3 Company moved back a short way and dug into "a knee-high grain field." The other two companies took up positions nearby. Krause reported having lost five men killed and twenty wounded.[26] However, as the situation was so confused and the Reginas and I Battalion continued trading bullets throughout the night and into the morning, a reliable casualty count was almost impossible.

Neither Tubb nor the Regina war diarist fully appreciated the strength of the attack thrown against them. Tubb remained convinced he had faced down no more than a single company, while the war diarist blandly noted that a minor counterattack "was repulsed by our troops."[27] A poorly executed attack carried out hastily and without artillery or tank support had resulted in the Reginas stopping a full battalion of about 1,000 Germans cold with only about 250 men. The outcome of the short firefight served as a testimony to the power of well-directed artillery.

At dawn, Lieutenant Colonel Matheson tightened his battalion's lines, withdrawing 'B' Company from Rots and ordering it to dig in astride the Caen-Bayeux highway immediately east of Bretteville, while 'D' Company moved across the battalion's front from la Ville-neuve to relieve the Winnipeg carrier company at la Ferme de Cardonville. News of the disaster that had befallen 9th Canadian Infantry Brigade also prompted his superior, Brigadier Harry Foster, to commit part of 7 CIB's reserve by moving the Canadian Scottish out on his flanks. He sent 'B' Company east of Bray to protect the 13th Field Regiment's gun position from possible attack and a 'D' Company platoon to the northwest of Bretteville to fortify la Bergerie Ferme.[28] The 13th Field's gunners had spent a long night providing near constant support to the Reginas, while simultaneously keeping a watchful eye out "for small parties of enemy snipers."[29]

Seeing that 7 CIB's forward position protruded like a butcher's blade into the German front, the 12th ss were determined to force Foster's battalions to withdraw. Until another major attack could be mounted, teams of snipers were filtered onto the brigade's flanks to harry the rear areas. By morning, so many snipers harassed the Canadian Scottish at Secqueville-en-Bessin and the gunners near Bray that the infantry found it impossible "to ferret them out." Finally, Canadian Scottish commander Lieutenant Colonel Fred Cabeldu asked Foster for tank support. The brigadier passed this request to 1st Hussars Lieutenant Colonel Ray Colwell, who dispatched Lieutenant W.A.P. Smith in a reconnaissance squadron Stuart. Unable to spot likely sniper positions with his turret hatch closed, Smith shoved it open and stood up with half his body exposed in order to see better. Instantly, a sniper round struck him in the arm, followed a second later by a bullet that "went through the side of his helmet and came out the top without causing any injury to his head."[30] Smith's crew rushed the wounded officer back to regimental headquarters at Secqueville, where he refused treatment until he passed on the location of several snipers he had located just before being shot.[31] For this and several earlier acts of bravery during the inland advance, Smith was awarded a Military Cross.

Two more Stuarts dashed to where Smith had been wounded, and succeeded in helping the Canadian Scottish carry out a determined sweep of the wheatfields the Germans were using as a route to sneak up on Secqueville. More than thirty snipers were either killed or captured, and thereafter incidents of sniping in the brigade rear areas significantly declined.[32]

To address the snipers pestering the 'D' Company platoon at la Bergerie Ferme, Cabeldu arranged some heavy support. The Cameron Highlanders of Ottawa sent No. 5 Platoon with its Vickers machine guns and No. 13 Platoon with its heavy mortars, while the 62nd Anti-Tank Regiment, Royal Artillery provided 'E' Battery and the 3rd Anti-Tank Regiment, Royal Canadian Artillery contributed a troop from the 94th Battery. When Captain Harold Gonder of No. 5 Platoon reported to Canadian Scottish commander Cabeldu for instructions, he was told to "build up as strong a redoubt there as you can. Make it impregnable and ready for any attacks during the night or the morning."[33]

Born in China to missionary parents, Gonder had lived overseas until his parents returned to Ontario when he was sixteen. He had entered the army during the Depression and worked his way up from the ranks. Prior to the invasion, he completed a stint as Major General Rod Keller's aide-de-camp. Normally, following such a posting an officer was appointed to headquarters staff, but Gonder had asked instead to return to the Camerons because he felt more at home in the ranks of a combat unit. The machine-gunner set to the task of fortifying the farm in close coordination with Lieutenant Gerry Blanchard of the 62nd's 'E' Battery, whose 17-pounders provided the greatest weight of firepower. Gonder found Blanchard to be "a very easy going, friendly, debonair, Errol Flynn type of fellow. We managed to emplace our guns, so we were well concealed but had an unobstructed field of fire and view ahead of us." Digging their antitank guns and the Vickers machine guns into firing positions on the edge of a wood immediately west of the farm, the two men agreed that "if enemy tanks should appear [Blanchard] should give first order to fire. This was only logical because machine guns couldn't do much damage to tanks, whereas an antitank crew—properly trained and with the advantages we enjoyed—could create a great deal of havoc."[34] The guns were positioned so that they had a clear field of fire along an arc swinging from the west to the south in order to cover all potential routes of approach likely to be used by the enemy.

FOSTER, MEANWHILE, was increasingly worried about the Regina Rifles. Tubb's 'C' Company was dangerously isolated in its forward position at Norrey. He urged Matheson to pull it back across the highway into a position to the front of Bretteville. The Regina Rifles commander "protested that he would just have to retake the position later." Reluctant to override the officer, Foster cautioned him to keep a close watch on the situation and to have an extraction plan in place should it be necessary.[35]

That Norrey was going to be hit hard was obvious to everyone. Early in the morning, Tubb evacuated its residents to a refugee camp established at Reviers. "Two families pleaded to remain," Tubb later wrote, "one an elderly couple living in a small, one-room cottage near Company HQ, the other a mother of about 30, with 2 or 3 children in a two-storey brick and stucco house close by. We gave way to both and put together a shelter of sorts to shield them somewhat in case of shelling."[36]

As 'D' Company marched through Bretteville en route to la Ferme de Cardonville, it picked up a new commander. Major Jack Love had died on D-Day and the company second-in-command, Captain "Hec" Jones, had been wounded in the leg the following day. To fill the senior officer post, Matheson had called Captain Gordon Brown, who for the past year had served as the battalion's transport officer. Brown was nervous about the change in duty, trying to remember those long-ago training lessons about the ins and outs of running a rifle company. Although most of his men had only two days' combat experience under their belts, Brown knew they had undoubtedly learned much in those hectic days while he was still "green as grass." Matheson warned Brown and his colleague, Major Eric Syme, who was taking the helm of 'B' Company (Major F.L. Peters having been killed by a mortar round late on June 6), "that the enemy was getting ready to launch an all-out attack to drive us back into the sea." He said they should expect to be attacked by armour sometime in the evening, but were to "just ignore the tanks. 'Your job is to stop the infantry that comes with them.'"[37]

A bemused Brown wondered "how one ignored enemy tanks... I was uncertain and very apprehensive. The prospect of being attacked

by a bunch of marauding Panthers was almost beyond my compre-
hension, especially since we had no tank support of our own."

The company walked out of Bretteville towards the farm and
Brown's combat initiation began immediately, as what seemed to be
more than a dozen German snipers started blasting away. Brown and
his men crawled on their hands and knees through the cover of the
tall grain or hunkered down below and alongside the armour-plated
sides of Bren carriers pulling two six-pound antitank guns from the
antitank platoon that were to support them. In this manner, 'D' Company arrived at Cardonville without loss, which relieved the Winnipeg
Bren carrier platoon. The Winnipeg troops left on the double, for the
sounds of a heavy gunfire exchange from their lines over by Putot-en-
Bessin indicated the Little Black Devils were hotly engaged. Brown
figured it would be 'D' Company's turn soon enough and that he had
best waste little time establishing a defensive perimeter.

Cardonville was built more like a small fort than a farm. Its two-
storey farmhouse faced east and was constructed of two-foot-thick
stone walls. An eight- to ten-foot-high wall extended out from the
house to enclose a courtyard, barn, several storage buildings, and
small field. Pressed up against the north wall was an orchard, while to
the south lay the railway track. Bordering the west wall was an open
field. Brown instructed two of his platoons to dig slit trenches inside
the courtyard but right against the base of the walls running along the
north, south, and eastern flanks of the farm. To gain fields of fire, the
men hacked holes in the walls through which they could aim rifles
and machine guns. Several Bren guns were set up on the farmhouse's
second storey to gain long-range fire fields in every direction except
east. That side of the farmhouse lacked any windows, but Brown decided this was acceptable, for in that direction lay the rest of the battalion. With insufficient manpower to defend the courtyard's almost
thousand-yard perimeter, Brown decided to leave the west wall unprotected except by a single Bren gun and several riflemen who could
cover the open field from a second-storey window.

Aware of "the conventional wisdom of 'don't put all your eggs in
one basket,'" Brown and his second-in-command, Lieutenant Dick
Roberts, "decided to leave one of the platoons in reserve in the small

orchard behind the back (north) wall. We also arranged to leave all
the vehicles there except two Bren carriers being kept inside the walls.
Finally, we placed our two antitank guns in the orchard to cover a mile
of open ground to our right. Some of these decisions we [came] to regret, as we learned that often war is not fought according to the book.
In the meantime, the signallers had strung the phone lines into position and communication with the battalion HQ was established. All
of this took a couple of hours after our arrival and the departure of
the Winnipegs' carriers" to complete.[38] Also positioned in the orchard
next to a hedge was a Bren carrier with Lieutenant Ronald Joseph
Macdonald, the Forward Observation Officer assigned to 'D' Company by 13th Field Regiment. The carrier was equipped with a wireless
set that the thirty-year-old artilleryman from Peake's Station, Prince
Edward Island would use to call in fire support for the rifle company.
Brown was grateful to have the gunner on hand because his own skills
at ranging artillery were greatly limited.

No sooner had 'D' Company finished its early afternoon preparations than the gunfire that had been constant from the direction of
Putot-en-Bessin rose to a fierce crescendo. Sprinting up the stairs to
the farmhouse's top floor, Brown peered through his binoculars and
saw a large German infantry and tank force charging the Winnipeg
positions. He was "stunned by the swiftness of the attack" and fearful
the Little Black Devils were being overrun.[39]

10

Now You Die

THINGS HAD BEEN GOING from bad to worse for the Winnipeg Rifles since just before dawn at 0400 hours, when 'A' Company's Major Fred Hodge reported hearing enemy tanks off in the far distance. The racket out to Hodge's front was generated by a "battle-ready scouting party" of Sturmbannführer Bernhard Siebken's 26th Panzer Grenadier Regiment's II Battalion, which was advancing in staggered formation to enable an immediate attack at the first hint of resistance. Unsure of the Canadian dispositions, Siebken opted to bull ahead with fighting teeth bared rather than try to feel out the enemy forward positions first by use of reconnaissance patrols. Siebken's scouting party advanced so rapidly it left the rest of the battalion far behind, strung out along a narrow road running from Cristot to Putot-en-Bessin. Despite its haste, II Battalion failed to gain the battlefield in time to coordinate with I Battalion's assault on the Regina Rifles.[1] The 26th Panzer Grenadiers' attack on 7th Canadian Infantry Brigade on June 8 thus developed piecemeal, with each battalion operating without coordination or communication with any other.

Just as a predawn light washed the eastern skyline, the German scouting party rolled through the wheat towards the bridge spanning the railroad on the Winnipegs' extreme right flank. Heavy artillery and mortar fire saturated the ground well ahead of the advancing force. The ground shaking around them from explosions and the air overhead whirring with steel shrapnel shards, Hodge's men crouched in their slit trenches. Taking a quick peek out of his hole, Hodge saw a cluster of infantry advancing in a tight pack around several vehicles, one of which was either an antiquated Mark III tank or a self-propelled gun.

Hodge let the Germans almost gain the bridge before ordering his two platoons to cut into them with Bren gun and rifle fire. Adding to this weight of steel were several Vickers machine guns from a Cameron Highlanders of Ottawa platoon commanded by Lieutenant Ashman. The heavily concentrated fire "swept the enemy infantry away like a scythe to hay," the Winnipeg regimental historian later wrote, while a six-pound antitank gun manned by Corporal Naylor's crew knocked out the armoured vehicle and an armoured car.[2] Badly blooded, the scouting party fell back and Siebken concluded he faced an enemy "ready to defend." There would be no easy dash to the beaches. II Battalion must first put in a well-prepared attack to clear the resistance discovered at Putot-en-Bessin.[3] Siebken was also painfully aware that his left flank was completely exposed to a possible counterstroke from the 50th British Infantry Division to his west. Panzer Lehr Division was to have covered that flank, but there was no sign of it and no news as to the division's whereabouts.

Siebken summoned his company commanders to a hastily established headquarters in a château outside le Mesnil-Patry. He ordered No. 7 Company under Leutnant August Henne to strike from the right, with Obersturmführer Heinz Schmolke's No. 6 Company on the left, while No. 5 and No. 8 companies provided supporting fire. "When should the attack begin?" Schmolke asked. "Half an hour ago," the battalion commander growled. Dashing back to his men, Schmolke saw smoke from a direct artillery hit blowing slowly away from the position. A single shell had killed two of his officers and left a couple more badly wounded. Hurriedly reorganizing the company command structure, Schmolke led his men towards battle.[4]

Unbeknown to Siebken, his flank was not threatened as feared, for a strong force of Panzer Lehr Division Panther tanks was already well north of his position grinding along a ridge parallelling the woods at la Bergerie Ferme. Captain Harold Gonder and Lieutenant Gerry Blanchard apprehensively watched this line of nine tanks cross the railroad west of Putot-en-Bessin and rattle towards their position. The 62nd Anti-Tank Regiment battery commander had only two 17-pound antitank guns and two 6-pounders from the 3rd Anti-Tank Regiment's 94th Battery capable of bringing sights to bear on the approaching Panthers.[5]

Gonder could hardly believe the cavalier manner of the German tank commanders. They were all sitting tall in their open turrets, looking straight ahead as if on a training manoeuvre. Glancing over at the antitank gunners quietly tracking the tanks with their guns, he thought it should be like shooting ducks in a row for them. The range was closing fast, down to about 1,200 yards, with the tanks approaching the farm in a tightly regimented single line. Everything was developing into a perfect ambush until one of his sergeants suddenly shouted in a panicky voice, "Fire!" Before Gonder could countermand the order, every Vickers machine gun in the line ripped off a long burst of fire. "Oh, boy, here we go," Gonder thought, as "immediately down came the turrets and the German tanks got into action... fast."[6]

The jig up, the four antitank guns cracked out an opening salvo that left four Panthers wrecked, and hastened to reload. Even as they did so, the remaining five Panthers swung towards them with long-barrelled 75-millimetre guns barking out rapid fusillades. Gonder watched in helpless horror as the crew of one antitank gun or Vickers machine gun after another was "literally slaughtered" by shells "fused to burst on impact. The uncanny skill of those tankers in finding us and getting the range was ghastly."[7]

In seconds, both 17-pounders were out of action, with many gunners dead or wounded. Blanchard rushed to the rear to bring up another 17-pounder and 6-pounder that had been covering the farm's northern flank, while Gonder shifted his machine guns to new positions not yet zeroed in by the tankers, who were now being supported by German mortar fire that was hammering the wood. "Fearing that the tanks were accompanied by infantry, [Gonder] exhorted his men to keep the guns in action," wrote the Camerons' regimental historian. "Sergeant Stanley and Private A.W. Bond picked up a gun whose crew had been disabled, and moving to an exposed bit of ground continued to fire at and around the tanks until the situation had been restored." The two men were subsequently awarded Military Medals and Gonder the Military Cross for their behaviour in this action.[8]

The company's casualties, however, were heavy. Although all his Vickers remained operational, Gonder lacked soldiers to man most of them. Having had their mortars wrecked by the opening salvo of German mortar fire, the surviving members of the Camerons' No. 13 Platoon jumped in, but were still too few to bring all the guns back on line. Fortunately, a number of the Canadian Scottish troops were "old 2nd Battalion men." This prewar battalion of the Canadian Scottish Regiment had been briefly reorganized in 1936 into a machine-gun battalion similar to the Camerons. Harkening back to their long unused training, the soldiers reacquainted themselves with the powerful, little-modified, .303-calibre workhorse that had served Commonwealth forces since before the Boer War.[9]

Smothered by artillery and mortar fire and raked from a distance by the Panthers, casualties among 'E' Troop grew to the point where Blanchard ended up "laying and firing one of the guns himself."[10] The rapid fire the British and Canadian antitank gunners kept throwing at the Panthers served to keep them at their distance, so the two sides engaged in a standoff from mid-morning to about 1630 hours. Then the tanks, undoubtedly low on ammunition, turned about and waddled home. The battle for la Bergerie Ferme was over. 'E' Troop's casualties were four dead, seven wounded, and two missing. Blanchard's cool bravery under fire earned a Military Cross.

When Canadian Scottish Major G.T. "Tony" MacEwan visited his 'D' Company platoon positioned in the wood, he was "surprised to find no casualties... although they were all shaken up. The mortars [No. 13 Platoon] were in a bad way [with] their transport—about four trucks—in all... hit and brewing. The MGS had many casualties." MacEwan's visit was in the mid-afternoon, and he thought the worst of the fight at the farm finished for the moment. The major reported the attack against la Bergerie as part of the offensive by 12th SS (Hitlerjugend) Panzer Division, not realizing that his men had faced down a probe by Panzer Lehr Division—just beginning to establish a presence on the battlefield. He was little worried about the situation at the farm, but greatly concerned by the ever increasing intensity of fire coming from Putot-en-Bessin. It seemed that the main focus of German attention was shifting inexorably to focus directly on that village.[11]

MEANWHILE, THE ATTACK ON PUTOT by the 12th ss 26th Panzer Grenadier Regiment's 11 Battalion had not developed with great immediate force despite Siebken's exhortations to his company commanders for haste. Not until about 1000 hours did Major Lochie Fulton spot a large force of German infantry advancing from le Mesnil-Patry towards where the railroad tracks fronted the Winnipeg Rifles' 'D' Company line. Unlike most of the battalion, Fulton's men enjoyed a good field of fire because they were dug in at a point where the railroad ran across their front at ground level. To the right of 'D' Company, the railroad continued to follow a ground-level grade past 'C' Company's front before dropping into a deep cutting to pass 'A' Company's lines. Fulton recognized that 'A' Company's position was the battalion's weakest defensive link, for the Germans could use the cutting as a deep trench from which to launch massed attacks on the two companies defending the right flank. They could also attempt, as they had earlier, to push armour across the railway bridge to support the infantry coming out of the trench.[12]

But, apparently unaware of the potential presented by the cutting, the Germans advanced in battle order directly towards 'D' Company's front under the cover of an increasingly violent mortar and artillery barrage. Fulton ordered his mortar sergeant to reply with the three-inch mortars, while No. 17 Platoon, closest to the railway, hit them with Bren gun fire. Meanwhile, 13th Field Regiment Forward Observation Officer Captain Ben Nixon called down a devastating concentration of artillery fire. A fierce firefight ensued between the Panzer Grenadiers and No. 17 Platoon, but after a few minutes of intense shooting the Germans fell back in disorder. The platoon's wireless operator reported to Fulton that casualties had been heavy and its commander, Lieutenant Jack Benham, was dead. But they had succeeded in staving off the German thrust.[13]

As Fulton had feared, a different story quickly developed on the front facing 'A' and 'C' companies. Shortly after noon, another push by No. 6 Company of the Panzer Grenadiers gained the railway cutting despite being smothered by heavy artillery concentrations. The Germans crept out of the trench by ones and twos to take up sniping positions along the railroad embankment south of the town. Hunkered down in slit trenches that faced tall stands of wheat, the Canadian riflemen found their view of the railway blocked, so they were unable to bring effective fire against either the strongpoint or the infiltrating troops. By late morning, the battalion's war diarist observed that snipers had come "to life in the buildings throughout the town and made it increasingly difficult to move in the whole [battalion] area... there was direct enemy machine gun, mortar, and artillery fire on our light machine-gun posts and individuals in slit trenches."[14] The two companies began taking heavy casualties.

Lieutenant Colonel John Meldram had been free to roam between rifle companies on foot all morning without great fear. Now the sniper fire was so thick he was only able to venture out from battalion headquarters to the front line inside the turret of a Sherman tank used by one of the 13th Field Artillery's FOOs. During one of their attempts to visit the companies, their tank was straddled by a concentration of 88-millimetre fire and forced to beat a hasty retreat. After this, Meldram decided it was irresponsible to continue taking the risks inherent in maintaining personal contact with his rifle companies, and depended instead on fitful and spotty wireless reports sent by the company commanders.[15] He still believed that the situation was under control—sending a wireless report to brigade at 1420 hours that assured Brigadier Harry Foster the battalion should "be able to handle the situation."[16]

But even as Meldram sent this report, the defensive wall held by the Royal Winnipeg Rifles started to crumble. Rifleman Robert Smellie of 'C' Company's No. 15 Platoon saw some infantry moving in the grain field south of the railway cutting. As he opened up with his Bren gun, "an artillery barrage started... which gradually swept through our position. One shell landed in a slit trench about 50 feet to my left." The two men inside were killed instantly. "As the shelling lessened and we put our heads up, I saw a rifleman from [No.] 13 Platoon climb out of his slit trench and run towards the enemy, throwing away his equipment and tearing off his clothes as he ran. He was very soon hit by fire from the other side of the rail track. We continued to fire and every time we saw a movement on the other side of the track, I would let go a short burst."[17]

The shelling and probes by infantry continued, with each attempt by the Germans to advance in strength repelled by the embattled companies, but casualties mounted and ammunition ran down. It became clear that the Germans had managed to not only surround 'A' and 'C' companies, but also 'B' Company to their rear. Other Panzer Grenadiers had infiltrated the lines of individual companies, cutting platoons off from each other. Fighting was increasingly at close quarters, with the artillery and mortars of both sides posing a hazard to friend and foe alike. All wireless communication within the three besieged Winnipeg companies broke down completely. Meldram lost all contact with most of his battalion and was helpless to regain it.

Major Fred Hodge's situation was desperate, made even worse by the fact that 'A' Company was short a full platoon because that of Lieutenant Frank Battershill was positioned almost a mile distant in Brouay. For his part, Battershill was pinned down by successive assaults that made it impossible for him to move towards Putot. First, a battalion from Panzer Lehr brushed up against his front while groping its way towards that division's planned forming-up position for a counterattack on Gold Beach. Lost and out of contact with the rest of the division, this battalion established a strongpoint on the southern edge of Brouay and started probing his position in strength. Concentrations of naval gunfire from ships standing off Juno Beach repelled the probes and inflicted heavy German casualties. Shortly after the Panzer Lehr unit had been thrown back, an attack was put in on Brouay by the 26th Panzer Grenadier's III Battalion. On the approach march, one company from this battalion passed through the area churned up by the naval guns. "Here," wrote Oberscharführer Hans-Georg Kesslau, "we encountered the most terrible image of the war. The enemy had virtually cut to pieces units of the Panzer Lehr Division with heavy weapons. Armoured personnel carriers and equipment had been ripped apart, next to them on the ground, and even hanging from trees, were body parts of dead comrades. A terrible silence covered all."[18]

The hasty attack on Brouay by III Battalion was thrown back, but only thanks to the firepower provided by 'F' Battery of the 62nd Anti-Tank Regiment, which caught the German infantry by surprise. Several of Battershill's men, however, were lost as prisoners when one section was overrun. The lieutenant reported by wireless to Meldram in the mid-afternoon that his "flank protection group remained intact" and in possession of Brouay, but was completely isolated from the rest of the battalion.[19]

At about the same time as Battershill was making his report, Hodge realized the rest of 'A' Company was surrounded and decided their only chance for survival was to break out towards Brouay by moving westwards inside the cover of the railway cutting. But just as 'A' Company fought through to the cutting, II Battalion's No. 6 Company launched a counterthrust supported by several self-propelled guns and armoured half-tracks that collided head-on with Hodge's men. Ammunition exhausted, hopelessly outgunned and outnumbered, the major decided only one option remained. "Lay down your arms and come in here," he shouted to his still desperately resisting soldiers. As most reluctantly moved to obey, Corporal Hank Grant of No. 9 Platoon "took off, along with a few others. I didn't go there to surrender that easy." Grant managed to dash through to 'B' Company's position, and seeing things were collapsing there as well, kept going right back to battalion headquarters.[20]

'C' Company's perimeter was also falling apart. Rifleman Smellie could hear No. 15 Platoon's Lieutenant Lew McQueen trying to raise Major Jimmy Jones on the wireless without success. Finally, McQueen sent a runner to try to get instructions. It took the man thirty minutes to return with news that the headquarters was abandoned. Jones and his men had apparently mounted the wireless in the company jeep and attempted to reach the forward platoons, but now there was no sign of them anywhere.

On No. 15 Platoon's flank, No. 13 Platoon "appeared to be overrun and without radio communications, we could not call down either mortar or artillery fire to support us. Lew McQueen ordered us to pull back to the hedgerow behind the orchard, at which time, we were to throw out some smoke bombs and make our way out by ourselves if we could. I fired about six magazines with the Bren by which time the barrel was nearly red hot. We threw out the smoke bombs and ran for our lives."[21]

Smellie reached the hedgerow, and along with a few others from the platoon crept eastwards. Reaching a point where the hedgerow butted up against a road, Smellie glanced out to see if they could dash across to the opposite hedgerow. He found himself "peering down the barrel of a heavy machine gun, which the Germans were just in the process of activating. We turned around and raced down the hedgerow till we came to the stone wall around a farmyard. It was obvious we would have to cross the road there if we wanted to get out of the orchard. McQueen told us to dash across in very small groups. The group I was with all made it. I never saw Lew McQueen again."[22] The popular twenty-four-year-old officer from Winnipeg was killed covering his men's escape.

Once 'A' and 'C' companies were overrun, the Panzer Grenadiers directed their full fury against 'B' Company, which was dug into an orchard. Company Sergeant Major Charles Belton, Lieutenant Don James, and Lieutenant Andrew Beiber formed a circle "wondering what to do as we were outnumbered, and we knew if this was to continue, we were going to be pushed right back to the beach again."[23] Some men from 'C' Company filtered into the position, including Lieutenant Douglas "Duke" Glasgow, a good friend of James. The two lieutenants had just crouched in a slit trench together when a German half-track burst into the perimeter with its heavy machine gun shrieking.

Those who could fled, but James, Glasgow, and a number of other men were forced to surrender. The Panzer Grenadiers quickly separated the officers from the men and then sent the other rankers marching up the road towards le Mesnil-Patry, while a soldier armed with a Schmeisser put James and Glasgow under guard. From the orchard, James watched the men marching up the road as a German fighter plane roared overhead, then cut a sharp turn that brought it back on a converging line of flight, and strafed the men with its machine guns. Several men were wounded, including Rifleman Albert Cook, who had his leg so badly shattered by a bullet that it had to be amputated.

The injured were piled onto a half-track and driven off for treatment. Then the rest of the prisoners were marched up the road. James had a sense of foreboding as he watched the way the Germans were acting and feared "something peculiar was going to happen down the road... because... they assembled several of our men together and made them sit down." His fears were confirmed when the young Nazis "proceeded to shoot them."[24]

WHILE THIS ATROCITY was unfolding, Company Sergeant Major Belton made to escape by taking the controls of the company's Bren carrier, a vehicle he had never before driven. When the half-track and other German troops broke into the orchard, he realized they were surrounded and also "that our Brigade HQ had no idea what was going on up forward because the Germans had infiltrated our lines and cut all our communications. I got the foolish idea I should jump in this carrier and see what I could do."[25]

Unable to figure out how to work the gearshift, Belton drove off "amid a deadly hail of fire... in low gear, the engine screaming, [at] about four miles an hour."[26] Heading along a road leading towards an intersection with the Caen-Bayeux highway, Belton kept trying to get the clutch and shifter working in concert, while looking nervously at an approaching grade that climbed sharply to the intersection. Just in time to prevent the carrier from stalling out, he forced the shifter into high gear and the vehicle lurched forward at rapidly increasing speed. As he roared into the intersection, Belton saw "two German SPs (self-propelled guns) sitting with their guns traversed in the opposite direction... I went through there so fast, and because their guns were hand traversed and couldn't swing back fast enough, I got through. They did get a couple of shots in that hit the dirt around me. I was going through a kind of cut bank and... this dirt [was] flying around and getting into the carrier, but I got away somehow."[27]

Belton drove straight to 7 CIB headquarters at Secqueville-en-Bessin, where he briefed a major standing at the gate of brigade headquarters. The CSM pulled out his map and drew exact positions of the three companies that had been eliminated. Belton said he was certain that not only his 'B' Company had been overrun, but that 'A' and 'C' companies had also been wiped out. When the major ran out of questions, Belton fired up the carrier again and headed back towards where the Winnipeg Rifles still held part of Putot, despite having lost almost three-quarters of their strength.[28] Major Lochie Fulton's 'D' Company and the Support Company were essentially all that remained of the battalion in terms of a coherent fighting force. Repeatedly, the Germans attempted to infiltrate and overrun Fulton's lines and were thrown back each time with heavy losses.

Then 'B' Company's reserve platoon, which had fallen back when the rest of the unit was overrun, crept out of the grain next to battalion headquarters, with Lieutenant Andy Beiber leading, and added its strength to the little battle group. With no wireless link to brigade and no idea of the fate of most of his men, Meldram clung to the hope that Brigadier Harry Foster would realize how dire circumstances were and send reinforcements.

In a slit trench nearby, Corporal G.V. McQueen of the headquarters section was worrying about his brother Lieutenant Lew McQueen, whose 'C' Company was no longer in wireless communication with battalion headquarters. It was Lew's twenty-fourth birthday and he had not had the chance to extend any good wishes. Now he worried that his older brother might be dead out there somewhere. "Lots of lead seemed to be flying around," he later wrote. "I decided that if it got to hand-to-hand fighting, I would need some movement. I decided to get rid of my small pack and webbing. I tied a bandolier of ammo around my waist, fixed my bayonet on the rifle, and started to crawl along the ditch. Who do I meet crawling toward me? My pal Tanner. We shook hands and I said: 'Tanner, if anything happens to me, tell Norma I didn't know what hit me.' He said: 'G.V., you tell the girlfriend the same thing.'" The two men huddled in the ditch and anxiously watched their front, sides, and rear, because they had no idea where the Germans might be.

All around Putot, men were being taken prisoner or attempting to evade that fate. Some were rounded up, only to have an opportunity to make a break for it. Lieutenants James and Glasgow had been loaded into a half-track, but when it struck a land mine they used the explosion to take flight. Dashing to a slit trench, the two men jumped in to find Lieutenant Basil Brown lying at the bottom practically dead from a terrible wound in his back. Also in the slit trench was a Panzer Grenadier with a Schmeisser, who immediately covered them. Suddenly, a heavy concentration of artillery slammed down around them and the young German jumped up and fled in terror.

Seeing there was nothing they could do for Brown, the men moved on, but were soon fired on by another Schmeisser-toting German as they approached an orchard outside Putot. A slug punched into the right side of James's jaw line and ripped out the other side. Blood was pumping from the wound as Glasgow dressed it as best he could with a field dressing. Then he stuck a finger into the wound to try stemming the bleeding and managed to find the point where an artery or vein had been punctured. Pressing down on it, Glasgow managed to prevent James bleeding to death and ignored his friend's pleas to leave him to die.

The pair were lying in a two-foot-high stand of wheat. Glasgow kept assuring James they would be all right, that the Germans would never find them there. Eventually, a half-track rumbled up and put paid to this tale as the two men were again taken prisoner. There were three Panzer Grenadiers aboard—a driver, a gunner, and a radio operator. James thought the Germans would take them to the rear, but instead the half-track headed towards Putot only to blow up on a mine that killed the gunner and radio operator. Another half-track quickly appeared and picked up the two Canadians and the surviving German. This time, the vehicle drove into the German lines to a place called Château d'Audrieu—a fine estate tucked into a small forest south of the village of Audrieu. James and Glasgow were escorted to a medical aid post inside the château compound, where the medical officer was astonished that Glasgow had "managed to contact the right place with my finger and save [James's] life."[29] Glasgow was marched off to join the uninjured prisoners, while James joined the wounded Germans in the aid post. Both men would spend the rest of the war in captivity.

AS HAD BEEN THE CASE with the 12th ss troops who had earlier over-run the North Nova Scotia Highlanders at Authie and Buron, some Panzer Grenadiers of II Battalion proved cold-blooded captors. During the action, the Winnipeg Rifles lost 256 men, of whom at least 175 were taken captive.[30] The majority of the prisoners were from 'A' company. Treatment varied wildly, seemingly dependent on the whim of the ss officers who held their fate.

Most of the Canadians were gathered into a large group at Putot, numbering about one hundred and guarded by a section of Feldgen-darmerie, or field police. They were then marched about four miles to the 26th Panzer Grenadier regimental headquarters at le Haut-du-Bosq, a cluster of houses on a rise of ground south of the village of Cheux. Another forty were initially crammed into a stable at Putot before being moved to II Battalion's headquarters at le Mesnil-Patry and housed in the barn of a Norman farmer, George Moulin. Acting under direct orders from Siebken, the ss troops guarding these men provided water and first aid treatment to the wounded.[31] Another party of twenty-four Canadians from 'A' Company and two 50th British Infantry Division soldiers was initially guarded by troops from the 26th Panzer Grenadier's III Battalion, who marched their captives towards their headquarters near Cristot. When they encoun-tered a 12th Reconnaissance Battalion patrol at a crossroads along the way, their custodians passed the prisoners into its hands. The patrol escorted the prisoners to that unit's headquarters at the Château d'Audrieu.

Having arrived only about two hours ahead of the party escorting the Canadian prisoners, Major Gerhard Bremer had established his command post behind the large château, under the cooling shade of a huge sycamore tree. A fanatical Nazi who had joined the ss at age nineteen, Bremer was a highly decorated veteran of the invasions of Poland, France, and Russia.

Shortly after the Canadians entered the compound at about 1400 hours, Bremer summoned Major Hodge, Lance Corporal Austin Fuller, and Rifleman Frederick Smith for interrogation. Under the sycamore's low-hanging branches, Bremer grilled the men for about fifteen minutes in flawless English without apparent success before angrily ordering the three men killed. Four ss troopers, including a lieutenant and a sergeant, escorted Hodge and the two other men into the woods and gunned them down. While this firing squad carried out its cruel work, Bremer more cursorily interrogated three more Canadians—riflemen David Gold, James McIntosh, and William Thomas. Frustrated at his inability to gain more than name, rank, and serial number, Bremer ordered the just returned firing squad detail to execute these men also. The three soldiers were ordered to lie on their stomachs with heads propped up on their arms and then were shot repeatedly in the back of the skull. Upon returning from this killing, the firing squad paused at the château kitchen for a quick snack washed down with apple cider.

Realizing he was unlikely to pry useful information from the Canadians, Bremer ordered the remaining prisoners placed under heavy guard in an orchard next to the château. At some point in the long, terrifying afternoon these prisoners endured, seven—including the two British soldiers—were marched into the woods and shot in the head, face, and chest at close range with small-calibre weapons. At 1603 hours, Bremer and several other officers strolled into the orchard and ordered the guards to bully the remaining thirteen men, all Royal Winnipeg Rifles, into a ragged line. Among the Canadians were two brothers, George and Frank Meakin. When the ss soldiers opened up on the helpless prisoners with rifles, machine pistols, and handguns, George Meakin stepped in front of his brother to shield the man's body with his own. Consequently unwounded, Lance Corporal Frank Meakin along with Rifleman Steve Slywchuk feigned being dead, but were both shot in the skull at close range by an officer who meticulously checked each body for signs of life. Two French farmers, Leon Leseigneur and Eugese Buchart, who were walking past the orchard on a nearby road, witnessed the execution of these thirteen Canadians.[32]

While Bremer and his men slaughtered their prisoners, Obersturmbannführer Wilhelm Mohnke was growing increasingly impatient with 11 Battalion commander Siebken's insistence on sending prisoners to the 26th Panzer Grenadier Regiment's headquarters. After about a hundred Canadians were escorted into the village, Mohnke demanded that no more be sent back. Stunned, Siebken interpreted this instruction as meaning that prisoners were to be shot upon capture. The officer announced with carefully phrased formality that he would send prisoners to the rear despite Mohnke's instruction. At about 2100 hours, he accordingly dispatched the forty men gathered in the Moulin barn towards le Haut-du-Bosq under a mixed guard of about eight Feldgendarmerie and ss troops.

About a mile and a half before le Haut-du-Bosq, this party was intercepted by a staff car bearing a high-ranking ss officer, who was overheard by a German-speaking Canadian to demand that the prisoners be eliminated. Soon after his departure, the prisoners were ordered off the road into a field and "bunched together in several rows, with the stretcher cases in the middle" while a convoy of tanks and half-tracks passed. As the last half-track rolled by, it abruptly turned into the field. Several ss soldiers jumped out and handed submachine guns to the prison detail in exchange for their rifles. When everyone was fully armed with automatic weapons, the guards and troops from the half-track advanced on the Canadians sitting on the ground. Realizing the inevitability of what was about to happen, Lieutenant Reg Barker of the 3rd Anti-Tank Regiment said in a calm, clear voice, "Whoever is left after they fire the first round, go to the left."

The Germans stomped to a halt thirty yards from the Canadians and one shouted in heavily accented English, "Now you die." Renewing their advance, the ss soldiers fired a fusillade of bullets from the hip that ripped into the still seated men. Most were either wounded or killed as the Germans burned off their first magazine of ammunition. As the ss troops calmly reloaded and moved in among the dead and dying to finish off any survivors, several men in the back row, who had been either only lightly wounded or unscathed, made a break for it. Only five managed to escape into the gathering night, the others gunned down and murdered with the rest. Those who escaped

were Corporal Hector McLean, riflemen Gordon Ferris, John Mac-
Dougall, and Arthur Desjarlais of the Royal Winnipeg Rifles and
Gunner Weldon Clark of the 3rd Anti-Tank Regiment. All were cap-
tured by other German units and imprisoned until war's end.[33]

While the identity of the ss officer in the staff car was never
confirmed, McLean later described him in a way that bore a remarkable likeness to Mohnke. And there was no doubt that the unstable
commander was out looking for blood on the night of June 8–9. Upon
learning that three more Canadians had been rounded up at Siebken's
headquarters, Mohnke demanded by phone that they be shot immediately. Siebken refused and a bitter argument ensued, during which
Mohnke accused the II Battalion commander of insubordination. The
moment Mohnke hung up, Siebken called 12th ss divisional headquarters and reported the matter to Major Hubert Meyer. The division's chief-of-staff assured him there was no standing order to
murder prisoners. In fact, he said, prisoners were valuable sources of
information and as many as possible should be captured and treated
in accordance with the rules of the Geneva Convention.

A relieved Siebken left his headquarters for the still raging
battlefront, fully expecting that Mohnke would be reined in by a
promised instruction from Meyer. However, Meyer was unable to
contact Mohnke directly because the regimental commander was
already en route by staff car to Siebken's headquarters.

Sometime in the early morning hours of June 9, Mohnke burst
into II Battalion's headquarters at le Mesnil-Patry and confronted Un-
tersturmführer Dietrich Schnabel, Siebken's special missions officer.
Drawing his pistol, Mohnke ordered the junior officer to execute the
three prisoners. Shaken and afraid to refuse a direct order, Schnabel
drove to Moulin farm where the three Canadians were being held.
Accompanied by three soldiers, two of whom were medical orderlies,
Schnabel had the prisoners taken out into a garden behind the barn.
The Canadians were Private Harold Angel of the Cameron Highlanders and riflemen Frederick Holness and Ernest Baskerville of
the Royal Winnipeg Rifles. Suffering a painful foot wound, Angel had
to be supported by Holness, while Baskerville limped along behind

because of a knee injury. Schnabel told the men to face away from the Germans, and then on his command the three accompanying soldiers fired a long burst of submachine-gun fire into their backs. To ensure the Canadians were dead, Schnabel then stepped forward and delivered a single pistol shot into the back of each man's head.[34]

11

One Hell of a Good Scrap

WHILE THE ROYAL WINNIPEG RIFLES taken prisoner were helpless players in a random lottery that determined whether they lived or died, many of their comrades were loose in the night trying to escape the cauldron of Putot-en-Bessin. Among these was Rifleman Jim Parks of the battalion's mortar platoon. Parks had considered himself lucky to have narrowly escaped drowning when his Bren carrier sank while disembarking from a LCT on June 6, but now thought surviving this terrible battle would be a sign that he was truly blessed. During the long, blood-soaked afternoon's fighting in Putot, Parks had become separated from his unit while trying to eliminate a sniper harrying battalion headquarters. When he spotted a number of Bren carriers and transport trucks careening out of Putot and heading for Secqueville-en-Bessin and 7th Canadian Infantry Brigade's rear, Parks decided the wiser part of valour was to follow suit. Creeping from one hedgerow to another, he followed a course that would hopefully lead him to the Canadian Scottish Regiment stronghold at la Bergerie Ferme.

Having expended all his Sten gun ammunition trying to silence the German sniper, Parks fervently hoped to avoid enemy contact. The young soldier was tired, hungry, thirsty, and dispirited at being alone in a hostile land. His spirits perked up momentarily, though, at the sound of voices to his left. But just as Parks thought to announce his presence, the shadowy images of five heavily camouflaged soldiers wearing distinctive coal-bucket German helmets emerged from the hedge. Faces covered with a mixture of black and sand camouflage paint, binder twine woven through web belts to break silhouettes, the men looked bizarrely like wraiths wrapped in bad-minton netting. Parks, who had enlisted in 1939 at the tender age of fifteen by outrageously representing himself as an eighteen-year-old, thought the Germans looked even younger than his now nineteen years. But they also looked hard-faced, and each soldier had a Schmeisser slung over a shoulder.

"My first thought was to get the hell out of there," Parks later re-called. "Even had I had a magazine for the gun there was no way I was going to have it out with them there. So I kept going as fast as I could without making much noise."[1]

A few minutes later, he looked across a field and saw the eight-foot-high wall surrounding la Bergerie Ferme on the opposite side. The field was being pounded by German artillery, each shell hurling large clots of dirt ten to twelve feet into the air. Glancing over his shoulder, Parks detected the Panzer Grenadiers flitting about in the hedge about fifty yards away and decided he either risked a run through the shellfire or "these guys" were going to catch him. Suck-ing down a deep breath, Parks bolted into the field, zigzagging through exploding shells until he banged up against the wall. A Cana-dian Scottish soldier glanced out at him through a loophole carved into the wall and then a length of thick rope dropped over the rim of the wall. Jumping to catch its trailing end, Parks quickly pulled him-self hand over hand up the wall and dropped over the other side.

As he hit the ground, the man who had thrown the rope said, "I'll switch my rifle for your Sten gun."

"I don't have any ammo for it," Parks replied.

"Don't worry about that. We're going into the attack in ten min-utes." Parks nodded and exchanged the automatic weapon for a Lee Enfield. So much for regulations, he thought, knowing that he could be placed on a charge for failing to retain possession of the weapon signed out to his care. He could easily imagine the battalion quarter-master reaming him out in a few days, but also realized the other soldier needed the gun more than he did at the moment. The soldier said his section had seen Parks poke his head out of the hedgerow before starting the dash across the field. They had also spotted the five Panzer Grenadiers and fired at them to cover him. "Don't think we hit any of them," the man said, "but they buggered off."

Parks was walked over to the farmhouse, where some tea stood in a can on the kitchen stove. A steel mug of the bitter brew was pressed into his hand. Stepping out of the kitchen, Parks crouched and leaned his back against the farmhouse wall. The courtyard was filled with Canadian Scottish all checking weapons or breaking extra ammunition and grenades out of boxes to fill every available web pouch or pocket with extra ordnance. It was about 2000 hours. Parks knew the Canadian Scottish were to try breaking through to Putot-en-Bessin to relieve the remnants of his battalion still holding out on the town's eastern flank. He hoped that they got there in time and that not too many of these brave lads would die doing it.[2]

Brigadier Harry Foster had decided to throw the Canadian Scottish Regiment into a hasty counterattack on Putot-en-Bessin in the late afternoon after it became obvious the Royal Winnipeg Rifles had been all but wiped out. At 1830 hours, the commander of 7 CIB walked into Lieutenant Colonel Fred Cabeldu's headquarters in Secqueville-en-Bessin and said he must attack in no more than two hours. The brigadier promised Cabeldu full support by the 12th and 13th Field Regiments, concentrated in firing positions at Bray, and the company of a 1st Hussars tank squadron. Foster then left the Canadian Scottish commander to work out the details of the attack.

"My plan," Cabeldu wrote, "was a simple one. We were in possession of the la Bergerie Farm woods. This was to be our start line. The road Secqueville-en-Bessin–Putot-en-Bessin was the centre line of the attack, with 'D' [Company] right, 'A' [Company] left, 'C' [Company] reserve right. 'B' [Company] was to disengage from its action at Vieux Cairon, be at the start-line as soon as possible and follow 'A' [Company's] axis. Tanks under [1st Hussars second-in-command] Major Frank White were to give right flank protection, our own Carriers left flank protection, and our 3-inch mortars were to fire from just [to the] rear of the start-line. The Camerons were to lay a smokescreen for us with their 4.2-inch mortars. We were on the extreme right of the division and British elements of the 50th [Division] were supposed to be holding the woods north of Brouay in small numbers. The artillery fire plan was difficult in view of the fact that enemy positions were not known, and, according to available information, the Winnipegs' [battalion] HQ was still in Putot. A creeping barrage commencing 300 yards in advance of the start-line was decided upon with a lift sufficient for a three-mile-an-hour advance, then lifting to concentrations south of the railway crossing and certain known enemy positions beyond. [Defensive Fire] tasks were to be prepared in advance on all crossroads leading into Putot-en-Bessin anticipating a completely successful attack."[3] Following immediately behind the infantry would also be the four 17-pounder self-propelled antitank guns of 248 Battery's 'K' Troop from the 62nd Anti-Tank Regiment to provide close-in support against any tanks or antitank guns the Germans might have deployed.[4]

Although he considered the plan simple enough, Cabeldu's men were going to have to scramble to attack on schedule. Only 'D' Company was situated at la Bergerie Ferme; the other companies had to start marching almost immediately to have any chance of being in place in time for the advance. Realizing this, Cabeldu had placed 'B' Company—almost four miles away in the area of Vieux Cairon—at the back of the attack column. Major R.M. Lendrum would also have to extract his men from the area covertly "in order not to give the enemy any idea that the situation [there] had changed"—nor that the gunners of the field regiments packed into firing positions at Bray were no longer protected by infantry.[5]

Even as he hastily cobbled his plan of attack together, Cabeldu issued orders summoning the company commanders to an 'O' Group at his headquarters. During the short meeting, Cabeldu "impressed on [them] the imperative need for success and haste. The Canadian Scottish *must* capture and hold Putot. There was no other infantry battalion between the enemy in Putot and the beaches."[6] The creeping artillery barrage would begin at 2030 hours, Cabeldu said, and the leading companies must jump off from the start line then or lose the advantage provided.

So quickly was the attack organized that the 1st Hussars were unable to send an officer to Secqueville in time for the briefing, so the Canadian Scottish second-in-command, Major Cyril Wightman, raced by motorcycle to the tank regiment's harbour area to personally brief the squadron commander. "I sort of said, 'Follow me to [the Squadron Leader,]'" he confided to his diary later, turned the bike around, and started heading towards la Bergerie with the Hussars trailing behind in their Shermans.[7]

Lendrum, who arrived only for the end of the briefing, also rode a motorcycle back to where his men were hotly engaged in a long-range duel with German forces that were pounding Vieux Cairon with artillery, mortar, and heavy machine-gun fire. Pulling out of the area while under fire and without revealing the fact that the village was being left undefended proved no easy matter, but soon Lendrum had his men behind a low rise that screened their movement as they marched "from one battle... cross-country... to get into another."[8]

Upon returning to 'C' Company, still in Secqueville, Major Desmond Crofton summoned the platoon commanders, while Company Sergeant Major W. Berry organized a distribution of extra ammunition and collected up antitank grenades and other supplies not needed in the attack. Being excluded from the briefing bothered Berry, because if the officers all ended up dead or wounded, responsibility for leading the company would fall on his shoulders and he would have little idea of the plan.[9] Among the young officers being briefed by Crofton was twenty-one-year-old Lieutenant Geoffrey D. Corry, who had only taken over No. 15 Platoon the day before as a reinforcement officer. Just getting to know his men, Corry had so far been impressed by their "great confidence and spirit" despite the losses suffered during the landings and advance inland. He listened with growing trepidation, however, to Crofton's briefly delivered orders. "The Winnipegs have been overrun by the Panzer Grenadiers," Crofton said sharply, "and it's the battalion's job to counterattack and retake Putot-en-Bessin. Our failure will allow the Germans to storm to the beach and jeopardize the whole invasion... There's no time to lose." Corry swallowed and thought, "Pretty heavy stuff." Gathering his platoon section leaders together, Corry explained the situation "quickly but clearly." Then it "was on with small packs, ammunition, and begin to move out."[10]

While waiting for Major Tony MacEwan to return to la Bergerie Ferme from the 'O' Group at Secqueville, Lieutenant Thomas Lowell Butters watched increasing numbers of Winnipeg Rifles straggling in from Putot. "They hobbled back, shot up, scared. Each man said that all hell was breaking loose out there." When MacEwan hustled into the farmyard and ordered 'D' Company to saddle up, Butters knew they were going into that hell. With the men marching behind, MacEwan led the way towards the wood south of the farm and "briefed his platoon commanders about what we were doing while on the move to the start line."[11]

'D' Company arrived at the edge of the wood, and Butters saw Cabeldu already there, staring through binoculars at "streams of troops crossing and running northeast towards [nearby] farm buildings." Fearing the soldiers might be Germans launching a pre-emptive strike, the lieutenant colonel dispatched the Bren carrier platoon to investigate. Its commander, Lieutenant Joseph James Andrews, quickly radioed back that Cabeldu was seeing Winnipeg Rifles on the run.

As MacEwan marched by at the head of his men, Cabeldu waved them forward and 'D' Company's "advance went in with terrific impetus."[12] The battalion had three miles to go, initially following a narrow lane until it met the Secqueville-Putot main road, and then directly by road to a bridge crossing the railway west of Putot. For the entire distance, the ground was almost perfectly flat and bordered on either side by grain standing four to five feet high, with a few scattered orchards breaking up the open fields until the road intersected the Caen-Bayeux highway. After that, the road passed through three wide grain fields divided only by thin hedgerows.

The company advanced in extended line, with Butters and No. 17 Platoon on the right, Lieutenant A.C. Peck's platoon to the left, and Lieutenant J.P.R. Mollison's men astride the road. MacEwan's company headquarters followed close behind Mollison's platoon and about fifteen yards farther back, Private R.H. Tutte trundled up the road in the company's Bren carrier. The carrier was heavily loaded with ammunition and medical supplies, so that it could serve as a mobile supply station. Riding shotgun beside Tutte was Private R.H. Rideout, a company stretcher-bearer. The battalion's three-inch mortar platoon was also tight on 'D' Company's heels. Given the speed of preparations, MacEwan considered the fact they crossed the start line on time "a miracle."[13]

Once on the advance, the lead platoons "spread out on either side of the road in the grain fields" and walked into a murderous rain of steel that the Germans—knowing the creeping barrage screened an attack—cast down immediately behind the Canadian artillery fire.[14] 'D' Company could only face this intense mortar and artillery fire, as the battalion "learned our first lesson" about German doctrine for meeting attacks. Cabeldu realized that the opening barrage supporting his attack equally betrayed the start line's position. Now the Germans had it marked and brought fire to bear on each company as it emerged from the wood. But without the artillery, Cabeldu believed his men would be slaughtered when they went forward.[15]

Even with the artillery support and the cover offered by a thick smokescreen created by the rapid 4.2-inch mortar fire of the Cameron Highlanders, 'D' Company started to take casualties. MacEwan was initially confused, unable "to tell whether we were walking into our own artillery or if it was enemy fire." From his position near the back of the company's advance, the major could see his leading platoons moving forward, but found it almost impossible to keep in touch with them as the officers were too busy to send regular wireless reports. Sensing that No. 17 Platoon was beginning to veer too far right, possibly in response to the heavy frontal fire it was taking, MacEwan dashed up the road to get directly behind the leading platoons and better control their movement.[16]

Rattling along behind in his carrier, Private Tutte "could see the full extent of our line, also I could see almost every man that fell and though the enemy fire was so heavy, not one man could I see hanging back. I had never known until this time that we had so many *men* in our company." When the first soldiers started falling, Private Rideout jumped off and raced to help the wounded.[17] Private W.A.P. Campbell of the mortar platoon later wrote of 'D' Company's advance that "it was really something to see, to watch the boys going across the fields. They just kept right on walking and getting shot down."[18]

The smoke boiling over the battlefield thickened, plunging the men into an early twilight through which heavy amounts of tracer rounds being fired by the Panzer Grenadiers to guide their aim "showed up brighter and brighter. The [company] passed through grain fields and orchards, pushing through each sparse hedgerow. Casualties were being suffered all along," MacEwan later wrote. Wounded himself, the major remained at the head of his men. "We passed over part of the Winnipegs' position with their arms and equipment left on the ground beside their slit trenches. Further on a German armoured car opened up from behind a hedgerow on the platoon on the left. After several heavy bursts of fire he moved off. Later it was hit and burned on the objective. Just before here I was hit for the second time and was out of action."[19] Lying where his wounds had rendered him helpless, MacEwan tried to draw the attention of second-in-command Captain Jack Bryden and Company Sergeant Major Kilner as the company headquarters section passed by, "but the smoke and flame and roar of exploding shells made this impossible." MacEwan was later picked up by a stretcher-bearer party and evacuated to the rear for treatment.[20]

As 'D' Company crossed the Caen-Bayeux highway, it entered the even deadlier killing ground presented by the three grain fields that had to be crossed in turn to gain the railroad crossing objective. Immediately, Butters wrote afterward, "the enemy mortaring increased and was supplemented by two or three enemy LMGs [light machine guns] firing from the centre and right edge of the first hedgerow. Casualties crossing the field increased. Similar conditions of opposition were met in crossing the second field, although mortaring appeared to increase in intensity.

"During the crossing of the third field many casualties were suffered. Enemy LMG fire opened up from an orchard on our right flank (about 4 guns)—further fire came from our front (about 2 guns) and fire was experienced coming from our right rear (the row of trees and hedgerow dividing the second and third field)."[21] Butters spotted a Panzer Grenadier in a tree blasting away at his men with a light machine gun, rushed the position, and shot the man, whose body plunged to the earth at his feet. But the rate of fire chopping at the platoon barely lessened. All his section leaders were down, either dead or wounded. Not that he needed them to help control the platoon, for only seven of the thirty-seven soldiers who had crossed the start line were still behind him.[22]

Tutte and his carrier were only about fifteen yards back of the company headquarters group as it moved out into the third field, when Bryden, Kilner, and signaller Private Sinclair "were instantly killed by a mortar bomb landing in their midst. Before I had passed them in the carrier another bomb dropped less than ten feet to my right. I got the dust on the side of my face and a terrific blast. My right ear was deaf for about three hours."[23]

A sniper with a light machine gun firing from the hedge behind the battalion concentrated his attention on Tutte, but he hunkered down below the height of the carrier's low armoured sides and these "turned the slugs away without any trouble. The sniper did manage to get one inside the carrier over my right shoulder, how it ever bounced around as it did inside the small space in the front without hitting me I'll leave for others to wonder. From there on to the bridge [there was] a lot of noise, smoke and dust, also a terrible ringing in my right ear from the mortar blast. But eventually we reached the bridge. I was only a few feet behind the first few to get there. The road leading to the bridge was a built up road with a drop off on either side, several of the men had taken cover, (the first they'd had) on the right of the road behind a bank facing the railway, so I swung the carrier around sideways and backed it down over the bank to the left of the road. We had reached our objective, now all we had to do was hold it."[24]

With MacEwan down and Bryden and Kilner dead, the company's senior subaltern Lieutenant Peck took over. When the remnants of

'D' Company reached the railroad, he quickly got the men digging in. Having managed to reach the objective despite crippling casualties, the lieutenant was determined to meet any German counterattack with extreme violence. Private Campbell and the rest of the mortar platoon meanwhile "set up our mortar out in the open under machine-gun fire. We usually fire at no less than seven hundred yards, but we tore out all the secondary charges from the bombs and were firing at four hundred. We soon ran out of ammunition and were going back for more when Peck came up and told us to let them know there was only twenty-six men left out of the company. What was he to do?"[25]

FORTUNATELY FOR PECK, 'D' Company was not, as the young officer feared, alone. 'A' Company had crossed the start line just minutes behind it and was now coming up on the left flank. This company's passage to Putot had been no less bloody. Stepping across the start line, the men were greeted by "a veritable wall of fire." With explosions churning up the ground all around, Corporal Bob Mayfield of No. 8 Platoon turned back to his mates with a fierce grin on his face. "Boy, this is going to be one hell of a good scrap," he shouted.

"That spirit was maintained throughout," the company's war diarist recorded soon afterward. "The casualties were naturally heavy, but never a wounded man whimpered, the opposite in fact was the case and time and again badly wounded men had to be ordered back. The air, red and black with flame, shot and shell, was also blue with the imprecations flung at the enemy by the wounded. Sergeant Bob Dickson, badly wounded in the knee, dragged his leg along almost two hundred yards until ordered back. Even then he had to be forcibly detained at the R.A.P. [Regimental Aid Post] after his wound had been dressed and, from then until evacuated, dug slits with other wounded for the most serious cases."[26]

'A' Company's platoon leaders suffered exceptionally high casualties during the advance, with Lieutenant Brian Carruthers wounded, along with sergeants Nettleton of No. 7 Platoon and Dickson of No. 8 Platoon. Nettleton's loss was a particularly heavy blow to the company, as he had been leading No. 7 Platoon with exceptional skill since its commanding officer had been wounded on D-Day. 'A' Company's commander, Major Arthur Plows, however, seemed to be everywhere at once during the assault—dashing back and forth from one platoon to the other to offer direction and chivvy the men onward.[27]

Private Jack Daubs hunched ever lower as he ran through the hornet storm of tracers buzzing past. Seeing a slit trench with a couple of soldiers in it, Daubs dived in. Noticing their Winnipeg Rifles shoulder patches, he said, "It's pretty hot, isn't it?" When neither man replied, the twenty-year-old from London, Ontario looked more closely and realized that both soldiers were dead. Dragging himself out of the trench, Daubs dashed onward to keep up with the rest of the company. Suddenly, he was staggered by something striking his helmet with terrific force and then giving his battle pack a hard yank. Crouching even lower, he paused to check his pack and discovered that a bullet had nicked the helmet and then penetrated the pack, where it had torn the pin off a two-inch mortar smoke bomb before punching a hole through his mess tin. Although the men were supposed to carry rounds for the platoon's two-inch mortars in pouches on the front of their webbing, Daubs habitually opted to put the two assigned to him into the pack, figuring this was safer than having the explosives draped against his chest. Seeing the damaged smoke round shook him badly because right next to it was a matching high explosive-bomb. Had the bullet struck that, Daubs knew, he "wouldn't be here anymore."[28]

'A' Company advanced so fast along a line more directly behind 'D' Company than originally planned that its leading platoons overtook Mollison's platoon and the men became intermixed. This led to Lieutenant Peck thinking his trail platoon had been lost and fearing 'D' Company's situation was direr than was the case. Fortunately for the shaken young officer, Major Plows quickly realized 'D' Company's disorganized state and rather than swinging 'A' Company immediately to its objective east of the bridge used his rightward platoon to bolster the other unit's strength. He also told his second-in-command, Captain W.H.V. Matthews, to consolidate the other two platoons on the objective while he sorted out 'D' Company.

When Peck reported that MacEwan had been wounded, Bryden and CSM Kilner killed, and the company almost destroyed in the attack, Plows decided to amalgamate it with his own.[29] While Plows tried to bring order to a chaotic situation, some men from the two companies, led by Lance Corporal Stan Kirchin and Corporal Hopkins, dashed across the bridge and established a toehold on the other side. Kirchin was killed moments later by German gunfire. The rest of the tiny force was immediately caught in a fierce firefight with a superior force of well-dug-in Panzer Grenadiers.

The moment Plows heard about this group's foray across the bridge, he realized that any attempt to reinforce their tenuous toehold would only expose the men committed to being "cut off and annihilated."[30] He ordered them to beat a hasty retreat back to the north side of the railroad cutting. He was, however, confident that the cutting's twenty-foot width made it an excellent front for a defensive position, because it effectively formed a "dry 'moat' and was a first-class antitank ditch at the same time."[31]

Plows proceeded to walk the length of the two-company defensive line "with magnificent coolness under hellish enemy fire of all kinds... organizing" his positions. "Particularly commendable is the fact that, despite the natural confusion, he bore in mind... that 'A' Company would have to leave this place and organized the defence accordingly" so that responsibility for 'D' Company's perimeter could be handed off smoothly once reinforcements were brought forward.[32]

Captain Matthews later stated that "Plows should have been given a VC [Victoria Cross] for his efforts. His coolness while organizing 'D' and 'A' companies at the bridge was an inspiration to all. With 'D' Company's headquarters knocked out lieutenants Peck, Mollison and Butters worked strenuously and with complete disregard for their own safety. But it was Major Plows with his cool, calm direction who stabilized the situation."[33]

Also showing a great deal of calm under fire was Lieutenant Peck, who mortarman Private Campbell thought "inspired the lesser beings... always walking around and talking to the boys no matter how heavy the fire. He was very English in his speech and the calm, cool way he strolled around and talked you'd have thought he was at a garden party."[34]

Shortly after Matthews started organizing the two platoons of 'A' Company that he had taken to the unit's objective, he was rendered senseless by a mortar blast and had to be guided back to the Regimental Aid Post. As there were now no officers other than Plows still functioning, Company Sergeant Major Grimmond took over the company.[35]

The ferocity of the battle was taking its toll even on the men and officers who were not killed or wounded. For the Canadian Scottish, D-Day had been a comparative walk in the park. Nothing had prepared them for the bloodletting they now endured. By the time he reached the railway bridge, Lieutenant Butters had been "terribly frightened. But I got myself together" and, drawing strength from the indefatigable Plows "who gathered that attack together," set to getting the men dug into defensible positions.

COMING UP FAST behind the two leading companies at about this time was 'C' Company, which had also made a long dash through the gauntlet of German fire. Lieutenant Corry's No. 15 Platoon had advanced with two sections forward, and the third and the small headquarters section in trail. Corry positioned himself directly between the two forward sections, so that everyone could see him. Soon after the advance was completed, he jotted down some impressions: "Fire beginning to get heavy. Bullets buzzing close. Okay, if you can hear them you're not hit. How far left to go. 1,000 yards." The company had reached a small orchard just to the north of Putot and dodged between the trees to gain the southern edge. Here lay another grain field whipped by machine-gun fire and exploding mortar rounds. The 1st Hussars tanks crashed up behind the infantry, shoving apple trees aside that blocked their progress, and started banging off shells towards the German positions, betrayed by their tracer rounds spitting out of their machine-gun barrels.

Convinced that the only way to keep the assault going was to never stop moving, Corry stepped out of the orchard into the field without pause. "Look around," he wrote. "No platoon. Gone to ground because of the fire. Wish I could do the same. Wave pistol in the direction of the enemy and yell, 'Come on guys, up the Scottish!' That gets everyone moving again. Suddenly we're passing the outskirts of Putot. Pass through an orchard and a hedge. See dead Germans, dead Scottish. See Scottish officer flattened into ground by tank.* Take up position to rear of 'D' Company. All hell is breaking loose. Tank, MG, mortar fire coming from everywhere. Can't tell which side bullets are on. Everyone digs in. Fastest slit trenches made in Normandy."[36]

At the bridge over the railway, the remnants of 'D' Company, supported by the 'A' Company platoon, were fighting desperately to gain control of the north side of the tracks. Private Tutte had been convinced to abandon his carrier when a sniper managed to get more bullets inside the driver's compartment. "Ducking behind the carrier I could hear a lot of shooting from the other side of the road, so I dashed across... to see if I could do anything over there to help out. Over on the right of the road, behind the bank facing the railway I found about a dozen of our lads all in different stages of mental [distress]. They were heavily engaged with two machine guns, which were sweeping the top of our covering bank. I was able to sneak around the end of the bank and throw five or six shots back to the position of one of the MGS. Though it was quite dark from all the smoke and dust, we could make out their position from the tracer they were using. Evidently 'Jerry' likes bright lights, he does use a lot of tracer. I'm not sure that I hit anything or not, but the MG I fired at did cut off for a moment, so I like to think that I knocked off the gunner and made it necessary for someone else to take his place.

"From under the bridge some of the men captured a German and his MG intact and well supplied with ammo. This turned to our own advantage as our... supply of Bren mags was getting perilously short. Soon after this we had to vacate our position in a hurry. A 3-inch

---

* This was Captain Bryden, who according to some accounts had only been badly wounded until being killed when a 1st Hussars tank ground overtop of him and CSM Kilner.

mortar bomb dropped only a few feet behind us. It so happened that it dug [into the] ground and the ground absorbed the shrapnel.

"From this time on all our fighting was on the left of the bridge and here we put in some heavy exchange of fire till about 2330. During this time I was kept well occupied, walking out wounded, searching dead and wounded as much as 500 yards to the rear and all along our front for extra Bren mags. I made four trips of this kind, each time returning with a dozen or more mags and before going out again helping one or two of our own boys wounded out to the side road and putting them as much under comfort as possible in a shallow ditch behind a hedge.

"About 2330 hours things began to quiet down and we started to dig. Not like we used to do on schemes, what I mean is—*We dug*. Badgers had nothing on us."

'B' Company and battalion headquarters had by now reached the outskirts of Putot and become entangled in a sharp fight with Panzer Grenadiers evacuating a string of ruined farm buildings. Major Wightman, the battalion's second-in-command, thought the fight for Putot "was quite hectic. One reason, perhaps, [was that] it was our first major attack and, secondly, it certainly was our very, very first night attack, which always leads to some confusion until after many months of experience."[37]

The Panzer Grenadiers finally broke just after midnight and fell back to the other side of the railway, digging in some thousand feet to the south. From here, they kept intermittently exchanging fire with the Canadians throughout the early morning hours of June 9. Strung out along the line of advance stretching from the wood south of la Bergerie Ferme to the bridge crossing the railway west of Putot were many dead and wounded Canadian Scottish, but nobody had time to tally the butcher's bill. That could wait for morning. For now the urgent task was to reorganize so that the battalion could meet any counterattack thrown at it in the morning and evacuate the wounded from the battleground.

While the Canadian Scottish rifle companies readied their defences, the headquarters company and 'D' Company of the Royal Winnipeg Rifles, which had been holding out on the eastern flank of

Putot, withdrew to la Bergerie Ferme—becoming the brigade's barely combat-capable reserve. In carrying out its hasty and costly counterattack against the 26th Panzer Grenadier Regiment, the Canadian Scottish Regiment had rescued 7 CIB from potential disaster. Had Putot-en-Bessin remained in German hands, the Regina Rifles would have been open to attack from three sides and might have been overrun like the Winnipeg Rifles. That would have effectively eliminated the brigade's combat effectiveness and exposed the western flank of 3rd Canadian Infantry Division to being turned by the 12th ss Panzer Division.

But the brigade's tenuous hold on the right flank of the division remained imperilled. Even as the gunfire around Putot dwindled to mere harassing fire, the sound of heavy fighting suddenly erupted from the direction of Norrey-en-Bessin and Bretteville-l'Orgueilleuse. Here, the Regina Rifles had been struck yet again by a 12th ss onslaught. This time, however, the fanatical young Panzer Grenadiers were attacking alongside armoured monsters—the division's Panther Mark v tanks.

12

Fight to the Death

GENERALFELDMARSCHALL Erwin Rommel had decided during
the afternoon of June 8 that a massed attack by the three Panzer
divisions across a solid front was strategically impracticable. Instead,
he ordered Panzer Lehr commander Generalleutnant Fritz Bayerlein
to abandon the advance immediately west of the 12th ss Panzer Division and concentrate before Tilly-sur-Seulles in order to recapture
Bayeux. The 12th ss would, meanwhile, seize the vital ground held
by 3rd Canadian Infantry Division that prevented its 25th and 26th
Panzer Grenadier regiments from linking up. Standartenführer Kurt
Meyer's 25th Regiment had troops in Franqueville and Authie while
Wilhelm Mohnke's 26th Regiment had no units east of St. Mauvieu.
For the 12th ss to renew its drive north to Juno Beach, it must gain
control of Norrey-en-Bessin, Bretteville-l'Orgueilleuse, and Rots.
Once these towns were returned to German control, the division
could use the Caen-Bayeux railway as a starting point for punching
through to Juno.

Brigadeführer Fritz Witt, 12th ss Panzer Division's commander,
arrived at the Abbaye d'Ardenne with personal instructions for
Meyer. While Mohnke seized Norrey, Meyer was to strike from the
east against the Canadians in Rots and Bretteville. By punching into
the lines of the Regina Rifles from both flanks, Witt hoped to smash
the Canadian battalion. Meyer's regiment would be bolstered by the
12th Panzer Regiment's 1 Battalion. In addition to these forty or so

Panthers, Meyer would also have at his disposal the Wespe Battery's 105-millimetre self-propelled guns. This would be a blitzkrieg night assault reminiscent of many such actions Meyer and Witt had successfully mounted on the Russian front. Meyer expected to take the Reginas by surprise at about 2200 hours and annihilate them.[1]

Shortly after this discussion, two ss troopers marched seven North Nova Scotia Highlanders into the compound and reported to Meyer that they had caught the men between Authie and Buron. Meyer turned angrily. "What should we do with these prisoners? They only eat up our rations." After whispering some instructions to an officer standing nearby, Meyer loudly declared, "In the future no more prisoners are to be taken!"

In short order, the Canadians were individually escorted from the stall in which they were being held through a narrow passageway that led into a garden. There, a sergeant armed with a machine pistol summarily shot each man in the back of the head. Privates Walter Doherty, Reg Keeping, Hugh MacDonald, George McNaughton, George Millar, Thomas Mont, and Raymond Moore were all executed in a matter of just ten minutes. When the killings were completed, the sergeant responsible exited the garden and casually reloaded his gun.

After the killer walked away, a young eastern European conscript named Jan Jesionek crept into the garden with three friends and found the Canadians lying in a ragged pile, around which a large pool of blood was forming. With grim irony, Jesionek, who had overheard Meyer's admonishment about having to feed the prisoners, noted that standing near the murdered soldiers was a bulky British ration canister.[2]

Whether Meyer ordered the killings or not was unclear. Certainly, his mind was barely focussed on such matters, for although Witt had showered Meyer with a wealth of armour and mobile artillery, he could do nothing to relieve the paltry offering of Panzer Grenadiers available for the upcoming attack. All three of Meyer's regular battalions were currently tied down in front of the 9th Canadian Infantry Brigade's front around les Buissons. Reluctant to pull any of these units away from there for fear of opening up a route for the Canadians to break through to Carpiquet airport, Meyer could only ante up small change in the form of No. 15 Motorcycle Company. Even this recon-naissance battalion unit had to be pulled out of the line and the result-ing gap filled by a company of heavily armed but less mobile engineers. Despite his paucity of infantry, the cocky Panzer Grenadier commander remained confident that speed and the sheer weight of armoured firepower would overwhelm the Reginas. Accordingly, Meyer mounted the majority of the infantry onto the hulls of the Panzers, with one platoon saddled up on their motorbikes. The tanks and motorcyclists were to go hell-bent for leather through Rots and along the Caen-Bayeux highway straight into Bretteville.[3]

Lacking a wireless link with Mohnke, Meyer teed up his attack ab-sent any coordination with the 26th Panzer Grenadier Regiment. He was confident of success. Exultantly, Meyer drove from tank to tank "calling out to the boys" in the crews and the mounted motorcycle troops. Having promised during training exercises in Belgium that he would personally accompany No. 15 Motorcycle Company into its battle-field debut, Meyer made it clear he would now honour that pledge.[4]

Going into the attack were several officers who had fought many campaigns at Meyer's side. Haupsturmführer Horst von Büttner commanded the motorcyclists. And Obersturmbannführer Max Wünsche—the 12th Panzer Regiment commander—personally led the Panthers in the absence of the battalion's leader, who had yet to reach the battlefield. Meyer swung onto the pillion behind his dispatch rider Helmut Belke, while in the sidecar next to him was Dr. Stift. Belke had been at Meyer's side since 1939. So, too, had Wün-sche. "We know each other," Meyer later wrote, "there is no need for discussion. [A] look, a sign, and the tanks are rolling into the night."[5]

As Meyer passed the tanks, he saw that the grenadiers sheltering behind the turrets of each Panzer "were waving to me... They slap each other on the back and probably remember my promise. They point to my motorcycle and shake their heads. My 'conveyance' seems slightly worrying to them."[6]

Belke gunned the motorbike out to the front of the column, so that Meyer led it at the Panthers' top speed to Rots, finding the village empty. The Panthers ground single file through the narrow streets, but on the other side spread into a wedge shape, with one company either side of the highway and two Panthers on point, barrelling along the road itself towards the next village. Coming within range of Bretteville, the Panthers began "firing round after round from their guns, shooting down the road to clear it for us, clanking into the village at full speed on their tracks. This is the way we fought in the east, but will these same surprise tactics achieve the same for us here?"[7]

MEYER SOON REALIZED the Reginas were unsurprised by the nighttime assault. Instead, the thorough reconnaissance his veteran officers and regimental scouts had conducted during the daytime, in order to know "every fold" of ground, had been detected by the Canadians, closely monitored, and its intent correctly interpreted. Lieutenant Colonel Foster Matheson cautioned his company commanders to expect an armoured night attack and insisted all troops maintain a state of full combat readiness despite the fact that everyone was verging on exhaustion.

That such precautionary measures were justified was confirmed at Norrey-en-Bessin shortly before Meyer's assault force hammered down on Bretteville. In Norrey, 'C' Company's No. 13 Platoon reported movement on its perimeter and Major Stu Tubb scrambled over. Standing next to Lieutenant Ray Smith, the company commander listened "to some highly suspicious noises in the darkness towards le Mesnil-Patry. There was talking and occasional calls back and forth, followed by sounds of pounding. We decided that someone unfriendly was starting to dig in and that we should put a stop to it, hopefully without disclosing our own position.

"Accordingly, two of 13 Platoon's Bren gun teams slipped off to the right to open fire. This ploy worked, as their opening bursts a few minutes later brought astonished shouts and, as they continued, sounds of a hasty retreat."[8] The Germans brought under fire were part of Mohnke's 26th Panzer Grenadier Regiment attempting to execute Witt's order by securing Norrey and linking up with the 25th Panzer Grenadiers.

While this action was playing out in front of Norrey, Meyer's combined force of tanks and infantry launched its attack and ran into an immediate hail of Bren gun fire from 'B' Company's position astride the Caen-Bayeux highway just east of Bretteville. Some of the mounted Panzer Grenadiers were shot off the tanks before the rest could dismount and scurry to the cover of roadside ditches. Using the ditches for cover, the Germans then advanced on the town by bounds as one section covered the forward movement of another, then passed through that section while it covered the next advance.

Casualties were mounting alarmingly as Meyer joined a cluster of Panzer Grenadiers in one of the ditches. He stumbled over a dead Canadian and heard someone groaning on the road to the left. Bren gun and Vickers fire from some of the surviving Camerons ripped towards the Germans. Meyer managed to reach the wounded man and looked down in horror at his old friend von Büttner. The motorcycle company commander had been shot in the stomach and was lying on his back. He squeezed Meyer's hand and said, "Tell my wife, I love her very much." Meyer knelt beside von Büttner as Dr. Stift dressed the wound, while Helmut Belke covered them with fire from a position off to the right. Suddenly, a Canadian dashed across the road and Belke killed the man with a head shot before sprawling to the ground himself. When Belke failed to stand up, Meyer ran over to find that he too had been shot in the stomach. Meyer tried to assure Belke he would survive, but the veteran soldier knew better. "No, I know this kind of wound," he said. "This is the end. Please tell my parents."

Tank commander Wünsche had meanwhile determined that his Panthers were not simply going to overrun the Canadians holding Bretteville as they had so many Russians in the past. He ordered one of the two tank companies to swing around the town's southern outskirts and attack it from the west, while the other struck it head on. The Panzers met an immediate wall of rapid and fierce fire thrown out by the six-pound antitank guns of 3rd Anti-Tank Regiment's 94th Battery, but still overran 'H' Troop's positions and killed or wounded all but twelve of its gun crews. 'G' Troop, however, was located more snugly inside the Regina perimeter and subjected the Panthers to fire that surprised the Germans with its accuracy.

Unable to locate the Canadian gunners, the Panzer company commander attempting to break into Bretteville from the east ordered his tankers to use incendiary rounds and set houses on fire for illumination.⁹ The sudden eruption of burning buildings on the town's southern outskirts also glaringly illuminated the other company of Panzers swinging around Bretteville. Despite mounting casualties, 'G' Troop swung its guns onto these new targets with deadly effect. Sergeant Herman Dumas single-handedly hauled his six-pounder along a hedge to fire round after round at almost point-blank range into the Panzers. Bombardier Cyril D. Askin managed to clear a jammed and abandoned gun, bringing it back into action for several accurately placed shots before being mortally wounded. Dumas would win a Military Medal, while Askin received a post-humous Mention in Despatches.¹⁰

The antitank guns pounding the Panthers zeroed in on one troop with shots that struck all three tanks at virtually the same moment. One tank exploded in flame when its engine compartment was pierced, and the crew narrowly escaped being burned alive. Another round punched through the troop commander's turret, blinding the loader and breaking many of his bones. The tank's electrical system failed. Quickly seizing command of the third tank, which was unscathed despite several hits from the six-pounders, the troop commander radioed a report to his company commander. He was ordered to break off the attack and withdraw, while the rest of the company would continue its flanking effort.¹¹

The Panzer Grenadiers to the east had by now bogged down on the edge of Bretteville and, according to platoon leader Untersturm-führer Reinhold Fuss, were forced "to withdraw under the vast enemy fire superiority."¹² Meyer hastily reorganized the battered infantry and flung one platoon at the town's far right, while the other tried to infiltrate through the outskirts to the left rather than drive directly up the main street to the church. Their objective was to rally on the church tower, where, if they found no Canadian tanks in place, they would fire signal flares and the Panzers and remaining infantry would then invest the town. Fuss commanded the rightward probe. The two-pronged attack failed as the leftward platoon was discovered and thrown back by 'A' company within minutes of its attempt to push into the town. Fuss, meanwhile, managed to reach the main square, but had only six men left "after a lot of violent shooting."

Seeing no tanks, he fired the signal flare and hurried his men into the dubious shelter of the church to await the Panzers.[13]

JUST BEFORE MIDNIGHT, Captain Gordon Brown, who had only assumed command of the Regina Rifles' 'D' Company that morning, looked out a hole in the wall surrounding la Ferme de Cardonville and saw his "worst fears... realized." Several massive tanks from the company trying to outflank the Bretteville defenders ground along the Caen-Bayeux highway directly towards the old farm. The captain cursed these Germans for not playing by the book. Sound military doctrine held that any armoured attack against the farm should have come from the open ground to his west, certainly not from out of the very middle of the Reginas' battalion area. Brown's antitank guns were all facing the wrong direction. Suddenly, from Bretteville, a salvo of small flares shot into the sky and in their glare Brown saw even more tanks heading to attack Bretteville from the east. "So much for the book," he thought.

Brown was about to run over to the gun crews and order them to swing the six-pounders around when he glanced one more time out a hole in the east wall of the courtyard. "Right in front of my eyes, a very large gun barrel appeared. It was mounted on a giant tank that moved very quietly along the little road beside the wall." The captain realized that the "tanks were using the rail crossing just a few yards to our left to move toward Bretteville, apparently oblivious of our presence in the farm." Uncertain "if they were aware of us or ignoring us, I realized the precariousness of our situation."

He was also surprised to see that the tanks appeared unaccompanied by any Panzer Grenadiers, rendering them better prey for antitank gunners or infantry armed with PIATS or antitank grenades. What the Panthers hoped to achieve baffled the young officer, for without "infantry support, the tanks were asking for a lot of trouble and could not hold, especially at night, any ground they might seize. It was against all the principles of tank warfare, as we understood them, to use armour in this fashion. I thought perhaps there was a glimmer of hope as I walked past the barn and through a hole in the wall into the orchard."

Brown made directly for the 13th Field Regiment's Forward Observation Officer, manning a radio aboard his Bren carrier, only to discover the FOO sitting perfectly upright but sound asleep despite all the flares and gunfire in the distance. Shaking him, Brown snapped, "For God's sake stay awake. We're being attacked by tanks. Try to get through to battalion HQ or to your regiment. We haven't been able to raise anybody back there at all."

"Sorry sir, I'm just so bloody tired. But I'll stay awake now," the young lieutenant said, and got busy with his radio. Brown moved next to the antitank gunners and, still unsure of his authority as a company commander, asked them politely to move their weapons to the other side of the orchard and open fire on the tanks passing the farm en route to Bretteville. "They opposed the idea on the grounds that we might draw enemy fire. I was exasperated and explained that the battalion HQ was in grave danger of being overrun in which case we would have little or no chance of survival." The sergeant in charge grudgingly agreed to move the guns as quickly as possible.

Dashing back to the farmhouse, Brown reported what he had done to his second-in-command, Lieutenant Dick Roberts, who confirmed that nobody had yet seen any Panzer Grenadiers accompanying the tanks. With a nervous grin, Roberts assured Brown that, in accordance with Matheson's advice, "he was doing his best to 'ignore' the tanks." Brown was impressed by the Regina native's steadiness and equally heartened to see that Company Sergeant Major Jimmy Jacobs, who seemed a "rough and ready NCO seemingly unafraid of anything," was also calmly going about organizing the company.

The company command post was set up in a lean-to attached to the stone farmhouse, with the wireless sets, telephone, and other equipment on a heavy wooden table. Brown found his signaller here trying to raise battalion, but "the phone line was dead and there was nothing but noise on the radio." Suddenly, the signaller shouted that he had Major Tubb over at 'C' Company on the wireless. Brown grabbed the microphone like a drowning man snatching at a rope, and asked how things were in Tubb's area. "Oh, we're fine," Tubb said. Brown wondered what they should do about the tanks "roaming all over the place?"

"Well, there's not much we *can* do, is there?" Tubb replied, with "no hint of alarm in his voice." Brown was certain Tubb's "calculated approach to battle was the way in which a first rate company commander should function. My trouble was that I lacked experience, that I had been away from infantry training for a year, and I felt I did not have Stu Tubb's and Dick Roberts's dedication and courage." The worried officer wished his friend good luck and the two cleared the airwaves in hopes of hearing some news from battalion.

By now, about twenty tanks had passed the farm. Most were standing outside Bretteville, hammering the town with their 75-millimetre guns and machine guns. A few, however, appeared to have pushed in among the buildings and Brown worried that Matheson's headquarters had been overrun. Even in the best-case scenario, the men at battalion HQ "were in a fight to the death, and it seemed possible to us that we might never hear from them again."[14]

CHAOS REIGNED IN BRETTEVILLE, as the Reginas' 'A' Company and headquarters personnel fought the Panthers at point-blank range. The first tanks roaring into the outskirts caught the Bren carrier platoon and the Cameron Highlanders of Canada's No. 4 Platoon digging into a fresh position.[15] Their own machine guns totally ineffectual against the thick armour, the Camerons suffered as the Panthers raked them with machine-gun fire. Several of the carriers were set ablaze by the powerful 75-millimetre guns. In disarray, the survivors scrambled through the streets to the dubious shelter of the perimeter established by 'A' Company and Matheson's headquarters troops across from the historic church.

In his command trench behind the farmhouse serving as battalion headquarters, Matheson saw several tanks push up the streets leading into the town from the east and halt three hundred yards off. Turrets swivelled, like a dog's snout pursuing the source of a tasty scent, and then the guns belched fire. For the next hour and a half, the Panthers slammed shot after shot into one building after another, while their machine guns ripped off continuous streams of bullets. The din of exploding rounds and collapsing buildings was terrific. Smoke and flame boiled in the streets.

At midnight, two Panthers prowled towards the headquarters building. From a slit trench about ten yards to the front of Matheson's command trench, Lance Corporal Bill Burton and Regimental Sergeant Major Wally Edwards watched helplessly as the two tanks "penetrated right up to the front gates" of the farmhouse's courtyard. The lead Panther started punching shells up the street towards the building and raking the courtyard with machine-gun fire. Hidden in a slit trench behind a stone wall next to the gateway, riflemen Gil Carnie, Clarence Hewitt, and Joe Lapointe waited until the Panther was directly beside them. Then Lapointe, knowing the thick armour protecting its front was virtually impenetrable, rose up and fired a round from his PIAT at the tank's more thinly protected flank from a range of just fifteen yards. The small two-and-a-half-pound hollow-charge explosive bomb struck home. The tank hesitated before rolling on another thirty yards as Lapointe and the other two men reloaded the awkward infantry antitank grenade launcher. When the rifleman's second round struck the Panther, it swivelled about and began withdrawing, but Lapointe quickly fired a third round that caused the big tank's rear end to slew into a wall. Here, RSM Edwards had stacked a necklace of Type 75 antitank grenades, intending to string it across the road in the event of a tank attack, but had been unable to finish the job before the tanks arrived. As the back of the tank struck the stack of explosive charges, it set them off and lit the Panther's engine compartment on fire. As the crew attempted to escape, the Reginas cut them down.[16]

"During this incident," Matheson wrote, "the second Panther had remained further up the road. Seeing the fate of its companion, it commenced to fire both 75-millimetre and MG wildly down the street 'like a child in a tantrum,' doing no damage whatsoever except... to the first Panther."[17] For his part in killing that first Panther, Lapointe was awarded a Military Medal.

Captain A.C. Vassar Hall disagreed with Matheson's assessment that the second Panther's fire caused little destruction. He arrived in Bretteville from Juno Beach at the same time Meyer's attack came in and, like Brown at la Ferme de Cardonville, realized the antitank gunners had their weapons pointed the wrong way to meet the tanks. As he tried to help the gunners rectify this error, "from the immediate area of battalion HQ there was a loud explosion and soon flames were visible above the intervening buildings." Running to the corner of a stone wall that surrounded the church, Hall glanced around it and was "astonished by the sight of a large German tank burning furiously and partially blocking the road right in front of battalion HQ." He watched "one of the crew scrambling out of the control tower, silhouetted by the flames coming from the rear of the tank. Though momentarily spellbound, I was suddenly aware of a tracer MG bullet coming directly at me, fired from a second tank which had been following the first one. I only had a fraction of a second to pull back to the shelter of the stone wall, but not before I received a blow to my cheek as the tracer clipped the corner of the stone wall. It knocked me down temporarily." After a sergeant next to Hall applied a field dressing to his wound, the captain hurried into the battalion headquarters courtyard and took shelter in a trench manned by quartermaster Captain Earl Rouatt. Here "we both watched the tracers flying overhead as the tanks stood off and contented themselves with shelling us for the rest of the night."[18]

Matheson estimated that twenty-two Panthers were circling Bretteville or making forays into the streets. "Fires and flares lit up the area, and the enemy several times appeared to be convinced that opposition had ceased." When a German dispatch rider roared past on a captured Canadian motorcycle, Matheson shot the man down with his Sten gun. Sometime later, a German officer "drove his Volkswagen [scout car] up before battalion HQ, dismounted and gazed about for a few seconds until an excited PIAT gunner let fly with a bomb, which hit him squarely." The officer disappeared in a spray of gore.[19]

It was 0230 hours of June 9 and the battle for Bretteville was stalemated. Although the Reginas were helpless to destroy the tanks unless they strayed into PIAT range, the tankers were equally unable to control the ground. But the German tankers were tough, determined foes, not given to accepting failure. Captain Brown at la Ferme de Cardonville could see the Panthers prowling outside Bretteville and was increasingly angered by the fact that the antitank gunners in the orchard had still not turned their guns to bring these tanks under fire. Until they did so, there was nothing he could do to help the town's defence. Stomping into the orchard, he demanded the antitank gun sergeant explain why they had yet to move. "What, sir, are we going to do about the six tanks that now surround this orchard?" the man asked with quiet resignation.

"'What tanks are you talking about?' I sputtered and he told me 'there are enemy tanks at each corner of the orchard and one on each side.' Peering into the night, I confirmed the tanks were indeed there. In the silence I could hear the quiet idling of their motors." The sergeant said the Panthers had been there for some time and yet seemed unaware of 'D' Company's presence.

Agreeing this was a blessing for the company, Brown set about spreading the word through the ranks that everyone should hold fire and not betray the position through unnecessary movement until he could organize a simultaneous attack on each tank by the two forward platoons. Envisioning an attack "by two or three men, jumping on each tank and slapping sticky grenades on their turrets," Brown knew success depended on achieving complete surprise. No sooner had he returned to company headquarters to put the ball in play than a Sten gun's chatter cut the night. "There goes the old ballgame," Brown muttered, as the tanks replied with a deluge of fire.

"All hell was breaking loose in the orchard. The tanks were firing wildly and tracer bullets darted everywhere. The barn, full of dry hay... had been set ablaze... [and] would burn to the ground quickly. Inside were two of our soldiers looking after our main ammo supply, which unwisely had been stored there. We grabbed as much as we could and... were able to get most of the ammunition out and over to the house. Then we took cover, as there was nothing we could do now for our comrades in the orchard. The tanks set all the vehicles on fire and were busy mopping up the slit trenches, running over weapons and crushing everyone and everything in their path."

The only thing barring the tanks from entering the compound itself was a thick, high wooden gate, behind which Brown strung a necklace of Type 75 grenades. No sooner were the grenades in place than "a tank lumbered up and knocked the gate back while we fired machine guns and rifles, the bullets bouncing wildly off the turret."

This meagre response surprisingly deterred the tank commander from pushing into the tight space. Instead, the Panther reversed and rumbled alongside the farm's east wall. The other tanks joined and ground around the farm like Hollywood Indians attacking a circled wagon train, pounding the wall with gunfire and machine-gunning the stone house. But Brown realized they were afraid to enter the compound without infantry support.

"We adopted an almost passive strategy... partly because we were trying to ignore the tanks and mostly because we couldn't do anything about them anyway. We no longer had the antitank guns... Some of our men fired machine guns through holes in the walls, just to remind the tank men we were still there.

"Casualties among our troops began to multiply as machine gun and shellfire were taking their toll... It seemed only a miracle could save us." Dawn was not far off and Brown prayed fervently that its arrival would bring Typhoon fighter-bombers to destroy the Panthers with rockets and bombs. Suddenly, there was a lull and then the tank fire trailed off altogether. Peeking out a loophole in the wall, Brown saw the tanks withdrawing across the railroad towards German lines.

Taking stock of the remnants of his company, Brown counted only fifty men still capable of fighting. "We were a motley looking bunch—uniforms muddy, wrinkled and shabby; several days growth of whiskers accentuated the grim and drawn appearance of the young faces. Most of the soldiers were in their late teens or early twenties, but they were aging rapidly as the horror of what they had seen began to sink in. Some were shivering, not from cold but from exhaustion, and all were apprehensive as to what would happen now."

A makeshift first-aid station in the house overflowed with wounded, and dead lay strewn through the orchard. Brown clustered the remaining soldiers at various points along the farm walls. "Everyone realized the house with its thick walls had now become a fortress and we were probably facing a fight to the finish... There was no choice but to see it through to the bitter end." With so few men, almost every man was able to set up behind an automatic weapon—some equipping themselves with German machine pistols. Brown expected the German infantry must have been waiting for the tanks to soften them up, and would come across the railway at dawn. "We didn't know if the rest of the Regina Rifle Regiment had survived the tank attack. Our prospects... were not encouraging."[20]

BROWN WAS UNAWARE that with the withdrawal of the Panthers from the farm, Meyer's assault had ended. Having thrown his men into the attack with such bravado, Meyer had soon looked upon a battleground where everywhere he turned old comrades from Russia sprawled dying on the ground. Tears streamed down his face. Leaping aboard a motorcycle, he had tried to drive into Bretteville to join the leading elements of the Panzer Grenadiers, only to have the fuel tank riddled with bullets and set alight. Several of the young troopers had grabbed Meyer, who was "burning like a torch," and rolled him in the muddy roadside ditch to smother the flames—quick action that left the officer uninjured.[21]

Having committed too few infantrymen, Meyer was unable to support the Panthers properly—a situation that only escalated as the motorcycle troops suffered heavy casualties in the intense fighting. Finally, after six hours of trying to press home the attack, Meyer bitterly conceded failure. At about 0430 hours, with the first hint of dawn tingeing the eastern skyline, the German force pulled back from Bretteville to a position east of the River Mue, near Rots. When Wünsche dismounted from his Panther, a concentration of artillery fire caught the cluster of tanks and the tank commander was slightly wounded in the knee by shrapnel fragments.

While Meyer received reports on his casualties, the 26th Panzer Grenadiers belatedly appeared on the battlefield stage left with the dawn assault on la Ferme de Cardonville that Brown had expected. The captain was just stepping out of the overflowing aid post when a soldier yelled, "Here they come," and opened up with automatic fire. Again, Brown was stunned by the attack's tactical stupidity. "If the infantry had not supported their tanks under cover of darkness, who would launch an attack in broad daylight without artillery or tank support?" he wondered. As Brown frantically tried to establish radio contact with Matheson's headquarters to seek artillery fire, CSM Jimmy Jacobs reported that there were about two hundred Germans "and they just keep coming."

"Every automatic weapon along the wall came into play. There was much shouting and cursing as the men called out warnings and there were screams from the wounded Germans as they fell. Guttural commands could be heard through the din." Lieutenant Roberts quickly rushed several men into the upper storey of the farmhouse, from where they could better bring the railway cutting being used by the Germans for a rally point under fire. Each time a wave was thrown back, the Panzer Grenadiers regrouped and tried again. Roberts pounded down the stairs from the attic and yelled that he had seen "a bunch of enemy crawling through the wheat and probably trying to surround us... We're in serious trouble." As the lieutenant ran back upstairs, he shouted over his shoulder that artillery was desperately needed.

Brown knew that, but had been stymied in trying to reach anyone on the wireless or phone. Just then, to his surprise, a voice over the wireless said, "Sunray [code for commander] here."

"Sunray, I'm sure glad to take this call," Brown cried excitedly.

His response was met by heavy breathing and then someone speaking English with a thick German accent inquired, "Allo, Englishman... Are you lonely?" over and over again.

Deciding that no divine intervention in the form of artillery was likely, Brown lugged one of the surviving Vickers heavy machine guns up to the farmhouse's top storey. As Brown, the Cameron gun crew, and a few Reginas began setting up the heavy weapon, a German soldier appeared about twenty yards from the farm wall and fired a burst through the window that Brown planned to use as a firing port. A tracer "snapped past me and struck a Cameron soldier setting up the gun. There was a violent explosion and the Cameron was thrown up to the ceiling. Shrapnel ricocheted around the room. The [Cameron] sergeant was hit and he jumped away from the gun shaking his wounded right arm with his left. Apparently the gunner who was hit had been carrying a couple grenades in the front of his tunic. The tracer had set them off causing a devastating blast in a confined area." Realizing the Vickers was too vulnerable in the up-stairs position, Brown ordered it taken back to the farm compound and deployed in a more traditional manner where it could fire along fixed lines from a dug-in position.

He then fetched a light machine gun and a German rifle from the weapons dump and found a place on the gun line. Infantrymen were more badly needed now than someone trying to exert command control, he reasoned, as he slipped into a trench in front of a loophole in one of the walls. Then a German artillery shell whistled in and ripped several of the heavy tiles off the roof of the house. Recognizing that this changed the balance, Brown decided he had to go back to being an officer and raced for his command post next to the farmhouse. "Shell after shell came over and exploded against the building and stone fences... [CSM] Jacobs and I lay on the floor, arms covering our heads while the barrage pounded around us." When the artillery lifted, a quick check surprisingly revealed that only two men by one wall had been slightly wounded by shrapnel.

Brown found Roberts still in the attic despite the fact that much of the roof had been blown away. The two men could see Germans form-ing up for a renewed attack in the cover of a smaller farm about two hundred yards south of the railroad. If he could bring artillery onto that position, Brown could seriously disrupt their preparations. But there was nothing he could do, as the "now familiar line of grey uni-forms and bucket style helmets were dashing across the railway to-ward us again... I went back to the command post as a burst of bullets splattered the wall just ahead of me. A gaping hole in the front wall was allowing the enemy to send MG fire through to the entrance of our post." Jacobs shouted that there were Germans gathering against the walls and they would soon start lobbing grenades into the compound. The normally unflappable CSM told Brown, "We're in real trouble."

Suddenly, the signaller yelled that he had battalion HQ on the wireless and this time it was for real. Brown shouted into the handset that he urgently needed to speak to Matheson. "Gord, is that you?" Matheson asked. "How are you?"

"Sir, we can't hold out much longer," Brown replied. "Can you help us? We need artillery and tank support. Heavy infantry attacks on us."

Without ado, Matheson got 13th Field Artillery's commander, Lieutenant Colonel F.P.T. Clifford, on the horn. Brown reported that the FOO from the artillery regiment assigned to the company was probably lying dead in the overrun orchard. He then described the situation and read off the map coordinates for Cardonville. "We need a good stonk on the [small] farm and then a barrage back from there to the rail line in front of our position. Can you see on the map what I'm talking about? We can't last much longer, sir."

Matheson broke in to ask how long Brown thought he could hold. After a quick consultation with Roberts, the captain said, "About twenty minutes, Sir. That's it."

Clifford cautioned that the barrage back from the farm to the rail line would roll up perilously close to Cardonville and "might hit your forward position."

"We'll have to take that chance, sir," Brown said.

Clifford said, "Tell your boys to take cover. They've only got a few minutes before the first shells come over their heads."

Brown and Roberts hurriedly spread the word and just two minutes later, the first 105-millimetre shells "came screeching over the farm and landed squarely in the enemy's farm. The roar was deafening as the mobile guns poured hundreds of rounds into the target. God Almighty it was marvellous. I'd never been so pleased with anything. It was a work of art. Col. Clifford had instructed his gunners well, as not one shell landed on us, although dozens struck no more than a few yards from our front wall... The concussion seemed earth shattering as the uproar lasted about 10 minutes."

When the firing lifted, Brown glanced out a hole in the south wall. The ground beyond "looked as though it had been ploughed over in the enemy's farm... Smoke was still rising from the shelling." The artillery fire had the desired effect—the Germans made no further attempts to take the farm by storm, confining themselves instead to aggressive sniper harassment and random concentrations of mortar fire. After the ferocity of the night and early morning assaults, 'D' Company considered such actions little more than a tiring nuisance.[22]

WITH 26TH PANZER GRENADIER Regiment's failure to take la Ferme de Cardonville, the 12th ss attempt to break through 7 CIB's front to Juno Beach was broken. The division paid a bloody price for the decisive defeat. Even though the 12th ss official statistics were generally overly conservative, the reported losses admitted 152 casualties—43 dead, 99 wounded, and 10 missing. As for tanks, the division confessed to the total loss of six Panthers. The 12th ss divisional historian conceded that while use of mobile, fast infantry, and Panzers organized into small battle groups had proven itself repeatedly in Russia, the tactic failed "here against a courageous and determined enemy."[23]

A byproduct of the defeat, Matheson noted, was that "the dreaded Panther, from being an invincible monster, became a clumsy machine which could be dealt with at close quarters by coolness and cunning." He estimated that half the tanks knocked out had fallen prey to PIATS.[24]

The Reginas counted only their fatal casualties in the battle, with eleven men killed during the night assault and thirty-three more on June 9.[25] The Camerons had been hard hit, with 'A' Company so badly shredded it was reduced from three platoons to two—No. 3 Platoon at Bretteville had greeted the dawn as a tattered remnant. The company reported eleven killed and ten wounded or missing, most from No. 3 Platoon. This was the heaviest casualty rate the battalion would suffer during any two-day period of the war.[26] The 3rd Anti-Tank Regiment also paid heavily, with the 94th Battery reporting that Lieutenant R.D. Barker and seventeen men were missing, five were dead, and five others wounded. Most of the missing had served in the overrun 'H' Troop. The regiment's war diarist dryly noted that, "while these casualties may be considered heavy, the battery gave a good account of themselves during the engagement."[27]

Although 7 CIB retained or reclaimed all vital portions of its front line by the morning of June 9, so that the 12th ss offensive was ultimately a complete failure, the Canadians protecting Juno Beach knew the battle was far from concluded. Nobody believed that the Germans were going to now go over to the defensive and abandon further attempts to throw the Allied invasion back into the sea.

13

Potential Menace Removed

O N JUNE 6, THE ALLIES had seized the initiative in Normandy. Seventy-two hours later, the Germans were no closer to tipping the balance in their favour. Although the invasion plan had envisioned far grander inland gains by D+3, the fact remained that simply by holding the bridgehead the Allies bought vital time to build up manpower, weaponry, and supplies inside the walls of Fortress Europe. Each day that the beaches remained secure from German land, air, and naval attack, the Allied position strengthened, proving that the increasingly defensive posture assumed by the invading divisions constituted an effective strategy. It was also about the only possible strategy, with divisions critically depleted by ever mounting casualties that outstripped the rate of reinforcement coming into Normandy from England. Until General Bernard Montgomery succeeded in putting fresh divisions ashore, a major breakout from the beaches towards Cherbourg or Caen was not feasible. Meanwhile, the seaward security of the beaches and the unfettered movement of shipping across the English Channel remained essential to the continued buildup and resupply of the front-line troops.

The Allies were fortunate that the Kriegsmarine failed to penetrate the defensive screen of aircraft and ships guarding the southern portion of the English Channel. This was not for want of trying. At times, it seemed impossible that the German U-boats and surface ships attempting to close on the beaches and convoy routes should all be thwarted. Certainly, the odds had seemed to favour the Germans on the night of June 7–8, when a 29th MTB Flotilla patrol of four craft commanded by Lieutenant Commander C.A. "Tony" Law aboard MTB 459 encountered two destroyers bearing down on it from Le Havre. Operating in a patrol grid also assigned to Royal Navy destroyers, Law was uncertain whether he faced friend or foe. Consequently, he opted to close on the fast-moving vessels and then issue a challenge. Before he could do so, the two destroyers made their identity known by opening fire at a range of 4,800 yards. The first salvo sent great towers of spray roaring up into the air on all sides of the little boats. Law ordered a charge with pom-pom guns blazing, because the Canadian MTBS had been stripped of their torpedo tubes and refitted with depth charge launchers for an anti-submarine role. Law's decision to attack rather than take flight, noted a later report, was akin to "going after an eagle with a flyswatter."[1]

As the MTB gunners opened fire, the lieutenant commander remembered that the guns were loaded so that the first rounds in the breech were star shells rather than high explosive. These "roared out and landed on the decks of the German destroyers, lighting them up like Christmas trees. The destroyers were a couple of the Möwe class, old, but still formidable. Soon the real stuff came out, and the scarlet glow of red-hot rivets appeared on the enemy's hulls. The range, now 500 yards, continued to close."

But not for long, as Law sensibly ordered the MTBS to turn away in line, with MTB 459 on the rear covering the others with a smokescreen. Having decided a quick bee sting was the best that could be achieved without imperilling the MTBS, Law now sought to break off the action. Racing along at twenty-five knots with shells still bracketing the MTBS, Law asked his coxswain what course they were steering. "Northeast, sir," the man replied.

"For God's sake, you're heading straight for Le Havre," Law snapped. And the destroyers were still "hot on our tails, shooting through the smokescreen." Law ordered the craft turned about to a northwest heading, and at about 0330 hours the destroyers lost interest in the chase. Frustrated by the lack of torpedo firing capability, which could have enabled the MTBS to damage or even sink the destroyers, Law thought the confrontation a total waste and a poor way to end a two-day-long patrol. Still, he breathed a sigh of relief when the boats sailed into their berths. His tired, unshaven crews were obviously looking forward to a well-deserved rest. That, however, would have to wait, as a visit by Vice-Admiral Percy W. Nelles—head of Canadian Naval Mission Overseas—was imminent.[2]

The men had barely enough time to clean up and render the MTBS fit for inspection before Nelles stepped aboard at 0800 hours. He quickly congratulated the sailors on their performance over the last two days, ending by congratulating Law and his men "on keeping the enemy away from the anchorages [off Normandy.]" By unwittingly drawing the destroyers into a northeasterly chase, Law had led them back towards their harbour at Le Havre, to which they opted to return after the MTBS escaped, rather than try again to penetrate the naval screen protecting the beaches.[3]

When Law's four-boat patrol ended its two-day operation, the other half of 29th MTB Flotilla took over the area of responsibility. With one boat down for repairs, the remaining three were commanded by Royal Canadian Naval Reserve Lieutenant C.A. Burk, who bore the curious nickname of "Daddy Bones," on MTB 461. The night of June 8–9 saw the seas running hard, with winds blowing force three out of the northwest. Three miles north of Sword Beach, the MTBS received a wireless message vectoring them towards Cap d'Antifer near Le Havre, but were unable to intercept the German ships suspected to be running for their home port. As Burk ordered the flotilla to cut engines so they could try covertly tracking the destroyers, a large star shell "burst overhead, displaying the three boats standing naked against the black background."[4]

Although illuminated by the star shell, the MTBS were not immediately fired upon—leading to the suspicion that the intent had been to light up the beaches in preparation for a bombardment. The destroyers were just five hundred yards from the MTBS, which were drifting silently on the flat sea. Burk ordered motors started and crept along in the destroyers' wake, shadowing their position in the hope of directing other MTBs or destroyers fitted with torpedo launchers against the German vessels. "But before they had more than got underway the enemy opened fire with rapid and accurate salvos for about ten minutes, [until] the MTBs were able to disengage under cover of smoke. MTB 464 took the brunt of the fire since [its] smoke was covering the others and one of [the] gunners, [Frederick T. Armstrong] was killed, while another crewman was seriously wounded in the back. All boats sustained slight damage but no other casualties, due mainly to the effectiveness of the smokescreen and the evasive tactics of the senior officer. Although it was impossible to claim more than a few hits on the enemy by pom-pom and Oerlikon, the enemy had again been successfully reported and stopped from attacking the anchorage," concluded an official report on the action.[5]

NOT ALL ROYAL CANADIAN NAVY vessels protecting the convoy routes to Normandy were forced to engage the Germans at such disadvantage in armament as the MTBs of 29th Flotilla. Royal Navy planners had long realized that the "greatest danger to the success of Operation Neptune, both during the assault and the buildup phase," was presented by the western approaches to the Channel because of the relative lack of geographical limitations on ship movement. The eastern entrance between Dover and Calais was a natural choke point that could be fairly easily barred to entry by German vessels coming out of ports north of Calais. Consequently, German ships based in Le Havre were the main threat on that front, but their numbers were limited. To the west, the situation was entirely different, for the western mouth "lay open to the broad reaches of the Atlantic and at its narrowest point, between Cap de la Hague on the Cherbourg Peninsula and Portland Bill in Dorsetshire, the Channel was 52 miles broad. Further to the west—the waters between Brittany and Cornwall and Devon—England and France were over 100 miles apart. The speed of modern warships had vastly reduced distance, but in this part of the Channel there was still scope for considerable effort on the part of the enemy" to inflict heavy losses on the invasion convoys or to bring guns to bear on the beaches.[6]

The Germans had many U-boats, small surface craft—such as E- and R-boats—and destroyers concentrated in the large naval bases at Bordeaux, La Rochelle, St. Nazaire, and Lorient. There was also the threat that German ships might move from bases in Norway down the coast of Ireland to gain the western approaches. By the early hours of June 9, the U-boat hazard had been largely thwarted by operations of six escort groups and the Royal Air Force Coastal Command bombers. The Royal Canadian Navy had provided four of these escort groups, of which two were made up of frigates and the other two of destroyers. Frigates *New Waterford, Waskesiu, Outremont, Cape Breton, Grou,* and *Teme* formed Escort Group 6, while *Matane, Swansea, Stormont, Port Colborne, St. John,* and *Meon* composed Escort Group 9. The destroyers *Ottawa, Gatineau, Kootenay, Chaudière,* and *St. Laurent* made up Escort Group 11, and *Skeena, Restigouche, Qu'Appelle, Saskatchewan,* and *Assiniboine* formed Escort Group 12.

For the most part, the frigates, operating outside the Channel in the hundred-mile-wide gap between England and France, endured a boring time trolling without success for U-boats—due to the fact that the German submarine effort was "tentative and uncertain." False contacts were irritatingly common for, as was true in the Channel itself, average depth in this area was sixty fathoms, the waters churned with strong tides and cross-currents, and the bottom was strewn with wrecks of many centuries of seagoing misfortune. Millions of herring swarming the waters in great schools little helped the situation.[7]

The same problems and lack of contact with U-boats plagued the destroyer escort groups working inside the Channel. At about 2000 hours on June 7, however, Escort Group 12 had become locked in a thirty-hour duel with a U-boat thirty miles southwest of Ushant. When Lieutenant Commander D.W. Groos's *Restigouche* picked up an asdic (sonar) contact, U-984 commander Oberleutnant Heinz Sieder attempted to "draw first blood" by launching a torpedo that ran out of control and exploded on the sea bottom.[8] *Restigouche* replied with a hedgehog attack, whereby a launching system fired twenty-four 7.2-inch depth charges in a pattern that struck the water ahead of the attacking ship. None of the charges would explode unless one or more actually clunked against the target submarine's hull, after which all the rest would detonate sympathetically. This avoided the surface ship's asdic being deafened by useless explosions, so there was a better chance of maintaining contact with detected submarines.

When *Restigouche*'s salvo missed, the four ships adopted a square search pattern. At 2057 hours, an explosion accompanied by an eighty-foot-high column of water about 175 yards abaft of *Saskatchewan*'s port beam warned that the sub commander was determined to stand and fight rather than using the confused waters to beat an escape. Eighteen minutes later, a shallow running torpedo sped close past *Skeena*.

Restigouche was coming about slowly at 2125 hours when a lookout sighted a periscope 100 yards off the starboard beam. Lacking sufficient speed for a depth charge attack, the destroyer fired all its guns at the sub. Again, contact was lost. The dance continued, with one destroyer after another establishing contact, sighting a periscope, or detecting great swirls in the water that might mean the U-boat was blowing its tanks to dive deeper.

At the very beginning of the action, the destroyers had deployed an ingenious device developed by the Canadian Navy, known as cat gear, short for Canadian Anti-Acoustic Torpedo. A series of metal bars linked together, it was dropped off the stern and trailed along behind the ship, disrupting the distinctive sound of the propeller that acoustic-guided torpedoes were programmed to seek. The value of this equipment was realized in an unintended way when a torpedo fired at Escort Group 12's command ship *Qu'Appelle* inadvertently struck *Saskatchewan*'s trailing cat gear and exploded. Although the cat gear was destroyed, it had prevented the U-boat from scoring a hit on *Qu'Appelle*.

Following this engagement, contact was lost, but Commander A.M. McKillop decided to linger in the area, hoping to force the U-boat to surface. Another box search was started at 2240 hours.[9] *Restigouche* gained two probable contacts over the next few hours and carried out two attacks, but without result. Finally, at 0600 hours on June 8, McKillop abandoned the square search and formed the ships up in a long line to sweep a greater area at fifteen knots of speed.

Until 0930 hours, nothing happened, then a torpedo exploded near where *Qu'Appelle* was steaming at one end of the line, followed five minutes later by a detonation between *Skeena* and *Restigouche* that threw a large column of water into the air just off *Skeena*'s bow.

Skeena's Lieutenant Commander P.F.X. Russell reported an excellent contact 950 yards away, with the target moving to the right. Then "a great pale blue swirl off [the] starboard bow" led him to believe the submarine was surfacing. *Skeena* charged to within 220 yards of the churning water and fired a hedgehog salvo. "Much air and black globules of oil were seen to rise to the surface," but Russell suspected the hedgehogs had detonated in the sub's wake. At best, the attack inflicted only limited damage, because no sooner did *Skeena* turn away than a torpedo passed her bow from left to right and a periscope was sighted off the port side. Shortly thereafter, another explosion erupted between *Qu'Appelle* and *Saskatchewan*. At 1000 hours, McKillop's ship picked up a good contact, but a hedgehog attack left the surface strewn with nothing but dead fish. When *Skeena* attacked the same contact, it merely added to the carnage. Undaunted, McKillop sent *Qu'Appelle* dashing towards another contact and launched ten depth charges with no discernible result. The water was now strewn with fish carcasses.

Seething with frustration, McKillop signalled Commander-in-Chief, Plymouth Vice-Admiral Sir Ralph Leatham: "An all day search in terrible asdic conditions produced nothing more than a few tons of fish."[10] Although the pursuit continued until 2100 hours, only a few fleeting contacts resulted and finally Escort Group 12 was ordered to clear the area to avoid being mistaken for a force of German destroyers being hunted nearby by 10th Destroyer Flotilla.

THIS FLOTILLA WAS DIVIDED into two divisions with four ships in each. Five of the destroyers were Tribal class, two Fleet class destroyers, and one a Polish-designed vessel. All four ships in 19th Division were Tribals: HMCS *Haida* and HMCS *Huron* were joined by HMS *Ashanti* and *Tartar*—which was the flotilla's command ship under the capable hands of Commander Basil Jones, RN. The Tribals were beautifully designed superdestroyers that displaced 1,960 tons when standard loaded and had twice the firepower of conventional British destroyer designs. Each ship boasted three twin-mounted 4.7-inch guns, one twin 4-inch high-angle gun, and four 21-inch torpedo tubes. Top speed was thirty-six knots and the ships' crews numbered between 238 and 259.

Haida's skipper was Commander Harry DeWolf and *Huron*'s was Lieutenant Commander H.S. Rayner. Both were regular RCN officers, who had built good wartime reputations. Rayner was considered an expert in torpedo warfare and held a Distinguished Service Cross for bravery in a previous action, but DeWolf's reputation placed him head and shoulders above all peers. Jones considered the Bedford, Nova Scotia native "an outstanding officer, not only in skill but aggressive spirit. Furthermore he had that priceless gift of fortune... of there always being a target in whatever area he was told to operate."[11]

On the morning of June 8, Vice-Admiral Leatham, in an unusual move, ordered all eight destroyers of 10th Destroyer Flotilla to concentrate at a point about fifty miles due south of Land's End. Leatham was responding to a warning from the Ultra cryptographers reading the Kriegsmarine's Enigma machine, which issued orders controlling surface ship movements. This report confirmed that four destroyers were departing the harbour at Brest, bound for the Channel. At about 1630 hours, Leatham, having in his hand from Ultra the full details of the enemy destroyers' course and speed, vectored the flotilla onto a northeasterly trending intercept course at twenty-two knots.[12] Leatham insisted that the flotilla be precisely sixteen miles north of Île de Bas no later than 2145 hours. From there, the ships would sweep westwards at twenty knots of speed to a point fifteen miles northeast of Île de Vierge and then patrol in a generally reversed direction until 0400 hours. The vice-admiral expected that the flotilla would have by then either encountered the German ships or that his intelligence would have been in error. If by 0400 hours no Germans had appeared, 10th Flotilla was to return to Plymouth.[13]

Aboard *Tartar*, Jones instructed his other ship commanders to form up by divisions, with 20th Division two miles off from 19th Division. Each division spread out, so that in the 19th *Tartar* led, with *Ashanti* 200 yards astern on her port quarter, *Haida* 1,200 yards astern on her starboard quarter, and *Huron* 2,000 yards directly astern of *Tartar*. In the 20th Division, the Polish-built ORP *Blyskawica*, HMS *Eskimo*, the British-built Fleet class ORP *Piorun*, and HMS *Javelin* adopted an identical formation.[14]

As 10th Flotilla began its search, the four German destroyers steamed north on the heading reported by Ultra. These ships constituted the 8th Zerstörerflotille and consisted of three destroyer types. z-32 and z-24 were Type 36A destroyers dubbed Narviks, which displaced 3,000 tons, had a top speed of thirty-eight knots, and were armed with five 5.9-inch guns and eight 21.7-inch torpedo tubes. A captured Dutch destroyer, redesignated ZH-1, was slower and smaller than the Narviks and mounted five 4.7-inch guns and eight 21.7-inch torpedo tubes. T-24 was not in the same class as the other three ships at all. A Type 39 fleet torpedo boat, T-24 weighed only 1,300 tons and carried four 4.1-inch guns and six 21.7-inch torpedo tubes for armament. It could also manage no more than twenty-eight knots, which meant that speed—the Narviks' greatest asset in battle—was compromised if the four ships were to fight as a unit.[15]

By 2200 hours, the 10th Flotilla was on stations north of Île de Bas and started a zigzagging sweep southeastwards at twenty knots. As the hours passed, the crews struggled to remain alert. The ships were blacked out. Everyone had been warned to prepare for surface action. In stuffy cabins below deck or on the bridge, some crewmen monitored various instrument panels, while the steel-helmeted "gunners waited beside the hatches of the opened magazines... grimly phantom-like with the white of anti-flash gloves running up their forearms and white canvas masks drooping from beneath their helmets to their shoulders, leaving only the eyes and noses visible... In the sick bays and wardrooms medical officers and attendants cleared extra space, laid out their instruments, drugs and blood plasma... Seamen off watch sat or lay or slept beside their action stations, on deck, along dimly-lighted companionways, at the foot of ladders; wherever there was room... Deep beneath them the throbbing engines, nursed by men who would have the least chance of escape from disaster, sent the destroyers weaving onward, twenty degrees to starboard, twenty degrees to port along the mean line of their course... The questing beams of radar sought out and returned with the numberless impressions which sent the running green ribbon of each operator's dial rising in jagged crests and falling away into troughs like the sea about it."[16]

It was a dirty night with intermittent rain squalls and thickening low cloud hampering the radar search. Midnight came and went with no contact, but at 0100 on June 9, about twenty miles northwest of Île de Bas, as the ships turned towards their westwards sweep, an echo off *Tartar*'s port bow was detected at a range of ten miles. *Huron* and *Haida* chimed in a few minutes later, with echo reports at 19,000 and 20,000 yards respectively. At 0120 hours, Jones ordered the ships to cease zigzagging and increase speed to twenty-seven knots. There was no question that the echo was a ship bearing eastwards. In short order, radar confirmed four echoes steering a course of 085 degrees at twenty-six knots and six miles off.

Jones ordered a turn to starboard to spread his ships across the enemy's bearing in a rough formation of line abreast. For 19th Destroyer Division, this put *Tartar* on one end of a long line with *Ashanti* off to port, then *Huron,* and finally *Haida*. The 20th Division was 20 degrees off the 19th's starboard quarter, but inexplicably ignored Jones's order and remained in the traditional British navy line ahead formation in which the ships advanced single file and those behind the leader were thus unable to bring fire to bear directly ahead of the column.[17] Suddenly, the moon broke through the clouds to bathe the racing ships in a ghostly white light. Lookouts on both the German ships and those of 19th Division could clearly see the opposing destroyers closing on each other, while 20th Division, two miles to the north, remained undetected by either the enemy's radar or lookouts.

Standard German destroyer doctrine when faced by attacking surface ships was to immediately fire torpedoes, and then break away to beat a hasty escape while the Allied ships scrambled to avoid the deadly charges. True to form, the Narviks and ZH-1 each fired four torpedoes at 19th Division from a distance of four miles and turned hard to port. But, expecting precisely this move, Jones had ordered his ships into the line abreast pattern in order to allow maximum flexibility for dodging torpedoes without losing the momentum of the charge. The formation also allowed each ship to bring both forward-mounted 4.7-inch gun turrets to bear. Jones's intention was to force the Germans to stand and fight in a "pell-mell battle" at close range.[18]

Having gained this opportunity, Jones ordered the four Tribals to open fire, while at the same time quickly shortening the range. *Tartar* scored four hits on the German flotilla leader's z-32 before she turned north and headed unknowingly straight towards 20th Division, at which point Jones shifted his attention to the other three destroyers. Instead of following the route taken by their leader, the other German ships turned 180 degrees to the west. *Tartar* and *Ashanti* both brought zh-1 under fire, registering several hits, while *Haida* blasted away at z-24 and *Huron* at t-24. All the German ships were spewing smoke to screen their movement, so that a thick oily pall hung over the water and the battle quickly degenerated into confusion, with ships blundering about half-blind.

Still advancing line ahead, 20th Division opened fire on z-32, scoring several hits before *Blyskawica* veered to starboard instead of towards the German destroyer when it replied with a torpedo launch. With the Polish ship streaming a smokescreen in its wake, the rest of the division followed, losing all contact with the enemy. The 19th Division was left to fight alone—at one-to-one odds.

z-32 wasted no time taking advantage of the new situation by doubling back in an attempt to regroup the German force and make for the English Channel, but at 0138 hours *Tartar* wheeled towards her. A brisk engagement ensued, with both ships scoring hits. Three 5.9-inch shells from z-32 tore into *Tartar*. The first started a raging fire in front of the foremost funnel, the second sprayed the bridge with splinters, and the third sliced through the foremast, wrecking all the wireless and radar aerials. The bridge was transformed into a slaughterhouse, with four officers killed and thirteen men wounded.

As most of the ship's crew turned to fighting the fire that threatened *Tartar*'s survival, Jones ordered the speed cut to six knots and turned the destroyer northwards to escape the wind fanning the blaze. The flotilla commander was out of the battle, forced to concentrate on saving his badly damaged vessel.

Before z-32 doubled back, *Tartar* and *Ashanti* had jointly savaged zh-1. Several shells punched through the engineering plant, cutting all power so she came to a complete halt. Groping through the dense pall caused by smokescreens and burning ships, *Ashanti* spotted the stricken vessel off to her port side. Swinging slightly starboard, the British destroyer fired four torpedoes at a range of 1,500 yards. Two struck home, one on the stern and the other the bow. A great explosion ripped the bow off, but still the vessel refused to sink. Circling zh-1, *Ashanti* battered her with shells fired at point-blank range, until at 0230 hours the crew took to lifeboats. Below decks, zh-1 was ablaze, and flames soon appeared on her superstructure. *Ashanti* ceased fire, and ten minutes later the ship "blew up with a terrific explosion... visible for miles."[19] After dawn, the British 14th Escort Group fished 120 survivors from the sea.

Despite zh-1's demise, the battle went on unabated. *Haida* and *Huron* gave chase to z-24 and T-24, now both trying to break contact. Initially, DeWolf aboard *Haida* concentrated his guns on the faster destroyer. Several hits caused severe damage and many casualties. But when the destroyer's covering smokescreen rendered accurate shooting impossible, DeWolf ordered the guns shifted to support *Huron*'s attack on T-24. Through deft manoeuvre, *Huron* gained an advantageous angle on the German ship and Rayner ordered three torpedoes fired. All missed. After successfully dodging the torpedoes, T-24 turned hard off its southwards line of travel and struck off to the east, plunging into the midst of a British minefield. Obviously a move of desperation, the ploy forced the Canadians to abandon their pursuit due to standing orders prohibiting any entry into Allied minefields. The two ships turned to starboard to clear the field, enabling T-24 to gain a significant lead. When the German ship emerged from the other side of the minefield, it sped at twenty-eight knots towards Brest, with *Haida* and *Huron* trying to get back into gun range at a speed of thirty-one knots. With a 19,000-yard lead, the

German ship managed to shake radar contact. The two Canadian ships finally abandoned the pursuit at 0215 hours and steamed back towards the rest of the division, looking for the stricken *Tartar* because Jones had broadcast a signal calling for the flotilla to rally on his position.

At 0227 hours, a ship steaming on a northwesterly heading at slow speed was sighted. DeWolf and Rayner both thought this was *Tartar,* so *Haida* flashed an identification light signal. Suspicions raised by an unintelligible reply, DeWolf ordered guns brought to bear on the ship, while issuing a new signals challenge that met the same response. Up to this point, the ship had been converging with the Canadian destroyers, but suddenly it swung southwards while dropping a smoke float to create a covering screen. The chase was on, with all the ships plunging through rough seas at speeds exceeding thirty knots, their decks awash with saltwater.

At 0255 hours, the Canadians had narrowed the distance to 7,000 yards and opened fire with a star shell that illuminated z-32 running before a thick white smokescreen. Caught in the glare of the illumination round, the German ship swerved eastwards before turning hard again to the south when *Haida* and *Huron* opened fire with their main armament. The German ship replied with illumination rounds and shells that kicked up waterspouts near the Canadian ships.[20]

On *Haida,* the gun crews responded with rapid salvoes until DeWolf decided they were wildly inaccurate and ordered the rate of fire slowed to between five and six salvoes a minute. Although neither DeWolf nor Rayner could see whether their fire was accurate, z-32 was being constantly straddled and taking numerous hits. At 0500 hours, three shells destroyed her forward turret and the port engine sputtered to a halt. Several more hits followed, until finally at 0513 hours, the starboard engine of the ship, now burning from end to end, also died. Her commander ordered the mortally damaged vessel run aground on the rocky shore of Île de Batz.[21]

Seeing the German ship reduced to a helpless wreck, *Haida* and *Huron* turned away to join the rest of the flotilla. The German destroyer flotilla no longer posed a threat to the invasion convoys. z-24 would be weeks in repair yards at Brest, while T-24 was too small to operate alone. The admiralty soon signalled 10th Flotilla with a message of congratulations to the effect that its action against the German destroyers had resulted in "a potential menace to the main operation [being] removed."

A veritable shower of awards poured down upon the officers and crew of the two Canadian ships. DeWolf, already having won the Distinguished Service Order in a previous engagement, was awarded the Distinguished Service Cross for his part in the action, while Rayner added a bar to his DSC. *Huron's* 1st Lieutenant B.C. Budge and *Haida's* Radar and Director Control Officer, Lieutenant C.N. Mawer, received DSCs. Three other *Haida* officers were Mentioned in Despatches. Six Distinguished Service Medals were awarded to ratings aboard the two ships and a further ten were Mentioned in Despatches.[22]

Canadian war correspondents rushed to capitalize on the success achieved by *Haida* and *Huron*, lionizing the ships and crews in countless stories. It was a welcome turn for the Royal Canadian Navy, which had "spent most of the war toiling in relative obscurity on the harsh North Atlantic."[23]

ONE ALLIED UNIT that never had to fear being out of the spotlight was the Royal Air Force's 617 Squadron, the renowned Dam Busters. Early in the morning hours of June 8, this squadron had debuted the use of a new type of bomb known as the Tallboy. Weighing 12,000 pounds, the cigar-shaped Tallboy contained 5,600 pounds of Torpex (torpedo explosive). Specially angled fins produced a rapid spin that, combined with a twenty-thousand-foot minimum release altitude, ensured the bomb attained supersonic speed. A Tallboy could penetrate sixteen feet of concrete on impact or bury itself two hundred feet into the earth before its detonators were triggered. A hundred-foot-wide crater would result, with shockwaves rippling out to create a localized earthquake capable of collapsing buildings.

On the night of June 8–9, twenty-five Lancaster bombers from 617 Squadron lumbered into the air heavily loaded with ordnance. Eighteen carried a single Tallboy, while the others were each loaded with eight standard 1,000-pound bombs. Their target was the Saumur Railway tunnel and a bridge crossing of the Loire River about 125 miles south of the Normandy battleground. Flying ahead of the bombers were ten Lancasters from 83 Squadron, RAF, equipped with marker flares to be dropped on the tunnel entrances. 617 Squadron had also added three Mosquitos, which were to precede the Lancasters with pinpoint bomb strikes on the tunnel mouths and to also mark these openings with flares. Wing Commander Leonard Cheshire was at the controls of one of these Mosquitos.

Piloting one of the Lancasters armed with a Tallboy was twenty-three-year-old Flying Officer Don Cheney of Ottawa. With more than twenty missions under their belt, Cheney and his crew were typical of the highly experienced Dam Busters, despite only having recently joined the squadron as part of a volunteer draft of veteran crews from other Bomber Command squadrons.

Cheney and the rest of the Dam Busters aloft had been thoroughly briefed on the critical importance of their mission. In the briefing hut, there had been the usual huge curtain-draped map from which the covering was removed only when everyone was settled and ready for the brief to begin. Cheney had noted that the ribbon fastened to the map with push-pins stretched from the base in England to a town in the Loire valley about forty miles west of Tours, and wondered what kind of target they would be attacking.

Cheshire quickly put the men in the picture. Intelligence sources had reported that a German Panzer battalion and other enemy forces, including the 13th ss Panzer Grenadiers Division, were moving by rail towards the Saumur tunnel. They were expected to begin passing through the tunnel on the morning of June 9, with other elements of both units moving by road over the bridge crossing. "We're going to take those targets out tonight," Cheshire said. "And if we can do that, we can delay their arrival at the front by weeks. Not just days, but by weeks."

From the briefing room, the crews had gone to the mess for a traditional pre-operational dinner of bacon and eggs. Then they had waited until the order to board the planes was issued, not long before midnight. When the green flare signalled start engines, Cheney was struck as always during a large raid by the great racket that one hundred Merlin engines winding up at the same time emitted as they coughed, spat, and then roared into life.

On takeoff, one of the Mosquitos had to abort because of a problem with its port engine, but the other planes all got away without incident and the crews settled in for a flight of more than two hours to the target. The two remaining Mosquitos struck first, trying to pitch their bombs into the tunnel openings during a dive from about 3,000 feet to a release altitude of 500 feet. As he pulled away at 0208 hours, Cheshire radioed for the approaching Lancasters to carry out their attack. With the Lancasters strung out in a long line, the bombing continued for thirty-seven minutes. Cheney arrived over the tunnel at 0217. The bombardier reported seeing ten huge explosions close to the target area and two certain Tallboy strikes within fifty yards of the marking flares. Cheney's Tallboy was released at an altitude of 10,500 feet, and the plane pulled away too rapidly for any of the crew to see whether it struck home.

One of the bombs the bombardier had noted landing virtually on target was the Tallboy dropped by Squadron Leader J.C. "Joe" McCarthy, a fellow Canadian, whose bomb pierced the roof of the tunnel, causing a major collapse. This explosion, combined with the earthquake effect of the other detonating Tallboys, caved in the entire roof, plugging the tunnel with thousands of tons of rock and soil. The bridge, too, was destroyed.[24]

The Dam Buster raid was only the most critical part of a major operation on the night of June 8–9 aimed against the railway system being used by German forces to move towards the Normandy beaches from southern France. More than 450 Lancasters, Halifaxes, and Mosquitos from Bomber Command struck railway crossings and vital junctions at Alençon, Fougères, Mayenne, Pontabault, and Rennes with stunning accuracy and a loss of only four aircraft.

14

With Rage and Sorrow

BLOODY TOIL was the order of the day for both the Germans and Allies on June 9, with neither able to gain significant advantage or to wrest control of essential ground from the other. Late the previous day, General Bernard Montgomery had realized that continuing to attempt seizing Caen with frontal attacks was futile. Despite his dislike for altering offensive plans midcourse, there was no alternative. Having established a tactical headquarters for himself in Creully's ancient castle, Montgomery pondered maps and considered the dispositions of units. "I have decided not to have a lot of casualties by butting up against the place," he then announced. "So I have ordered Second Army to keep up a good pressure [in front of Caen] and to make its main effort toward Villers-Bocage and Evrecy, and thence southeast toward Falaise."[1]

This shifted the impetus of operations from directly north of Caen, where 3rd British Infantry Division and 3rd Canadian Infantry Division had originally been tasked with battering their way head-on into the city, in favour of a flanking attack. Too cautious and shrewd a tactician to believe a single southeast hook could necessarily reach Caen, he decided to simultaneously pass the 51st Highland Division through 6th Airborne Division's lines east of the River Orne to strike the city from that flank. These two pincers would encircle the city, and when their dagger-like leading edges met, any enemy within the city and environs would be trapped. To ensure that the Germans were prevented from taking flight before the pincers closed on the Falaise plain, Montgomery intended to drop the 1st British Airborne Division in the Odon valley at Noyers and Evrecy to block the obvious escape route.

Montgomery knew he was in a race with his nemesis Generalfeldmarschall Erwin Rommel to develop an offensive plan and be first out of the gate, for surely the German commander was doing precisely the same thing. "If the Germans wish to be offensive and drive in our lodgement area between Caen and Bayeux, the best way to defeat them is to be offensive ourselves and the plan will checkmate the enemy completely if we can pull it off," he said.[2]

The biggest threat to success was the necessary delay before his operation could begin. Although the 7th Armoured Division—tasked with executing the right hook—had landed on D+1, the left-hook force of the 51st Highland Division and supporting 4th Armoured Brigade were still straggling ashore. Landings since D+1 had been severely hampered by the continually worsening maritime conditions created by a series of storm tracks. Montgomery complained that the "bad weather is a great nuisance as what we want now is to be able to take quick advantage of our good position by striking deep before the enemy can build up strength against us."[3] Despite these problems, he hoped to kick off the offensive on June 10.

No sooner was his plan formulated than Allied Expeditionary Air Force commander Air Marshal Sir Trafford Leigh-Mallory scotched the airborne drop, scheduled for daylight to avoid the chaos that had plagued the D-Day landings. To adequately protect the planes carrying the airborne division, Leigh-Mallory would have to shift fighters away from the tight protective cap cast over the sea lanes and Normandy beaches to fend off incursions by the Luftwaffe. While the German air force seldom made more than fleeting appearances, Leigh-Mallory refused to take such a risk. It was also true that the air marshal had little stomach for the dangers inherent in dropping lightly armed troops deep in enemy territory, with nothing but the expectation of army generals that a fast-moving armoured division would arrive in time to rescue them from annihilation.

Montgomery considered Leigh-Mallory's worries baseless, but he also faced opposition from a grave Admiral Sir Bertram Ramsay, who did not like any idea of exposing his precious ships to possible Luftwaffe attack. The airborne troops would hardly be fighting alone, Montgomery insisted, for they would not be dropped until 7th Armoured Division was within reach of Villers-Bocage. Delaying the landings until that moment ensured that artillery regiments would be in range to support the airborne troops. Neither man was swayed by Montgomery's assurances, and as each was his equal in the power structure of Supreme Headquarters Allied Expeditionary Force (SHAEF), he had to reluctantly abandon the airborne feature. "Obviously [Leigh-Mallory] is a gutless bugger who refuses to take a chance and plays for safety on all occasions," Montgomery fumed. "I have no use for him."[4]

Although stripped of his desired airborne division, Montgomery remained confident of success. He just had to beat the Germans off the mark.

Montgomery clearly grasped German intentions, but it was the plan of Panzer Group West commander, General der Panzertruppen Leo Freiherr Geyr von Schweppenburg, that he was in a race to forestall rather than Rommel's. The tank general had little respect for Montgomery, and expected him to dally before launching any major offensive until he had enough strength on the ground that he could attack across a broad front. Rather than passively await the inevitable, von Schweppenburg planned to strike first.

By June 9, he had a battered but still formidable Panzergruppe in Normandy that consisted of three Panzer divisions—the 21st, the 12th, and Panzer Lehr. Driving to the Abbaye d'Ardenne, the veteran tanker ascended the tower that served as Standartenführer Kurt Meyer's observation post and the two men discussed the situation. He worried that Panzer Lehr's left flank might be exposed to attack by the Americans, but there was nothing that could be done to alleviate this threat. If he were to gain the initiative, a coordinated attack by all three divisions was absolutely necessary. On the night of June 10, he warned Meyer, all three divisions must press north on a front extending from

Gold Beach through Juno to just west of Sword. The focal point of the attack would be along either side of the rail spur running from immediately west of Caen to Luc-sur-Mer on the coast.[5]

A fundamental weak link in the British Second Army line still existed here, where the opposing flanks of 3rd British Division and 3rd Canadian Division had not been tightly married. 21st Panzer Division had failed due to a lack of strength and determination to break through to the beachhead on the night of June 6. With three divisions applying overwhelming pressure across a wider front, von Schweppenburg believed he could succeed where one division had met frustration.

To narrow the breadth of the front the divisions must attack, von Schweppenburg ordered Panzer Lehr to shift slightly eastwards and assume responsibility for the ground west of the River Mue— essentially the entire front facing 7th Canadian Infantry Brigade's battalions at Putot-en-Bessin and Bretteville-l'Orgueilleuse. This would enable the 12th ss's 26th Panzer Grenadier Regiment to hand off responsibility for le Mesnil-Patry and Cristot, and move east of the River Mue to fill the gap between its lines and Meyer's, which ran from the bank of the Mue east to Franqueville. The 21st Panzer Division's boundary with the 12th Division's right flank would remain the Caen–Luc-sur-Mer rail line.[6]

Even as von Schweppenburg decided his final deployments, he expressed concern that Norrey-en-Bessin remained in Canadian hands—jutting dagger-like into the belly of the German lines. He and Meyer agreed that Norrey must be recaptured before any future counterattack could be launched in that area.[7]

MEYER, STILL SMARTING from the defeat handed him by the Regina Rifles, intended to eliminate the nuisance of Norrey with typical decisive, bold action. Just that morning, the 12th Panzer Regiment's No. 3 Company, consisting of twelve Panther vs, had arrived in the area of Rots as part of the division's ongoing deployment to the area. Meyer ordered the tanks to attack the village immediately. Lacking any infantry to support the tankers, he promised that the 26th Panzer

Grenadier Regiment's 1 Battalion would carry out a simultaneous assault from the southwest. Both units were to cross their start lines at 1300 hours.

Obersturmführer Rudolf von Ribbentrop, son of the Reich's Foreign Minister Joachim von Ribbentrop, commanded No. 3 Company, but was unable this day to lead his tanks into action due to a wound inflicted by a strafing Allied fighter-bomber earlier. Although the Knight's Cross holder had since discharged himself from hospital without permission to rejoin the company, his arm was swathed in splints and commanding a tank was simply impossible. Instead, Hauptmann Lüddemann, the company's second-in-command, took charge and von Ribbentrop was left to fret on the sidelines.[8] Standing beside von Ribbentrop, as the company commander quickly briefed Lüddemann on how to carry out the assault, was 12th Panzer Regiment leader Obersturmbannführer Max Wünsche. Both officers urged Lüddemann to advance at top speed, the Panzers pausing only to fire their 75-millimetre main guns—highly inaccurate when fired on the move—at tactically important targets.

The attack was scheduled for 1300 hours for a reason. German intelligence had noted an almost clockwork pattern to Allied fighter-bomber operations over Normandy, whereby the pilots stood down around noon for a couple of hours. It was as if pilots all took a break for lunch and a quick nap. Whatever its cause, the regular respite opened a window during daylight hours—normally suicidal for movement without overhanging trees to camouflage vehicles—when tanks could roam freely. No. 3 Company used this opening to jump off from close by la Villeneuve towards Norrey, following the Caen-Bayeux railway. For the first five hundred yards, the ground rose gently, then they passed onto a wide expanse of perfectly level meadows and fields. In the middle of this open ground stood the smoking ruin of Norrey. The only cover for the tanks consisted of a hedge that might mask their approach to the village.

Lüddemann knew the company's only chance was to break into Norrey with lightning speed, allowing no time for the Canadians there to react in a coordinated manner. Drivers slammed accelerators to the limit and the tanks plunged forward and spread out on a broad front, with orders to stop for nothing.

The moment the tanks entered the open plain, the Reginas in Norrey spotted them, but the infantrymen of 'C' Company neither panicked nor scrambled to meet the onslaught headed in their direction. Instead, Major Stu Tubb and his men settled back to confidently watch events develop, for at 0515 hours that morning they had been reinforced by an ad hoc force of nine Shermans from the 1st Hussars. These tanks were positioned outside the village on the eastern flank behind a low ridge that screened their presence from the charging Panthers. In fact, as the Germans closed on Norrey, Lüddemann ordered a leftward swing towards the railroad station on the village's outskirts that brought the tank company to within a thousand yards of the hidden Shermans.

Several of the Canadian tanks were of the Firefly variety. And looking through the aiming sight of Lieutenant G.K. Henry's Firefly was crack gunner Trooper A. Chapman. When six Panthers bore across his front, Chapman coolly held fire until they lined up like ducks in a row. "Then with Trooper 'Sass' Seaman slapping the rounds into the 17-pounder, he fired five times. Five rounds—five Panthers. Before he got to the sixth one another 'C' Squadron tank, commanded by Sergeant Boyle, had accounted for it."9 While the 17-pounders tore into the sides of the Panthers with armour-piercing rounds, the Shermans mounting standard 75-millimetre guns hurled down a heavy, disorienting rain of high-explosive shells that tore up great gouts of earth around the German tanks.

Unterscharführer Alois Morawetz, commanding a lead Panther, heard a muffled bang on the outside of the turret and then the tank swayed as if it had lost a track to an exploding mine. Glancing out of the cupola, he saw an explosion rip the turret off another Panzer. Suddenly, the MG 42 ammunition inside his tank began cooking off and a fire broke out. Morawetz looked down into the main compartment to see that his gunner had been rendered helpless by steel splinter wounds. With flames engulfing the tank's interior, Morawetz frantically wrenched the turret hatch open, bailed out, fell onto the rear engine compartment, and briefly lost consciousness. When he awoke, smoke and fire poured out of the turret hatch. Several other Panzers burned nearby. Morawetz and the other survivors from the tanks, many badly wounded with severe burns, headed back on foot towards the attack starting point. As he set out for the rear, the officer saw five Panthers withdrawing at speed, firing rapidly as they fled. No. 3 Company's attack had ended almost as abruptly as it had started. Of the thirty-five crewmen in the seven Panthers that had been knocked out in a matter of seconds, the 12th ss would record two killed, two officers, four NCOs, and eleven men wounded, and one officer, two NCOs, and eleven trooopers missing. The missing were probably immolated in the tanks.[10]

From near la Villeneuve, Wünsche had watched the Panthers burst into flames and later wrote: "I could have cried with rage and sorrow."[11] Among the wounded was Lüddemann, who was evacuated to hospital and never returned to active duty.[12] As for the Panzer Grenadiers of the 26th's 1 Battalion that Meyer had promised would attack at the same time, they never appeared. The tanks had fought alone and been dealt a stunning defeat.

Not only had No. 3 Company utterly failed, but the rapidity of their defeat greatly bolstered the morale of the 1st Hussars. Until now, the Canadian tankers had dreaded the inevitable day they would encounter Panthers instead of the Mark IVs against which they were more evenly matched. Thirty-two-year-old Sergeant Léo Gariépy figured that "such scores made the enemy hesitate about forcing the issue, and boosted our morale as well as that of the infantry. We found our Shermans were much more maneuverable than their clumsy, low-slung tanks, and we could traverse and fire with much greater rapidity. True, they could out-range us by far, but if you were fortunate enough to see him before he saw you, you could easily work circles round him. We could fire three rounds to his one, and in any given position, stopped or going full speed, forward or in reverse; but he apparently had trouble to fire on the run. We saw that we could not only take it, but dish it out, and this we did that day with gusto."[13]

WHILE THE IST HUSSARS had been shooting up No. 3 Company, the 26th Panzer Grenadiers had been about a mile to the west busily launching a series of determined counterattacks against the Canadian Scottish at Putot-en-Bessin. Meyer's orders that this regiment support the armour were never acknowledged by Obersturmbannführer Wilhelm Mohnke and, given the communication gaps between the two 12th ss regiments and the 26th commander's unsteady leadership the day before, may not have reached Mohnke.

At first light on June 9, Lieutenant Colonel Fred Cabeldu had walked through the positions established during the previous night's fierce fighting. Across the Caen-Bayeux railway cutting, the Germans were heavily dug in and likely to counterattack at any moment. Facing the Germans, in front of the bridge crossing the railroad west of Putot, were the remnants of 'A' and 'D' companies. 'B' and 'C' companies were positioned out on either side but back of the two forward companies, so they could both guard the flanks and serve as a reserve. The battalion perimeter looked much like an arrowhead. It was an uninvitingly grey, drizzly morning, and the men shivered from the combined effects of cold, damp, fatigue, and hunger.

Cabeldu considered the merits of pulling the two forward companies out of the front and replacing them with those in reserve, but decided a switch now would just create disorganization. If the Germans counterattacked before the switch was complete, disaster was assured. Also he "was anxious to hold a strong counterattack force in hand, and therefore reluctant to use either of my reserve companies to reinforce them at this time."[14] Instead, he told Major Arthur Plows, still commanding both forward companies, that there was to be no retreat. They were to fight in place to the last man. He positioned the antitank, mortar, and carrier platoons where they could give the two rifle companies supporting fire.[15]

In his slit trench in 'D' Company's small perimeter, Private R.H. Tutte found "our position in daylight made me wonder a bit. Our whole position took in no more than a piece of ground on the left of the bridge about 200-feet square. Most of our defensive position was in a small orchard between a thick hedge and up to within a few feet of the bridge, this small area under the eye of Lieutenant Butters of 17 Platoon. On the other side of the hedge (away from the bridge) was Coy HQ and most of the remainder of 18 Platoon under Mr. Peck, this all facing the railroad over an open field. Our rear being covered by a few men under Mr. Mollison of 16 Platoon."[16]

Smack in the centre of the orchard stood a disabled German half-track with a heavy gun mounted in its troop compartment. The gun's barrel still covered the road up which Tutte had driven the Bren carrier during the night counterattack. On seeing it, he "wondered how I had ever reached the bridge at all in the carrier."[17]

While 'A' and 'D' companies took stock of their situation, Private Joe Rumney led a patrol through the wreckage of Putot itself and found that the villagers had abandoned the place. As he led the patrol out of a small orchard, a large force of Panzer Grenadiers came through a hedge on the opposite side. The two startled groups of soldiers immediately opened fire and Rumney pulled his men back on the run, managing to effect a hasty escape without loss except for the wounding of one soldier in the foot. Private G.A. Percival, mindful of his hunger, managed to somehow scoop up two chickens as he dashed through a large flock and quickly broke their necks while on the run.[18]

The patrol had no sooner returned to the battalion perimeter than heavy mortar fire slammed down on 'D' Company. From his slit trench, Tutte saw Panzer Grenadiers—many armed with light machine guns—approaching under the covering fire's protection. 'D' Company quickly slashed into the Germans and the attack dissolved in the face of this fire, aided by "a bit of fast action from our own 3-inch mortar."

At 0900 hours, Tutte spotted German tanks prowling behind a hedgerow south of the railroad and Plows was alerted.[19] A few minutes later, the tanks closed to hull-down positions across the tracks and soon "fire from [the] tanks, infantry and artillery [was] brought to bear. Our position was unquestionably critical, the enemy infantry and armour being only 100 to 150 yards away, but the conduct of the men was as usual exemplary and unquenchable. Several times the enemy attempted to launch an attack and each time were forced to retire under the fierce onslaught from our troops small-arms fire. No. 7

Platoon with Sandy Clark was particularly excellent in this regard answering the enemy shot for shot... The position held firm despite a terrific pounding."[20]

Although the tanks kept hammering 'D' and 'A' companies from the other side of the rail cutting, they were unable to cross it and appeared hesitant to try using the bridge. From behind the forward companies, the battalion's six-pound antitank guns and three-inch mortars replied with rapid fire that succeeded in repeatedly breaking up attacks by the Panzer Grenadiers every time they attempted to cross the cutting.

Just before noon, a shell from one German tank plowed into the knocked-out half-track in the middle of the orchard and set it alight. The vehicle proved to be heavily loaded with ammunition of every conceivable type—possibly including some 88-millimetre rounds— which all started cooking off in spectacular explosions. Machine-gun rounds whipped through the air, tracer bullets sizzled brightly over-head, and shrapnel from high-explosive shells sprayed the nearby slit trenches. Whenever a heavy shell detonated, the carrier skittered back about two feet on its rear tracks. Tutte watched in astonishment as the half-track lurched towards a slit trench occupied by two 'D' Company soldiers. The men seemed frozen, unsure whether to risk exposing themselves to all the shrapnel flying about or staying in place and facing the probability of being run over by the vehicle's steel tracks. Finally, as an explosion chugged the half-track to within a foot of the trench, they broke cover and sprinted to safety just before another shell cooked off and the tracks obliterated their slit trench.[21]

Major Plows, meanwhile, had been calling down artillery fire from 12th Field Regiment to help keep the Germans at bay. Suddenly, his radio ceased operating and, lacking grid coordinates, the guns fell silent. Plows looked over to his second-in-command, Captain W.H.V. Matthews, recovered from the effects of a shell blast that had badly dazed him during the night attack, and held up a coin. When the toss went against Matthews, the captain jumped into 'A' Company's Bren carrier and with Private Hank Morrison at the controls raced through intense fire to reach battalion headquarters and re-establish a link to the artillery regiment.[22]

The heavy fire ripping into the company perimeter hit No. 9 Platoon particularly hard, as Lieutenant Bernard Clarke and Sergeant W.A. Paterson were both badly wounded. Then, in the midst of the fury, Private Percival was seen dodging from one slit trench to another, pausing at each hole and "inquiring if anyone had any salt for the chicken he had procured earlier." None of the other soldiers ever knew if he managed to find the precious condiment.[23]

When a tank shell exploded practically on top of one of the two six-pound antitank guns firing briskly from behind 'D' Company, shrapnel wounded the entire crew, but the men on the other gun split up in order to keep both in action. Finally, the German fire slackened, soon slowing to nothing more than intermittent machine-gun bursts from concealed gun positions and desultory sniping by Panzer Grenadiers who had managed to infiltrate nearby hedgerows.[24]

Tutte was kept busy during the fight helping the ever mounting numbers of wounded caught in the front-line position. He even managed to whip up a pot of tea and serve it to two casualties in an attempt to bolster their spirits, because the intense fire made it impossible for him to evacuate them in the still operational Bren carrier. When the main attack petered out, he and some other men hurriedly loaded the wounded and Tutte drove them back to the battalion's aid post. "Some of these wounded men," he noted, "had been lying out since midnight previous, that they were hard hit was evident though they all took it without a murmur."[25]

With the lull in battle, the men turned to eating whatever they could lay hands on. (Presumably Private Percival and his mates in 'A' Company's headquarters section also enjoyed the chicken.) Tutte thought "it was certainly very decent of 'Jerry' to allow a pause for refreshments."[26] For most of the men, however, the meal was limited to hard chocolate pulled from emergency rations, as food was in desperately short supply in the front trenches.

The company commanders took advantage of this relatively quiet time to have "all ranks... take off their shoes and socks for the first time since landing and in many cases shrapnel from the beach area was still imbedded in the fleshy part of their legs. Some were quite badly swollen. There was great danger of gangrenous infection in some of these cases and one or two were evacuated." That these men had borne these discomforts without complaint struck Captain P.F. Ramsay, second-in-command of 'B' Company, as "proof conclusive of the morale and determination of these relatively green troops to do their bit and to keep doing it regardless."[27]

LIEUTENANT COLONEL CABELDU put what he expected would merely be a short interlude before the battle regained its previous feverish pitch to good use by scrounging the rear area and sending every spare soldier—whether cook, clerk, or driver—forward to support the hard-pressed riflemen in the two forward companies. He also attached Lieutenant Bowen's Bren carrier platoon to 'D' Company, a step that not only beefed up its thinning ranks but also provided the extra fire-power of the Bren guns mounted on the carriers.

Major Larry Henderson had arrived from Juno Beach as a replace-ment officer, and Cabeldu assigned 'D' Company to his command. Although Major Plows remained in overall command of the forward two companies, Henderson's presence freed the overextended officer from having to attempt to be everywhere at once. Tagging along with Henderson was a Forward Observation Officer from 12th Field Regi-ment, who introduced himself to Cabeldu simply as Freddie. His presence, and more importantly the accompanying wireless set tuned to the gunners back at Bray, enabled Henderson and Plows to bring down withering fire on the Germans when they attempted another determined counterattack around mid-afternoon.

Henderson noted that the "efforts of our FOO were excellent and very heartening to everyone. Arty support was limited of course when the enemy reached the embankment [railway cutting]. We risked one shoot on the bridge area, which I believe was influential in driving the enemy out, but found it too dangerous to ourselves to repeat. Late in the [afternoon] unfortunately other elements of our arty proceeded to shell us while we were being mortared... at the same time. This, I think, did more to shake our morale than anything throughout the entire day."[28]

The intentional artillery fire laid on by the FOO proved decisive. The Panzer Grenadiers ceased further major assaults, returning

again to long-range harassment by machine guns and close-in sniping with rifles and Schmeissers. As night fell, Plows asked permission to pull 'A' and 'D' Company back about one hundred yards from
the position virtually on top of the railway cutting, to where they
could overlook the ground from a slight rise that offered a better field
of fire. The lieutenant colonel agreed, but again pressed on Plows
that it was essential no further ground be given up no matter how
much pressure was put on the forward companies.[29]

For 'A' Company, noted its war diarist, "it was with a mingled feeling of relief and regret that we gave up that piece of ground so fiercely
wrested and so gallantly defended. Balm, however, was poured on our
wounds by the fact that we knew that, though we would not be there
on the ground, we covered it well by fire, and the Bosche would not
have it."[30]

Cabeldu was frustrated at not being able to pinpoint German positions and movement due to the fact that many of his men, still short
on ammunition for their own weapons, delighted in spraying no
man's land with the vast store of captured Schmeissers and light machine guns in their possession. He sharply demanded this practice
cease "because the difference in the sound of the MGS [makes] it
difficult for us to pinpoint the German tactics." He soon ordered a
virtual ceasefire altogether, when it became apparent that the ss
troops were using the covering darkness to take up positions in the
fields surrounding the battalion and then attempting to draw fire
with searching shots aimed randomly towards the Canadian lines.
Cabeldu issued orders "to withhold all fire unless attacked" to prevent
betraying the location of company perimeters.[31]

At last, battalion headquarters had opportunity to take a full roll
call and determine its casualties during more than twenty-four hours
of near continual combat. The results were sobering, for the Canadian Scottish counted forty-five officers and men dead and another
eighty wounded. Most had fallen during the bloody counterassault
from la Bergerie Ferme to Putot. Cabeldu grimly noted that, taken together with the eighty-eight casualties the battalion had suffered over
the course of D-Day and D+1, one-third of its total pre-invasion
strength was now lost.

For the lieutenant colonel's pivotal role in the long action, during which he responded with strong leadership to one emergency after another, Cabeldu was awarded the Distinguished Service Order. Lieutenant A.C. Peck, who had been wounded during the June 9 German counterattacks but remained on the field until finally ordered by Henderson to report to the regimental aid post, earned a Military Cross.

During the middle of the battle, Padre Robert Seaborn looked about the badly exposed battleground, particularly up the road towards la Bergerie, and noted the many Canadian corpses strewn along it and in the adjacent fields. "Time some of those men were brought in and buried," he decided, but could find no jeep for such a task, and all the carriers were busy with the more pressing duty of running ammunition up to the front and bringing the wounded back to the RAP.

Normally, Seaborn stayed in the RAP during combat in order to succour the wounded. This could range from lighting a cigarette for those too weak to hold a match, fetching a cup of tea for anyone shivering with shock and cold, or, less commonly, sitting by a soldier's side and offering either conversation or prayer to help ease his passage into death. But with the rate of casualties slowing, Seaborn felt it time to turn attention to this other essential task of chaplaincy.

Wandering about the farmyard that battalion headquarters had taken over, Seaborn eventually found a horse in a shed. Ranging farther afield, he discovered an old two-wheeled cart standing by a battered stone farmhouse. He then fetched Sergeant Watkins, who ran the officer's mess, and drafted him as a willing assistant. Horse hitched to wagon, the two men set off and gathered up one wagonload of dead Canadians after another.

Each load was taken to "a quiet little spot protected by a hill that was in an orchard. Here I had some reinforcement troops that had arrived dig some graves and started burying them. The days were hot so I'd wrap them in a blanket and take off their tags and pay books and anything else like personal papers, put these together, and then take the [men] into that field and bury them. Say a few prayers and then I'd sit down and write as soon as I could to the next of kin. It was very exhausting and difficult psychologically. I was pretty young. Didn't do those letters the next day. What you tried to do was you had the information from their pay book, who the next of kin was. Sometimes I knew them, some I knew fairly well. Others might have come up two days before as reinforcements, so I'd always try and have a word with the company commander, the platoon commander, or someone if I didn't know them. Then I'd just have to write a letter saying that their son had been killed and where and when. Killed in action, always. Didn't go into gory details. That wouldn't make sense to anybody. So I'd just write a short letter.

"I was the Anglican padre so I wrote all letters to the non-Romans. We had a Roman [Catholic] padre too. And I wrote some of the Roman letters if I couldn't get hold of him. He was at brigade and many of the Romans had been killed. If he wasn't there to say the Roman prayers [when men were dying or being buried] I would say them. We had the little book, so we could say some of the general ones."[32]

Seaborn was somewhat glad that he was not a native of Vancouver Island, particularly Victoria, from which most of the battalion hailed. The thirty-two-year-old son of an Anglican priest had been born in Toronto and taken a classics degree at the University of Toronto, followed by attendance at Divinity School there. After completing divinity training in 1932, he served various parishes in the city before accepting a position as the incumbent of the congregation in Cobourg, Ontario in 1941. A year later, he joined the army when the Queen's Own Rifles raised a new battalion, but soon after being posted overseas in 1943 was assigned to the Canadian Scottish battalion deployed in England.

One soldier in the battalion described Seaborn as having been the most unpopular man in the regiment before D-Day because his religious zeal was only matched by his nervousness, which seemed to make him incapable of appearing sincere in his desire to be friends with the troops. Then came the invasion, and the same soldier watched with admiration as Seaborn openly faced concentrated machine-gun and mortar fire to bandage and carry wounded soldiers to safety. During one such rescue, he had suffered a flesh wound to the leg, but that never slowed his pace. The soldier wrote his cousin in

Canada, saying another man in his section had told him, "Gee, I wish I was half the man that guy is."[33] For his actions on D-Day, Seaborn had been decorated with a Military Cross.

Not being from Vancouver Island, Seaborn found writing the letters to families of deceased soldiers an easier task because "I didn't know their fathers and mothers. Some of the fellows I got to know quite well and others I just knew by name or even hardly that... Mostly if they died of wounds in the next few hours, I'd just say they were killed in action. I didn't see any sense in making the people at home feel worse."

As for missing soldiers, Seaborn and the battalion adjutant determined early on to delay sending notices that men were missing in action as long as possible. This gave the padre time to "go around and try to find out if anybody could tell me what had happened. Sometimes a man would say something like, 'Yeah, his buddy's over there or that his buddy had just put him in the ground over there.' And so we were able to keep those messages of missing believed killed down to a minimum. I thought one of my responsibilities at this point was to see that they were buried and their graves marked and the location sent into the graves commission with a cross reference on a map, so they could be found and later brought into central graveyards."[34]

Almost as soon as Seaborn started venturing out into no man's land, sometimes with Sergeant Watkins in tow and sometimes alone, Cabeldu expressed concern for the padre's safety. He called Seaborn into his office and ordered him to stop going so far out looking for people. But the padre considered recovering the dead a vital part of his duty. "I'm not able to rush around with a machine gun, but at least I can look after this side of things," he thought. With careful consideration of his actions, Seaborn avoided answering Cabeldu's order with either a yes or no. Thereafter, he was "just a little more circumspect because I thought we couldn't leave them lying out there in such exposed positions."[35]

15

Too Great a Risk

THE HEAVY CASUALTIES 3rd Canadian Infantry Division suffered in the first three days of fighting after D-Day put tremendous pressure on the medical units tasked with caring for the wounded. Three Canadian Field Ambulance units, Nos. 14, 22, and 23, accompanied the division ashore, respectively assigned to the 7th, 8th, and 9th infantry brigades. By June 9, No. 14 Canadian Field Ambulance had established a mobile advanced dressing station at Pierrepont, to which 7th Canadian Infantry Brigade casualties were sent, usually after having their conditions first stabilized at the Regimental Aid Posts. On June 8, the field unit opened a special casualty clearing station in Secqueville-en-Bessin to deal with the collection and treatment of the many Regina and Royal Winnipeg casualties. On that day alone, jeep and ambulance drivers evacuated 115 casualties through Secqueville back to Pierrepont.

Faced with soldiers cracking under the stress of combat, Dr. Robert Gregory, the divisional neuropsychiatrist, organized an exhaustion centre on June 9 in a house next to the Pierrepont facility. Here the division's first battle exhaustion cases were assessed on an individual basis and given what Gregory deemed appropriate care on a soldier-by-soldier basis.[1] Although only Gregory could authorize the evacuation of battle exhaustion cases beyond this facility, a medical officer from each field unit had earlier been trained in initial rudimentary treatment. This intervention consisted of little more than a sedation program of battle exhaustion cases, combined with immediate separation from soldiers suffering physical wounds so as to "not upset the morale of the others."[2]

Prior to the invasion, Gregory had strived to weed out anyone he felt was "neurotic," mentally inadequate, or "apt to give trouble in action" due to psychological reasons. He removed 127 men on psychiatric grounds and afterward declared the division shipshape. "The general morale throughout the whole division is excellent," he reported. "The troops are relaxed and in high spirits." More worrisome was the state of reinforcements expected to be required as the division went through the meat grinder of D-Day and the inland advance. He felt that reinforcement troops, held at depots in England, were neither well trained while they loitered awaiting assignment nor managed in a morale-boosting manner.

Gregory expected that battle exhaustion cases during the first days in Normandy should be relatively few in relation to the ratio of physically wounded. Allied psychiatrists had noted that during the initial days of battle few men broke down—a phenomenon they were at a loss to explain. The best theory was that soldiers of questionable psychological stability had an impressive ability to hold together for a short time through willpower alone. As the fighting continued, stress levels would naturally rise, resulting in a breakdown.

For this reason, Gregory was unsurprised that virtually no exhaustion cases were reported on D-Day, and as the fighting inland continued, only a trickle of men were sent to the rear for psychological reasons. In the first forty-eight hours after opening the exhaustion unit, Gregory diagnosed just forty men as requiring treatment.[3]

This was a remarkably low ratio of psychological cases relative to wounded, considering that statistics gathered during the Italian campaign—particularly following the bloody street fight in Ortona—led to an expectation that 10 to 15 per cent of all battle casualties would be neuropsychiatric. Gregory figured that the early low statistics validated the initial weeding-out process, and that those men now evidencing battle exhaustion symptoms proved that "a division cannot be completely weeded." He did, however, note the beginning of a pattern whereby the numbers of battle exhaustion cases appeared to increase when troops were "very tired, very static, dug-in and under heavy counterattack." In almost every case, the diagnosed soldier "complained bitterly of mortar fire and 88-millimetre artillery."[4] With 3 CID locked in a developing stalemate on its front, Gregory feared that the number of battle exhaustion cases was going to rise rapidly.

Meanwhile, the medical units treating far greater numbers of men suffering physical wounds rapidly established an efficient, systematic funnelling process for evacuating casualties from the front to the beach and then on to hospitals in England. By D+2, the majority of Second British Army's casualty clearing stations, field, surgical hospitals, and blood transfusion units were concentrated in three designated medical areas—Hermanville, Reviers, and Ryes. The one at Reviers was principally concerned with treating casualties suffered by 3 CID and other units operating out of Juno Beach. On June 8, the beach evacuation system was formalized when a specially outfitted Landing Ship, Tank (LST), capable of evacuating about three hundred casualties per trip to England, came into service. As the LST was unable to dock on the sand, the wounded had to be first loaded aboard DUKW's—2.5-ton amphibious six-wheeled trucks capable of six knots in water—for shuttling to the LST. On board, the casualties were treated in improvised operating rooms on the lower deck.[5]

To save lives, the surgeons in the Normandy beachhead had to act quickly during emergency operations. Canadian surgeon J.B. Hillsman's experience with a soldier badly wounded in the leg was typical. Despite the severity of the wound, Hillsman puzzled as to why the patient's pulse was already "very weak and thready." When the surgeon turned the man over, he discovered a dry hole in his back and realized he was bleeding internally. In whispers, the surgical team worked out their plan to "save this boy. Pour the blood into him fast then a quick attempt to stop the bleeding." Hillsman glanced at the anaesthetist, who nodded. The surgeon quickly made his incision and blood spurted all over, making it impossible for him to find the severed vessel. He frantically groped for clamps while shouting for suction, unable to see, the gushing blood making it impossible to find the point vital to save the man. "He's bleeding too fast," Hillsman cried.

"A Pack! Press Hard! It's still flowing. Big forceps, quick! I'll have to clamp blind. *Oh God, I hope it get it,*" he thought. But he couldn't find the spot. Nothing to do but a greater incision to reach the main artery, a terrible decision to have to make. "The vessel is tied. Back again to the first incision." Seeing the flow of blood slowed but not stopped, he ordered, "Suction! Pack! Sponge! Quick." Deftly retying the vessel to completely stem the blood flow, Hillsman straightened, cracked his back, and sighed with relief. Then a voice in his ear said gently, "I'm afraid he's gone." The surgeon stared down on the boy lying dead on the table. "Sorry, old man," he thought, "I'm a lousy surgeon." But there was no respite from the tragedy, as an orderly tapped his shoulder. "The Resuscitation Officer wants to see you. Another belly."[6]

In their letters home, the surgeons seldom discussed the dramatic contrast between peacetime surgery in Canadian hospitals and army field hospitals. Dr. Joseph Greenblatt of the 14th Canadian Field Unit typically downplayed his role in saving the lives of many men brought to the surgery with bodies torn and smashed by bullets and shrapnel. The doctor, who before the war had been on the staff of Ottawa Civic Hospital, was among the first to land on Juno Beach. On the morning of June 10, he was enjoying a well-deserved rest from front-line surgical duty and turned to writing sweetheart Fran Trachtenberg. Since D-Day, he wrote, "things at times are a bit sticky and are slightly more dangerous than being in England, but I want you to know that things are going very well and I am confident that not only will we emerge successful but we will do so quickly... As far as my own little sector of this show is concerned everything is going ok. It is by no means a walk but we are definitely winning, so there you are. Until yesterday I was pretty well up front and as a result didn't get very much in the way of sleep, but the 'boss' pulled me out and relieved me and I slept yesterday. I slept for about 24 hours and now I really feel chipper again."[7]

That it was possible for medical officers to be rotated out of the front-line surgeries showed that the Royal Canadian Army Medical Corps (RCAMC) units and their British counterparts serving 3 CID had adequately prepared to cope with the heavy rates of casualties.

Although food and even ammunition were often scarce on the front lines, medical supplies were seldom insufficient. Each medical unit landed on D-Day equipped with everything from bandages to blood for transfusions to ensure self-reliance for two days. Additional supplies had been packaged before the invasion into shipping blocks that were put ashore on Juno Beach according to a strict schedule. Even extra stretchers and blankets were slotted into the buildup schedule. The division had been allotted 750 stretchers and 2,250 blankets to take ashore with it on D-Day. Thereafter, that number was increased according to a strict regimen, to maintain the same ratio of stretchers and blankets versus men ashore as the division increased its numbers on the sand. "At no time among Canadian medical units was there any shortage of essential medical equipment," the RCAMC official historian wrote.[8]

The wounded brought back from the front lines to the beach and then evacuated to England were generally impressed by how smoothly the medical units operated. Knowing that wounded soldiers could generally rely on being quickly cared for greatly heightened morale on the front lines.

High morale was essential for the assault divisions, for they still carried the full weight of the battle and must continue to do so at least until General Bernard Montgomery began his two-pronged offensive against Caen. This attack was now unlikely to start before June 11 or 12, Montgomery had conceded. Meantime, the Germans were expected to launch a pre-emptive counterattack that, were it to succeed, might derail his entire operational plan. Second British Army intelligence staff warned repeatedly that such an attack would probably concentrate on the boundary line between 3rd Canadian Infantry Division and 3rd British Infantry Division and against the 6th Airborne Division lines east of the River Orne.

On June 9, however, the heaviest fighting the Canadians faced was on the division's western flank in the form of the 12th Panzer Regiment's No. 3 Company assault on Norrey-en-Bessin and the persistent counterattacks 26th Panzer Grenadier Regiment threw against the Canadian Scottish at Putot-en-Bessin. Elsewhere along the Canadian front, the battleground was quieter, but by no means inactive.

A MAJOR PROBLEM for divisional headquarters on June 9 was the threat to its rear areas posed by pockets of Germans from the 716th Infantry Division that had been cut off during the advance inland on D-Day and D+1. In those two days, this division had been all but annihilated. The isolated elements that were bypassed by the assault units during their rapid inland advance lost all contact with their divisional command and with each other. From the front line back to the beach, soldiers of the 716th still crept about or were dug into hidden strongpoints. Some sought to sneak past the Canadians and regain German lines, others waited to be relieved by a German counterattack, and a lesser number continued to inflict what damage they could with ambushes and sniper attacks.

As each day passed and their situation grew obviously more hopeless, the number of men who surrendered increased. They straggled out of the brush, fields, and hedgerows looking hungry, tired, beaten. But for every man who surrendered, there seemed to be a greater number either ready to continue the fight or too frightened to risk giving up. Prior to the invasion, German propagandists had warned that the Allies "did not take the Geneva Convention very seriously" and that the assault battalions had been instructed not to take prisoners.[9] Taking these warnings at face value, many German soldiers did their utmost to avoid capture even after being cut off and stranded behind enemy lines.

Soldiers understand the inherent dangers of surrender in the midst of combat. Pumped up by fear and adrenaline, opposing troops can all too easily shoot before appreciating that a man actually has risen out of the ground or stepped from a treeline unarmed, with no intention to fight. Rarely, though, do civilized, well-trained soldiers kill surrendering opponents except in cases where they are enraged by the deaths of men at their sides inflicted by those now laying down arms. How quickly such incidents are halted depends on the rapidity with which officers and non-commissioned officers exert control over their men. Once those first hazardous moments pass and a soldier's surrender is accepted, the likelihood of his being killed rapidly diminishes. At this point, the shooting of a surrendered soldier can no longer be the result of misjudging an enemy's intentions while under fire. It constitutes an execution and can be considered a war crime. While many Hitlerjugend of the 12th ss Panzer Division engaged in such post-surrender murders, there is little evidence to suggest that Canadian soldiers responded in kind.

Even so, for German soldiers to hide out behind Canadian lines often proved fatal. Twenty-year-old Roger Chevalier was visiting the farm where he had worked as a farmhand before marrying and establishing his own operation near Anguerny. In the farmhouse, he joined his former employer and a handful of Canadian soldiers at the kitchen table, sharing a bottle of calvados the farmer had broken out for an impromptu liberation celebration. When the farmer's wife responded to a knock on the front door, she gaped at the sight of ten German soldiers standing there. In broken French, one demanded that she provide them with civilian clothing. While this discussion was going on, the Canadians exchanged glasses for weapons. Several ducked out the back as others moved to cover the front door from within the house. Suddenly surrounded, the Germans dropped their guns and were led off to the nearest prisoners' cage.

On June 9, however, Chevalier was called to the same farm to do a small job for his former employer. While Chevalier mended a piece of machinery near the barn, he heard the farmer's wife complaining that one of her cows had produced no milk and that this had been the case for several mornings. Then the woman heard some rustling in the branches of a walnut tree near the cow paddock. A wary glance revealed the outline of a German soldier hidden in the foliage. While Chevalier kept watch on the tree, the woman rushed to report her discovery to a nearby Le Régiment de la Chaudière patrol. Chevalier watched smugly as a couple of these soldiers moved towards the tree with their rifles at the ready. Another Bosche in the bag, he thought. Then, to the young farmer's horror, instead of calling for the hidden soldier to come down and surrender, the two men simply raised their rifles and "shot him like a rabbit." Chevalier knew the image of the young soldier dangling lifelessly from the branches as the Canadians strolled away would forever haunt him. He could not imagine how these men, who looked no older than himself or the man they had just killed, could have become so brutalized by war.[10]

Chevalier might have more readily understood their actions if he had been aware that the Chaudières were routinely being fired on by snipers hiding in trees precisely like the young German. As the soldier failed to drop a weapon from the tree or call out an intention to surrender when they approached the tree, the Canadians could easily have decided he was probably armed and dangerous. Few soldiers would put their own lives at risk attempting to take an armed enemy prisoner.

The Chaudières bore the brunt of responsibility for cleaning up the Germans still operating in the Canadian rear. Their policing duties extended from Reviers in the west to Anguerny. They also had companies assigned to holding a section of front running north from Anguerny to Basly. This left the battalion badly overextended. Its Bren carrier platoon was kept particularly busy pursuing persistent enemy snipers or mopping up detected pockets of larger forces operating behind Canadian lines.[11] That one of 8th Canadian Infantry Brigade's battalions had to perform rear-area policing actions while also maintaining a presence in the battle lines was symptomatic of the increasing shortage of combat troops 3 CID had on the ground— hampering its ability to continue offensive operations.

Rooting out German snipers and isolated pockets was just one aspect of the Chaudières' rear-area details. The battalion's patrols also had to determine whether to leave civilians alone or to place them in detention. Each patrol had to assess whether the civilians were in danger if they remained in their farmhouses, villages, or hiding places, and whether they posed a security threat. Since the landings, there had been sporadic incidents of fascist civilians joining the Germans in sniping at the Canadians, while others were picked up attempting to pass intelligence on the division's dispositions to the enemy. Faced with any semblance of hostility by a group of civilians, it became common for Chaudière patrols to round the lot up and march them back to the British Beach Group responsible for incarceration of POWs and civilian suspects. By June 9, several hundred civilians had been detained in a loosely guarded wire enclosure at Reviers, and overcrowding was becoming a concern. This led to an incident when a Chaudière patrol attempting to hand off about 120 civilians taken into custody the previous day was told that "the Beach Group would not take... them." An urgent request from Chaudière Lieutenant Colonel Paul Mathieu to division asked, "What to do with them?" At a loss for an answer, Major General Keller and his staff tossed the matter back in the battalion commander's lap. Deciding his men were perhaps becoming too zealous detaining civilians, he had them more thoroughly interrogated about their sympathies, issued some stern warnings, and then ordered the entire group released.[12]

Most civilians were almost euphoric at being free of the German boot and went out of their way to provide vital intelligence to the French-Canadian troops, particularly as the Québécois dialect was similar to that of Normandy. On June 8 when the Chaudières patrolled through Colomby-sur-Thaon and beyond to the River Seulles, they were intermittently harassed by snipers identified as left-behind members of 716th Division. The soldiers had no luck eliminating these snipers until several civilians guided Captain Michel Gauvin and his Bren carrier section to where four Germans slept in a nearby barn. The Germans were taken prisoner without a fuss. Near Colomby, another patrol received a civilian report that a large group of Germans was hiding in a château. A quickly organized fighting force closed on the building and surrounded the Germans. After lengthy negotiations, a 716th Infantry colonel, his staff, and about sixty soldiers marched out of the building and stacked their arms. The troops accepting the surrender were delighted to also capture a large Swastika flag. Meanwhile, in the front-line positions, wrote the regiment's war diarist, "snipers continued to harass us all day."[13]

JUST HOW INSECURE the divisional lines of communication from the front to the beach were had been made very clear early on June 9 to Captain George Eckenfelder, the Royal Canadian Corps of Signalers officer assigned to 7 CIB. The thirty-four-year-old, who had been a civil engineer in peacetime, set off in a jeep from Secqueville-en-Bessin to Bény-sur-Mer to attend a meeting at divisional headquarters. He drove through a pleasant "little wooded valley near Fontaine-Henry and on the outskirts of that village I met some Canadians who had just landed that day. It was a provost unit setting up a

POW cage in a field and they were setting up MGs to cover the cage. I spoke to the lieutenant in charge and told him where I was going and asked if he knew anything about the road.

"'Oh, it's okay,' he said. So I took off in my jeep and only drove for about five minutes before I came to a barbed wire entanglement across the road. I knew right away something wasn't right, but when I started to back up to get out of there a machine gun opened up on me. I bailed out into the ditch and almost immediately there were two Germans on top of me. They put me back in the jeep and said, 'Drive on.' Which I did and we went up a hill and around a corner to where there was a very large cave. It was an underground quarry in which this unit had holed up. On the ridge above the cave they had a perimeter defence set up with machine guns and mortars and it was a very tough little position. Already they had gathered up about twenty prisoners and there were some of our people wounded and some of their own wounded too."[14]

The quarry was a vast underground chamber with spur shafts running off in various directions that contained copious amounts of German supplies. In one of these rooms, a large number of trucks were parked. Eckenfelder realized the quarry had been a major supply dump for the 716th Infantry Division.

Not long after Eckenfelder was taken prisoner, some Germans marched in with the provost officer and his sergeant in tow. They had been rounded up while driving the same road the officer had assured Eckenfelder was safe.

About an hour later, a Chaudière fighting patrol under command of Major G.O. "Gus" Taschereau discovered the quarry position and a sharp firefight broke out. Deep in the cave, Eckenfelder could hear mortars and machine guns firing from the defensive position on top of the ridge and explosions that sounded as if they were made by rounds fired from a two-inch mortar. As the day wore on, it was obvious the Germans were under siege and the Canadian force outside the cave was being reinforced. Around him, the Germans "became more and more agitated and eventually the commanding officer came to me and said, 'You're the senior officer among my prisoners and I would like to surrender. We've fought a good fight, but we're surrounded and have no hope of getting out of this.'" The German spoke to Ecken-felder in excellent French, which the signals captain spoke also.

In that language, Eckenfelder replied, "Fine. You call in your troops and disarm them right here."

The German officer did exactly that and soon Eckenfelder "had a pile of... rifles, Schmeissers, and other weapons in front of me." But the "shooting outside was still pretty hot," although now, with the bulk of the Germans disarmed, most was coming from the Canadian positions. "We have to stop this shooting before anyone goes out there in the open," Eckenfelder told the officer. "So you better have someone go out in front there with a white flag."

When the commander detailed a junior officer to the task, the man groused that "no self-respecting German officer ever waves a white flag." By this time, Eckenfelder had armed himself with a Luger pistol that he waved airily in the junior officer's direction. "Well, this time, sonny, you'll have to wave a white flag," he said.

"I don't have a white flag," the man complained.

"There's a hospital at the end of the cave there and they have white sheets and there's a long handled shovel over there. So get a sheet and tie it to the end of the shovel," Eckenfelder ordered. Grudgingly, the officer fetched a sheet and rigged it to the shovel. Then he "poked his head out of the cave with me right behind him and waved the white flag." Eventually the shooting stopped.[15]

At the same time as the fight for this cave wound up, another fierce firefight started in front of the mouth of another section of the quarry that was not linked to the one occupied by Eckenfelder's group. Here, more Germans were deeply entrenched inside the cave and on the overhanging ridge. During an attempt to rush the posi-tion, several Chaudières were wounded and stranded in no man's land between the cave and the Canadian positions. Desperate to help them, but unable to do so because of the intense German fire, several Chaudières stepped out into the open with their arms up. "We have come to look for our wounded," one of the men yelled.

Not a shot was fired as this mission of mercy was carried out. A German soldier then emerged from the cave with a large Red Cross flag and approached Captain Gauvin, who was in command of the Chaudière platoon. The man asked Gauvin to accompany him into the cave for a parley. Warily, Gauvin entered a "quarry honeycombed with caves in which, by the flickering light of candles, he could see some fifty wounded Germans and Canadians. The German doctor in charge asked Gauvin to remove the Canadian wounded, as some would not live if they did not receive proper attention immediately. Gauvin replied that all the wounded would be taken to a hospital if the German garrison would surrender; a few minutes later, the Germans agreed to do so."[16]

These actions on June 8 and 9 eliminated most of the organized pockets of resistance, but snipers roaming the countryside continued to plague the division. At 2045 hours on June 9, divisional headquarters issued a stern message to all units and formations that "every effort must be made by... all troops to clear up individual snipers and gun or mortar positions behind [front lines]. The existence of these enemy are a constant menace and cannot be accepted."[17]

The single major enemy strongpoint in Second British Army's rear area was the radar station near Douvres-la-Délivrande, still holding out despite major attacks against it by 3rd British Infantry Division, which had taken over responsibility for securing this position from the North Shore (New Brunswick) Regiment on June 7. About three hundred enemy troops composed of a Luftwaffe security detachment and a company of Panzer Grenadiers from 21st Panzer Division were dug into heavily fortified positions around the radar towers. All attempts to overrun the position had been thrown back, and the Germans there showed no sign of considering surrender.*

---

* Not until June 17, when No. 41 Royal Marine Commando launched an assault supported by several petard-mounted AVRE Churchills and heavy shelling by artillery and naval ships, did the Germans at the radar station give up. By then, they were out of supplies and ammunition. Six officers and 214 men were still alive to surrender, and no determination of how many were killed during the siege was compiled. (Stacey, *Victory Campaign*, 144)

The presence of this lodgement inside the Allied lines continued to plague movement of vehicles along all roads east of Basly, which were subject to fire from an 88-millimetre antitank gun positioned in front of the radar station.[18]

WHILE 3 CID's rear areas were judged far more secure by the end of June 9, the same could not be said of its front lines, where a broad gap still existed between 9th Canadian Infantry Brigade on the left and 7th Canadian Infantry Brigade to the right. The latter brigade could do little more than continue holding its own in the area of Bretteville-en-Bessin and Putot-en-Bessin until the rest of the division came up on its eastern flank and 50th British Infantry Division moved up on the other.

Major General Rod Keller recognized that the only way his division could return to the offensive was to close the gap between his two leading brigades, but it was not possible to cobble together an attack that could succeed with the depleted manpower available. He also needed to regain Authie and Buron on 9 CIB's front. If he pushed into the Mue valley to secure Vieux Cairon and then advanced through Rots to gain the Caen-Bayeux highway at la Villeneuve, those battalions involved would be in the same left-flank-exposed position that currently imperilled 7 CIB. The challenge was to create a front line that looked like a gradually sloping shoulder running down from a high point at Norrey-en-Bessin through Rots and on to Buron. Such a continuous front would save 7 CIB's hard-won salient, while providing a firm base from which the division could renew its offensive thrust towards Carpiquet airport.

Currently, the only screening force in position on that flank was provided by the Sherbrooke Fusiliers, which had tanks positioned on a line of higher ground between Secqueville-en-Bessin and Bretteville-l'Orgueilleuse. Keller had moved the armoured regiment to this position on June 8. Still rebuilding from its heavy June 7 losses, the regiment's surviving tanks and crews were divided into two composite squadrons, with Major V.O. Walsh commanding one and Major E.W.L. Arnold the other. Walsh's squadron set up southeast of Bretteville, while Arnold formed up just outside the southern outskirts of Secqueville.

The most forward tank troop in Walsh's squadron had rolled up onto a low hill overlooking a large orchard immediately west of la Villeneuve. From this position, the tankers monitored and shelled German vehicles attempting to move along the Caen-Bayeux highway, but were soon targeted by enemy artillery. Having not yet been fully briefed on the dispositions of 7 CIB's infantry battalions, Walsh decided the accurate artillery fire was likely being directed by a German forward observer using the stately church tower in Norrey-en-Bessin for an observation post. Walsh's gunner quickly shot the tower down with a few well-placed rounds.[19] In Norrey, Major Stu Tubb watched with dismay as the "tower crumbled into rubble along with adjacent buildings. It was sad to watch this happening to such an old structure."[20]

Despite the Sherbrooke Fusiliers' presence on 7 CIB's left flank, the gap there still greatly worried Keller and his staff. Of particular concern was its threat to the safety of the division's two artillery regiments dug into firing positions at Bray. Before 7 CIB's Brigadier Harry Foster sent the Canadian Scottish into the counterattack on Putot-en-Bessin, this battalion had provided security for the gunners. Through the night of June 8, the artillery regiments had been forced to take men off the guns to carry out their own perimeter defence. But with daylight, the calls for artillery support across 7 CIB's front came in fast and furious, so the gunners were too busy crewing their 105-millimetre Priests to defend their own perimeter, leaving them dangerously vulnerable to a raid by enemy infantry from the Mue valley.

Although merely a creek to Canadian eyes, the River Mue had spent centuries cutting a comparatively deep valley in the Norman soil that the farmers little bothered to clear for cultivation. It was still densely forested and presented ideal ground for use by 12th ss troops to infiltrate into the Canadian rear areas. Snipers posed a constant hazard to the gunners, and both the 12th and 13th Field Regiments lost men to such fire during the early morning of June 9. In the

13th Field Regiment's gun position, Sergeant C.R. Fox and Gunner Ronald Casselman, both manning guns in the 44th Battery, were shot by snipers—the latter dying of his wound.[21]

Realizing that 7 CIB's infantry battalions were too depleted and strung out along a hotly contested front to cover the artillery regiments, Keller decided to detach 8 CIB's Queen's Own Rifles and put it under Foster's command. By mid-morning on June 9, he had this battalion moving by truck from Anguerny to clear the Germans out of the woods near Bray.[22] With the Chaudières patrolling the division's rear areas and the North Shore (New Brunswick) Regiment assuming responsibility for securing Anguerny while continuing to protect the division's eastern flank, 8 CIB was rendered virtually impotent in terms of offensive capability. Second British Army commander Miles Dempsey accordingly placed No. 46 Royal Marine Commando under command of 8 CIB's Brigadier Ken Blackader. At 1945 hours, as the Queen's Own disembarked from trucks at Basly, No. 46 Commando reported to 8 CIB headquarters.[23]

Although the arrival of the commandos strengthened the brigade, it would still be some time before it was organized for offensive actions, so any attempt to advance the Canadian front meanwhile fell to 9 CIB. This brigade had hardly been sitting on its hands since the North Novas were pushed back from Authie and Buron on June 7. Throughout the following day, the three battalions of the 12th SS Division's 25th Panzer Grenadier Regiment had repeatedly attempted to wrest les Buissons from the firm grip of the Stormont, Dundas and Glengarry Highlanders. Intensive shelling by German 105-millimetre and 88-millimetre artillery preceded each Panzer Grenadier infiltration attempt. These barrages were hellishly drawn out, with one starting at 1040 and grinding on for two hours.[24] Then German infantry were spotted "crawling through the long grass in front" of 'A' Company's front. The Glens drove off this attack with assistance from the Highland Light Infantry mortars stationed at Villons-les-Buissons.[25]

Keen to regain the initiative, Keller and Brigadier Ben Cunningham alerted the Highland Light Infantry to be ready for a noon counterattack intended to seize Buron. Lieutenant Colonel F.M. Griffiths informed his company commanders they were to "break out of the

Fortress and attack Buron and then push on to our final objective" of Carpiquet airport. "An 'O' Group was held, a plan made, and then we were told to hold." Keller had decided that "it was... too great a risk to advance further until the 3rd British Division on our left straightened up the line."[26]

That division's 9th Infantry Brigade attempted to complete its task in the mid-afternoon on June 9 with a four-phase drive to successively clear Cambes, Galmanche, Mâlon, and St.-Contest. The Royal Ulster Regiment advanced behind a creeping artillery barrage that walked to the outskirts of Cambes, where a small wood faced the village. An immediate German counterattack, however, prevented the battalion from pushing out of the trees into the streets until it was reinforced by the King's Own Scottish Borderers. The two battalions bullied their way into Cambes. From Villons-les-Buissons, the HLI watched in awe and increasing terror as artillery regiments on both sides turned guns on the doomed village. "A terrific rain of shells fell on the place from every direction. Unfortunately, we were in the middle of the counter battery [crossfire] and many rounds from both sides fell upon our area."[27] Fighting raged until about 0200 hours the next morning before the village was reported cleared by the two British battalions, but by then they were so beaten up that the rest of the offensive plan was abandoned.

Breaking off the British attack left the Highland Light Infantry, whose positions around Villons-les-Buissons were on the most easterly flank of the Canadian division, still exposed to observation by German spotters operating in Galmanche and St.-Contest. During daylight hours, 'C' Company's men were forced to cower in their slit trenches, for "every time they appear on top they come under fire from enemy mortars, MGS, 88-[millimetre] and whatever else Bosche can throw at them... Our mortars cannot fire except when there is other arty activity as when they do, there is an immediate rain of counter battery fire... [German fire] seems to be pretty accurate, indicating that they had previously taped our positions."[28]

16

Fix Bayonets

BY LATE AFTERNOON on June 9, the 12th ss (Hitlerjugend) Panzer Division and elements of the 21st Panzer Division had stymied 3rd British Infantry Division's attempt to bring 9th Infantry Brigade up parallel with the Canadian left flank. Having blocked the British advance, the Germans redirected the fury of their artillery from embattled Cambes to where the Stormont, Dundas and Glengarry had been holding 9th Canadian Infantry Brigade's most forward front at les Buissons since the night of June 7. Lieutenant G.D. Utman was killed and most of his mortar platoon were killed or wounded, putting all the tubes out of action. Several nearby soldiers, who had rudimentary mortar training, raced to help the survivors get the weapons back into action.[1] 9th Canadian Infantry Brigade's Brigadier Ben Cunningham arrived at that point on a front-line reconnaissance, with the Glens' Major Archie Hamilton in tow. Seeing the calamity that had befallen the mortar crews, Cunningham dashed through the fire and smoke of exploding shells to personally reorganize the stricken unit. "What a brigadier," the regiment's historian later exalted, "a living inspiration to his command!"[2]

Casualties mounted throughout the ranks, with Captain Charlie Thom taking shrapnel in the neck and thirty others wounded by shrapnel and concussion. By now, the Glens had taken to calling les Buissons Hell's Corners, particularly the intersection next to the walled Paix de Coeur Château, where fighting seemed heaviest.

Realizing these attacks were coming from Vieux Cairon, Cunningham and Glens commander Lieutenant Colonel G.H. Christiansen decided to have 'C' Company, supported by a troop of Fort Garry Horse tanks, seize the village. Both men knew this thrust faced stiff opposition, particularly as the Germans had an 88-millimetre gun line dug in to the front of Vieux Cairon.

While this attack was being teed up, Fort Garry Horse Lieutenant Colonel Ronald Morton strode up to 'B' Squadron's acting commander, Captain Robert D. Grant. "You have to do something to take the pressure off the infantry," he said. "I want you to go out around in front of les Buissons through the wheatfields and draw fire off the infantry." 'B' Squadron's Major Jack Meindl had been wounded in action on D-Day and its second-in-command, Captain Jim Hill, killed on June 8 when a German artillery round exploded in a les Buissons courtyard in which he happened to be standing. As the senior surviving officer, Grant had suddenly found himself in charge of the squadron, a job he felt ill prepared for, as he had previously served as the rear-link officer stationed at regimental headquarters.

Despite his lack of combat experience, Grant thought Morton's order "seemed... like a crazy idea." But he also recognized that the lieutenant colonel "was the boss." Not only had the squadron lost its senior commanders, but it was also so badly shot up that Grant only had four tanks left out of the twenty-one that had come ashore on D-Day. Trundling out into the open wheatfields in broad daylight with so few tanks and no screening infantry sounded suicidal.

Nevertheless, the four tanks growled out into the field as instructed, and promptly achieved the purpose of drawing fire off the infantry and onto themselves, with disastrous effect. After travelling only a half-mile, the Shermans were zeroed in by the 88-millimetre guns in front of Vieux Cairon and all knocked out of action in a matter of seconds. A shell punched through the side of Grant's tank, passed right between the driver and co-driver, missed the ammunition racks, and then sliced an exit hole in the other side. Everyone in Grant's tank bailed out before it went up in flames, but one man was wounded. The tankers started working their way on foot back to les Buissons. En route, one of Grant's troopers butted head-on into a

Panzer Grenadier creeping through the tall wheat, and fearing a gun shot would betray their presence to other Germans, strangled the soldier with his bare hands. Grant was grimly impressed, thinking that if he had encountered the German "I'd have dropped dead."

Because the wheat was so tall, it was hard for the men to keep track of each other's location and soon Grant was alone. After about an hour of crawling along, he reached the edge of the field and looked out at the ruins of les Buissons. The air over the village was black with the smoke of dozens of fires burning in the shell-blasted buildings. Several trucks and Bren carriers were also burning in the narrow streets, but otherwise the village looked abandoned. Yet Grant knew that hundreds of infantrymen were hunkered deep in slit trenches all along the front, and he was on the wrong side. As he lay in the wheat pondering how to approach the lines without being shot by a twitchy infantryman, most of the other tankers crawled up beside him. They were all right down on their bellies, knowing the risk they faced. Finally, Grant "stuck my helmet up in the air on the end of my pistol over the wheat to let them know which side I was on." Creeping through the last few feet of wheat, Grant kept the helmet up as high as he could and was relieved to hear someone from the village holler, "Come on in."[3] The tankers scuttled into the dubious protection offered by les Buissons.

About the time Grant got back to the village, 'C' Company and its supporting tanks kicked off the attack on Vieux Cairon. Captain R.P. Milligan, the company's second-in-command, led this attack as Major Archie MacDonald was designated Left Out of Battle. This standard policy required a rotating cadre of officers and non-commissioned officers to not participate in an action. In this way, should the unit be wiped out, there would be a leadership reserve around which it could be reformed.[4]

Private Mervyn K.R. Williams's section moved out with the rest of the company, the Bren gunners burning off one magazine after another as they tried to force the Germans to keep their heads down. Williams noticed that the gunners were pouring out such a rapid rate of fire that they had to change gun barrels every three to five minutes because of overheating. Halfway across the open ground between les

Buissons and Vieux Cairon, the company was driven to ground by a "terrific barrage of fire" from the 88-millimetre gun line and what seemed a solid wall of machine-gun positions dug in ahead of the artillery.[5] At 1900 hours, less than sixty minutes after the attack had started, 'C' Company pulled back under fire to les Buissons.

A short time after the failed attack, Christiansen ordered Milligan to take his company and round up all the civilians still in the village for evacuation to the beach. The lieutenant colonel believed the accuracy of the German artillery resulted from someone relaying information on the battalion's dispositions over a clandestine wireless set. In addition, the continual pounding to which les Buissons was being subjected was sure to produce heavy civilian casualties, so they would be safer in the rear.

Williams and the other soldiers led civilians out of homes and basements, loading them aboard several trucks. Older people were put in the trucks first, so that they could sit on the benches for a more comfortable ride. Just as the last of the elderly were put into one of the trucks, a scuffle broke out in its back. When the soldiers jumped on to investigate, they discovered two Germans in civilian clothes, who had attracted the ire of the old people by claiming seats on the benches. They were quickly jerked out of the truck and marched to a POW cage.[6]

In the village's churchyard, meanwhile, a 'C' Company platoon commanded by Lieutenant D.C. Stewart discovered an underground air-raid shelter crowded with about a hundred civilians. An elderly midwife was assisting an obviously very pregnant woman who appeared on the verge of going into labour. The soldiers left the two in the shelter and loaded the rest into the trucks, which then headed for the beach. Stewart told Milligan about the two women. When Milligan reported to Christiansen, the lieutenant colonel made it plain that he wanted all civilians evacuated regardless of their circumstances. He particularly didn't want two women and a newborn baby left on the battalion's hands in the middle of a bloodily contested battleground.

A chastened Stewart could rustle up no better transport than a two-wheeled milk cart to serve as an ambulance in which the pregnant woman could lie while some of his men pushed it back to one of the rear-area surgical units.[7] That evening, the men returned with the happy news that she had given birth to a girl—Mademoiselle Roger Maillard—quickly claimed by the Glens as the first "baby of Hell's Corners."[8]

THE 9TH BRIGADE'S inability to rekindle offensive operations on June 9 corresponded with similar failures all across the invasion front. Virtually every plan for a concerted Allied advance quickly went awry as the committed battalions found the Norman countryside too restricted for tanks and infantry to work well together. Casualties by now had so thinned the ranks of armoured and infantry battalions alike that neither could support the other in significant strength. Fighting from well-fortified strongpoints, the Germans easily blocked any attempt to press home an assault by tanks and infantry working in concert, while either tanks or infantry advancing alone proved easy game.

The use of heavily prepared fortresses had been adopted effectively by both sides. In the Canadian lines, "fortresses" such as Villons-les-Buissons and les Buissons on the left, and Norrey-en-Bessin and Bretteville-l'Orgueilleuse to the right, had proven unassailable. The 12th ss had been foiled at every turn from gaining an advantage over the Canadians and had been dealt a sharp reversal when the Canadian Scottish wrested Putot-en-Bessin back from its grasp. Counterattacks thrown in by Panzer Grenadiers supported by Panzers, infantry operating alone, or an independent Panzer company had all been roundly defeated. The fact that the Canadians remained intent on renewing the offensive at first opportunity forced the 12th ss to commit forces piecemeal on narrow fronts to forestall the possibility. The Canadian resolve also prevented the Hitlerjugend from weakening one point of its broad line to concentrate forces for a counterattack on another point. These same handicaps hindered the Germans throughout Normandy, so that plans for a major counteroffensive capable of breaching Allied defences in any decisive manner all came to naught on June 9.[9]

The German response was further hampered by continued poor intelligence and an unwillingness throughout the higher levels of the ponderous command chain to abandon preconceived notions of how the Allied invasion strategy must develop. By June 9, Oberkommando der Wehrmacht staff, with the primary exception of Operations Chief Generaloberst Alfred Jodl, who still called for immediate elimination of the beachhead despite the lack of forces to carry out such a mission, recognized that throwing the Allies back into the sea was no longer feasible. Yet okw offered no instructions to Army Group B's Generalfeldmarschall Erwin Rommel to develop a new strategic response. Effectively, Rommel was left to his own devices and then severely hobbled when Hitler decreed there could be no reallocation of Fifteenth Army divisions away from the Pas de Calais area to Normandy.

Remarkably, almost everyone at okw, as well as Commander-in-Chief West Generalfeldmarschall Gerd von Rundstedt and Rommel, still clung to the notion—encouraged by the continuing Operation Fortitude deception—that a second, grander invasion was imminent. So Fifteenth Army remained pinned on the coastline northeast of Normandy, while Rommel received vague promises that divisions from far distant fronts would be forthcoming. That these could not possibly arrive in time to contribute to the outcome of the beachhead phase of the battle went unsaid. Despite the fact that most okw staff acknowledged the beachhead could not be eliminated with the divisions Rommel had on hand, Hitler countenanced no other strategy. okw directives continued to urge Rommel to "recover the entire length of the Normandy coastline." Lacking sufficient forces to deliver a major offensive capable of overwhelming the Allied divisions, okw messages, drafted to assure Hitler that the staff were not adopting defeatist attitudes, insisted the beachhead could be "broken down by concentrated local counterattacks and then 'demolished in detail.'"[10]

Panzer Group West commander, General der Panzertruppen Leo Freiherr Geyr von Schweppenburg, still hoped to launch precisely such an operation by unleashing the three divisions of 1 Panzer Corps gathered along the Normandy front against the Second British Army lines early on June 10. Rommel, however, recognized that these divisions had all become so entangled in checking the British-Canadian advance towards Caen and Carpiquet airport that they could not effectively switch to the offensive from their current positions and hope to achieve any gains of consequence. More likely, they would end up "demolished in detail" and that could not be allowed.

He decided that a pause was needed, during which the Panzer divisions could be extracted from the front line and replaced by infantry divisions. While these fresh divisions kept the Allies contained, I Panzer Corps could reorganize and then perform its proper battlefield function by forming the spearhead for a well-coordinated counterstrike that might just succeed in carrying out Hitler's directives. At 1730 hours on June 9, Rommel issued an instruction to Seventh Army and I SS Panzer Corps. "There should be a return to the defensive in the sector between the Vire and Orne and the counterattack should be postponed until all preparations had been completed."[11] Rommel planned to await the arrival of II Parachute Corps, which would replace the Panzer divisions in the line with a highly competent and determined force. The question, of course, remained of when this corps would actually be detached by Hitler from where it was positioned in Brittany and sent marching to Normandy.

Yet Rommel could not afford to simply go on the defensive until the paratroops arrived. To do so would allow General Bernard Montgomery to set the pace of offensive operations. Consequently, while directing German forces between the Vire and Orne to assume a defensive posture, those east of the Orne were to counterattack 6th Airborne Division on the morning of June 10. On this front, Rommel was fortunate to have available two largely unscathed divisions—the 711th Infantry Division and 346th Grenadier Division—as well as elements of the badly mauled 716th Infantry Division and the still formidable 21st Panzer Division.

This latter division had, in accordance with instructions from von Schweppenburg, launched a localized counterattack on June 9. A battle group, formed around the nucleus of Major Hans von Luck's 125th Panzer Grenadier Regiment, was ordered to launch "a decisive attack on Escoville, advance on Ranville, and take possession of the Orne bridges." Seizing these bridges would isolate 6th Airborne Division and the British battalions that had marched from Sword to reinforce its hold east of the river. Capture of the bridges would also fully expose 3rd British Infantry Division's left flank and put its hold on Sword in jeopardy. It was an ambitious and audacious plan, and von Luck's regiment was bolstered with significant artillery and armour for its execution. Tanks and self-propelled guns were provided by 22nd Panzer Regiment's No. 4 Company and three batteries of the 200th Assault-Gun Battalion, while a company of 88-millimetre guns from the 220th Antitank Battalion would provide covering fire protection from any British armour in the area. The 21st Panzer Reconnaissance Battalion would lead the attack. Generalleutnant Edgar Feuchtinger, 21st Panzer Division's commander, assured von Luck he would have all the division's artillery supporting the attack for as long as its ammunition held out.[12]

Assembling the battle group before dawn, von Luck deployed the antitank guns on a hill south of Escoville to cover the battle group's advance. The major placed his small command group immediately behind the reconnaissance battalion troops to enable him to exert combat control. To avoid detection by artillery and naval gun spotters, the battle group struck out of the darkness at Escoville and quickly fought its way into the village against heavy resistance from British paratroopers. The moment it turned light, however, the paratroops called naval gunfire down on the centre of Escoville and the German attack collapsed. Four of the ten Panzers were knocked out by the naval guns and about forty Panzer Grenadiers died before von Luck pulled back to the start line.[13]

WHILE THE 21ST Panzer Division had attempted this breakthrough at Escoville, the 857th and 858th regiments of the 346th Grenadier Division were still licking their wounds from a botched attack launched the previous day against 1st Canadian Parachute Battalion. Having had their first assault on le Mesnil crossroads driven off by a counter-bayonet charge on June 7, these two regiments had tried to overrun the crossroads again on June 8. Nightlong concentrations of artillery and mortar fire preceded the attempt. Then, in the dull predawn light, the paratroops had looked along the road approaching the intersection from the south and spotted a column of infantry supported by several Mark IV tanks and self-propelled guns forming up. Advancing in marching ranks, as if on parade, the grenadiers headed their way.

As the parachute battalion's mortar crews zeroed in the three-inch mortars that had fortuitously arrived the day before from the beachhead, the only explanation they could muster for the bizarre German advance is that they believed the paratroops lacked mortars. If so, they were rudely disabused of this notion as the tubes started coughing out rounds as quickly as the mortar men could drop them down the spout. Explosions ripped ragged holes in the advancing column before the grenadiers realized their mistake and broke out into an extended line to continue closing on the crossroads inside the cover of dense orchards lining the roadway. The tanks, meanwhile, pressed up the road, disdainfully shrugging off the exploding mortar rounds, while the SPGs pulled into sheltered positions from which they enjoyed clear fields of fire on the Canadian lines.[14]

'B' and 'C' Company directly faced the advancing Germans, with 'A' Company near the brickworks unable to bring any fire to bear at all. This meant that only about 160 Canadians were squared off against a far superior force backed by tanks, against which the paratroops could do nothing until they came within the hundred-yard range of the PIAT guns. The torrent of fire thrown out by the paratroops forced the grenadiers back as they tried to cross the field directly in front of the Canadian line, but one Mark IV ground on alone directly into the point where the two company lines met. From here, it raked the slit trenches on either side with its machine guns and 75-millimetre gun, inflicting heavy casualties on the nearest platoons. Faced with such devastating fire, several precious minutes passed before one of the battalion's PIAT gunners was able to crawl close to the tank. He quickly punched two explosive charges against its hide, and although these failed to penetrate, they convinced the tank crew to call it a day. The tank rolled two hundred yards back across the field to where the grenadiers had taken up position around a large farmhouse surrounded by an orchard, which on one side extended almost to the Canadian lines.[15]

From here, the Germans raked the Canadian lines with heavy machine guns and accurate sniper fire. Leaving the Germans in possession of the farm put the entire battalion position at risk, yet this was a typical Norman fortress, with its courtyard enclosed by a high stone wall, through which the grenadiers had carved firing slits for the machine guns. Lieutenant Colonel G.F.P. Bradbrooke told 'B' Company commander Captain Peter Griffin that he must wrest control of the farmhouse from the Germans no matter the cost.

With the entire battalion now numbering fewer than three hundred men, Griffin could only scrape together an assault force of seventy-five men, composed of fifty men from two of his platoons and twenty-five soldiers from Headquarters Company. Griffin's plan was simple. The 'B' Company component under his command would conduct a frontal assault, while Lieutenant Norm Toseland flanked the German position with the other troops and hit the farm from the south.[16]

After briefing the men, Griffin said, "Fix bayonets." Hearing that chilling command, Private Mark Lockyer thought, "This is idiotic." To attack a heavily defended position without artillery or tank support seemed certain suicide and counter to their training. Turning to the man next to him, Lockyer said, "This is like 1914. Is he serious?" Griffin showed just how serious he was by racking a bayonet onto the end of a Lee Enfield and yelling, "Charge!" Without a moment's hesitation, the men in the two groups all dashed forward to do their duty.[17]

Sprinting across the orchard, Griffin's men caught the grenadiers by surprise and overran a line of about six machine guns that had been unmanned. But as they closed on the farm the German defence hardened, despite the fact that the parachute battalion's three-inch mortars were thumping the farmhouse and enclosed courtyard with a fierce barrage. Unable to push forward in the face of the stiffening fire, Griffin's force spread through the orchard and began shooting it out with the defenders.

Meanwhile, Toseland's little band of twenty-five men had jogged along the road until they had passed by the farm and turned to move in from the flank in a full-tilt charge towards a facing hedgerow. The Germans here were alert, manning several machine guns dug into the reverse side of the hedge. As the guns opened up, Lockyer saw Sergeant C.E. Huard die. Then Corporal O.M. Bastien and Private

W.W. Shawluk fell. Seconds later, just ten yards from the hedgerow, a slug pierced Lockyer's right lung and knocked him down hard. Toseland urged the others on, with Private T. Davies inspiring the survivors as he met the German fire with a Bren gun fired from the hip while on the run. But Davies soon fell wounded, along with Private H.W. Hughes. Four other men were killed before the charge reached the hedgerow. Toseland and the men still on their feet cleared the position in bitter hand-to-hand fighting. Then they pressed through to come up on Griffin's flank and provide covering fire from behind another hedgerow.

Griffin's mauled force managed to finally seize the farmhouse after a close-quarters fight and set out to secure several outbuildings farther to the south. But as they closed on the new position, they came under intense fire from a large force of grenadiers dug into the buildings, and spotted a number of armoured vehicles parked close by. Realizing he lacked the numbers to prevail, Griffin fell back on the farmhouse. Recovering from their initial surprise, grenadiers and supporting armour moved towards the farm from the outbuildings, while heavy mortars pounded the old stone building. To try holding the farm would mean death, so Griffin ordered a withdrawal to 'B' Company's original lines.

The paratroops had to fight their way back by moving in bounds, with one section covering another while it retreated a short distance and then protected the backs of the first section. Several men were wounded or killed along the way. Some of the wounded, including Private Davies, suffered a second injury but still remained in the fight. Griffin's men probably would have been butchered during this phase if not for the covering fire from the remnants of Toseland's little group. Privates Russell Geddes and W. Noval, respectively using a Bren gun and sniper's rifle, proved particularly deadly—credited jointly with killing about fifty Germans during the withdrawal. Both men were awarded the Military Medal, as were sergeants Joe LaCasse and Harvey Morgan. Sergeant George Capraru earned a Mentioned in Despatches citation. For his part in the assault, Griffin received a Military Cross.

When Griffin's force was clear, Toseland and his badly cut-up group began a fighting withdrawal of their own. There was no time to check the ground for immobilized wounded before the men fell back with guns blazing. Several paratroopers were left in no man's land. Barely conscious, Private Lockyer was vaguely aware of his comrades leapfrogging past him as they headed for the rear. They were all gone by the time he heard another of the wounded yell, "Help! Help! Somebody help me!" Lockyer could see the fellow and a couple of others sprawled nearby who showed faint signs of life.

Eventually, two Germans approached through the orchard. The dirty uniform and baggy pants worn by one indicated he was a common grenadier, but the other man was spiffed out in a pristinely clean and pressed officer's uniform. As he approached the wounded soldier who had cried out for help, the officer calmly drew a Luger and shot the man in the head. Then he strolled over to another of the wounded and shot him. Lockyer frantically stuck a hand inside his camouflaged paratrooper's smock, soaked it in the blood oozing out of the bullet hole in his chest, and smeared his face liberally. Taking a deep breath, he lay absolutely still as the two Germans walked over. One kicked him with terrific force in the stomach, but the private stifled a groan and kept his body loose so that he flopped lifelessly. Twice more a boot slammed into him, eliciting the same response, before the two men walked towards another paratrooper who was pleading for help. Lockyer heard the man moan, "Help," and then sob, "Oh no!" A pistol cracked and then the Germans walked away.

Passing out, Lockyer awoke again only after dark. Finding a morphine syringe, he injected himself and felt a little stronger after that. Eventually, he started crawling towards the Canadian lines. It took a long time, but at last he recognized the roadside hedgerow where the paratroops were dug in. From the darkness, someone hissed, "What's the password?"

"Christ, I dunno. I've been lying out all day," Lockyer groaned. A couple of paratroopers scurried out and dragged the wounded man into the lines. Three days later, he was evacuated to hospital in England.[18]

WHILE GRIFFIN'S FORCE fought its battle, the paratroopers at le Mesnil brickworks had received a welcome surprise when Lieutenant John Madden and four other paratroopers from 'C' Company stick marched wearily into the perimeter. On D-Day, the twenty-year-old lieutenant's stick had been one of the most poorly dropped in the battalion, landing on the west side of the River Orne about 1,200 yards from Sword Beach. Determined to rejoin the battalion, Madden had led a handful of his men across country, including a hazardous dash over Pegasus Bridge while the battle for control of it still raged, and finally made it home four days later. Along the way, the Canadians had occasionally supported British units they passed in quelling German resistance, or been forced to crawl past enemy positions in still-contested parts of the battlefield. Despite the fact that the various parachute battalions and brigades had become badly intermixed after the D-Day drop, Madden never considered joining one of the units he encountered along the way. Training had instilled in him that paratroops stuck to their objective and the Canadian final objective was to rally on le Mesnil, so that is what he determined to do.[19]

Madden reported to 'C' Company's headquarters in a two-storey house. The lower floor served as the farm stable, while the family lived above it in crude quarters. The lieutenant was shocked to learn that Major Murray MacLeod and Lieutenant H.M. "Chuck" Walker were dead. Major John Hanson was in command, and as Madden was senior to the other surviving 'C' Company officer, Lieutenant Sam McGowan, he became the company's second-in-command. Hanson confided that he was happy to see Madden, because they had written him off for dead. Then Hanson told him to get out on the line and see to the men, who numbered just sixty-eight. Despite the fact that he was exhausted, Madden recognized that the paratroopers holding the line at le Mesnil were practically zombies after four days of almost constant action. Faces were gaunt, expressions flat, and filth and dried blood grimed their tattered uniforms and bodies. Almost every man had a ragged bandage covering one wound or another. But when he spoke with each in turn, he heard a quiet, understated confidence in their voices. Madden figured these men could take on just about anything the Germans threw at them and win. He surely hoped that was the case, for even as Griffin led his mauled band of troops into the battalion's lines, it was obvious the battle for the crossroads was far from over.[20]

Despite being unable to hold onto the farmhouse, Griffin's charge proved a success because the Germans chose not to reoccupy it, confining themselves instead to sniping at the Canadian lines from the orchard. No tally of the losses suffered by Griffin's frontal assault group were compiled, but Toseland's smaller band suffered terribly. Of the twenty-five who went into the attack, eight were killed and thirteen wounded. Toseland amazingly escaped without a scratch, despite the fact that several bullets pierced his clothing during the charge on the hedgerow.[21]

Although the Canadian paratroops didn't know it, their decisive counterstrike against the two grenadier regiments meant that most of the 346th Grenadier Division were still reorganizing on the morning of June 9 and so unable to launch an offensive alongside 21st Panzer Division at Escoville. Once again, a failure on the part of German divisional and regimental commanders to communicate intentions clearly had resulted in attacks being launched piecemeal, with nothing achieved but the spilling of blood on both sides.

The June 8 fighting also bought 1st Canadian Parachute Battalion a relative lull in combat the following day, which the men took advantage of to try getting a bit of rest. On 'C' Company's front line, Corporal Dan Hartigan envied those who could easily find sleep despite the distant sounds of war. As evening settled in on June 9, temperatures remained warm, and the corporal watched wearily as "flares coursed into the sky... The crump-crump-crump of sporadic artillery fire chilled the lonely, sleepless senses of the infantrymen."[22]

PART THREE

SLUGGING MATCHES: D+4 TO D+6

17

Getting Nowhere

DURING THE NIGHT of June 9–10, Major General Rod Keller's headquarters bustled with activity while staff drafted plans aimed at closing the gap between its two leading brigades, as well as establishing firm control over all ground north of the Caen-Bayeux highway. As these plans were developed, the officers started looking beyond the highway, with a mind to carrying out an armoured thrust from the Bretteville-l'Orgueilleuse strongpoint to occupy a steep hill immediately south of Cheux that dominated the surrounding country. In the original invasion plan, 2nd Canadian Armoured Brigade was to have cleared both the village and hill as its last action on D-Day. But the brigade's three fighting regiments had come up well short of this objective due to problems getting ashore and then stiff resistance met throughout the inland advance.

The 1st Hussars and Fort Garry Horse regiments, which had landed close behind the assaulting infantry battalions, had experienced heavy losses among their squadrons equipped with the experimental amphibious duplex-drive Sherman tank. Many of these self-propelled tanks had foundered in the rough seas, while others were immobilized or sunk by mines and beach obstacles. Once ashore, the tankers were exposed on the open stretches of sand, facing antitank guns that were dug into concrete pillboxes. Even when the beach was taken, the tanks were badly delayed heading inland due to the difficulty of getting over or around the steep seawalls. During the inland advance, the armoured regiments had been forced to crawl along at the pace of the infantry, who were often driven to ground by well-concealed machine-gun positions. To press on alone without the infantry was to risk being knocked out by fire from equally well-hidden antitank guns and Grenadiers firing Panzerfausts—shoulder-fired antitank weapons. By day's end on June 6, tank losses within 2 CAB's regiments had reached a state of crisis, with the 1st Hussars and Fort Garry Horse mustering barely half their strength.

But now Keller believed the time had come when tanks could regain the initiative on the battlefield and achieve the D-Day objectives. He summoned 2 CAB's Brigadier Bob Wyman and instructed him to put together two operational plans for his tanks, whereby one regiment participated in clearing the Mue valley to the highway while another broke out of Bretteville and secured what was dubbed the Cheux hill feature.[1]

Having gone through the Sicily invasion and up the Italian boot to Ortona as the brigadier of 1st Canadian Armoured Brigade, Wyman had the most battle experience of all Keller's brigadiers. During the fight for Ortona, he had drawn the ire of 1st Canadian Infantry Division's Major General Chris Vokes for a perceived hesitance to fully support operations with his tank regiments. Vokes had been so angry at the conclusion of the December 1943 fighting he had made it known to Eighth Army headquarters staff that he would welcome the replacement of 1 CAB as the division's armoured support by any British tank brigade. As the British considered 1 CAB the finest tank brigade in Eighth Army's complement, the staff quickly removed it from Vokes, retaining it as a fire brigade to send to whatever division most needed tank assistance.

Vokes had almost immediate cause to regret his hasty outburst when Wyman was assigned to a stint in England on the First Canadian Army staff as brigadier of Royal Artillery, and 1 CAB received a new brigadier that the notoriously outspoken divisional commander greatly respected. He did not, however, miss Wyman, who he considered "a bull-headed guy, a little lord unto himself." That he believed

Wyman felt that infantry but not tanks were expendable only fuelled his disdain for the man.[2]

Wyman's time at First Canadian Army headquarters was short, for once it was confirmed that 3 CID would be among the invasion assault divisions he was appointed to command 2 CAB. The division's Deputy Adjutant and Quarter Master General Lieutenant Colonel Ernest Côté particularly appreciated Wyman's tough, no-nonsense approach. On the first day ashore, when Keller sometimes appeared uncertain of what to do, Wyman was often at his shoulder providing advice based on his combat experience. Such advice, Côté noted, was "appreciated" by the divisional commander.[3]

Because the armour was expected to carry out these two operations in a bold dash, Wyman and his regimental commanders were placed in control, with the assigned infantry acting under their direction. This would be the combat debut for the division in an operation where infantry supported and were directed by tankers. During all earlier operations, the infantry brigadiers or their battalion commanders had had authority to assign specific supporting roles to the tankers, even those that saw the tanks ranging ahead of the foot soldiers.

This infantry-dominant command structure reflected standard Western Allied doctrine. Tanks were normally intended to act as well-armoured and highly mobile forward-based gun platforms capable of backing up advancing infantry at close quarters. This view was a major cause of the Allied failure to upgrade the Sherman tank in either firepower or armour thickness to enable it to engage in tank-versus-tank battle against German Tigers and Panthers. The only major improvement offered Commonwealth tankers by the time of the invasion was the provision of one 17-pounder fitted Firefly tank to each troop, which gave the unit a powerful antitank capability. But no thought had been given to equipping all Shermans with the heavier gun because the 75-millimetre was judged a better weapon for delivering high-explosive, armour-piercing, and phosphorous rounds at close range in support of infantry. The Americans showed no interest at all—dismissing the Firefly as unnecessary—in increasing the main gun power of the Sherman. Instead, they adopted a doctrine of putting enough tanks on the ground to ensure they outnumbered German armour.

For the forthcoming two Canadian assaults, however, there could be no assurance that the Shermans would enjoy anything close to superior armoured mass. Keller could give little intelligence to Wyman with regard to the number or dispositions of enemy units operating in the Mue valley or between Bretteville and the Cheux hill feature. Whatever his failings might have been in the Mediterranean, Wyman had demonstrated no hesitance in committing his three tank regiments to battle either during the assault landings or the drive inland. The result was that all three regiments were still badly depleted by the heavy losses suffered. Although the personnel of 2nd Canadian Armoured Brigade Workshop worked tirelessly to repair tanks as fast as they were recovered and new armour was delivered to the front as soon as it arrived on the beach, the rebuilding efforts were frustrated by continuing high daily losses. Crews were also badly depleted, although there were generally spare tankers sitting around at the regimental headquarters for lack of Shermans.

By the end of June 9, the situation had worsened significantly. On June 7, the brigade's first post-landing operational tank status report showed 115 Shermans fit for action, with 21 to be ready in twenty-four hours, and 36 knocked completely out. Among the fit Shermans, the Firefly model numbered 17 fit, 3 on the to-be-fit roster, and none knocked out. As for Stuart Honeys, 15 were fit, 3 to be fit, and 6 knocked out.[4]

At the end of June 9, the brigade reported only 112 Shermans still fit for a fight, with one Sherman scheduled for service in twenty-four hours. This despite having lost only 11 Shermans in battle that day. Of the fit Shermans, 13 were Firefly models, and no more of these would be available for twenty-four hours. Of those lost during the day, three were Fireflies.[5]

Wyman's immediate concern was to get as many functioning tanks as possible up to the regiments that were to carry out the two-phased operation. To speed the process of moving tanks from the beach landing sites or 2nd Canadian Armoured Brigade's Workshop,

top · Canadian troops welcomed by French civilians as they liberate an unidentified village on June 10. Donald I. Grant, LAC PA–137978.

above · Canadian soldier armed with a Sten gun stands guard inland from Juno Beach on June 9. R. Bell, LAC PA–132802.

top left · Men from Regina Rifles 'D' Company using a hole in the wall surrounding la Ferme de Cardonville as an observation point for monitoring German movement. Donald I. Grant, LAC PA-129042.

left · Regina Rifles 'D' Company soldier at a loophole cut into the wall at la Ferme de Cardonville. Donald I. Grant, LAC PA-131423.

above · Panther tank that Rifleman Joe Lapointe knocked out in Bretteville on the night of June 8–9 with a PIAT gun. Frank L. Dubervill, LAC PA-130149.

above · Canadian tanks in distance engage advancing German infantry on June 9, a battle that appeared to little disturb the cow in the foreground. R. Bell, LAC PA–137444.

top right · Private Alvin Guitar and Gunner W.M. Holmes guard Hitler Youth prisoners that were rounded up by Le Régiment de la Chaudière on June 12. Frank L. Dubervill, LAC PA–133958.

right · The aftermath of battle in Bretteville. Building in foreground was Regina Rifles battalion headquarters. Behind, the ruins of the cathedral. Frank L. Dubervill, LAC PA–133735.

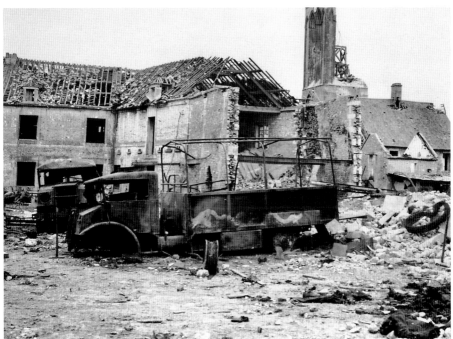

top left · During a brief lull in the fighting, a group of Canadians improvise a meal with compo rations and some fresh farm eggs. Left to right: Lance Corporal W.T. Haggerty, Lance Corporal B.J. Doucette, Corporal A. Boudreau, Company Sergeant Major R.M. Cooper. In the background is Lance Corporal Tellum. R. Bell, LAC PA–142037.

left · One of the Fort Garry Horse tanks knocked out in Rots. In the background stands the village's badly damaged church. Frank L. Dubervill, LAC PA–169307.

above · Temporary cemetery established outside Bernières-sur-Mer by 8th Canadian Infantry Brigade for its soldiers killed during the fighting of June 6–12. Frank L. Dubervill, LAC PA–133753.

Sherman tank at the back of a column moving inland from Juno Beach on June 8, its turret reversed to guard the rear. The French tricolour it is flying serves as a recognition signal. Donald I. Grant, LAC PA–131424.

he issued immediate orders for all regiments to send back "all tank crews for which tanks are presently lacking." Only three or four surplus tankers were to remain on hand to replace men who became unfit for duty. Those sent to the rear were cobbled into crews and assigned to the next available Sherman.[6]

He also ordered the workshop to pull out the stops and get as many Shermans operational as possible before dawn of June 11. By mid-afternoon on June 10, the workshop was able to report to brigade headquarters that it would have "11 tanks ready for return to units tonight." Unfortunately, only two were destined to a regiment tasked with the attack.

On June 9, the 1st Hussars had thirty-five Shermans mounting 75-millimetre guns and six with 17-pounders, and had been promised two more 75-millimetre Shermans by the end of June 10. The Fort Garry Horse could field only thirty-four regular Shermans and four Fireflys. The Sherbrooke Fusiliers would not participate in the forthcoming attacks as this regiment was the most depleted, having lost most of its strength in the desperate Authie-Buron battle of June 7. By June 9, it still had only twenty-seven fit-to-fight 75-millimetre Shermans and three Fireflys. The Sherbrookes would be the division's armoured reserve when the other two regiments went into action. Wyman bulked it up by sending nine fit-to-fight tanks its way.[7]

Wyman assigned the job of taking Cheux to the 1st Hussars, and clearing the Mue valley to the Fort Garry Horse. When Lieutenant Colonel Ray Colwell heard this news, he was still so short of both tanks and manpower that his 1st Hussars could only field two squadrons rather than the normal three. Colwell pleaded for reinforcements, and Wyman promised to see what was possible. He assured the worried officer that he would not commit the regiment into action until June 12. Between now and then, the brigadier said the 1st Hussars should make use of the time to "get as much rest as possible for tank crews, who are thoroughly tired out."[8]

Keller, Wyman, and their respective staffs spent the first part of the day working out a general operational plan. The divisional commander informed the brigadier that the 1st Hussars would be accompanied in their attack by the Queen's Own Rifles, while No. 46 Royal Marine Commando supported the Fort Garry Horse. Wyman and his people next got to work laying out the full sequence and timing schedules for each assault to attain a series of waypoints en route to the final objective.

At 2100 hours, Wyman held an information conference during which he briefed regimental staffs. Wyman told the assembled officers that the 1st Hussars, supported by the Queen's Own and probably two troops of self-propelled antitank guns, would advance across six miles of ground from Bretteville to the Cheux hill feature on the division's right flank. This would happen on June 12. On June 11, the Fort Garry Horse, he said, would "make good an intermediate objective," by clearing the Mue valley from Vieux Cairon through to la Villeneuve. Once this hamlet was taken, the tenuous hold that the Regina Rifles had on Norrey-en-Bessin south of the Caen-Bayeux highway would be much more secure, enabling the village garrison to support the 1st Hussars and Queen's Own Rifles during their ensuing assault. The Fort Garry force was to reach la Villeneuve by "last light." The Canadian division would be free by June 13 to begin advancing in force south of the Caen-Bayeux highway to align with the long thrust into the German defences that the 1st Hussars and Queen's Own would have won on the 12th.[9]

The attack by 2 CAB, Wyman understood, would loosely coincide with a planned major operation by the British 7th Armoured Division through the 50th Infantry Division towards Villers-Bocage. This was the first phase of General Bernard Montgomery's flanking offensive from the right towards Caen. The 50th Division would also put in an assault to the left of Cheux between Cristot and Tilly-sur-Seulles. While the British and Canadian operations were not coordinated, they might strain the Germans' ability to concentrate reserves to stem a massed assault developing over a couple of days across a broad front. Wyman had no information, though, on the specific timing Second Army had set out for the beginning of the 7th Armoured Division–50th Infantry Division offensive. He only knew that it was to occur sometime in the next few days. So it was likely that by the time the British offensive began, 2 CAB would have already cleared the Mue and be established at Cheux, enabling the Canadians to anchor 50th Division's left flank as it and the 7th Division pivoted eastwards once Tilly and Villers-Bocage were taken.

WHILE WYMAN was carrying out his briefing on the night of June 10, Second British Army commander General Sir Miles Dempsey was ironing out final details with his own staff for Montgomery's two-pincer scheme. Originally, the operation was to have involved not only 7th Armoured Division's major thrust west of Caen, but also a matching effort by the 51st Highland Division striking out from 6th Airborne Division's perimeter east of Caen. Dempsey's hopes to execute the operation in this manner were frustrated early on June 10 by German counterattacks against the paratroops.

The major thrust of these attacks launched by the 346th Grenadier Division was to achieve a breakout from the centre of a dangerous inward bend in the airborne division lines at Bréville, less than two miles from Ranville and Pegasus Bridge. This deep indentation in the airborne division's lines had existed since the close of battle on June 6, when the casualty-riddled British 9th Parachute Battalion had been unable to eliminate the German defenders holding Bréville. While Bréville was the focal point on June 10, the paratroops holding the line all along le Plein–Bois de Bavent ridge were subjected to heavy artillery fire and sporadic probes by infantry seeking to exploit any weak point.

At le Mesnil crossroads, 1st Canadian Parachute Battalion was hammered repeatedly by shellfire, probed by patrols, and harassed by continuous sniper fire. Over the course of June 9–10, two strictly defensive days, the Canadians had sixteen casualties, of which six were fatal. This represented 4 per cent of the total Canadian strength at le Mesnil, which "indicated just how severe the results could be when a methodical, calculating and efficient enemy put their long experience to work," noted paratrooper Corporal Dan Hartigan. "On an attack day casualties were to be expected. On a defensive day they seemed less necessary and so all the sadder." It was obvious to the men holding the line that the battalion's combat ability was being slowly whittled away.[10]

Gravely concerned that 6th Airborne Division's grinding attrition rates jeopardized its ability to hold the lodgement east of the River Orne, 1 British Corps commander Lieutenant General John Crocker decided the 51st Division should take over responsibility for the southern half of the perimeter. He also placed 5th Battalion, The Black Watch, under 6th Airborne Division command, as part of its 9th Battalion, with specific orders to eliminate the Bréville inward bend on June 11.[11] Although necessary, the commitment of the 51st Division to stabilizing the front east of the Orne meant it would be unable to carry out Montgomery's left-hand pincer movement in anything more than a localized manner.

Unaware of Crocker's decision, 2 CAB Brigadier Wyman and his staff were badly hobbled on June 10 by a lack of intelligence on the strength or composition of German forces in either the Mue valley or south of the Caen-Bayeux highway opposite 7th Canadian Infantry Brigade's front. Vigorous reconnaissance patrolling was ordered in both of these areas, with little success. The North Nova Scotia Highlanders attempted to slip a patrol into Vieux Cairon, but it was quickly pinned down by fire from the Germans holding there and had to withdraw without learning anything of value. Meanwhile, the Stormont, Dundas and Glengarry Highlanders pushed a patrol out towards Buron, which they found to be heavily occupied. Bypassing the village, the patrol pressed on towards Authie but turned back about halfway because of heavy German activity in the area. The Highland Light Infantry carried out a patrol to the east of the division's area of operations that failed to find either British or German troops.[12]

While patrols beyond the Canadian front lines were coming up dry, this was not the case for one small unauthorized patrol in friendly territory. The North Novas were still recovering from the debacle of June 7 and taking fresh casualties every day from the persistent shelling as well as patrols that the 9 CIB battalions were sending out on a nightly basis. On June 10, the arrival of a fresh draft of officers to replace those lost in the fighting led to a reorganization of the battalion and the re-imposition of a higher level of discipline. The men were ordered to shave and wash, but also treated to a welcome addition of an egg for breakfast. Then they were ordered to get what rest was possible.

A few enterprising troops, however, took the opportunity to stand down from sentry duty and explore the farm buildings near their position. In one, a 750-gallon barrel of wine was discovered in the basement. Word was quickly sent out and a large group of North Novas queued up in the cellar to fill canteens only to have, lamented the battalion war diarist, "the 'dirty new adjutant' stop them and place a guard on it."[13]

While things were quieting down somewhat on 9 CIB's front, snipers remained a persistent problem for the Canadian Scottish holding Putot-en-Bessin. The Germans were based in a strongpoint in a woods south of the railroad between Brouay and Putot. This same position posed a threat to both 7 CIB's right flank security and also the forthcoming attack, as the 1st Hussars must pass through le Mesnil-Patry, only about a mile to the east. For these reasons, brigade ordered the strongpoint eliminated. Lieutenant Colonel Fred Cabeldu decided to wait until after dark to send a fighting patrol into the wood to wipe out the Germans, but in the meantime wanted to rid the area around his perimeter of snipers. Captain J.D.M. "Doug" Gillan offered to take some men outside the perimeter in his platoon's Bren carriers and carry out a sweep of the area with the intent of deliberately drawing fire, determining the location of each sniper, and then killing him. As Gillan was explaining his idea, Captain Harold Gonder of the Cameron Highlanders' No. 5 Platoon volunteered a couple of carriers mounting Vickers heavy machine guns. These guns were fitted to a pintle that enabled them to be fired perpendicularly—perfect for blasting snipers out of trees.

The carriers set off at high speed along a road routinely subjected to heavy sniper activity. When the snipers brought their guns to bear on the carriers, the Camerons ripped into the trees with the Vickers, and Gonder saw several enemy soldiers shot out of the branches during the first quarter mile of their run. Just ahead, the road was crossed by another, and Gillan and Gonder had planned that the carriers should make a sharp turn onto this road, follow it for a ways, and then

take another that dogged back to the battalion perimeter. Glancing behind him, Gonder noticed that the other carrier had fallen about fifty
yards behind while slowing to take out a sniper. Gonder worried that
its driver would fail to make the turn and end up running straight
down the current road, possibly driving into an enemy ambush.

Proper procedure called for a commander issuing orders to other
carriers in a column to wave one or the other of specially designated
signal flags above the little vehicle's armoured side while remaining
inside its protected cover. Forgetting the flag procedure in the urgency
of the moment, Gonder stood up "to wave my hand. The instant I
stood up I saw a great flash and it was just as if a giant hand poked
me back in the seat and I knew I had been hit." The driver jammed on
the brakes and said, "Oh my God, sir." Gonder snapped at him to get
moving or they would all get hit. The captain was angry, knowing
"I wouldn't have been hit if I hadn't made this mistake, my silly behaviour. One of my corporals reached over with a knife and cut my
clothing right down to the skin and put on the field dressing."

Back in the perimeter lines, Gonder walked into the Canadian
Scottish headquarters and reported to Cabeldu, who said, "Get somebody else to give your report. You go see the [Medical Officer]." Gonder
was so furious with himself that when he got to the Regimental Aid
Post he "started gabbling away to the MO, who said, 'Don't talk, Hal.'
He was a gentle man and he poked around and told me I had been hit
in the throat and he was afraid my vocal cords might have been damaged and so didn't want me to talk." Gonder was quickly evacuated to a
rear area hospital and from there to hospital in England.[14]

As darkness fell, Lieutenants S.R. Ross and I.P. MacDonald
formed up No. 11 and No. 12 platoons of 'B' Company for the patrol
that was to clear the woods. Earlier reconnaissance indicated that the
enemy position contained several machine guns and possibly some
antitank guns or mortars. To force the Germans to take cover during
the patrol's approach, the rest of the battalion would pound the wood
with its 3-inch and 4.2-inch mortars while two troops of Sherbrooke
Fusiliers tanks banged it up with their 75-millimetre guns.

The two officers planned to cross the railway cutting by slipping
over the bridge that had been the focus of much fighting during the

counterattack of June 8–9. As MacDonald's No. 12 Platoon led the way onto the bridge, however, it "came under heavy mortar and MG fire from down the track on either side. No. 11 Platoon, less two sections which were held up, made their way across the track, taking out at least one MG on the track and one beyond it. From then on," a battalion after-action report stated, "the situation was one of very close confused fighting, our troops in the open taking on enemy machine guns in fortified positions and deep slit trenches and trying to avoid mortar fire and fire from our tanks. Two MGs were taken out for certain and losses, at least as heavy as our own, inflicted on the enemy. Our losses were fairly heavy—Lt. MacDonald was killed at the bridge and 17 [other ranks were] killed or missing.

"Noteworthy during the raid was the aggressiveness of our troops in the face of terrific fire; the skill of the enemy in the handling of his fixed lines of fire... and finally the devotion of the stretcher bearers and patrols sent to look after the wounded."[15] When Corporal A.L. Frost, who was pinch-hitting as MacDonald's Acting Sergeant, saw his commander shot down and killed, he took over the platoon without hesitation. As he guided the men back towards the north side of the railroad, Frost discovered Private D.W.M. Ives lying on the ground incapacitated by a wound. Frost hefted the man over his shoulder and carried him through enemy fire to safety, an act that won him a Military Medal.[16]

The speed with which the patrol had been discovered and torn into by well-hidden German troops provided some telling intelligence, despite the failure to come anywhere close to reaching the strongpoint in the woods. It was clear that the 12th SS Panzer Grenadiers still had strong and determined forces immediately south of the railway and were determined to prevent any major push by the Canadians into that area—sobering news for those planning the 1st Hussars–Queen's Own Rifles phase of the forthcoming attack.

JUNE 10 PROVED a day fraught with crisis and frustration for the Germans. East of the River Orne, the counterattack out of Bréville had failed to make any progress, with the grenadiers and supporting self-propelled guns quickly forced back into a defensive position centred on the village. For all their efforts during three days of concerted attacks against the paratroopers, the Germans had failed to gain any ground or to annihilate any airborne battalions. Instead, the forces fighting east of the Orne were tied down in a costly war of attrition with little in the way of reserves to make up their losses.

The 12th ss (Hitlerjugend) Panzer Division's 25th Panzer Grenadier Regiment facing the 3rd British Infantry Division and 3 CID's 9th Infantry Brigade had also been forced back onto a defensive posture, a fact that mightily chafed its aggressive commander. After the disastrous failures of his attacks on Bretteville-l'Orgueilleuse and Norrey-en-Bessin, Standartenführer Kurt Meyer knew he lacked sufficient strength to both hold his sections of the line and carry out further offensive actions. Yet the obstacle that Norrey presented, jutting deeply into the German lines, remained, and General der Panzertruppen Leo Freiherr Geyr von Schweppenburg had once again ordered the Canadians kicked out. Although Army Group B Generalfeldmarschall Erwin Rommel had instructed 1 Panzer Corps's divisions west of the River Orne to assume defensive postures, von Schweppenburg still hoped to have that decision reversed. Then on the night of June 10–11, he would commit the 21st Panzer, 12th ss, and Panzer Lehr divisions against the British-Canadian front in one massive assault that might yet hurl the Allies into the sea.

Accordingly, the 12th ss had scrambled to gather some semblance of a force that could strike Norrey before day dawned on June 10. All that Brigadeführer Fritz Witt could call on, however, was the infantry of the 12th ss Panzerpionier Battalion. Deployed behind the 26th Panzer Grenadier Regiment's perimeter south of the village, the battalion began a hasty assault unsupported by any artillery or mortar fire. Immediately greeted by withering artillery, mortar, and machine-gun fire, the attack—the battalion's first—quickly faltered. While some platoons managed to reach the edge of Norrey, none could get in among the fiercely resisting Regina Rifles. Dawn found much of the German battalion helplessly pinned down. Although a withdrawal was ordered, some sections were unable to comply until nightfall because of the intensity of fire directed their way. The butcher's bill for a fight the Regina Rifles war diarist felt so insignificant as to not mention tallied eighty Germans killed, wounded, or missing.[17] The Reginas reported no casualties worth mentioning from the action. While the Reginas were perhaps modest to a fault, one veteran British divisional commander later wrote that: "The Canadian defence of Norrey and Bretteville over the 8th to 10th June must surely go down as one of the finest small unit actions of WWII."[18]

The Regina war diarist did remark with somewhat bland enthusiasm on the welcome presence of Typhoon dive-bombers striking positions near Cheux at about 1900 hours on June 10.[19] In fact, despite the continuing cloudy and cool weather, most of the Canadian battalions on the front lines witnessed a great increase in Allied air operations, with fighter-bombers swarming overhead throughout the day. By June 10, Allied control of the skies over Normandy was virtually complete, the Luftwaffe seldom venturing from its airfields to give battle. The Allied air superiority was greatly aided by the fact that air force and army engineers had managed to open several temporary airstrips in the Normandy beachhead to serve as refuelling stations. These had received their first customers on June 9 when planes from No. 144 Wing, Royal Canadian Air Force set down mid-morning. Later that afternoon, thinking they were the first to carry out such a feat, 401 Squadron, RCAF landed for refuelling and received the disappointing news that 144 Wing had got there first.[20]

Plans were afoot for all of No. 144 Wing, under command of the famed fighter ace Wing Commander J.E. "Johnnie" Johnson, to be the first RCAF or RAF wing to set up permanent shop at a Normandy landing strip on June 11. Already an advanced headquarters party was on the ground at St. Croix-sur-Mer. The field, Flying Officer Frederick A.W.J. Wilson of 441 Squadron noted, "was just a bulldozed strip of land. Bulldozers had cleaned up a strip of farmer's field and made us a little runway." Tents were set up nearby for use as quarters, mess halls, and supply depots.[21]

Now able to rapidly refuel and re-arm in Normandy rather than having to return to bases in England, the fighter-bomber squadrons could spend far more hours conducting operational sorties in the battle zone. For the Germans, this meant that attempting to move by day anywhere in the rear became all the more hazardous.

The Allies were also able to use airpower to deadly effect due to an intelligence coup by Ultra. Montgomery's staff received word that Panzer Group West's headquarters was to be established in the village of la Caine about twelve miles south of Caen, effective the evening of June 9. This report filed at 0439 hours on June 10 included detailed information on which houses the Germans were using.[22]

Such precise targeting information was too tempting for Supreme Headquarters Allied Expeditionary Force to pass up and a hastily planned air strike was launched. Deciding on a maximum effort, Allied Expeditionary Air Force put together a joint fighter-bomber and medium bomber operation that included the B-25 Mitchell bombers of No. 139 Wing, RAF of No. 2 Group, 2nd Tactical Air Force, commanded by Wing Commander Clarence "Larry" Dunlap.

A thirty-six-year-old Cape Bretoner from Sydney Mines—who traced his Canadian ancestry back ten generations to 1761—Dunlap's fascination with flight had begun when he was eleven. Adulthood failed to diminish his interest, so at the urging of Royal Canadian Air Force recruiters he enlisted upon completion of an electrical engineering science baccalaureate degree in July 1928. When war broke out, Dunlap was director of armament at RCAF headquarters in Ottawa. Going overseas in 1942, he first commanded RCAF Station Leeming in Yorkshire before taking command of No. 331 Wing, RCAF in May 1943. Posted to North Africa, this Wellington Bomber wing supported the Allied invasions of Sicily and Italy—flying almost 2,200 missions with a loss of only eighteen planes. Appointed a Commander of the Order of the British Empire for this effort, Dunlap returned to England to take command of No. 139 Wing, RAF stationed in Cunsfold, Surrey, with the rank of Group Captain.

Dunlap's wing headed for the target at about 1900 hours on June 10. Although trained for pinpoint daylight bombing attacks, the Mitchells would this evening be forced to carry out a blind drop because heavy cloud cover was encountered the moment the planes crossed the Normandy coast.[23] The bombers successfully searched out la Caine, however, and hot on the heels of a low-level strike by four squadrons of rocket-firing Typhoons at 2030 hours, the seventy-one medium bombers dumped their payloads on the little village.

The attack annihilated the headquarters, turning it into a flaming ruin. While von Schweppenburg, who had arrived minutes before the attack, escaped with minor injuries, his Chief of Staff Generalmajor Edler von Dawans and sixteen others were killed. Among the dead was I ss Panzer Corps liaison officer Hauptsturmführer Wilhelm Beck. Those staff officers who survived the raid were evacuated—the wounded to hospitals, the merely shaken to a new location where the command might slowly rebuild.

The destruction of Panzer Group West's headquarters threw the German operational command structure in Normandy into even greater chaos. To fill the gap in the command chain, I ss Panzer Corps was placed under direct control of Seventh Army's Generaloberst Friederich Dollman, with corps commander Obergruppenführer Sepp Dietrich once again left as the senior commander in the Caen area. Any thought of the Panzer divisions carrying out offensive actions in the next few days died with the destruction of Panzer Group West. Dietrich was increasingly fatalistic, complaining to Rommel after his corps passed to Seventh Army control that no further offensive action was possible and that without major reinforcement by additional Panzer divisions the Germans could hold the existing line around the Allies no more than three weeks. That such a hardened Nazi loyalist would talk with such open defeatism took many of his subordinates by surprise, but one commented later that if nothing else Dietrich had always been "a realist." Told by Rommel that a limited offensive posture must be maintained, Dietrich growled, "With what? We need another eight or ten divisions in a day or two, or we are finished... I am being bled to death and getting nowhere."[24]

News of Panzer Group West's destruction hit staff at Oberkommando der Wehrmacht hard, prompting the war diarist there to note that the event caused a "crisis." Nobody in the German intelligence community had any suspicions that the headquarters at la Caine had been so precisely located through Allied ability to read its wireless codes. Instead, it was believed that either the French underground had reported the location or a British reconnaissance plane spotted circling the village earlier in the day had determined that the village housed a high-value target.

One thing was clear to everyone, from OKW staffers to Rommel—Dollman was no von Schweppenburg, and without the veteran tanker's steely leadership 1 ss Panzer Corps was incapable of delivering the concentrated blow necessary to split the beachhead into two. At best, all that Dietrich could probably muster was the kind of "penny-packet" tank attacks that had frittered away much of the strength of the three divisions.[25]

At 12th ss Division's headquarters, Witt's staff had managed to canvass its regiments and battalions to determine the casualties suffered during the past four days of fighting. For a division that considered itself a cut above the Canadians they fought, the statistics were grim—about 900 killed, wounded, or missing, with 220 of these being fatal. Twenty-five tanks had been wrecked beyond repair. For all these casualties, the division had achieved precious little. Although they had stemmed the Canadian advance on Carpiquet airport, the Hitlerjugend had failed totally to achieve its intention—a major breakthrough to the landing beaches and victory over the Allies. It was now bogged down in static, defensive warfare—which every Panzer commander knew was a tragic waste of such a division's armoured potential.

And there was no doubt June 11 would bring more fighting and increasing casualties. Although the Canadians had been thrown back into a largely defensive posture on their left flank, wireless intercepts by the Hitlerjugend suggested an assault was shaping up around Norrey-en-Bessin. The Reginas' dagger continued to threaten the German front.[26]

18

Attack at Once

LATE ON JUNE 10, while still putting finishing touches to his Villers-Bocage offensive, Second British Army's General Miles Dempsey received an intelligence warning that the Germans were massing a major counterattack from Caen into the still existing wedge between the 3rd British and 3rd Canadian divisions. Anxious to prevent his operation being pre-empted by the German action, Dempsey immediately ordered 1 British Corps commander Lieutenant General John Crocker to concentrate most of the armour available in the Sword Beach area on the high ground south of Douvres-la-Délivrande to meet any such attack.

As dawn broke over Normandy on June 11, the sudden buildup of British tanks in the area was duly noted by the besieged Luftwaffe stronghold at the Douvres radar station and reported to Obergruppenführer Sepp Dietrich, the 1 ss Panzer Corps commander. "Continuous movement, heavy and medium tanks, towards southwest," the radar station lookouts informed Dietrich by wireless message. "More than eighty tanks counted in one hour." Somewhat later, they reported about two hundred medium tanks gathering in the Anguerny area "with transport echelon facing south."[1]

General Bernard Montgomery happily monitored this buildup of armoured force, hoping the Germans would attempt a counterattack into the gap. If they came, the British armour would fix the German tanks in place and destroy them. "We are VERY strong now astride the road Caen-Bayeux about the junction of 3 Div and 3 Canadian Div, and if the enemy attacks he should be seen off. I have 400 tanks there," he said in a note to his Chief of Staff at 21st Army Group.[2]

Dietrich, who had neither instructions from Army Group B nor intent to launch a major counterattack into this area, interpreted this concentration of tanks as a sign of a forthcoming major offensive in that area. An alert was sent to his Panzer divisions that they should prepare to meet strong Allied attacks.

Contributing to Dietrich's anxiety was the heightened level of activity on the front where 12th ss (Hitlerjugend) Panzer Division faced the 9th Canadian Infantry Brigade, falling as it did to the immediate left of the tanks concentrating near Anguerny. Here, Brigadier Ben Cunningham had launched an aggressive program of patrolling during the night, with two battalions sending company-sized patrols out to prowl no man's land and wreak havoc behind the German front held by 25th ss Panzer Grenadier Regiment. The Stormont, Dundas and Glengarry Highlanders sent 'B' Company out into the dangerous ground between les Buissons and Vieux Cairon, while 'A' Company swept the cluster of farms designated as le Vey, a little to a mile northwest of Vieux Cairon, to ensure against German infiltration to their rear. While not venturing into Vieux Cairon, the first patrol circled the village without detecting any Germans.[3] At 0140 hours, the second patrol filtered through le Vey, passing a line of abandoned German slit trenches on the edge of the clustered buildings. A careful sweep turned up no further signs of the enemy and only a single civilian the patrol decided was harmless. By 0230 hours, the patrol had returned to the battalion lines at les Buissons.[4]

Cunningham had grander plans for the Highland Light Infantry, instructing that a company-strength fighting patrol probe Buron during the night of June 10–11. A total of one hundred men were mustered for this operation—the eighty-eight strong 'C' Company supported by twelve sappers from 18 Field Company, Royal Canadian Engineers. Their orders were not only to check enemy strength in the village but to undertake the "engagement and destruction of enemy and equipment."[5] The patrol was to pass through the Glens at les Buissons and travel cross-country to Buron.

When Major R.D. Hodgins reported to Lieutenant Colonel H.S. Griffiths, he found the HLI commander staring out into the darkness on the edge of les Buissons. "Brigadier wants a night fighting patrol of company strength taken through to stir things up. Hodge, I want you to take that patrol." Still getting used to being a combat company commander, Hodgins's first thought was that he was out of his depth with responsibility for "all these guys."

He also considered it crazy to go out into no man's land with such a large force on what was supposed to be a stealthy mission, and argued "to just take about twelve people as over 100 was too many, some would get lost. I didn't want to take any radio sets either as they crackled too loudly. Griffiths allowed me to cut back to three Platoons of twenty-five men each [plus the sappers]. We worked out a set of signals using Very pistols and flares."[6]

With faces blackened and stocking caps on, the patrol slipped out of les Buissons at 2223 hours. Thin cloud obscured the moon and Hodgins hoped to hell it stayed that way until this business was finished. A short distance out, the pointman spotted a clutch of Germans digging away and talking to each other in soft voices. The word "minen" kept cropping up, so it was easy to figure the men were planting mines. Not wanting to tip his hand so early, Hodgins quietly backed away from the Germans and pushed on for Buron.

Outside Buron, Hodgins and his men looked over the situation and noted four machine-gun positions set up on each corner of the village. There seemed to be a small number of Germans dug in around the houses on Buron's northern edge. Pressing into the village itself, several buildings were found to contain bodies of dead Germans, but there seemed to be no military equipment or ammunition stored anywhere.

As the patrol began pulling out of Buron, the clouds abruptly parted and an almost full moon beamed down on "all these guys strung out behind me." In for a penny, Hodgins thought, and ordered the company to spread into an assault line as they headed for a German forward outpost that had been bypassed on the way in and now stood between them and a safe extraction route. From behind, gunfire suddenly broke out. Looking over his shoulder, the major saw tracers flashing to and fro. Then someone reported that one platoon was missing, apparently locked in a firefight with some Germans.

That left him with fifty men and most of the sappers. But everyone "was armed to the teeth," so he figured that number would suffice and led them into a sharp firefight that ended when the Highlanders over-ran the position. At one moment in the battle, with bullets cracking through the air all around, someone started yelling "Major Hodgins, Major Hodgins." The officer wished the lad would shut up because "the Germans are going to shoot for this Major Hodgins guy!"[7]

With the enemy position silenced, Hodgins ordered his men back to les Buissons. They dashed back, pursued all the way by searching German mortar fire that was able to keep the large force spotted in the moonlight. But the fear of fire paled in comparison to tripping over rotting corpses of North Nova Scotia Highlanders and Panzer Grenadiers who had been killed during the withdrawal from Buron on June 7. Several times, the mortaring drove Hodgins to dive into slit trenches or craters and each time he shared the hole with dead men.[8]

Arriving back at les Buissons at 0330 hours, Hodgins found the missing platoon had already made it home. They had bumped into and killed a two-man German mine-laying party.[9] This had initiated a running fight between the platoon and some Panzer Grenadiers that resulted in Lieutenant R.L. Harvey and Corporal Hedrich being slightly wounded. They, however, were the patrol's only casualties. Hodgins looked around at his men and noted that "everyone was high as a kite... first action and made it back!"[10] The HLI war diarist wrote in conclusion that "it would seem a fighting patrol of this size is too unwieldy and could well have got into serious trouble, if there had been enemy [in force] in the village."[11]

NOT LONG AFTER this patrol had set out, Dempsey—concerned about the report that the Germans were teeing up a counterattack into the gap to the left of 9 CIB—decided to look more closely at 3rd Canadian Infantry Division's planned two-day offensive. The scheme worked up by 2nd Canadian Armoured Brigade's Brigadier Bob Wyman called for clearing of the Mue valley from Vieux Cairon through Rots to la Villeneuve on June 11, followed by a second-phase drive from Bretteville-l'Orgueilleuse through to the Cheux hill feature on June 12. This limited drive towards Cheux was now discussed in detail, with Dempsey's primary concern using this operation to support the larger British offensive.

By the end of that meeting, Dempsey reached a decision that drastically impacted the Canadians, but nobody from 2 CAB or 3 CID was consulted.[12] Nor was the revised role Dempsey envisioned for the 2 CAB attack passed immediately down the command chain to inform Wyman and his staff that the current operational plan needed to be reconfigured and rescheduled.[13] Deciding 2 CAB's schedule was too slow to benefit his grander operation, Dempsey instructed Crocker to order the Canadians to carry out both phases concurrently. Doing so would ensure that the 1st Hussars–Queen's Own Rifles drive to the Cheux hill feature conformed with the June 11 offensive by 7th Armoured Division and 50th British Infantry Division to the right. The decision, made in haste and based on faulty intelligence, would have tragic consequences.

Although Dempsey stated his intentions sometime before midnight on June 10, the process by which these instructions wound through the command chain to the affected battalions proved tortuously slow. Only at 0300 hours did Crocker's staff signal 3rd Canadian Division that 2 CAB, with one 8 CIB battalion under its command, would advance "NOT before 1200 [hours] 11 Jun[e] along axis Bretteville-l'Orgueilleuse, Norrey-en-Bessin, St. Mauvieu, Cheux, to [le Haut-du-Bosq]."[14] Here the orders inexplicably rested until 0730 hours when divisional staff informed 2 CAB that it was "to advance the timing of the attack towards Cheux, and carry it out as early as possible today, instead of tomorrow." With No. 46 Royal Marine Commando and its supporting squadron of Fort Garry Horse tanks already moving from near Anguerny to begin clearing the Mue valley, Brigadier Wyman had expected to put finishing touches to the Cheux phase of the attack that afternoon. Accordingly, he had scheduled a move of 2 CAB headquarters forward from Basly to Bray, where he would be close to the action developing during either phase of the offensive.[15] This move was already underway when the new orders arrived, but Wyman quickly alerted Lieutenant Colonel Ray Colwell at

0800 hours that the attack schedule was changed and the 1st Hussars "were to attack at 1300 hours."[16] Colwell, who had returned from an earlier O Group held in Basly at 0400 hours with assurances to his staff that they would have twenty-four hours to prepare for the forthcoming attack, was stunned. With the operation to begin in only five hours, the 1st Hussars began a frenzied attempt to get ready.

Fortunately, during the late evening of June 10, the regiment had received twenty tanks from the rear and the loan of an additional seven tanks and crews from the Fort Garry Horse. This brought the 1st Hussars' total Sherman tank strength to seventy-six, enabling Colwell to reconstitute the regiment's third squadron—'B'—under command of 'C' Squadron's second-in-command Captain Harry Harrison.[17] As many of the new crews who arrived with the reinforcement tanks had never seen combat, tank crews were shuffled to ensure that all had at least one or two veterans.[18]

The seven Fort Garry Horse tanks and their crews on loan were not the first that this regiment had provided to bolster the 1st Hussars. On June 8, Captain Cyril Tweedale's tank troop had been assigned to the Hussars and reported to 'C' Squadron's Major D'Arcy Marks. They had served with this squadron ever since.[19]

Within an hour, Colwell received further instructions to attend a final O Group convening at 1100 hours at 2 CAB's new headquarters in Bray.[20] Before departing, Colwell advised his staff to have all the squadron commanders and other relevant officers gathered for a last briefing on the attack plan at noon.[21] It all seemed dangerously accelerated.

The Queen's Own Rifles were even more surprised than the 1st Hussars to learn that the attack was advanced a day, for they had only arrived at their new assembly area of Neuf Mer—about a mile northeast of Bray—the previous evening. At 1000 hours, the battalion war diarist wrote that the day was to be "spent in clean up and further digging of slit trenches—rumours of an attack to be put in but nothing definite as yet." That all changed in a matter of minutes when Wyman signalled Lieutenant Colonel J.G. "Jock" Spragge with instructions "that the battalion will attack and seize the high ground south of Cheux. This is to be done by 'D' Company passing through the Regina Rifles at Norrey-en-Bessin and seizing le Mesnil-Patry. The balance of the battalion will then swing through them and by-pass Cheux, seizing the high ground at [le Haut-du-Bosq]."[22]

At 1100 hours, two very worried lieutenant colonels reported to Wyman at his newly established Bray headquarters. Again, the brigadier set out the attack plan and schedule. Spragge and Colwell both protested against embarking on the operation so hastily. There were many problems, not the least being that the Queen's Own and 1st Hussars had never worked together. Both commanders pointed out the other three glaring flaws in the plan. "First, no time was al-lowed for reconnaissance; secondly, no artillery preparation was pro-vided despite the fact that it was known that the place [le Mesnil] was strongly held; and thirdly, the men were expected to go riding on tanks through flat wheatfields, thus providing perfect targets for the defenders."[23] That the tanks would also be dangerously exposed to antitank fire was a given that Wyman and Colwell both recognized. After hearing the commanders out, the brigadier told them the orders held and they were to "get [the attack] in at once."[24] Realizing nothing could be done to delay the operation, Spragge and Colwell rushed back to their units.

BY THE TIME Wyman had started his final briefing for the Cheux as-sault, the first phase of 2 CAB's operation to clear the Mue valley had been underway for almost three hours. The Fort Garry Horse's 'A' Squadron under command of Major Harry Blanshard had married up with No. 46 Royal Marine Commando at about 0800 hours in front of the hamlet of Barbière just east of Thaon. The plan was sim-ple. From Barbière, the commandos and tankers would bear down on Vieux Cairon and clear any Germans out of this stubborn stronghold that threatened 9 CIB's right flank at les Buissons. Once Vieux Cairon was secured, the combat team would advance in two prongs, with one crossing to the west side of the Mue to sweep Lasson while the other stayed on the east bank and moved through Rosel. Beyond these vil-lages, the two groups would rejoin and go up either side of the creek to break into le Hamel and Rots simultaneously. Upon capturing Rots, the team would complete the operation by pushing on to la Villeneuve astride the Caen-Bayeux highway.

'A' Squadron numbered five troops of three tanks each—including one Firefly—and a two-tank headquarters section. Blanshard commanded one of the headquarters tanks and Captain E.A. Goodman the other. Goodman, who had joined the army in 1940 after finishing university, had always been nicknamed Eddy before assignment to the Fort Garry Horse. As that regiment was already awash with Eddys, some wag took to calling him Benny, after the bandleader Benny Goodman, and it stuck. When the tankers met the No. 46 at Barbière, most of the commandos proved to be Scots, who immediately insisted on calling him Jock.

The commandos seemed a rough and ready bunch, but also acted like very professional soldiers. Numbering 24 officers and 440 NCOs and other ranks, each marine commando group was subdivided into seven troops and a small headquarters section. No. 46's commander was Lieutenant Colonel C.R. Hardy. Normally employed on coastal assaults and raids without lingering long on dry land, the commandos were equipped with only light weapons and almost no vehicles. Although the men were mainly Scottish, their commander was "a very soft-spoken Englishman," who seldom raised his voice to be heard even in the midst of combat.[25]

From Barbière, the commandos advanced with No. 1 Troop under Lieutenant N.S. Rushforth providing close support, while the other tanks held back some distance in order to serve as mobile artillery if needed or to quickly come up to cover the flanks should German tanks be encountered. The ground was thickly wooded from Barbière to Vieux Cairon, so the Shermans were confined to a narrow track that hugged the creek. If the commandos wanted a section of forest or a building subjected to a few 75-millimetre gun rounds, they fired flares to mark it as a target.

With the road switching occasionally from one side of the Mue to the other via narrow bridges, the first problem the tankers encountered came when Blanshard's tank skidded off the side of one to dangle precariously over the water, with the main body of Shermans stuck behind it. A considerable delay ensued as the tankers ran cables between the major's Sherman and several of the others to winch the tank off the bridge. Throughout this effort, the men outside the tanks were under sporadic fire from several well-hidden German snipers, but no casualties resulted.

When the forest opened up beyond the bridge, Lieutenant J.G. Jeffries came up beside Rushforth with No. 5 Troop, and the six tanks accompanied the commandos towards Vieux Cairon. Resistance stiffened as scattered pockets of Germans fighting from dugouts attempted to delay the advance, with support from a number of heavy mortars firing from somewhere south of the village. Rather than get held up clearing the dugouts, Lieutenant Rushforth radioed No. 2 Troop's Lieutenant D.M. McPherson and asked him to carry out mopping up these positions so the commandos and lead tanks could maintain the attack's momentum. McPherson readily agreed, and with guns blazing, he and sergeants E.H. Crabb and H.S. Strawn roared into the German positions. As McPherson's tanks wiped out the German dugouts, Blanshard brought the remaining two supporting troops of tanks into a line and "shot up the town" while the commandos moved in among the buildings and swept the Germans out of Vieux Cairon. A number of prisoners were taken in this action and identified as forward elements of a company from the 12th ss, 26th Panzer Grenadier Regiment.[26]

The Panzer Grenadiers had abandoned any plans to defend the northern part of the Mue valley in strength, opting instead to mass available units into a strong defensive line centred on Rots. Here, Obersturmbannführer Wilhelm Mohnke had deployed one company of Panzer Grenadiers, a company of escort troops, a platoon of pioneers, two 75-millimetre antitank guns, and the Panther vs of No. 4 Company from the division's 12th Panzer Regiment. From a barn's loft out front of Rots, a forward observation officer of the III Artillery Battalion enjoyed an ideal view of "the valley of Mue creek, running northeast and covered with trees and bushes, as well as the open terrain in the direction of Rosel and Vieux Cairon."[27] In Rots, Panzer commander Hauptsturmführer Hans Pfeiffer had set several Panthers in well-covered positions near the village's school and church, from which they had clear fields of fire to the north and northwest. Other tanks were massed into a quick reaction team standing at a road junction on the corner of a little park on the southern edge of Rots. The village itself was a long, narrow stretch of buildings straggling along the highway that linked Vieux Cairon to la Villeneuve.

Holding Rots was considered vital. Its position three quarters of a mile north of the Caen-Bayeux highway meant that a strong German presence there threatened the left flank of the Regina Rifles at Norrey-en-Bessin and Bretteville-l'Orgueilleuse. Maintaining control over this penetration into the Reginas' flank somewhat mitigated the effects of the deep thrust Norrey represented into the heart of the 12th ss lines, which had so disrupted the Germans' attempts to regain the initiative. The infantry commander in Rots, Hauptsturmführer Helmut Eggert, had established strong defensive positions inside the village and along a line facing the Reginas extending south to la Villeneuve, so that his defensive front was directed to the northwest. But the commandos and Fort Garry Horse tanks approached from the northeast, driving into the Panzer Grenadier rear from the right flank. With his forces already stretched thin, Eggert had to pull men from his main line and send them rushing through Rots to meet this suddenly appearing threat to the whole position.[28]

The commandos and tanks easily brushed aside the German screening forces between Vieux Cairon and the villages of Lasson and Rosel, with Hardy reporting them secure at 1500 hours. Capturing these villages concluded three-quarters of the planned operation. Until now, all had gone much as expected; the next stage was more uncertain. No intelligence estimates of German defences in the villages of le Hamel and Rots had been collected, but recent probing attacks by the Reginas had met stiff resistance.

Hardy's plan was to attack le Hamel first, while Canadian artillery kept any troops in Rots contained by steady concentrations of high-explosive and smoke rounds. Once le Hamel was taken, two troops of commandos supported by tanks would drive into Rots and clean up the opposition there. If all went as planned, the commandos would then press on to la Villeneuve to complete an impressively rapid six-mile advance.[29]

No. 1 Troop, Fort Garry Horse still led the tanks as the combat team pushed out of Rosel towards le Hamel. Driving easily up to the edge of le Hamel, Blanshard ordered the entire squadron to form up in line and subjected the village to a heavy direct shelling that covered the entry by the commandos. Rots was also saturated with explosives from the artillery and the tanks. With le Hamel quickly subdued, No. 2 Troop was ordered to take over the lead and head for Rots with the headquarters tanks immediately behind. The commandos moving up around the leading tanks were struck by heavy fire from the village, but Sergeant Strawn, commanding No. 2 Troop's Firefly, admired how "they walked right into it" despite taking "quite a beating."[30]

Just as Blanshard prepared to order the squadron into a charge on Rots, a series of jumbled instructions from headquarters convinced the major that he was being instructed to send No. 1 and No. 5 troops back to the regimental lines. Although baffled, he told the two troop commanders to take their six tanks home and carried on the operation with the three troops he had left and his two headquarters tanks.[31]

Despite the intensifying fire, the commandos and about eight tanks pushed into Rots, fighting towards the square where the school and church stood. No. 2 Troop still led with Captain Goodman's tank snug behind Major Blanshard's and another troop behind the headquarters section. Standing back was No. 4 Troop, to cover the flanks. There seemed to be German infantry fighting from every house lining the main street, and the tanks "were going almost house by house through the streets... blowing in windows and trying to assist the marines by shell fire through the windows." Goodman kept anxiously thinking, this is "not exactly an area for tanks."[32]

LIEUTENANT MCPHERSON's tank led the way up the narrow street. His driver, Trooper L. Ballantyne, nervously reported what he took to be Panther track marks in the street's dirt surface. Cautiously, the Sherman moved on until it came alongside the church. Strawn, whose tank was third in line behind McPherson, saw a Panther tank standing no more than thirty yards up a side street. The big tank's 75-millimetre gun "barked... and hit Lieutenant McPherson's tank in the front, killing... Ballantyne, and taking off [Lance Corporal L.L.] Paulson's foot. The crew immediately bailed out, taking... Paulson with them. The Hun, from a concealed position started throwing grenades and... McPherson and Corporal [W.K.] French were wounded by fragments."[33] Trooper F. Stokotelny, the only member of the tank crew unwounded, tried dragging Paulson to cover, but a machine-gun burst killed the injured man and tore a chunk off one of Stokotelny's fingers.

The other tanks had all come into the square and assumed positions with their backs pushed up close to the shelter of a stout building or tucked into the opening of a narrow alley. The rear of the tanks provided protection from the heavy machine-gun fire tearing up the square. Into the middle of this mess a lightly armoured Canadian scout car suddenly drove with the Fort Garry's brigade liaison officer, Lieutenant W.E. "Eddie" McMitchell and his driver sitting side by side. Goodman and McMitchell had shared a room back in England. "Why the hell he was there," the captain didn't know, but figured that McMitchell—frustrated at being posted to brigade—had come looking for some action. "Poor guy, he got too much," Goodman said later. One of the Panthers emerged from a lane leading into the square behind the Canadian tanks seconds after McMitchell's appearance and blasted the scout car. Goodman watched in horror as the vehicle started burning. "I saw [McMitchell open] the top, trying to get out and then sink back and burn to death right before me. That is my most vivid battle memory."[34] Somehow the wounded driver managed to escape before the car was completely engulfed.

Sergeant Strawn's tank was on one side of the square beside Major Blanshard's, with Goodman's and Sergeant Crabb's Shermans across the way. Strawn couldn't believe how confused things were or how badly the Germans "had us bottled in." Through the smoke choking the square, he saw Goodman and Crabb both backing their tanks away from a building that had provided them with some scant cover in an attempt to find a better angle of fire. A Panther in an alley that neither Strawn nor Blanshard could draw a bead on blasted off two rounds. Both tanks shuddered, halted, and started burning.[35]

In the turret, Goodman's gunner scrambled past the captain in a frantic effort to escape through the hatch. Goodman hefted him up through the opening and pushed him out towards the tank's rear. Ten feet above the tank, a Panzer Grenadier leaned out a window, levelled a light machine gun, and killed the man with a burst of fire. The loader/operator had been killed by the armour-piercing round that had sliced through the turret, while the driver and co-driver had either escaped from their isolated front compartment or not, so Goodman decided it was time to go. As the captain started to crawl out of the turret hatch, his jacket snagged, trapping him in place. Flames were already licking his body, the clothes smouldering. "Goddamn, don't burn to death," he grunted while tearing the jacket off. Pitching out onto the ground, Goodman ran towards a ditch where some other tankers had taken refuge. The German firing from the window chased him every inch of the way with a steady stream of fire that chewed up the ground without scoring a single hit. Once he gained the ditch, Goodman started crawling along it with the other tankers, heading east out of Rots for the cover of an adjacent wheatfield.[36]

Sergeant Crabb's tank had been knocked out at the same time as Goodman's. The crew commander had suffered a bad chest wound, while troopers R.F.R. Holmes and G.N. McKinlay were killed. Trooper A.K. McMasters was injured in the leg. Only Trooper Stephenson escaped unscathed from the tank. He assisted the two wounded men in getting to safety, treated their wounds, and stayed with them to fight off any Germans who might discover their hiding place.

Meanwhile, the Panther that had shot the two tanks crept directly into the square. Sergeant Strawn watched the massive tank come and then fired a round from his Firefly's 17-pounder right through a corner of a beat-up building, scoring a hit on the Panther's armoured front that caused it to scamper in reverse back to cover. The sergeant also blasted a machine-gunner he saw trying to bring fire to bear on some wounded tankers. Beside him, Major Blanshard's tank was firing off rounds at a frantic rate. Finally, the major had two of the most seriously wounded men loaded up on the back of his tank and ordered Strawn to follow him in a withdrawal from the square.

Strawn had swung his turret around so that the gun barrel faced the rear during the fight with the Panther, and momentarily forgot that his tank faced the opposite direction when he ordered the driver to advance. As the Sherman headed in one direction and the major in the other, Strawn realized his mistake and got the driver started on the awkward process of turning the tank around in the narrow square. By the time the procedure was completed, Blanshard's tank had disappeared.

Attempting to catch up, Strawn ordered his driver to go down a road that he soon realized was heading the wrong way, into enemy territory. His driver, Trooper W.G. Taylor, was running flat out and as the tank careened around a corner it came face to face with a Panther blocking the path. "The driver," Strawn later wrote, "just about stood the tank on her nose and the gunner rapped two shots into the Panther from 100 yards setting it on fire. I told my driver to advance around the burning tank, but the gunner with the excitement, forgot the long-barrelled 17[-pounder], and it caught on the burning tank, breaking the hand and the power traverse. Seeing that we could not bring our gun on any target I told the driver that it was up to him, that speed was what we required. I knew that if we stayed on the road it would eventually bring us into Bray which was in our hands, but first we had to go through la Villeneuve which was still in enemy hands. As we came out of Rots with the tank going at full speed there was a Panther... about 800 yards to our right. Whether or not he didn't see us or was too taken by surprise is debatable, but we were under cover again before he could fire a shot. We then hit la Villeneuve which had more Germans in it than a hick town has farmers on a Saturday night. We managed to get halfway... through when a Panther nosed out about 300 yards in front, blocking the road."

Realizing the game was about to end abruptly, Strawn shouted for Trooper Taylor to stop on the side of the road and for everyone to bail out. As the Sherman skidded to a stop, Strawn got halfway out of the turret before it shook with a terrible bang. The German round sliced through the front of the driver's hatch, killing Taylor instantly. Piling out of the turret, Strawn went one way while his loader and gunner went another. Strawn reached a lane behind the Sherman and looked back to see Trooper C.W.D. Wright die in the street as a machine-gun burst tore into him. The other man disappeared among some houses.

Making his way carefully forward, Strawn passed out of the village, through a wheatfield, and into the country. As darkness fell, he became disoriented and decided to stay put until dawn. With first light, the sergeant was able to see the barrage balloons hovering high over the ships at the beach and used them as a beacon to guide him north towards the Canadian lines. He was picked up by a Queen's Own Rifles patrol in the late morning of June 12. Strawn's courage during the engagement in Rots would be rewarded with a Military Medal.[37]

EVEN AS STRAWN'S TANK had evacuated Rots by heading into enemy lines, the battle for the village had raged on. The commandos refused to give up, and the Germans fought with their usual fanatical determination. Men squared off against each other with bayonets, knives, submachine guns fired at point-blank range, and grenades. Soldiers grappled in the dark of basements and in the mud of garden plots. Bodies lay strewn around the church and school.

In a wheatfield next to the village, Captain Goodman joined an O Group. Lieutenant Colonel Hardy was planning a final assault to relieve those commandos still fighting in Rots and to secure the place once and for all. Goodman was feeling the pain of his burns, but considered himself still in the game because the injuries weren't agonizing. Lacking a tank, he would fight at the side of the commandos. Just how bad the burns were, he had no idea, but his face didn't feel as seared as one hand did. The other burns were mostly on his back, so he couldn't see them.

The marine commander gave his orders in the same calm, soft voice he had used at the beginning of the long assault. There were precious few commandos gathered around, but they seemed undaunted by the task ahead. Hardy pointed out where the Germans were concentrated around the school and church. Then he told one man toting a Bren gun to take up a position from which he could cover the commandos by forcing those Germans to keep their heads down. "You cover," he said to the man, "and I'll stay with you and use a gun and the rest of you men just go for the high [wheat] and get in over there." He pointed to where a lane entered Rots.

Goodman went forward with a marine corporal and soon the two men were lying in the grain beside a road, watching a group of ten to twelve Germans coming their way through the wheat. Whenever the enemy soldiers encountered wounded commandos or tankers, Goodman was shocked to see them pause and shoot them. It dawned on the captain that he had lost his personal weapon and was unarmed. He didn't want to die without putting up a fight. When he mentioned this, the commando pulled out his fighting knife, "still dripping with blood from his earlier hand-to-hand fighting and said, 'Ok, Jock, so let's at least get one of the bastards before they kill us.'

"I still can't believe," Goodman said later, "I was so relaxed. I knew I was going to die but that wasn't the big thing. I knew I was going to get one of these guys beforehand."

When the Germans were no more than ten yards from where Goodman and the commando were holed up, a troop of Fort Garry tanks came over a rise above the wheatfield and opened fire. The Panzer Grenadiers took off, dashing behind a house to regain the shelter of embattled Rots. One tank roared up and down the road past Goodman's hiding spot, raking both sides indiscriminately with machine-gun fire, so that the captain wondered whether the Germans or the tankers were going to kill him.

As the tank moved farther down the road, Goodman saw his chance and jumped up. Knowing there were marines and tankers, many of them wounded, hiding through the wheat, he yelled, "Okay, fellows, come on and make for the tanks." Goodman led a loose gaggle of soldiers through to the tanks and then took command of the troop by commandeering a Sherman with a broken turret and gun. The engine ran fine, though, and the machine guns worked, so Goodman clanked out to the front of the troop and made for Rots.[38]

Already in the village wreaking havoc was No. 4 Troop under command of Lieutenant F.J. Curtin. The troop had first swept a circle right around Rots, firing at any signs of enemy resistance, and managed to knock out one Panther.[39] This may have been Panzer company commander Hauptsturmführer Hans Pfeiffer's tank, which was destroyed while attempting to withdraw from a hill that had been serving as a German strongpoint until overrun by commandos and Canadian tanks.[40]

Curtin then led these tanks into the village "and shot it up completely." As night fell, the last of the German defenders gave Rots up. While the commandos took up fighting positions throughout the village, the surviving Shermans still fit for action deployed alongside them.[41] Taking charge of three tanks, including the damaged one he had been using, Goodman loaded them up with wounded tankers and drove directly to 2 CAB's brigade headquarters to get the wounded treated.[42]

Still little appreciating the extent of his own injuries, Goodman intended to get back into action. "What can I do to help you?" he asked Brigadier Ron Wyman. Goodman was thinking that they needed to round up some more tanks and crews to reinforce Rots before the Germans counterattacked. And there was the unfinished business of taking la Villeneuve.

"You don't look so good," Wyman said.

"I guess I'm not feeling too good, but that's not important. What can I do?"

Wyman told him that he would put the two operational tanks under command of a reinforcement lieutenant and that Goodman should get over to the hospital forthwith for treatment. "It won't make any difference whether I go now or later," Goodman objected.

Growing impatient with this brave but recalcitrant young soldier, Wyman snapped, "No, no, that tank's no good anyway with the gun out of action, so you get the hell out of here and leave me the two good tanks."

Goodman realized he had better take his leave and did so, but rather than heading to the hospital he returned to regimental headquarters.[43] When he walked in, everyone looked as if they were seeing a ghost, and one officer hastily explained that Major Blanshard had radioed during the confused battle that Goodman had been killed.[44]

This time, he obeyed the orders to seek medical attention and soon learned that his injuries were serious enough. Goodman's hand had suffered third-degree burns, his face second-degree, and he had many other second-degree burns over his body. The doctor swathed his face in so many bandages that only his eyes showed and told him it would take two to three weeks for his injuries to heal, but that he would be fit for duty again once they had. Goodman realized he was happy to learn that his war was not yet over.[45]

'A' Squadron had lost seven men killed and eight wounded in the fight.[46] For their part, the Marine commandos had suffered twenty killed, nine wounded, and thirty-one missing.[47] The 12th ss admitted to having lost twenty-two men killed, thirty wounded, and fifteen missing, but the commandos and tankers believed the number of dead enemy far surpassed this report. Among the German dead was Pfeiffer, the Panzer commander.[48] At midnight, Brigadier Ken Black-ader at 8 cib headquarters and Major General Rod Keller's staff at 3 cid were arguing whether the marine commandos and fragment of tankers left in Rots were capable of withstanding a counterattack, which they expected to fall on the village at any moment. Blackader wanted to send Le Régiment de la Chaudière to reinforce the position, but the decision process seemed inexplicably stalled.

19

We've Been Sucked In

MAJOR GENERAL ROD KELLER's uncertainty over whether to re-inforce the tankers and commandos holding Rots was linked to 2nd Canadian Armoured Brigade's hastily undertaken second June 11 assault. While 'A' Squadron of the Fort Garry Horse's and No. 46 Royal Marine Commando had been clearing the Mue valley, Brigadier Ron Wyman spent the morning of June 11 feverishly issuing instructions to advance the assault on the Cheux hill feature a full twenty-four hours. Whatever reservations he held about the order from Second British Army commander General Miles Dempsey to move up the attack, the brigadier kept to himself. Protests by both Queen's Own Rifles Lieutenant Colonel Jock Spragge and 1st Hussars Lieutenant Colonel Ray Colwell were brushed aside. Wyman insisted the lead element of the two battalions must "cross its start line by 1300 hours."

The overriding need for haste had been forcibly impressed upon Wyman at 1130 hours by the division's General Staff Officer, Lieutenant Colonel Don Mingay, who personally carried a message to this effect from Major General Rod Keller. Keller's right-hand senior staff officer playing courier emphasized the importance of the note. In a couple of terse sentences, Keller directed Wyman that "it was imperative the attack be mounted at the earliest moment."[1]

Despite the ambitious nature of 2 CAB's operational plan for June 12, Wyman undertook no modifications to compensate for lack of preparation time. With less than five hours to get the attack rolling, the brigadier and his staff were unable to prepare either an artillery support-firing plan or to have units conduct any prior reconnaissance to identify enemy positions. Wyman could only hope that speed, the combat prowess of the Sherman tank, and the courage of the tankers and infantry would prevail.

Leading the attack would be 'D' Company of the Queen's Own Rifles piggybacking on tanks of the 1st Hussars' 'B' Squadron, closely followed by 'C' Squadron. Colwell's regimental headquarters would tail 'C' Squadron, while 'A' Squadron brought up the rear. 'A' Company of the Queen's Own would spread out by platoons on the tanks of 'C' and 'A' squadrons.[2]

Wyman intended to be right behind this potent force with a small tactical brigade headquarters aboard three Shermans, each mounting a wooden gun barrel instead of the 75-millimetre in order to provide room for additional wireless sets. Wyman would ride in the lead Sherman, his brigade major in the second, and his chief signals officer, Major F.R. Pratten, Royal Canadian Corps of Signals, in the third. Being close to the action, Wyman hoped, would allow him to exert strong command presence and assure the attack was carried out with determination.[3] Trailing Wyman's headquarters would be a second wave consisting of the Fort Garry Horse's 'B' and 'C' squadrons with the remaining two companies of the Queen's Own aboard, while the Sherbrooke Fusiliers formed a reserve back at Bray.

The start line for the attack was the Caen-Bayeux railroad about half a mile south of Bretteville-l'Orgueilleuse. From this point, the assault force would carry out a right hook through le Mesnil-Patry and then cross a wide stretch of about three miles of open country to gain the Cheux hill feature from the west.[4] Clearing le Mesnil-Patry was considered vital to the operation's success, in order to secure the flanks of the attacking force and the 50th British Infantry Division, which would attack to the west as part of Second Army's major offensive towards Villers-Bocage. Responsibility for seizing the village lay with 'B' Squadron and 'D' Company, while 'C' Squadron would support this effort by clearing the ground on its right flank.

Once le Mesnil-Patry fell, the Queen's Own would rush its mortar and antitank platoons forward to reinforce the Canadian hold there.

'B' Squadron would remain in the village with the infantry, while the remaining two tank squadrons along with 'A' Company dashed on to the final objective.[5] By last light, 2 CAB should have established a strong armoured presence supported by the Queen's Own Rifles south of the Caen-Bayeux highway that would shake off the stalemate threatening to freeze the front lines in place. Possessing a salient south of the railroad that extended deep into German lines and was hinged on the right by 50th Infantry Division would enable Keller to begin working his infantry brigades forward on the left flank, to gain Carpiquet airport.

One cautionary note clearly stated by Wyman during briefing sessions was that under no circumstances should the assault forces remain on the road when it passed through Norrey-en-Bessin. Although 'C' Company of the Regina Rifles held Norrey firmly in its grip, the narrow streets were a natural choke point for tanks and strewn with rubble from shell-blasted buildings. And an unknown number of 26th Panzer Grenadier Regiment troops facing the village from the south could potentially block the advance.

What opposition the attackers would meet once across the railroad tracks was a mystery to the division's intelligence officers. The divisional daily intelligence summary for June 9 had reported the presence of some self-propelled guns and up to "twenty-five [tanks]... in the area le Mesnil-Patry," but whether these still lurked in the vicinity was uncertain.[6] Wyman imparted the impression to Colwell and Spragge that opposition should be light, but provided no information source for his assessment.

Advancing the attack by a full day had another consequence that gravely worried Colwell and Spragge. Normally, this kind of attack would be heavily supported by artillery fire ranging in on pre-plotted targets to soften or eliminate enemy strongpoints. Plotted firing traces would be developed so that the guns could be summoned at any time to deliver accurate fire against enemy pockets of resistance, or to carry out counter-battery fire against German guns or mortars shooting at the assault force. Little of this preparatory work had been undertaken and there was insufficient time to complete it now before the attack began. In the absence of an artillery plan, the two forward observation officers from 12th Field Regiment, RCA—Captain Charles Rivaz and Lieutenant E.J. Hooper—could only provide firing missions to the artillery via on-the-spot radio calls.[7] Forty-year-old Rivaz—one of the regiment's original wartime officers and a former lecturer at Guelph's Ontario Agricultural College—was a highly competent gunnery officer. He, Hooper, and two gunners serving as wireless operators worked out of an outmoded Canadian RAM tank fitted with radios. They would advance in concert with Colwell's regimental headquarters.

When Rivaz arrived late in the morning at the 1st Hussars forming-up position near Bray, he found the tankers still loading ammunition and fuel into their Shermans. Tracking down 'B' Squadron's Captain Harry Harrison, Rivaz conferred with the squadron commander's loader/operator Trooper I.O. Dodds, who helped the artillery officer link his radio into the squadron net.

Aboard a Sherman that sank off Juno Beach on D-Day, Dodds had been in the reinforcement pool awaiting reassignment until becoming part of the draft sent to reconstitute 'B' Squadron. As the command tank's wireless operator, it was his responsibility to establish the squadron's communication net. Most of the loader/operators assigned to the squadron were green and found it difficult to properly adjust the delicate tuning mechanism of the No. 19 set.[8] Dodds spent hours on June 10 at his radio "chanting into his microphone" while periodically pausing to check if everyone was netted in on him. Inevitably, one or more of the twenty-one tanks that were to be included in the net was absent and the process had to continue. By noon on June 11, the net was still barely operational.

Inordinately long netting efforts not only frustrated the squadron's wireless control operator, but also posed a serious security risk. German radio intercept teams constantly cruised the wireless bandwidth, seeking frequencies used by Allied units. They were greatly aided by the capture of a copy of 2 CAB's radio procedures and codes dug out of a wrecked Sherbrooke Fusilier tank near Authie on June 9.[9] The 12th SS (Hitlerjugend) Panzer Division radio surveillance team hit paydirt on the morning of June 11 when it picked up the signals coming from the 1st Hussars, enabling the Germans to determine the location of the armoured regiment's assembly area. Translators quickly determined an attack was going to develop out of 7 CIB's front against le Mesnil-Patry.[10]

Facing 7 CIB's front were Panzer Grenadiers of the 26th Regiment and the division's Pioneer Battalion. Obersturmbannführer Wilhelm Mohnke ordered these units to remain hidden while the Canadian tanks passed them by, and then to strike the infantry that would be following close behind. Once the Canadian foot soldiers were eliminated, the Shermans would prove easy prey for German tanks, anti-tank guns, and Panzer Grenadiers attacking with shoulder-launched Faustpatrones and magnetic mines. Mohnke put all available artillery and mortar units in range on immediate alert and ensured that artillery spotters were able to cover all routes of approach that could be used by an armoured force. As most of these routes had already been pre-plotted, fire could be brought to bear quickly whenever needed.[11]

IN THE 1ST HUSSARS assembly area, Captain Harry Harrison and the other squadron commanders gathered around Lieutenant Colonel Colwell at 1215 for a final briefing. Besides giving the order of march, there was little he could offer except the grim news that there would be no divisional artillery plan and that no reliable estimate was available of the German forces they might face. The squadron commanders grumbled that forty-five minutes was ridiculously short to properly brief their troop commanders, but were told there was nothing that could be done about it.[12]

By the time Harrison got back to 'B' Squadron, it was time for everyone to mount up and roll. The Queen's Own Rifles had marched out of Neuf Mer at 1215 hours to join the Hussars and were tromping into the tank assembly area. Major Neil Gordon, commander of 'D' Company, climbed onto Harrison's tank so the two officers could coordinate their actions. They had never met. As the riflemen spread themselves among the Shermans, it was obvious to both men that they could never make the railroad start line for a 1300 hours attack, only minutes away.

Gordon, who had rushed to enlist in the Queen's Own as an Upper Canada College Cadet on the outbreak of the war, was a highly trained infantry officer and graduate of both the British and Canadian battle schools. While serving on loan to the British Eighth Army's Loyal North Lancashire Regiment during the North African campaign, the officer had gained a great deal of combat experience. This was not true, however, for the men in his company. Landing behind the battalion's assault companies on D-Day, his company had suffered few casualties and seen little action in subsequent fighting.

Like most everyone in the Queen's Own, Gordon considered Spragge a topnotch battalion commander and had been shocked when the man could only set out the orders for the attack on a scruffy map, without time for any kind of visual reconnaissance to check its accuracy. Spragge had somehow come to the understanding that the attack was required to head off one the Germans were mounting on the division's extreme right flank in order to get between the Canadians and 50th British Infantry Division. When the briefing ended, Spragge singled Gordon out "and said not to rush it, but he had no control over the action. He obviously felt as concerned as I did," Gordon later said. "We had no idea of what we were going on, no recce and we just looked at a map. Crazy. This, after all we had been taught, and it was the one thing you shouldn't do."[13] The major estimated that to tee up an attack such as this properly would have delayed its start to at least 1800 hours.[14] Gordon considered himself lucky to at least be attacking with a full-strength company of 135 men who were virtually all pre-invasion Queen's Own regulars, rather than inexperienced reinforcements sent to rebuild the assault companies that had been shredded on the beach.

Perched aboard one of the tanks, Rifleman Dave Arksey saw Lieutenant Colonel Spragge watching the company roll towards combat. A soldier shouted down to the battalion commander, "This'll make you a brigadier, Jock." Arksey uneasily noted that Spragge, normally an affable commander, never smiled.[15] The rifleman was sitting next to new-found friend Rifleman Llewellyn Louis "Lew" Bridges, a replacement from Vancouver who was built like a heavyweight wrestler and had joined the regiment just a few days before. "They build them big in Vancouver," the twenty-two-year-old from Ontario said when the man had passed over a Jersey Milk chocolate bar gripped in a massive paw by way of introduction.

"Look, I've never been in action before," Bridges said. "Mind if I stick with you." The two men had shared a slit trench since.[16]

For his part, 1st Hussars' Captain Harrison did not share Gordon's anxiety. A graduate of Royal Military College, the twenty-four-year-old Montrealer had a reputation for arrogance and had considered his skills underutilized as 'C' Squadron's second-in-command. Now at the head of his own squadron, the captain was looking for a chance to prove himself and his theories. Chief among these was a belief that the regiment's older officers, particularly his former squadron commander Major D'Arcy Marks, little understood the proper employment of armour. The militia-trained Marks, Harrison thought, was overly cautious.[17] When the opportunity arose for a bold dash by armour, with or without infantry support, Harrison felt that Marks and the other squadron commanders inevitably failed to act. Today would be a chance to show what those who dared could achieve.

And what a day it was. On this Sunday, the June sun shone out of a perfectly blue sky. The overgrown fields of grain shimmered golden in the midday light. In blissful ignorance, many riflemen aboard 'B' Squadron's Shermans lit cigarettes and pressed their backs up against the turrets, heads tipped back to enjoy the warm sun on their faces. They were in shirtsleeves and carrying a welcomely light equipment load—a weapon, ammunition, web gear, and small packs. So many rumours had circulated in the absence of any formal briefing that nobody in the rank and file had the foggiest idea what they were doing. Some thought they were headed to meet a counterattack. Others that they were to provide security for the tankers, assigned to carry out a shoot from the front lines against distant German targets. Dodds, the loader/operator in Harrison's Sherman, believed they headed for "a quiet HE [high-explosive] shoot with the artillery." The exercise of netting artillery officer Captain Rivaz into the squadron wavelength had strengthened this understanding.[18]

In the squadron lead tank at the head of the attack column, Sergeant Léo Gariépy thought the emphasis on speed meant the operation was to be a "piece of cake. It was a beautiful sunny day, warm, with hardly any wind, the men in high spirits and planning on teaching the 'rookies' how to behave themselves in action." The twenty-one-year-old Gariépy had been in some tough shootouts since coming ashore as one of the lead assault tanks on June 6 and had no qualms about being on point. Right behind him was No. 2 Troop's new commander, Lieutenant Jimmy Martin, and then Trooper Jim Simpson.[19] Martin was a replacement officer Simpson and Gariépy had never met before No. 2 Troop's reconstitution. The hasty O Group Martin had held before the troop saddled up failed to give either of his subordinate crew commanders a clue as to what they were embarked upon.[20]

As 'B' Squadron rolled out of the Bray assembly area, 'C' Squadron's Lieutenant Bill McCormick, whose No. 2 Troop was to lead this squadron's advance, saw smoke coming out of the engine compartment. After dousing the small fire with extinguishers, McCormick discovered a fuel line leakage had caused the problem. Leaving his crew to get the tank repaired, the lieutenant ran over to Corporal Bill Talbot's tank and took command of it.[21] By the time this exchange was carried out, a large gap had opened between 'B' Squadron and the rest of the column. McCormick ordered his new tank driver, a replacement he remembered only as Trooper Smith, to try and catch up. Tracks squealing, the Sherman led 'C' Squadron in pursuit.

In Harrison's tank, Trooper Dodds was increasingly irritated by the lack of wireless discipline clogging the squadron's airwaves. Someone kept asking for Harrison to come up on the net, while even more persistently another tanker sought to be re-netted. "He had time to net a dozen sets by that time, so I finally told him to 'lock up and shut up.' He was okay at the time and so were the rest of the stations."[22]

Gariépy was more disturbed by a tank officer who insisted on providing a step-by-step travelogue of their progress towards the start line. As the tanks edged past a knocked-out Panther V, the officer called that they were "nearing dead enemy bear (code for tank)." Then it was that they were going past a schoolhouse, then a wheatfield, until finally the sergeant snapped the wireless off to spare his ears from this chatter so he could concentrate.[23] The 12th ss wireless intercept team happily continued to eavesdrop, able to use the officer's folly to track the column's progress on a minute-by-minute basis.[24]

As the lead tanks passed Bretteville and approached the point where they were to leave the Norrey-en-Bessin road rather than pass through the village, an urgent radio warning from the Regina Rifles caused Colwell to order an immediate change of plan. Never advised of the attack, the Reginas had sown a minefield that stretched across the open fields between Bretteville and Norrey-en-Bessin. Having been instructed to bypass Norrey, the 1st Hussars now had no choice but to remain on the road and navigate through the village to get past the minefield.[25]

A hurried Orders Group assembled as the tank commanders and Major Neil Gordon gathered around Colwell on the road. The lieutenant colonel gave them a new line of march to a start line on the southwestern edge of Norrey. Gordon just had time to get back to 'D' Company, "point out the axis of advance to [his] platoon commanders and get cracking" before the tanks started moving again.[26]

Norrey proved to be precisely the choke point Wyman and his staff had feared when they ordered it bypassed. The main street was so narrow the tanks were forced to move in single file, with sides almost scraping the buildings. A sharp, almost 90-degree right-hand turn at the church required each tank to go backward and then forward several times to navigate it. Between the late start departing the assembly area and the difficulty passing through Norrey, 'B' Squadron reached the new start line outside the village at 1420 hours.[27] Harrison reported that the squadron was beginning the attack. Although the rest of the regiment was still far behind, Dodds heard the captain tell his crew commanders by wireless to "speed up the attack."[28] With 'D' Company clinging to the Shermans, 'B' Squadron ground out of Norrey and into a line of attack, while Gariépy's No. 2 Troop remained on the road to le Mesnil-Patry, and the rest of the squadron swung to the left into the two- to three-foot-high wheat.[29]

It was only about 1,200 yards from Norrey to le Mesnil-Patry across fields of standing grain interspersed with apple orchards and occasional beet fields. The road Gariépy's troop followed cut sharply to the right beyond the village to approach le Mesnil-Patry from the northeast, so the Canadians were advancing on an oblique angle directly into a pocket created by the 12th ss troops defending the area. To the right of the squadron were No. 5 and No. 6 companies of the 26th Panzer Grenadier Regiment's II Battalion. Immediately to its front, No. 7 Company formed a defensive ring around the Château du Mesnil-Patry, a two-storey stone mansion that served as the battalion's headquarters. Two companies—Nos. 2 and 3—of the Pioneer Battalion were to the left of the château, and it was directly towards these Panzer Grenadiers that most of Harrison's tanks were headed.[30]

'B' SQUADRON was well on its way when 'C' Squadron started through Norrey. As it did so, the Germans started blasting the village with artillery and mortar fire in an attempt to disrupt the developing attack. When Colwell's regimental headquarters section ground up to the village's northern edge and he saw how easily the main street could be blocked if the shelling smashed an adjacent building, the lieutenant colonel headed out on the flank hoping to find a way around Norrey. His tank struck a mine and was disabled after going no more than a few hundred feet off the road. Running into the village on foot, Colwell ignored the shells exploding all around him and directed the tanks passing so that they remained on the only viable route through.[31]

Queen's Own commander Lieutenant Colonel Spragge, meanwhile, had decided that something had to be done to give the advancing column some support in the absence of a proper divisional artillery fire plan. He ordered the battalion's mortar platoon commander, Lieutenant Ben Dunkleman, a thirty-one-year-old former professional Toronto football player, to set up the three-inch tubes in Norrey and lay down whatever fire support he could. The mortar platoon set up in a barnyard surrounded by a thick fieldstone wall on the village's northwestern flank, just to the front of the railroad tracks. It was a good position, allowing the mortar crews to cover the breadth of ground that the Hussars and Queen's Own were advancing across.[32]

'C' Squadron was now through the village and heading to the right of 'B' Squadron's line of advance. Aboard its Shermans were some men from 'A' Company. Most of this unit, however, was mounted on 'A' Squadron and only just beginning to move through Norrey. The company commander, Major Elliot Dalton, was back with the larger group. Dalton was still grieving over the news that Charlie, his older brother by six years, had died from a head wound suffered when he led 'B' Company ashore on D-Day just up the beach from Elliot's own assault company. The last time the twenty-seven-year-old had seen his brother had been on the landing ship before they boarded the small landing craft for the run into shore. "I'll see you tonight," Charlie had said simply before going towards his men. Elliot was still coming to terms with the thought that he would never again see his brother.[33]

Out on the road to le Mesnil-Patry, Gariépy had his head stuck well above the edge of the turret hatch in defiance of Harrison's order that crew commanders were to keep the hatch buttoned up during the advance. Bottling himself up would make it next to impossible to spot any mines the Germans might have sown into the roadbed, so Gariépy thought the risk necessary. From overhead came the sickening, slithering rustle noise emanated by artillery shells passing through air. Looking back over his shoulder, he saw the village exploding under a fierce barrage. The sergeant glanced into the wheatfield beside the road and met the eyes of several men lying in its cover. They wore German helmets and just lay there as the Sherman roared past.[34]

Hell broke loose a moment later as Panzer Grenadiers popped out of the grain all over the place, and antitank guns concealed in haystacks and folds in the ground opened fire. It was 1452 hours, little more than a half-hour since the squadron had passed out from Norrey. Trooper Jim Simpson was out in the grain near the road on the extreme right flank of the squadron, with Lieutenant Martin on his left and Gariépy up on the road. He had half a dozen Queen's Own on the tank and they just disappeared the moment the firing started. Bullets pinged off the armour. The tanks kept going, with Simpson's gunner blazing away at everything and anything. The gunner slammed rounds out so fast that Simpson barely had time to offer any fire direction. He saw a shell smash into a chicken house. Feathers and bloody chunks of poultry flew every which way. Then they were past it and barrelling onward.[35]

Simpson had lost track of Gariépy's tank. Gaining the orchard, he and Lieutenant Martin held up on the southern edge in order to fire on the open ground in front of le Mesnil-Patry and the village itself. Martin's tank was about twenty yards to Simpson's right. When an infantry officer ran up to the lieutenant's tank, Martin stuck his head out to confer and was immediately struck in the head by a sniper shot. "He just disappeared into the turret." Martin's loader/operator started yelling over the wireless in a panicked voice that his commander needed help. The tank then turned around and took off for the rear, leaving Simpson alone in the orchard. The trooper shrugged and stayed where he was, raking the ground to his front with high-explosive and co-axial machine-gun fire in an attempt to suppress the heavy small-arms fire coming his way. He could hear bullets rattling off the turret. Glancing up at his hatch, which was slightly open, Simpson saw that big gouges had been scraped in the steel by bullets. He figured the same sniper who had shot Martin was trying to pick him off.[36]

Back in the barnyard on the edge of Norrey, Lieutenant Dunkleman saw puffs of smoke coming from four large stacks of grain out in the fields about 1,200 yards from his position and quickly ordered them fired on with smoke rounds. Dunkleman noted that "they burned in a peculiar manner, just like a big black ball, and... were evidently camouflage over pillboxes or tanks, as screams were heard emanating from them."[37]

German artillery observers noted the fire from the mortars. Mere seconds after the first tubes started shooting at the stacks of grain, the barnyard was hammered by heavy counter-artillery and mortar fire. Rifleman Jack Martin, who manned one of the mortars, heard shrapnel "flying all over the place" and figured they were in a pretty unhealthy spot.[38] But not as bad as the soldiers out front. The mortar crews could see that they were getting massacred.

Out in the middle of this killing ground, Rifleman Dave Arksey saw flashes of antitank guns firing from only about three hundred yards ahead of the leading tanks. Every shell fired seemed to knock out a Sherman. When the tank he was riding on took a hit and suddenly lurched to a halt, Arksey and his pal Bridges bailed off into the tall wheat. One of the other men on the tank, Rifleman Rene Arsenault, was nearby. "He had a compound fracture," Arksey noticed, "all the flesh and muscles were showing." A Panzer Grenadier rose up out of the grain and chucked a potato-masher-style grenade, which struck one of the Canadians in the hip with shrapnel. As the German popped up after the explosion to check his throw, a single Lee Enfield cracked and the man pitched back dead.

"Do you know any prayers, Lew?" Arksey asked.

Bridges looked at him, puzzled. "What?"

"Didn't you ever go to Sunday School? It would be a good idea to use whatever you got. I think we've been sucked in."[39]

Having lost sight of any of the other soldiers in the tall grain, the two men got down on their stomachs and started crawling. Arksey led the way back towards the Canadian lines.

Their company commander, Major Neil Gordon, was down in the grain near Harrison's tank trying to rally his men. He figured that half were already down, either dead or wounded, and could only see about twenty-five still capable of fighting.[40] The air was thick with German bullets, but Gordon had yet to see a single enemy soldier and realized they must be incredibly well dug into camouflaged trenches. The major tried to get the attention of Harrison or any of the tank crew commanders, but they were all buttoned down inside their turrets. Tank-infantry coordination had gone out the window the moment the battle had been joined. In North Africa, the British Churchill tanks had been fitted with a phone at the rear that an infantryman could use to talk directly with the crew commander. But the Shermans were not so equipped. Gordon knew his company was on its own and probably didn't have a chance.

The next moment he was on the ground with blood pumping out of his face. A bullet had hit him in the mouth, ripped out a chunk of gum and teeth, and exited through a cheek. His brother-in-law, Lieutenant Bob Fleming, ran up and tenderly applied a field dressing to the wound. "I can't stop the bleeding," he told Gordon.

"You're not supposed to be here," the major replied through a mouth frothing with blood. "Get busy. You're the company commander now." Fleming headed forward, but was quickly shot and killed. As Gordon struggled to his feet, a bullet punched into his left knee and knocked him unconscious. When a Hussars tank came by headed towards the rear, some of Gordon's men flagged it down and put the wounded officer on its back.[41]

STUCK INSIDE THE TURRET of Captain Harrison's command tank, Trooper Dodds tried to follow the raging battle over the wireless set. He could hear the sheet-ripping sound of German MG 42s coming from all around and tankers were shouting over the wireless that they couldn't see the antitank guns that were killing them. The gunner next to him, Sergeant Johnstone, was switching back and forth from banging out high-explosive rounds with the 75-millimetre and raking the haystacks with the co-axial machine gun. Fitted into the turret alongside the main gun, the co-axial was a 30-calibre Browning machine gun used when fighting infantry at close range. Glancing through his periscope, Dodds saw a gunner in the tank ahead of him chuck a misfired 75-millimetre round out the turret hatch. Over the wireless, someone kept demanding to know 'B' Squadron's position. Not recognizing the voice and having no desire to interrupt Harrison with such nonsense, Dodds ignored the orders to report.

The Sherman moved into a field of what seemed to be red clover, where Dodds spotted a couple of Panzer Grenadiers running about trying to duck all the shells and co-axial fire Johnstone was putting out. Then the tank entered an orchard where there seemed to be even more Germans. Dugouts were everywhere, and Johnstone started punching high-explosive rounds into them. At times, the driver had to back up so the gun barrel could be depressed enough to fire into the holes.

Dodds noticed that at least half the Browning machine-gun ammunition was used up, the rack behind the co-driver emptied, along with the one right behind the driver. Reaching for another high-explosive shell, Dodds discovered this was all gone, too. Harrison hollered, "Let him have AP [armour-piercing] down the dugouts," indicating one that was only fifteen yards away. Dodds was snagging shells one-armed that the driver passed up to him for loading into the 75-millimetre, while using his free hand to keep the co-axial machine gun cover in place. If he lifted his hand, the cover was so hot from the continual firing that it popped up and the ammunition belt stopped feeding through. Seeing a German in front of the tank that Johnstone had failed to notice, Dodds took over the co-axial himself and ripped off a burst that sent the man spinning into the trees. When he stopped firing, the rest of the belt in the gun ripped off spontaneously in one continuous burst, each round ignited by the gun's intense heat as it passed through the breech.

Harrison had the turret hatch open, frantically tossing grenades out at the German infantry. He threw the entire allotment of twenty No. 36 grenades that the tankers had on board and then chucked out eleven of the dozen No. 77 smoke grenades. Each time he yelled for a smoke grenade, Dodds passed it up. The last grenade Dodds stuck in his pocket when the battle lulled for a second and Harrison took advantage of the moment to try and gain some control over his squadron. The captain called for each nearby tank to move one at a time at his request so he could see who was who. A minute or two into this procedure, a bullet struck him in the head, causing a flesh wound that bled heavily.

While Dodds passed him a field dressing, Sergeant Johnstone assumed momentary command. He yelled to the driver, "Speed up, Huckell. Follow the tank in front till I tell you different." When the sergeant moved as if to replace Harrison in the turret, the captain grabbed his radio mike and resumed command. Dodds dropped down onto the Sherman's floor, knelt, and started rearranging ammunition for the next inevitable bout of fighting. There was a hellish bang as a German shell ripped the driver's hatch cover off and the breech of the 75-millimetre gun shook violently before dropping downwards. Johnstone screamed, "Bail out." Dodds looked up to see Harrison give "one hesitant look skywards and then both were gone."

"Not relishing the idea of jumping out of the turret in enemy machine-gun fire I said, 'Get the escape hatch off.'" Located in the centre of the tank floor, this hatch opened between the tracks, providing good cover. Dodds handed the co-driver a hammer. As the man banged the hatch open, "the tank appeared to be rolling backwards and Huckell turned to put it out of gear. At this point something hit the tracks twice in quick succession and sparks appeared in the escape hatch. I went out the turret top with all the speed I could, dropping to the ground and running twenty yards into some bushes. I did not see or hear any more of Huckell until he was found dead beside the tank several days later. From the brush I peered through a hedge only to see a German about fifty yards away, he had a rifle and looked ready for anything. I ducked back into the brush and moved a few feet and lay down. Three shots went over me, none really close. Looking in the other direction I saw two of our fellows beside one of our tanks, which was burning. I ran the fifteen yards to them and crouched beside them."

One of the men was Harrison's co-driver, the other an officer with two bullets in his left shoulder that didn't prevent him from crawling. Fifty yards away, another Sherman burned and the men crawled to it, finding three more tankers hiding in a hedge there. From here, they crawled northwards to another burning tank, picking up anything useful from the Canadian kit lying on the ground. When they reached this tank, the men assessed their situation. It was pretty grim. Dodds had a couple of grenades. The co-driver was the only one with a hat of any kind, and that was a black tanker's beret. Only the officer had a gun, just a pistol. Discipline suddenly broke down as the other troopers took off in whatever direction they felt best—some running, others crawling. Dodds and the officer stuck together, crawling under the tank and staying there even as it started to smoulder. In the distance, Dodds heard Sherman tanks moving in the nearby fields. He could also make out the sounds of Panzer Grenadiers closing in on their position.[42]

[20]

Guess We Go

'**B**' SQUADRON AND 'D' COMPANY had rolled into the maw of the German killing zone, with disastrous results. In a matter of minutes, Captain Harrison and Major Neil Gordon's commands were shredded. The Panzer Grenadier pioneers lying in wait had been initially surprised to see the infantry riding on the tanks, but had quickly responded by ignoring their instructions to let the tanks pass and launching an immediate assault. The infantry tangled hand-to-hand in desperate battle, while the Panzer Grenadiers also attacked the tanks with Faustpatrones and magnetic mines.

When one of the Hitlerjugend soldiers jumped off a Sherman on which he had fitted a magnetic mine, he stumbled into the sights of the gunner inside and was cut down by a machine-gun burst. Seconds later, the tank blew up in a fiery ball as the mine detonated.

Nearby, Pionier Horst Lütgens had three Faustpatrones (meaning fist cartridge) in his dugout as the tanks rolled around him and a sergeant yelling at him to take them on. Depending on the model, these hand-held disposable antitank rocket launchers—popularly called Panzerfausts or Tank Fist—fired either a 5.5-pound or 6.39-pound projectile, respectively capable of penetrating armour 140 to 200 millimetres thick at a range of less than ninety feet. The biggest flaw in both weapon models was an effective range of only about one hundred feet, so that they had to be brought to bear perilously close to the target.

Moments before the attack, he had been sitting on the side of his hole writing a letter home in the warm spring sunshine. Now he scrambled to fit detonators to charges and stepped out into a landscape boiling with smoke and flames, whipped by bullets and shrapnel from exploding tank rounds. As he started crawling through the wheat towards one Sherman, more appeared on either side of it. A blue haze of gunpowder smoke shrouded the tanks as he closed in. The tank Lütgens headed for had its gun barrel pointing directly at the château that was the headquarters for 11 Battalion, 26th Panzer Grenadier Regiment.

Closing to within sixty feet, Lütgens shouldered the weapon and squeezed the trigger. Nothing happened. The Panzerfaust had jammed. Recocking the firing mechanism, he tried again with the same result. Panicked and beginning to shake almost uncontrollably, the young ss trooper tried again. This time, the bomb roared towards its target. Without waiting to see the result, Lütgens fled, with bullets tearing up the earth around him as one of the other tanks opened up with its co-axial machine gun. Diving into his dugout, Lütgens turned over to see that the Canadian tanks were all swinging away in an attempt to meet the sudden onslaught of three Panzers that had appeared.[1]

The tanks were from No. 8 Panzer Company of 11 Battalion, 12th Panzer Regiment under command of Obersturmführer Hans Siegel. En route to an award ceremony at the battalion headquarters, Siegel had heard the sounds of battle in the distance and decided to check what was happening. His tanks rolled up on the eastern side of the orchard and into the right flank of most of Harrison's squadron. The shootout was short and fierce, with six Shermans dying in seconds.[2] One of these was Harrison's, another that of his second-in-command, Captain John Smuck.[3] (Both officers managed to escape from their tanks, although Smuck was badly burned.) Then, intent on taking advantage of the confusion among the Canadians and thinking more Panzer Grenadiers were forward of his position, Siegel ordered his tanks to charge forward. Suddenly, the lead Panzer Mark IV blew up as it pushed through a hedge. Everyone jumped clear except for the driver, who burned to death inside. Siegel looked around wildly as his own tank emerged from the hedge, convinced they were being fired on by a hidden antitank gun. A second later, the tank shook hard as an armour-piercing round penetrated the front of Siegel's Mark IV and killed the wireless operator. As the tank began to burn, Siegel and the rest of the crew abandoned it. The surviving Panzer was knocked out at the same time.[4]

There was no antitank gun. The fire came from 'A' Squadron, which had deployed in a defensive line on a height of ground between Norrey-en-Bessin and Bretteville-l'Orgueilleuse. They were to meet and repel any German counterattack, while also providing covering fire for the retreating tankers and infantry. Realizing the attack was a disastrous failure, 1st Hussars commander Lieutenant Colonel Ray Colwell had held back the only squadron not yet committed to the advance on le Mesnil-Patry.

When Siegel's three Mark IVs emerged from the hedge, several of the Hussars tanks zeroed in on them with deadly accuracy. Chief among these was Corporal Art Boyle, who commanded a 17-pounder Firefly Sherman, and had been leaning out of the turret hatch chatting with the half-dozen Queen's Own still perched on his tank. Suddenly, the men "started getting shot off the tank." Spinning around, he saw a Mark IV Panzer coming through a hedge about 1,500 yards away, quickly sighted it in, and put an armour-piercing round into the air. The shot hit home and the German tank brewed. Fire from the other Shermans knocked out the remaining two Panzers in Siegel's troop. Boyle didn't see any more signs of Germans trying to advance on Norrey, just scattered remnants of Hussars and Queen's Own trickling back.[5]

And to the front the sounds of battle kept growing in intensity.

WHILE THE MAIN BODY of 'B' Squadron and 'D' Company had been virtually wiped out in the opening thirty minutes of battle, a handful of infantry under command of twenty-two-year-old Lieutenant

George Bean managed to break into le Mesnil-Patry from the right-hand flank. Also inside the village ahead of the infantry were two tanks of No. 4 Troop led by Captain Richard Wildgoose, a former newspaperman from London, Ontario. Bean had only nine men with him as the platoon pushed up to the edge of the village. During a short firefight with some Panzer Grenadiers fighting from slit trenches, Bean was shot in the leg. The young officer refused to quit, turning instead to his men. "Shall we go in and clean it out ourselves?" he shouted, while gesturing towards le Mesnil-Patry.[6] When Rifleman John Lloyd Wardell and the others answered that they should, Bean, limping badly, led them forward.[7]

Using a sunken road for cover, they moved in among a group of buildings on the outskirts. Bean and his men wiped out several more German positions before reaching a clearing and taking cover in a large bomb crater because of heavy incoming mortar fire. Out front of the crater, the two tanks from Wildgoose's troop were blasting away at the heart of the village with their main guns. Running over to the tanks, Bean stood in the open trying to attract their attention and was wounded in the back. As he stumbled back towards the crater, he was wounded a third time and collapsed about fifty yards away. Seconds later, Wardell was hit and knocked unconscious.[8]

Lying out in the open, Bean waved for Sergeant Samuel Scrutton to take over and press the attack home. An army brat, who as the son of a Princess Patricia's Light Infantry regimental sergeant major had been virtually raised in barracks, Scrutton was a tough and decisive non-commissioned officer. He quickly decided that going on was plain suicide and instead dragged the wounded officer back into the crater. Meanwhile, Wildgoose's tank had been knocked out and the officer killed. When the surviving tank started withdrawing, Corporal A. Jackson dashed out and flagged it down. He and Scrutton loaded Bean onto the back while Wardell, who had regained consciousness, "and those [others] of us who were still able to move, climbed aboard."[9]

The badly shot-up little band had to fight its way out while riding on the tank. Scrutton managed to kill about a dozen Panzer

Grenadiers who attempted to prevent their escape. Pausing at about 1500 hours just beyond the worst concentrations of Germans, Scrutton counted two of the nine men in the party dead, discovered he had one missing, and two were so badly wounded they were unable to walk.[10] Scrutton earned a Distinguished Conduct Medal, while, for his leadership, Bean was awarded the Military Cross.

While Bean's little group made its escape from le Mesnil-Patry, 'C' Squadron headed towards the village after finally working its way through the narrow streets of Norrey to gain the battlefield. Squadron commander Major D'Arcy Marks deployed his tanks with three troops out front—No. 4 left, No. 2 in the centre and on the tip, No. 1 to the right.[11] The other two troops were back of those on the flanks and his squadron headquarters held the centre of a loose diamond formation.

Leading the way were the two tanks of Lieutenant Bill McCormick's No. 2 Troop. Because of the earlier fuel line leak in his own tank, McCormick was riding into battle with a different crew than normal. But except for the driver, a fresh replacement with the last name of Smith, the men had served in his troop for a long time. The others were gunner Trooper Len Magee, loader/operator Trooper William Wallace Millar (whom everyone just called W.W.), and co-driver Trooper Euclid "Frenchie" Moreau. No. 2 Troop's second tank was commanded by Corporal Jackie Simmons, whose brother, Sergeant William "Foo" Simmons, was also somewhere out in the middle of this battle. The two brothers hailed from Timmins and so were inevitably known as "the Simmons from Timmins." Aboard this tank were troopers Alf Cooper, Cy Bleakley, Rolly Parsons, and Bill Mugford.[12]

'C' Squadron pushed out into the wheatfields and McCormick lost sight of most of the tanks in the tall grain. Soon the world seemed cut down to just five Shermans—the two from his troop and the three of another. An eerie silence hung over the landscape as they advanced towards le Mesnil-Patry with no sign of friend or foe—just the yellow grain from which smudges of smoke billowed darkly into the blue sky. A few minutes later, McCormick saw a tank burning out to his front, then another, and then a whole bunch. The lieutenant had expected to see an exchange of fire going on between 'B' Squadron and the enemy, but not this. He still could detect no Germans and didn't see any Queen's Own riflemen either. Finding the whole scenario "very ominous," he ordered the tank halted. "I'm not going into this," he said over the wireless. Switching to the internal communication net, McCormick said, "Driver, reverse."

As the driver moved to comply, Major D'Arcy Marks came up on the squadron net. In a very calm voice, the commander said, "We got to attack. This is a job we've been given to do and we have to do it."

"To hell with this," McCormick replied. None of the other tanks were moving, as everyone waited to see how this conversation played out. Nobody who knew McCormick would consider that he balked at proceeding out of cowardice. On D-Day, the lieutenant had taken his tank far out in front of the entire 3rd Canadian Infantry Division in a bold dash that carried almost through to Carpiquet airport. Had the rest of the squadron received his wireless messages urging them to come up in support and responded to them, many in the 1st Hussars believed the division would have been spared the fierce fighting that had been going on these past days.

There was a pause and then Marks spoke. "I'm calling for volunteers."

McCormick chewed on that a second. What was being proposed ran counter to the old military maxim that you reinforce success rather than failure. Those burning tanks stood as evidence that 'B' Squadron had suffered disastrous failure in the initial attack and to go forward courted more of the same for 'C' Squadron. But McCormick admired Marks greatly and was also a good soldier. "Guess we go," he responded.

Countermanding his earlier order, the lieutenant said, "Driver, forward." As his tank started moving, so did the rest.

A few minutes later, McCormick saw Panzer Grenadiers moving to his left and opened up on them with high-explosive and the co-axial. Then something moved in the bushes to his right and he raked them with shells and bullets. With what seemed to be all of 'B'

Squadron sitting out there burning, the lieutenant was sure there must be German tanks or antitank guns around, so he was blasting every likely hiding spot.[13]

'C' Squadron's advance descended into the same chaotic pandemonium of slaughter that had befallen 'B' Squadron. When tanks suddenly started taking hits and blowing up at 1615 hours, Marks yelled into the regimental net that the squadron was under attack by enemy tanks firing from his right flank.[14] Colwell immediately passed this report to brigade headquarters and was warned by someone on Brigadier Ron Wyman's staff to "not fire on them as they were friendly tanks... Colwell, thinking the tanks must be British armour supporting the 50th Infantry Division off on that flank, ordered [Marks] to hold fire and fly his recognition flags."[15] The major dutifully climbed out of the turret hatch and fastened the recognition flag to the radio aerial, but the tanks to the right kept closing in while continuing to fire on the squadron. Marks reported this to Colwell at 1623 hours.[16] The situation, he added, was becoming untenable as his squadron casualties were escalating rapidly. Before Colwell could countermand his no-fire order, all contact with 'C' Squadron was abruptly lost.[17]

By now, the tanks to the right were coming within point-blank range and more Shermans were being hit and bursting into flames. Peering through the smoke and tall grain, few Canadian tankers could see any of the tanks firing on them. They shot back blindly, but without any noticeable effect as the rate of fire coming their way kept increasing in volume and accuracy.

Bearing down on 'C' Squadron was an entire company of 12th Panzer Regiment—No. 5 Company of 11 Battalion under command of Sturmbannführer Karl-Heinz Prinz. The German tanker had been ordered to support the Panzer Grenadiers. Enjoying the advantage of higher ground, Prinz and his company could bring the Shermans under fire without betraying their own position. They proceeded to pick the Canadians off one by one.

Things went from bad to worse for Marks after losing the wireless link to Colwell's headquarters. His second-in-command, Captain

Gerry Stoner, hobbled up to report that his tank had been hard hit minutes earlier and he had ordered the crew to bail out. No sooner had everyone got clear than a second round punched into the Sherman and it burst into flames. Stoner was struck in the right knee by shrapnel, but was game to stay in the fight if Marks wanted. The major ordered him instead to get back on foot to Norrey and re-establish contact with Colwell.[18] He was desperate for orders permitting a withdrawal. Stoner hurried to the village, passing 12th Field Regiment's Captain Charles Rivaz on the outskirts. The artillery officer lamented that his radios had failed and he could do nothing to summon artillery support for the embattled tankers and infantry. When Stoner reported how badly things were going out front, Colwell summoned a scout car and sent him to brigade headquarters with orders to get Wyman to release the Fort Garry Horse squadrons and remaining Queen's Own to reinforce the attack.[19]

Meanwhile, 'C' Squadron's wireless net was clogged with jumbled messages from excited and desperate loader/operators. Trooper Larry Allen in Corporal R.C. "Reg" Pike's tank recognized the voice of one man who kept pleading, "Our crew commander is killed, what do we do now?" Another operator stammered, "Our guns are getting hot. What should we do?" Someone responded tersely, "Piss on 'em and get off the air. You're jamming."

AT THE SAME TIME as Colwell tried to summon reinforcements, Queen's Own Rifles commander Lieutenant Colonel Jock Spragge reluctantly ordered Major Elliot Dalton to take the majority of 'A' Company holding in Norrey forward to pass through 'D' Company and get into le Mesnil-Patry. Neither man knew that 'D' Company no longer existed. As Dalton led his men out from the village, he saw Major Neil Gordon "on a tank being taken out and he had been shot through the face. He was a rather messy looking individual.

"I got a look at the ground to see how I was going to use it and then a mortar bomb came over and lit at my feet and tore most of my uniform off and the base plug [of the bomb] went through my leg. I had actually gotten up to where the Start Line was supposed to be.

"I had said to my batman and Bren gunner 'Run' and they both went to ground, and I ran and got hit, proving that the riflemen were a hell of a lot smarter than their majors in the [Queen's Own]. I got hit and they didn't get a scratch."[20]*

That was the end of 'A' Company's supporting attack. Spragge ordered the men back into Norrey. There was nothing more that infantry could do, and Colwell was holding back his last squadron while waiting for reinforcement. The tankers and infantry still out there would have to cope on their own, for neither commander had any more than fleeting contact with them over the wireless and consequently could not order a retreat. Colwell feared the German tanks were going to turn his flank, so he kept calling over the radio for 'B' and 'C' Squadrons to come back and form up alongside 'A' Squadron.[21] But there was no response from the battlefield. Then abruptly Marks came up on the radio and acknowledged.

Marks no longer had contact with the rest of his squadron, however, and nobody could raise 'B' Squadron. Captain Cyril Tweedale was in a tank next to Marks and the two officers concurred by wireless that their tanks "were the only ones left, so we laid smoke and retired."[22] The time was about 1700 hours.

Everyone was coming independently to the conclusion that to stay on the battlefield was to die, so an uncoordinated retreat started. Few tankers got out with their Shermans, but Trooper Jim Simpson of 'B' Squadron was an exception. He had rapidly burned through all the machine-gun ammunition, high-explosive rounds, and most of the armour-piercing shells. When the traverse, which the gunner had

---

* Dalton soon found himself in a hospital in England being challenged as to why he was on a stretcher instead of in his bed. The nurse bustled him into a ward only to find another man sleeping in the bed that was supposedly Dalton's. Waiting at the doorway, Dalton was unable to see the man, who had been sleeping with the sheet pulled up over his face. When the nurse said the soldier in the bed claimed to be Major Dalton of the Queen's Own, Dalton declared he must be nuts, for that was who he was. Suddenly, the sheet fell away and Elliot stared into his brother's eyes. Both Charlie and Elliot recovered from their wounds within a few weeks and returned to duty.

been wildly ratcheting around to bring the guns to bear, started acting up, he decided it was time to make a break for it. His troop sergeant, Léo Gariépy, had disappeared in the opening moments of battle, his lieutenant Jimmy Martin was dead, and the officer's tank crew had fled. The infantry were either dead on the ground near the tank or also gone. Ordering his driver to turn the Sherman around, Simpson guided it back towards Norrey. Off to one side, he spotted a half-dozen wounded Queen's Own lying in the roadside ditch. Wary of snipers, he called to them without sticking his head out of the turret hatch, "If you can get those guys on the back, I can get them the hell out of here." A couple of walking wounded helped the others climb onboard. Looking around, Simpson saw nothing but burning tanks stretching across the horizon all the way back to Norrey. He told the driver, "If you ever got this thing into high gear, get it into high gear now. We don't want to be dawdling here."

As the tank broke out of the orchard into the wheatfield, Simpson could see German infantry and what he was sure were Panzers swarming in the open in front of Norrey. The driver had the Sherman running flat out. "The steel tracks were screaming on the blacktop" as they raced towards Norrey. Arriving safely, Simpson dropped the wounded Queen's Own at an aid station before heading for the regiment's base at Bray.[23]

Simpson's troop mate, Sergeant Gariépy, had a penchant for solo operating in hostile country. Rapidly outdistancing the rest of the troop, he had pushed into the streets of le Mesnil-Patry alone and was soon caught in a running fight with Panzer Grenadiers aboard half-tracks that appeared to be reinforcing the units already engaged. Gariépy sent three of the half-tracks up in flames before an explosion on the outside hull set the crew's bedrolls and some spare machine-gun ammunition ablaze. Using the smoke pouring off the tank as a screen, Gariépy reversed out of the immediate gun battle, and once clear of the shooting ordered everyone out. The five tankers crawled along a roadside ditch "over dead Germans and Canadians" back to the safety of Norrey.[24]

Sergeant William "Foo" Simmons, brother of Corporal Jackie Simmons, had his tank shot out. As the crew pulled itself together after escaping the Sherman, Simmons saw a German tank traverse its turret to bear on the group. "Shouting at his men to scatter he ran towards the [tank] to draw its fire and was never seen again. Thus two brothers who came overseas with the Hussars distinguished themselves on the battlefield with unselfish heroism," the regiment's historian later wrote.[25]

Trooper Larry Allen in Corporal Reg Pike's 'C' Squadron Sherman didn't like the spot they were in, with a high stone wall to their right and thick brush to the left. More dense brush barred the way ahead. There was no room to turn around. To get out, the driver would have to reverse back the way they had come. Pike said there were German infantry all around them. Then he shouted, "There's a Jerry out here with an antitank gun and he's going to shoot us!"

Allen yelled, "Shoot him first." Pike yanked back the action on his Sten gun, but it jammed on sand that had got into it on the beach during the invasion landing. A round from the German slammed into the engine compartment, followed by several others that knocked the tank's power out. "Abandon tank," Pike yelled. As he tumbled out of the turret, Allen and the gunner decided to first fire some high-explosive shells into the brush to clear an escape route. Then they jumped out. Pike was there with a German machine gun in his hands. "Coming with me, Allen?" he said.

"No," Allen replied. "We're going to find a hiding place in the bush."

Acting confused and barely coherent, Pike turned and walked off towards le Mesnil-Patry rather than the rear. Allen quickly lost sight of the man, whose body would be found later.

Allen and the rest of the crew took cover in the brush while trying to figure out what to do next. As they hid there, the survivors from three other tanks moved towards them. "What a mess they were in! Burned beyond recognition. Their flesh hanging in shreds from their faces and hands. We went to assist them. As I approached a fellow who was crawling on his knees and the *backs* of his hands, I asked why he was using the backs of his hands. He turned them over; the cooked flesh had been worn off in his trip across the field. I must have looked horror stricken.

"'Don't you know me, Allen?' he asked pitifully.

"'Silversberg!'

"'You're in bad shape,' I said. 'Come on all you guys. Let's get out of sight.'" Allen was shocked that he had failed to recognize Trooper Frank Silversberg. The two men had entertained the regiment often with a comedy routine where Allen was the straight guy for the comic's wide repertoire of jokes. Allen was now in charge of about nine men, of whom five were badly burned. He hid the injured men, who were helpless to suppress their pitiful moans, separately from the unwounded so any Germans drawn by the sounds would not discover the whole group.

Among the burned men was Captain John Smuck of 'B' Squadron. An ex-Toronto policeman, Smuck drew his .38-pistol and said, "Come on Allen, we've been in tougher spots than this and got out." Suffering from burns and a bullet wound, the captain was clearly in shock. Allen calmly told him, "I know where we are. I know where the hedgerows are. If we're going to get out of here, either our fellows will put in a counterattack and get us out, or we will get out after dark. Right now that area is alive with angry Germans with MGs and grenades, so come with me!"

The captain "broke down and allowed me to lead him to a place of hiding." Everyone hunkered down and hoped for counterattacking Canadians to reach them or darkness to fall before the Germans found their position.[26]

LIEUTENANT BILL MCCORMICK had glimpsed Trooper Allen escaping from Pike's knocked-out Sherman off to the left of his own position. Then he looked to the right and saw Corporal Jackie Simmons and his crew out on the ground beside their burning tank. A gun flashed to the right behind McCormick and a shell slammed into the track on that side of the Sherman. Hoping to beat the German tank to the next shot, the lieutenant swung the turret towards where he had seen the gun flash, but a second shell slammed into the turret with deadly effect. McCormick's gunner, Trooper Len Magee, and loader/operator Trooper W.W. Millar were both killed. Somehow, McCormick found himself lying on the ground outside the tank. It felt like his "feet were on fire. I couldn't figure out why there wasn't flame or smoke coming from them. They were burning. I looked down and could see bone."

Simmons and his crew crawled up and joined the survivors from McCormick's tank. None of them knew which way they should go to escape. McCormick pointed back towards Norrey. "We go that way. I can't go, though. Get out of here." He was mad, angry with himself for not ordering the tank abandoned when the first shot hit it, angry at the stupidity of orders that had brought so much death and destruction down on them all.

The other tankers refused to leave him. "That's an order," McCormick snapped. McCormick's small co-driver, "Frenchie" Moreau replied firmly, "We're all getting out of this and that's that." After a couple of the men bandaged McCormick's injuries as best they could, they grabbed his web belt and crawled off through the wheat pulling the lieutenant along with them. A few seconds later, German mortar bombs started tearing up the field. The bombardment seemed to go on forever. "It was just whistle, wham. Whistle, wham." McCormick thought, "If I get out of this, I'm not going to take shit from anyone again as long as I live."

When the mortars stopped firing, the men carried on. In the tall grain, it was impossible to keep together. McCormick saw Simmons head off in the direction of another injured man lying in the wheat. (The corporal managed to carry the wounded tanker to safety.) Then McCormick was alone with Trooper Alf Cooper from Simmons's tank. Cooper was helping McCormick—a big, heavily built man—single-handedly by lying on his side and dragging the lieutenant. McCormick could help somewhat by hauling with his arms, but his legs were useless. They came to a stretch of elliptically shaped open ground where the wheat had been harvested. "I don't think I've enough strength to crawl around it," McCormick said.

Cooper didn't hesitate. Lying on his side, he just crawled out into the open, pulling McCormick along in his wake. The two men were about halfway across when McCormick "felt as if somebody had taken a crowbar and slapped me." A rifle slug had torn a chunk out of his backside. They lay still for a bit after that, hoping the round was only a wild shot and not deliberately aimed. When nothing further happened, Cooper started moving again. More than an hour after they had set out from the knocked-out tanks, they reached an orchard occupied by the Regina Rifles. A couple of soldiers helped McCormick into the cover of a slit trench and one handed him a bottle of cognac.

McCormick had the presence of mind to refuse. "If I get out of this," he said, "I'm going to be on an operating table and I won't have any, thanks." He was told that the Reginas were trying to get jeeps up to evacuate the wounded coming into the orchard but that the ground between them and Bretteville was under German fire and it was presently too dangerous. He would just have to hang on.

Finally, a jeep appeared and he was taken to Bretteville and put in a barn on a stretcher. "Take my boots off. My feet are burning," he said to an orderly. The man began untying the laces. "For Christ's sake cut them off," McCormick moaned. He was exhausted, couldn't remember ever sleeping since the invasion. Sometime later, the orderly passed him again. "Please take my boots off," the lieutenant said.

"I cut them off fifteen minutes ago." McCormick realized grimly that "things weren't very good down there." It was a verdict confirmed when 1st Hussars second-in-command Major Frank White came by and said, "I'd lose my leg. That it was just like gelatin." Two days later, McCormick's right leg was amputated in a field hospital back at the beach. When he awoke and learned the news, his first thought was, "This is never going to get me down." As he heard how many Hussars had died that day out in the wheat, McCormick decided that losing a leg was scant price to pay compared to what those men had lost.[27]

By the time McCormick and Cooper had completed their slow, agonizing crawl back to the Canadian lines, all surviving tanks from 'B' and 'C' squadrons had withdrawn through Norrey. The heavy German shelling of the village during the day had realized Colwell's fears—choking the narrow streets with rubble so that they were blocked to use by armour. Yet because of the surrounding minefields, the Shermans had no choice but to go through the place. Another lane was blocked when Lieutenant George "Flash" Gordon of 'C' Squadron's No. 1 Troop turned a corner at such speed that his Sherman rolled, its steel tracks gouging the side of building.

In the barnyard where Lieutenant Ben Dunkleman had set up the Queen's Own mortar platoon, Rifleman Jack Martin was still hotly firing his three-inch tube despite the heavy incoming mortar and artillery fire hammering the position. Suddenly, no more than twenty-five feet away, a Sherman tank crashed through the two-foot wall sending "stone and mortar all over the place. If we had been a few feet to the tank's right it would have crushed and mashed us like potatoes." The tank barrelled on into Norrey and the men went back to their mortars.[28] Another tank smashed through the wall of a building on the outskirts of the village and plunged into a basement, while others used their guns to blast open paths through walls and buildings to gain the northern outskirts.[29]

The fire the mortar platoon put out into the fields was the only support given the withdrawing troops. Artillery officer Captain Rivaz was dead, killed by a shell. No communication with the artillery regiments could be established.[30] Finally, when his men had barely any rounds left to fire, Dunkleman gave the order to withdraw. They piled the mortars onto their Bren carriers, only to find that there was so much rubble blocking the barnyard and road that turning the vehicles around was impossible. Instead, they backed them along the narrow lane towards Norrey. At the junction with the main road, everything was in chaos. An explosion just as the mortar carriers pulled up killed a soldier from the Canadian Provost Corps, who was trying to direct traffic. Mortarman Corporal Gordie Sullivan jumped off the lead carrier, dragged the man to the side, and took over. Sullivan no sooner passed the mortar platoon out of the intersection than a second shell killed him. The carriers fled Norrey and withdrew to where the Queen's Own were rallying in Bretteville.[31] Here, Sergeant John Missions of 'B' Company watched grimly as his friend Sergeant Sam Scrutton brought in the little party that had escaped from le Mesnil-Patry.

"How you doin', Sam?" Missions asked.

"That was a real son-of-a-bitch," Scrutton replied.[32]

In Bretteville, meanwhile, the 1st Hussars were trying to tally their losses. Only two 'B' Squadron tanks out of twenty-one had made it back and both were damaged. One was Trooper Jim Simpson's. Nine 'C' Squadron tanks had escaped. Total tank losses were three Fireflys and thirty-four standard Shermans.[33]

Simpson and Captain Bob Rogers stood on the road outside Bretteville as night fell, hoping and praying for more survivors to come in. With so few men left from 'B' Squadron, the regiment was having trouble even piecing together a picture of who was missing because the reinforcement schedule had been in Captain Smuck's tank. As the veteran crews had been broken up and spread among the tanks, nobody knew who had been where. Finally, it was completely dark, and Simpson turned to Rogers. "There isn't any more of 'B' Squadron coming back." The two men trudged dispiritedly back to the regimental harbour.[34]

Vive le Canada!

OUT IN NO MAN'S LAND, 1st Hussars and Queen's Own Rifles were still trying to get back to the Canadian lines. Trooper I.O. Dodds and the wounded lieutenant had been hiding under a knocked-out Sherman tank when a group of Panzer Grenadiers started milling around. Dodds threw a grenade from the front of the tank into a nearby hedge, and when it exploded the Germans all went quiet for a moment before they started talking again. The lieutenant "lay on his back at the rear of the tank, pulling the pin from his grenade cost him a great deal of pain and effort with his wounded shoulder, but he got it out and threw the grenade... from the rear of the tank." Again there was silence, followed by a resumption of chatter and then Dodds saw several Panzer Grenadiers moving deliberately towards the smouldering tank. Drawing his revolver, the lieutenant said, "Give yourself up, kid."

"No," Dodds replied and crawled quickly into the hedge. Gaining the road, he ran along it before breaking through a hedge on the right-hand side. Coming out into a pasture, he saw a German about forty yards off, and rolling into some brush, "burrowed under like a rabbit. Several shots went by me. I stopped and lay flat. More shots came into the brush, ticking off leaves a few feet from me." Ducking and dodging from one hedge to another, dashing across pastures when there was no alternative, and using a compass to keep bearing northwards, Dodds finally reached the lines of the 50th British Infantry Division.[1]

Many were less fortunate. Trooper Larry Allen's little group holed up in the brush, hoping for either rescue by a counterattack or night-fall. They watched tensely as some German soldiers came along with a two-wheeled wagon they were using to pick up their dead and wounded. When the Panzer Grenadiers discovered the injured tankers that Allen had bedded down away from the fit men, he heard shots from that direction. Then a German challenged, "Englander? Soldaten?" More shots followed. Gradually, the moans of the wounded ceased as challenges were issued, followed by shots.

"I heard one of the boys say, 'Did you get yours?'" Allen later wrote. "And one groaned and answered: 'Yeah, where did he shoot you?'

"'In the guts.'

"'Me too, the dirty bastards.'

"The last sound I heard from our men was [one] calling his wife's name. Then I heard some German boys as they died calling for their mothers. What an equalizer death is! I felt sorry for these youths who were calling, 'Mütter, Mütter.'"

A few minutes later, the Germans closed on Allen's position and a challenge was shouted. Allen stayed put, hoping he had not been seen. Then he heard a bayonet being rasped onto a rifle barrel and, deciding the game was definitely up, surrendered. Expecting to be killed like the others, Allen was surprised when they just motioned for him to join the procession. When he stepped out onto the road, the soldiers saw he was barefoot and demanded to know why. With gestures and pidgin English, he explained he'd taken his shoes off in order to allow for silent movement, and hoped they didn't search the brush. Had they done so, they would have discovered that he had been "wearing a lovely pair of German jackboots" picked up on the beach on June 6.[2] Allen was led off into captivity.

As before when the 12th ss (Hitlerjugend) Panzer Division faced a surfeit of prisoners, some were treated correctly under the rules of the Geneva Convention, some faced mistreatment but had their lives spared, and others were murdered without cause. Sergeant William "Foo" Simmons was among the murdered, his body dumped into a ditch near the château outside le Mesnil-Patry serving as II Battalion, 26th Panzer Grenadiers' headquarters. Whereas Sturmbannführer

Bernhard Siebken had gone out of his way to protect prisoners from the Royal Winnipeg Rifles on June 7, he exerted no restraining hand on his young soldiers this day.

Rifleman Dave Arksey and his new friend Rifleman Lew Bridges were crawling through the grain towards Canadian lines in the late afternoon when a shot rang out. The bullet caught Bridges in the head, killing him. Arksey was ordered to his feet and added to a group of five other prisoners. Among them was twenty-six-year-old Sergeant Major Jack Forbes, who had been shot in both legs. As Arksey joined the men, one of them reported that Forbes had been wounded after capture. Nearby, the body of one of the company's runners was sprawled, and the man said that he had been killed by the same burst of fire that had wounded Forbes.

Ordered to start marching towards the German rear, two of the men picked Forbes up, but the officer in charge said, "Lean him against that tree. He'll be looked after. Now come over here."

Reluctantly, the men obeyed the order and Forbes was abandoned, ultimately bleeding to death. Marched over to where two wounded Panzer Grenadiers lay, the German officer instructed the Canadians to "pick them up and go to First Aid." Arksey and the rest "were all dead scared, and nobody was saying a word... every move was very, very careful. One of the guys, [thirty-two-year-old Charles Stuart] Hood, with no weapons at all, still had a bandolier on. He sensibly thought he'd get rid of it. Maybe he moved a little too quickly; as he was taking it off, a nervous German fired and killed him."

At the headquarters, they were interrogated but refused to give anything beyond their ranks and serial numbers. The man conducting the interrogation was a major wearing a black leather coat with ss death's head emblems, who looked as if he had stepped out of central casting in wartime Hollywood to play the villain's role. Waving a letter he claimed to have taken off a Royal Winnipeg officer, the officer shouted that it instructed the Canadians to take no prisoners. Considering the letter, he said, they were fortunate to be alive.

Arksey spoke up. "Tuesday [June 6] was our first day and we took sixty of you people prisoner on that day alone. That letter's counterfeit." The major refused to show him the letter and eventually tired of

346 / HOLDING JUNO

trying to get answers out of the men. Finally, he ordered Arksey and two of the others taken to a "little rise of ground" by two privates and the lieutenant. The two privates ratcheted back the cocking levers on their Schmeissers and aimed them at the Canadians. "We're standing there waiting for it, legs shaking. Ten minutes go by. Then another ten minutes. Then another ten. By that time I'd told myself... I won't even hear the shot. So what. Then we realized they weren't going to do it, and when they told us to sit down we all just kind of collapsed." They were soon transferred to Caen and sent on their way to POW camps.[3]

Despite the self-sacrifice by Sergeant William "Foo" Simmons, who charged an enemy tank to give his men a chance to escape, Sergeant E.S. Payne and troopers R.C. McClean and Lee Preston were rounded up. While being marched towards 11 Battalion head-quarters, the Germans escorting them suddenly opened fire from be-hind. Shot through the back, Preston dropped dead. Although the fire came from almost point-blank range, Payne only had an ear grazed and McClean was untouched. Both men collapsed and feigned death. Surprisingly, their wards assumed all three Canadians were dead and strode off. The two survivors escaped.

Also captured were Captain John Smuck and troopers Arthur Hancock, Albert Charron, and Joseph Leclaire. A single guard as-signed to march them back to headquarters forced the men into a field en route and executed them. Their bodies were later exhumed from a single grave.[4]

Four other 1st Hussars taken prisoner were troopers Albert Joseph Cybulski, John Dumont, Leslie Soroke, and Lawrence Sutton—all of 'B' Squadron. Cybulski had lost several teeth when their tank had been hit, and Soroke had applied a field dressing to his mouth to stem the bleeding. They were picked up by about fifteen Panzer Grenadiers who formed themselves into two lines with seven men on each side, while the remaining soldier forced the four tankers to run through single file. As the men passed along the line, they were beaten with rifle butts. Then one of the Germans gestured for them to start walk-ing up the road. Put on edge by the man's manner, Soroke started walking backwards so he could watch the German. After only a few steps, the German raised his gun and shot Sutton in the back. The force of the bullet threw Sutton against Soroke, who held the dying soldier in front of him as a shield while the German turned the rifle on Dumont and gunned him down. As the man fired at Cybulski, Soroke dropped Sutton and dove into a hedge.

Hiding out until nightfall, Soroke then returned to the scene, finding the corpses of Sutton and Dumont but seeing no sign of Cybulski, although the man lay dead in a nearby ditch. After wandering for three days in no man's land, hiding out in barns and fields, scavenging food wherever he could find it, Soroke was finally taken prisoner again. This time he was properly treated and spent the rest of the war as a POW.[5]

The 1st Hussars Regiment would forever remember June 11 as Black Sabbath, because it accounted for the heaviest losses suffered in a single day of the war and almost a third of the Hussars' casualties for the entire European campaign. Eighty men were casualties, 59 of these fatal.[6] The Queen's Own Rifles counted 55 killed, 33 wounded, and 11 taken prisoner. In the battle's aftermath, one Queen's Own officer described the attack as "conceived in sin and born in iniquity."[7]

Although the 12th ss held the ground at le Mesnil-Patry, it paid a heavy price. The 26th Panzer Grenadier Regiment reported 18 dead, 32 wounded, and one missing, while the pioneer battalion had 29 killed, 49 wounded, and 5 missing. Losses among the 12th Panzer Regiment's tankers tallied one dead, 7 wounded, and 5 missing. In all, the division had suffered 189 casualties in the fight for the village.[8] While the 1st Hussars' war diarist reported that the regiment "knocked out definitely 14 tanks, 11 of them Panthers and many probables," the 12th ss admitted losing only the three Mark iv Panzers of Obersturmführer Hans Siegel's reconnaissance group.[9] The diarist was wrong, however, for there were no Panthers on the June 11 battlefield. One of the Mark iv tanks was subsequently repaired and returned to duty.[10]

NO SOONER was the battle concluded than the surviving Queen's Own and 1st Hussars began trying to understand why it had gone so badly wrong. Rifleman Jack Martin heard various Queen's Own officers "put it down just to plain lousy intelligence" that led to a belief that le Mesnil-Patry was either abandoned by the enemy or only lightly held.[11]

There was an immediate scramble by brass all the way up the command chain to justify the operation. On June 12, First Canadian Army waded in with a minute to the 1st Hussars from Lieutenant General Guy Simonds, commander of 11 Canadian Corps, under whom 3rd Canadian Infantry Division and the 2nd Canadian Armoured Brigade normally served. "While the battle yesterday seemed futile, it actually put a Panzer Div[ision] attack on skids, thereby saving 7 CIB from being cut off and in the broader picture it helped 7 British Armoured Division to advance on our right flank."[12] Even the media pitched in, with one English newspaper summing the action of June 11 as "a modern version of The Charge of the Light Brigade."[13]

It was all nonsense, of course, for there was no offensive brewing on the German front facing the Canadian and British beaches. By the end of June 11, the 12th SS was so depleted by casualties it could barely man its defensive front. Panzer Lehr was fully engaged trying to stem the offensive launched by the British from Gold Beach to the Canadian right. On the morning of June 11, before battle had been joined in either the Mue valley or at le Mesnil-Patry, the 12th SS reported having suffered about 900 casualties, of which 220 were fatal. It had also lost at least 25 tanks, or 13 per cent of its entire armoured force.[14] The ensuing fighting in front of le Mesnil-Patry and in the Mue valley cost the division a further 256 dead, wounded, or missing. Although the division had a full strength of 20,540 men and officers, only 12,000 were part of its "bayonet strength" and assigned to combat sections. So by day's end on June 11, the division had lost slightly more than 10 per cent of its total fighting strength.

While Second British Army and 3rd Canadian Infantry Division commanders strove to justify the operation against le Mesnil-Patry, the surviving Queen's Own and 1st Hussars mourned comrades lost and looked forward to revenge. Platoon Sergeant Dave Kingston in 'C' Company of the Queen's Own noted that the morale of the battalion was high after the battle. "The attitude was, 'Let's go.' Exact opposite of what you would expect. Instead it was, 'We'll pay those bastards back.'"[15]

These feelings only intensified after 'A' Company Sergeant Major Charlie Martin led a three-man patrol towards le Mesnil-Patry on the morning of June 12 and discovered some men from 'D' Company who had obviously been executed. With him on the patrol were the company's two snipers, riflemen Bill Bettridge and Bert Shepherd. The three men crept through the grain right up to the village and were surprised to find that the ss seemed to have withdrawn. It was ghostly. No wrecked German vehicles or dead German soldiers could be found anywhere. But strewn through the grain and hedges in front of the village and in its streets were many Canadian corpses.

Crossing one wheatfield, Martin came across Sergeant Tommy McLaughlin and his five-man section. They lay in a row close to a low stone wall, and the csm immediately thought the entire thing looked wrong. Each of the men had a field dressing covering one wound or another. Lying on the ground beside every man was the pocket-sized New Testament soldiers were given. Looking closer, Martin saw that each man had been killed by a single shot to the temple. He could only surmise that the section had been initially machine-gunned in the advance, taken cover behind the wall to treat their wounds, then surrendered. Realizing they were to be murdered, the soldiers had sought comfort in their Bibles before one of their captors fired the fatal shots. Lying beside Sergeant McLaughlin were Corporal J.E. Cook and riflemen P. Bullock, J. Campbell, E.W. Cranfield, and G.L. Willett.[16]

Soon after Martin returned from this patrol, he said to one of 'D' Company's few survivors, Rifleman Jim McCullough: "Well, if that's how they want to play the game that's how we do it."[17] It was a feeling shared by many Queen's Own and 1st Hussars as news of the atrocities committed against their comrades filtered through the ranks. Padre H.C. Creelman moved to head off the dangerous mood simmering in the 1st Hussars by counselling the men during a commemoration service on June 12 "not to seek revenge by doing likewise."[18] In the end, men like Charlie Martin could not steel their hearts to mercilessly execute men who surrendered. This humanity, the csm realized, was one of the things that ultimately separated the Canadians from the fanatic Hitler Youth they had fought.[19]

THE MURDEROUS IMPULSE within the 12th ss had made itself felt on Le Régiment de la Chaudière on June 11 when one of its patrols ran afoul of the enemy near le Hamel. Corporal P. Desbiens had led seven men out from Bray towards the village in the Mue valley in the early morning, before the assault by No. 46 Royal Marine Commando and 'A' Squadron of the Fort Garry Horse got underway. The patrol was to test enemy strength along the route the Chaudières were to take in order to reinforce or relieve the marines once they had completed their attack. As the patrol would be operating in open country during broad daylight, Lieutenant Willy Foy's platoon positioned itself well forward to provide support if the small group ran into trouble. Also in a covering position was Captain J.Y. Gosselin's mortar platoon.

Desbiens and the men met no opposition and saw no sign of the enemy during the passage cross-country into the streets of le Hamel. But the moment they entered the village, the eight soldiers were brought under heavy fire by what seemed to be a full company of Panzer Grenadiers. Watching from Foy's position, Major George Sévigny ordered Gosselin to cover the patrol as it began a desperate retreat from le Hamel. Desbiens had just four men with him as he fled the village. The other three men had been too badly wounded to get back unaided—something that the other men, all walking wounded themselves and returning gunfire to keep the Germans at bay, could not provide. As it was, one of the men with Desbiens collapsed from loss of blood halfway back to the Canadian lines and had to be abandoned.

When Desbiens told Foy that he had lost a man on the way back from le Hamel the lieutenant headed alone into no man's land. Foy found the wounded soldier moments before several Panzer Grenadiers arrived from the opposite direction. A short firefight between Foy and the Germans ensued until they backed away. Scooping the man up, Foy dashed "under a rain of bullets" back to safety. His actions earned a Military Cross while Desbiens won a Military Medal.[20]

In the early morning hours of June 12, the Chaudières pushed through le Hamel en route to relieve the badly mauled commandos and discovered the bodies of their three missing soldiers. Each showed signs of having been wounded in the firefight and then murdered instead of being taken prisoner and given first aid. One of the men had been finished off with a bayonet or knife.

Major Hugues Lapointe led his 'A' Company with a detachment of antitank guns in support through the streets of Rots at 0300 hours on June 12. Uncertain how much of the village was in the hands of the commandos, the men "searched every house, every courtyard to avoid ambush. Here is the confirmation of how ferocious last night's battle must have been. The commandos lie dead in rows beside the dead ss. Grenades are scattered all over the road and in the porches of the houses. Here we see a commando and an ss man, literally dead in each other's arms, having slaughtered each other. There a German and a Canadian tank have engaged each other to destruction and are still smouldering, and from each blackened turret hangs [a] charred corpse. Over here are a group who ran towards a wall for shelter and were shot down before they got there. And then, near the church, as the advance guard of [the] company and the carriers turn the corner there are three Germans. One of them instantly draws his pistol and hits one of our men. A Bren gunner kills two of the three ss men, but the survivor does not surrender; he dodges us and gets away. Now we understand with what kind of fanatic we have to deal."[21]

After this encounter, Lapointe reported to No. 46 Royal Marine Commando commander Lieutenant Colonel C.R. Hardy and was told the unit had only a tenuous hold on Rots and le Hamel. He expected a counterattack at first light and wanted 'A' Company to stand in reserve so that it could move immediately to meet the Germans wherever they might strike his lines. Lapointe thought Hardy "felt far from certain of holding the village if the counterattack took place."

With the dawn, no counterattack proved forthcoming and Lapointe was just moving to take over responsibility for le Hamel's defence so that the commandos could concentrate their strength in Rots when Hardy told him the marines were pulling back to Vieux Cairon. As the commandos withdrew, Chaudière commander Lieutenant Colonel Paul Mathieu moved the other companies into a defensive ring centred on the two villages. When the battalion intelligence officer, Captain Gérard Leroux, arrived at the new battalion headquarters in le Hamel that evening, he was called over to the house across the street by its owners Monsieur and Madame Lalonde. Although the retreating Germans had looted their home of most of its food and carried off their livestock and any objects of value, the woman had somehow rustled up ingredients to bake a cake. Engraved on its top in sugar were the words, "Vive le Canada!"[22]

Leroux was touched by her generosity and also surprised that the woman had managed to calmly go about baking a cake in her kitchen during a day when the 12th ss were relentlessly shelling the two villages with artillery and mortar rounds.[23] The Chaudières dug their slit trenches deep and were thankful that the Germans facing 3rd Canadian Infantry Division seemed content to confine themselves to such fire rather than counterattacking to regain the ground lost the previous day.

THAT THE GERMANS were determined to keep up the pressure on the Allies holding the beachhead was made clearly evident on June 12 to the paratroopers of 6th Airborne Division, in fierce fighting centred on the dangerous inward bend in its front line at Bréville. The day before, the Black Watch, 5th Battalion had carried out an attack intended to eliminate this German stronghold and walked into a tragedy. Advancing at 0400 hours towards the height of ground on which the village stood, the battalion was ripped to pieces by intense machine-gun fire. In mere minutes, almost two hundred men were killed or wounded, while every man in the leading platoon "died with his face to the foe."[24] This brought an abrupt halt to any chance that the 51st British Infantry Division might achieve a major breakout through the lines of the airborne troops holding east of the River Orne.

Falling back from the Château St. Côme–Bréville, the Black Watch dug in beside the remnants of the 9th British Parachute Battalion, with woods on one flank and the estate grounds to their front. The battleground was dormant at first, but then at about 1500 hours on June 12, the Germans counterattacked on the heels of a forty-five-minute artillery and mortar barrage with a battalion of infantry supported by half a dozen tanks and self-propelled guns. Falling primarily on the Black Watch positions near the château, the Germans overran several forward platoons. A distress call for reinforcements was issued, and Brigadier James Hill raced to the brickworks at le Mesnil crossroads. "Could 1st Canadian Parachute Battalion send a reaction force to relieve the Black Watch?" he asked Lieutenant Colonel George Bradbrooke.[25]

The Canadian commander was badly pressed by his own depleted ranks and the need to continuously meet probes against the crossroads by the Germans, but he agreed to send 'C' Company. Replacing its section of the line with every man he could free up from headquarters company, Bradbrooke sent Major John Hanson's men marching. It was a pitifully small force, just sixty strong. At the head of one of the company's three platoons was Lieutenant John Madden.

When he led his men through the Black Watch and saw one Scottish sergeant major bugging out for the rear despite showing no signs of being wounded, Madden "wondered what the hell we were getting into."[26]

Ever a fire-breather, Hanson had no intention of merely taking up positions in front of the Black Watch and waiting for the Germans to grind his small force down through attrition. The best way to meet overwhelming force, he figured, was to hit it head-on with a spoiling attack of your own. Hanson decided to clear the woods on his flank.

Having double-timed the march from le Mesnil crossroads to reach the position before the Black Watch were overrun, Hanson barely gave his paratroopers pause before leading them through the British troops towards the forest. "Here come the Canadians!" many of the obviously exhausted and dispirited infantry called out as the paratroopers entered their lines. Then, as they realized Hanson and his men were going to keep right on going, some cautioned, "You chaps should not be going into that forest."

But the paratroopers never hesitated and soon were fighting the Germans spread through the woods at close quarters. Corporal Dan Hartigan quickly noted that "as soon as they recognized that they were faced with paratroopers... they backed out of the woods completely." Having shaken up the enemy sufficiently to buy a breather during which his men could take over the Black Watch position in an orderly manner, the major ordered the company to fall back. As the battered Black Watch trudged gratefully off to the rear, 'C' Company's little force pulled tight into a horseshoe-shaped defensive perimeter facing both the château and its spacious grounds and retaining a toehold on the edge of the woods. In the short fight to clear the Germans from the trees, only Private C.A. Allen had been wounded, his abdomen torn open by a burst of MG 42 fire.[27]

During the wood-clearing operation, Madden had lacked sufficient time to get a good feel for the lay of land on the other side of the trees that obstructed his northeasterly view. Deciding he would like to gain a better appreciation of the area, the lieutenant took his runner and ventured into the woods. Encountering no opposition, the two men were soon on the other side looking out across a large horse pasture about six hundred yards wide. In front of some brush on the other side, a German half-track was parked, and next to it a cluster of troops was setting up a large mortar. Madden's Sten gun had a maximum range of only about three hundred yards and the runner's Lee Enfield would be shooting almost beyond its effective range at that distance, so he decided to leave the Germans unmolested and head back to the defensive perimeter.

Just as the two men started back into the woods, Madden heard the thump of the mortar firing and then the piercing shriek of a falling round that exploded mere yards away. Realizing the Germans had spotted them, Madden yelled, "We better get the hell out of here." By running a few yards and then throwing themselves flat, they managed to outrun the exploding rounds that chased them all the way back to the Canadian line. The runner had taken a small piece of shrapnel in his back near the kidney, but said he was okay. Madden bandaged the wound, then set his platoon up in a mortar pit that the Black Watch had dug well out to the front of their main position.

The pit was about six feet by six feet and strewn around inside it were boxes of rations the British soldiers had left behind in their hasty withdrawal. Food had been in short supply at le Mesnil crossroads, so Madden and his men pounced on the boxes, ripping them open with wild abandon. "To have all these lovely goodies, particularly the many chocolate bars, was wonderful. We dug them out and ate them like we were at a kid's feast."

Even more valued than the food were the couple of Vickers .303-calibre machine guns and plenty of matching belted ammunition that the British had left behind, which seriously boosted their fire-power. Madden also gathered in several German MG 42 machine guns from no man's land and added these to his automatic weapon strength. By the time they were finished setting up the weapons, half his platoon were armed with machine guns.[28]

In order to reach the Black Watch as quickly as possible, the Canadians had travelled light, taking with them nothing more than weapons, ammunition, and grenades. Figuring they would be taking over prepared positions, Hanson had given no thought to picks, shovels, or entrenching tools. But the Black Watch positions were out in the open rather than right up on the edge of the woods, and Hanson had no intention of backing off and letting the Germans control the treeline. So other than for the few men from Madden's platoon using the gun pit, the paratroopers hunkered down behind fallen trees and scraped out what holes they could with rifle butts and helmets.

They had barely started this process when the Germans opened a heavy artillery and mortar barrage. Madden and the five men with him huddled deeply in their hole as "shells crashed all around and trees fell down." The lieutenant was thinking how one shell falling smack into the middle of the dugout would kill them all when his bat-man ran up and shouted that he had found a good shelter for Madden and himself that had overhead cover. He led Madden at a run to what turned out to be a three-ton truck. There was nothing to do but crawl in under the truck to escape the rain of shrapnel and hope nothing scored a direct hit. When the barrage lifted a few minutes later, Madden looked into the back of the truck and stared at a full load of crates containing three-inch mortar bombs. "Jesus, what overhead cover," he barked at the sheepish runner.[29]

As soon as the shellfire ceased, the Germans counterattacked in strength from out of the château grounds and through the woods. Several tanks and self-propelled guns backed up the infantry. One tank stopped just outside of effective PIAT gun range and started raking the Canadian lines. Hartigan lay on the ground as bullets chopped off bramble bushes above his head. "We pressed our cheeks into the turf and rolled our eyes upward to watch the brambles being mowed down as though by a scythe about a foot above our faces."

To his right, Private Cliff Douglas "blasted away at the tanks with his Bren gun, hoping to spray a few bullets through one of their machine-gun ports. At the same time Bill Chaddock... equipped with a sniper's rifle, was trying to achieve the same thing with his telescopic sight. Cliff Douglas and Ralph Mokelki were ripped through their thighs by the tanks' medium machine guns. They were helped and patched up with tourniquets by Private Eddie Mallon."[30]

When the tanks and infantry pulled up outside PIAT range rather than rolling forward to overwhelm the paratroopers, the Germans started their artillery and mortar barrage again. The Canadians were subjected to withering fire from the infantry and tankers to their immediate front, and a simultaneous rain of shellfire. Every few minutes, the shelling would ease off and the infantry would make an attempt to close on 'C' Company's position. Each attack was immediately scattered as the paratroopers opened up with intense and accurate fire.

"That's where the company's soldiers earned their greatest credit," Hartigan later wrote. "With no way to effectively attack the enemy's superior numbers or heavy equipment and with no trenches in which to protect themselves, the paratroopers refused to give up an inch of ground. They held their positions and fought back from the edge of the forest floor with their machine guns, their... PIAT antitank guns and their little 2-inch mortars."[31]

Hartigan's section of No. 7 Platoon was taking a beating as the battle dragged on. A heavy mortar that had found their range was pounding the position and the only cover the seven soldiers had was the three-to-four-foot-high bramble bushes in front of the woods. When one round struck a tree behind Hartigan and Chaddock, chunks of shrapnel ripped into Chaddock's back. Moments later, a storm of shellfire erupted behind Hartigan and he was struck by five bits of steel. By now, five men in the section were wounded badly enough that they could barely function. The only uninjured man was Mallon. Chaddock was dying, too badly wounded for the company medics to save. No. 7 Platoon had a dozen men needing evacuation, and a half dozen paratroopers in the other platoons were as badly off. Douglas and Mokelki were too badly wounded to walk. Hartigan was bleeding less heavily than these two men and still mobile, so he had Mallon concentrate on the other two men.

Then Hartigan tried to help Chaddock. "I slit open his camouflaged battle smock and his trousers and pulled off his boots. He was terribly injured from head to foot. I gave him an ampoule of morphine... and put a tourniquet and sling on his upper left arm.

"My section was a shambles... I wanted to cry but had no time. Nine out of the ten of us who had landed six days earlier on D-Day were now dead or wounded. Lieutenant Sam McGowan came and examined my right foot, hit by four of the five shell fragments my body had taken. He ordered me off the battle-line immediately. 'In ten to fifteen minutes you'll be of no more use here,' he said. 'You won't be able to walk.'" Hartigan and one of the other wounded men took turns carrying Chaddock towards the company headquarters. Other walking wounded carried those who were unable to move independently, while anyone who could manage a hobble fended for himself. As Hartigan's decimated section moved out, Eddie Mallon picked up his gun and prepared to defend a sixty-yard-wide section of the perimeter single-handedly.

At company headquarters, the wounded were collected into a group and then sent on foot towards a British aid post a quarter-mile behind the front line. The place was packed with Black Watch and paratroopers suffering every imaginable wound. "Men with missing legs or arms or both. Men hit in the lungs, bleeding from their mouths. Men groaning, gurgling or crying, because they were in unbearable pain or suffering from... battle exhaustion... Men vomiting, others chewing on bread, others dying or dead."[32] Hartigan was soon évacuated to a hospital in England.

By the time he and the other wounded paratroopers reached the aid station, the German attack against 'C' Company had petered out. The enemy tanks growled off past the château with the infantry in tow, and the artillery fire slowly wound down. 'C' Company triumphed, holding the line that had threatened to collapse and expose the River Orne bridge crossings to German attack, but at a terrible cost. Of its sixty men, twenty-three had been killed or wounded. Late that night, the 6th Airborne Division launched a massed counterattack of its own through 'C' Company's line that succeeded in wresting Bréville from the Germans and straightened out the dangerous inward bend. With the morning, the remaining soldiers marched back to le Mesnil crossroads and took up their positions on the still embattled 1st Canadian Parachute Battalion front line.[33]

As Madden took his place in a slit trench facing the enemy, he looked around at the remnants of the company and was struck by how determined they still looked despite all they had endured since jumping into Normandy such a long time ago. Before that jump, the invasion planners had promised the paratroops they would only have to fight for four days at the most and then would be withdrawn in keeping with the doctrine for use of airborne divisions. They were shock troops, not to be wasted in protracted combat or defensive operations. But there was no sign they would be relieved anytime soon. Madden knew that the men felt somewhat betrayed that they had been kept in the line, but he knew nobody would hesitate to do his duty. They would hold the crossroads as long as they had to and if necessary to the last man.[34]

ACROSS THE BREADTH of 3rd Canadian Infantry Division's front, June 12 saw a stalemate develop with neither side capable of anything more than sending fighting patrols to harry the other. An uneasy quiet settled over the battlefield. Conditions on the front lines remained rough. There was nowhere for soldiers to wash, shave, or clean and mend uniforms. Men sported ragged beards. Rations were limited and hot meals rare. Sleep was something snatched fitfully between stands on watch, patrols, and the persistent harassing fire of artillery and mortars. The stench of death permeated the air, with hundreds of corpses still strewn across no man's land.

In the Regina Rifles sector at la Ferme de Cardonville, Captain Gordon Brown decided something had to be done about the German

dead lying close by the farm. Although the Germans had ceased trying to overrun 'D' Company's position, the farm remained a fortress
around which 12th ss Panzer Grenadiers roamed with deadly intent
towards anyone venturing from its protective walls.

Brown and his second-in-command, Lieutenant Dick Roberts,
stared out at the thirty to forty corpses near the farm walls and discussed what to do. Finally, after consulting with Company Sergeant
Major Jimmy Jacobs, they agreed that "a carrying party made up of
mature soldiers would handle the dead bodies." Arranging to borrow
a bulldozer and operator from the Royal Canadian Engineers, they set
about the grim job. While the bulldozer carved out a large trench in a
field next to the farm, screened by the railway embankment from
German observation, Roberts led the carrying party out to retrieve the
bodies on stretchers. As the Germans were brought in, Jacobs and
Brown "would remove all ID tags, the wallets or other personal be-
longings, package them up with the dog tags and then bury the bodies. We all went about our tasks in something of a daze. It was a
numbing experience, this first time burial of dead enemy soldiers.
Some had tried to bandage themselves, apply tourniquets... in order
to try to save their lives."

The captain looked at the corpses and was saddened to see that
they "were so young, these blond, handsome German boys. They
were fanatical Nazis, victims of the brainwashing they had received.
What a senseless loss of life on both sides."

When the job was done and the bulldozer had completed covering
the dead with earth, Brown, Roberts, and Jacobs walked back to the
farm. They drafted a report that detailed the number of Germans
buried and provided map references for the burial ground, which was
sent up to battalion headquarters along with the personal effects and
identification. Brown hoped the personal effects would eventually
find their way to next of kin in Germany, but doubted that receiving
them would lessen the pain of having a son dead in a foreign land.
The three men then "decided that perhaps we should try some of the
local Calvados to help us forget."[35]

He could not, however, push aside the memory of how many
Regina Rifles—most little older than the boys they had just buried—

had fallen during these past six days. The ferocity of the fighting still shook him. Later he would say, "the fighting in Normandy... against the ss... had a bitterness about it that did not prevail in later battles against the regular German army units."[36]

Although they had given as good as they took, the price in Canadian lives was terribly high, which had also served to fuel the fierce nature of the fighting. Between June 7 and June 12, Canadian casualties suffered holding Juno Beach totalled 196 officers and 2,635 other ranks. Of these, 72 officers and 945 other ranks died.[37] Added to the 340 dead and 574 wounded on D-Day, the infantry battalions and the supporting tank regiments of 2nd Canadian Armoured Brigade were barely fit for action. They could hold, but the impetus of any offensive would have to come from elsewhere.

In fact, none of the divisions that had assaulted the beaches on June 6 remained capable of more than holding actions. But in their determined defence of the beaches, these Canadian, British, and American soldiers had ensured the survival of the Allied beachhead in Normandy. For on the beaches behind the infantry, tankers, and artillery gunners engaged in bitter battle inland, a great tide of men and matériel had poured ashore. By the night of June 11–12, 326,547 men, 54,186 vehicles, and 104,428 tons of supplies had been landed.[38] The Allies were ashore, and there was no longer any chance they could be thrown back into the sea. The battle to hold Juno and the other beaches was won.

In the Shadow of D-Day

I STAND IN BRETTEVILLE-L'ORGUEILLEUSE looking at the side of a three-storey triplex that stands close to the street. The outside wall is stuccoed and brightly whitewashed, but the distinctive roofline that cuts sharply down from the third storey to a single storey at the building's back is impossible to mistake. Sixty years ago, Rifleman Joe Lapointe of the Regina Rifles waited until a Panther v tank rumbled just past this outside wall, and then fired his PIAT gun. An army photographer later shot an image of the knocked-out Panther with the roofline of this building clearly visible in the background. Its brick walls were unpainted then, window shutters on the front of the building splintered by battle, doors torn off hinges by soldiers conducting a hasty search.

Nearby, Bretteville's church, which had all but one side of its steeple blown down in the battle, has been mostly restored. The steeple is square and incomplete-looking, however, because the elegant belltower that originally rose above the wider base column was never replaced. Across the street, the château that served as headquarters for the Reginas throughout the June 7 to 12 fighting has been fully restored as well. There is a plaque commemorating the events of those days.

Norrey-en-Bessin also has a plaque, although the village itself has few buildings from the war remaining. One such structure still carries the scars left when Lieutenant George "Flash" Gordon rolled his

1st Hussars Sherman against its side during the retreat by 'B' and 'C' squadrons on June 11. The church here also had its steeple blown off, but it has been rebuilt. From here, I take a right turn and follow the route travelled by the tankers and 'D' Company of the Queen's Own Rifles out into the farmland that stretches off to le Mesnil-Patry. Passing through Norrey, it is hard to see how difficult the tanks found navigating its narrow streets, as they have been widened and straightened.

Today, the grain fields are carefully tended, crops recently harvested rather than growing wild and abandoned to heights of four and five feet. No perfect cover for ss Panzer Grenadiers now. There is little relief to the ground, just wide flat fields. The Norman farmer seldom borders his land with hedgerows these days, as they would impede the manoeuvring of large tractors and other machinery. Most of the orchards that once grew here are also gone, given over to grain fields instead.

In le Mesnil-Patry, a modern church stands. Outside is a memorial plaque that bears the badges of the 1st Hussars and Queen's Own Rifles, with a dedication to the men who fell on June 11. Plaques and monuments abound inland from Juno Beach wherever young Canadians fought and died during those six blood-soaked days that followed D-Day. In les Buissons, a plaque notes that this is Hell's Corner and bears the inscription "In grateful memory of the soldiers of the 9th Canadian Brigade." It was erected in 1984 on the invasion's fortieth anniversary. Authie has a grey limestone memorial to the North Nova Scotia Highlanders and a sobering little blue sign that denotes one street as Place des 37 Canadiens in memory of the thirty-seven Highlanders and Sherbrooke Fusiliers murdered in the village by the 12th ss on June 7. In Buron, a small square is flanked on either side by flagpoles—one the Canadian maple leaf, the other the French tricolour. Two monuments stand in the square. One for the Sherbrooke Fusiliers and the other the Highland Light Infantry, who paid heavily recapturing this village on July 8, 1944 and appropriately dubbed it "Bloody Buron."

East of Buron, the ground rises towards St.-Contest. From atop this low rise, barely more than thirty feet higher than the ground below, it is easy to see how such a low profile still dominated the battle-ground. The Norman landscape between Juno Beach and the Caen-Bayeux highway is a study in subtle topography. There is the long slow rise from the coastline, with few undulations. The Canadians could never escape the watchful German eye. To the east of the ridge, the favoured outpost of Kurt Meyer and 12th ss artillery spotters stands. The Abbaye d'Ardenne where twenty Canadians were exe-cuted has been mostly restored to its former grandeur. Its great cathe-dral with wide shoulderlike balustrades is as imposing as it would have been on June 8. In the garden where the murders took place, a monument commemorates the eighteen soldiers killed on the night of June 8–9 and two others who died while prisoners on June 17. The names of the men are inscribed on the memorial.

Elsewhere across the breadth of the Canadian battlefield there are other plaques, other interpretive signs that explain various events during the six days' fighting. Memory of the battle to hold Juno Beach—the so-called bridgehead battle in official military parlance—is alive and well here in France.

Hardly so in Canada. Mention Normandy and, after the media frenzy of the sixtieth anniversary celebration coverage in 2004 com-bined with endless television reruns of *Saving Private Ryan*—most Canadians will recall that the D-Day landings happened there. A far smaller number will be aware of some of the more infamous battles that followed during the long summer of fighting to break out from the beachhead. Verrières Ridge and the Falaise Gap might be recog-nized. Putot-en-Bessin, Authie, Buron, le Mesnil-Patry? Probably not. Outside of the regimental memory kept alive by the units that fought these battles little attention has been shone on them.

The official history by Colonel C.P. Stacey allowed this period of battle fifteen pages of text and maps. Most other histories of the Canadian participation in the Normandy campaign grant it far less space, if bothering to mention it at all. Bookended by D-Day and the greater battles of July and August, the fighting of June 7–12 was re-duced to little more than a footnote in the historical record. Yet over 1,000 men who were the sons, brothers, husbands, and fathers of many Canadians died here in just six short days. About 1,700 more carried the scars of wounds suffered for the rest of their lives. There were also the mental scars so many soldiers bore afterward, for as Captain Gordon Brown of the Regina Rifles later noted, there was "a bitterness" to the fighting, as the Canadians squared off against the 12th ss in this battle, that was uncommon to other engagements.

If the June 6 to 12 fighting is ill remembered, there is greater knowledge of the murders of Canadians that took place during this time. The subject of several documentaries and books, the 12th ss atrocities are usually linked almost exclusively to Standartenführer Kurt Meyer. Most veterans I interview forget that Meyer was not yet the divisional commander of the 12th ss. Only on June 14, when shrapnel from a naval shell killed Brigadeführer Fritz Witt, did Meyer assume its command. But Meyer had the misfortune to be captured on September 6, 1944, and was the only 12th ss officer to be tried for war crimes by Canada.

An unrepentant Nazi even after the war's end, Meyer's stony and dismissive composure during the proceedings did little to advance his claims of innocence in any of the killings. Presided over by Major General Harry Foster, who had commanded 7th Canadian Infantry Brigade and had many of his Royal Winnipeg Rifles and some Regina Rifles murdered at the time, the court returned a guilty verdict on three of five counts. Meyer was sentenced to death by firing squad, but Canadian Army Occupation Force commander Major General Chris Vokes commuted the verdict to a life sentence. Vokes thought the evidence that Meyer was directly responsible for specific murders was vicarious rather than direct. Confined in New Brunswick's Dorchester prison, Meyer served only five years before being released in 1954. He returned to Germany and worked for a brewery while becoming a prime advocate for Waffen-ss seeking military pensions, until his death from a heart attack in 1961 at age fifty-one. More than five thousand veterans, mostly former ss, attended his funeral.

The Canadians killed by the 12th ss are mostly buried in the Canadian War Cemetery at Bény-sur-Mer. Here lie 2,043 Canadians in tidy rows, one after another. Only five servicemen from other countries are buried here, so the evenly spaced white headstones overwhelmingly bear the official maple leaf national emblem used by the graves commission. Enlistment number, rank, name, regiment, date of death, and generally age are listed. A cross, or less commonly, Star of David might also be engraved below the vital statistics. Whether religious affiliation was indicated rested with the family, who were also able to add a personal inscription not exceeding sixty-six characters if they wished.

Most did, and the moving voices of remembrance for those who fell are heard here. "To the world he was just another one. To us he was our darling son," wrote twenty-six-year-old Private Lawrence Burton Perkins' family. Perkins, a Stormont, Dundas and Glengarry Highlander, died on June 7. "In loving memory of Ewalt, a dear husband and daddy. Every day in silence we remember. Sadly missed by his loving wife and daughter Connie." This for Private Ewalt Brandt of the Canadian Scottish Regiment, killed on June 10.

Repeatedly, the theme of remembrance is etched into the hard white stone. Often it is coupled with a sense of bewilderment mingled with pride in sacrifice. Why did this life have to be cut short? "God alone understands," wrote the family of Regina Rifles Captain Robert Gibson Shinnan, who died on June 9.

We do well as a nation to seek more than divine understanding. The Canada we live in today exists because of the sacrifice of these young men who marched to a call to fight in foreign lands against fascism. They gave their all. Walking out of the cemetery at Bény-sur-Mer on a gentle spring day in Normandy, it is hard to imagine this landscape when it was torn by the blast of shells, gunfire, and the screams of young men dying. Birdsong seems to be everywhere this fine morning. Looking back, I see the Canadian flag snapping in the breeze among the headstones and hope that the trend of record attendance at memorial services on November 11 will continue. That more people will seek to remember and to understand how these young men came to lie in this place so far from home.

3RD CANADIAN INFANTRY DIVISION
  7th Reconnaissance Regiment
  (17th Duke of York's Royal Canadian Hussars)
  —observer elements only

The Royal Canadian Artillery:
  12th Field Regiment
  13th Field Regiment
  14th Field Regiment
  19th Army Field Regiment (attached)
  3rd Anti-tank Regiment
  4th Light Anti-Aircraft Regiment

Corps of Royal Canadian Engineers:
  6th Field Company
  16th Field Company
  18th Field Company
  3rd Field Park Company
  5th Field Company (attached)

Brigade Support Group:
  The Cameron Highlanders of Ottawa (MG Battalion)

7th Canadian Infantry Brigade:
  The Royal Winnipeg Rifles
  The Regina Rifle Regiment
  1st Battalion, Canadian Scottish Regiment

8th Canadian Infantry Brigade:
   The Queen's Own Rifles of Canada
   Le Régiment de la Chaudière
   The North Shore (New Brunswick) Regiment

9th Canadian Infantry Brigade:
   The Highland Light Infantry of Canada
   The Stormont, Dundas and Glengarry Highlanders
   The North Nova Scotia Highlanders

2ND CANADIAN ARMOURED BRIGADE
   6th Armoured Regiment (1st Hussars)
   10th Armoured Regiment (The Fort Garry Horse)
   27th Armoured Regiment (The Sherbrooke Fusiliers Regiment)

1ST CANADIAN PARACHUTE BATTALION
   (Landed Drop Zone V near River Dives)

APPENDIX B:
CANADIAN INFANTRY BATTALION
(TYPICAL ORGANIZATION)

HQ COMPANY:

No. 1: Signals Platoon

No. 2: Administrative Platoon

SUPPORT COMPANY:

No. 3: Mortar Platoon (3-inch)

No. 4: Bren Carrier Platoon

No. 5: Assault Pioneer Platoon

No. 6: Antitank Platoon (6-pounder)

A COMPANY:

No. 7 Platoon

No. 8 Platoon

No. 9 Platoon

B COMPANY:

No. 10 Platoon

No. 11 Platoon

No. 12 Platoon

C COMPANY:

No. 13 Platoon

No. 14 Platoon

No. 15 Platoon

D COMPANY:

No. 16 Platoon

No. 17 Platoon

No. 18 Platoon

APPENDIX C:
CANADIAN ARMY, GERMAN ARMY, WAFFEN-SS ORDER OF RANKS (LOWEST TO HIGHEST)

LIKE MOST Commonwealth nations, the Canadian Army used the British ranking system. Except for the lower ranks, this system little differed from one service arm to another. The German Army system, however, tended to identify service and rank throughout most of its command chain, while the ss ranking system was further complicated by the fact many of its ranks harked back to the organization's clandestine paramilitary roots. The translations are roughly based on the Canadian ranking system, although there is no Canadian equivalent for many German ranks and some differentiation in responsibility each rank bestowed on its holder.

CANADIAN ARMY	GERMAN ARMY	SS
Private, infantry	Schütze	Schütze
Rifleman, rifle regiments	Schütze	Schütze
Private	Grenadier	Grenadier
Gunner (artillery equivalent of private)	Kanonier	Kanonier
Trooper (armoured equivalent of private)	Panzerschütze	Panzerschütze
Sapper (engineer equivalent of private)	Pionier	Pionier
Signaller (signals equivalent of private)	Funker	Funker

CANADIAN ARMY	GERMAN ARMY	SS
Lance Corporal	Gefreiter	Sturmmann
Corporal	Obergefreiter	Rottenführer
Lance Sergeant	Unteroffizier	Unterscharführer
Sergeant	Unterfeldwebel	Scharführer
Company Sergeant Major	Feldwebel	Oberscharführer
Battalion Sergeant Major	Oberfeldwebel	Hauptscharführer
Regimental Sergeant Major	Stabsfeldwebel	Sturmscharführer
Second Lieutenant	Leutnant	Untersturmführer
Lieutenant	Oberleutnant	Obersturmführer
Captain	Hauptmann	Hauptsturmführer
Major	Major	Sturmbannführer
Lieutenant Colonel	Oberstleutnant	Obersturmbannführer
Colonel	Oberst	Standartenführer
Brigadier	Generalmajor	Brigadeführer
Major General	Generalleutnant	Gruppenführer
Lieutenant General	General der (service arm)	Obergruppenführer
(no differentiation)	General der Artillerie General der Infanterie General der Kavallerie General der Pioniere General der Panzertruppen	(no differentiation)
General	Generaloberst	Oberstgruppenführer
Field Marshal	Generalfeldmarschall	None

Canadian military personnel won many military decorations between June 7 and 12, 1944. The decoration system that Canada used in World War II, like most other aspects of its military organization and tradition, derived from Britain. A class-based system, most military decorations can be awarded either to officers or to "other ranks," but not both. The Canadian army, navy, and air force also have distinct decorations. Only the Victoria Cross—the nation's highest award—can be won by personnel from any arm of the service or rank.

The decorations and qualifying ranks are:

VICTORIA CROSS (VC): Awarded for gallantry in the presence of the enemy. Instituted in 1856. Open to all ranks. The only award that can be granted for action in which the recipient was killed, other than Mentioned in Despatches—a less formal honour whereby an act of bravery was given specific credit in a formal report.

DISTINGUISHED SERVICE ORDER (DSO): Army officers of all ranks, but more commonly awarded to officers with ranks of major or higher.

DISTINGUISHED SERVICE CROSS (DSC): Navy officers ranging in rank from commander down to lieutenant.

MILITARY CROSS (MC): Army officers with a rank normally below major and, rarely, warrant officers.

DISTINGUISHED FLYING CROSS (DFC): Air Force officers and warrant officers for acts of valour while flying in active operations against the enemy.

AIR FORCE CROSS (AFC): Air Force officers and warrant officers for valour while flying, but not while in active operations against the enemy.

DISTINGUISHED CONDUCT MEDAL (DCM): Army warrant officers and all lower ranks.

CONSPICUOUS GALLANTRY MEDAL (CGM): Navy chief petty officers, petty officers, and men.

DISTINGUISHED SERVICE MEDAL (DSM): Navy chief petty officers, petty officers, and men.

MILITARY MEDAL (MM): Army warrant officers and all lower ranks.

DISTINGUISHED FLYING MEDAL (DFM): Air Force non-commissioned officers and men for valour while flying in active operations against the enemy.

AIR FORCE MEDAL (AFM): Air Force non-commissioned officers and men for valour while flying, but not in active operations against the enemy.

NOTES

INTRODUCTION: WORSE THAN THE BEACH

1 Col. C.P. Stacey, *The Victory Campaign: The Operations in North-West Europe, 1944–1945*, vol. 3 (Ottawa: Queen's Printer, 1960), 650.

2 Charles Martin, *Battle Diary: From D-Day and Normandy to the Zuider Zee* (Toronto: Dundurn Press, 1994), xii–xiv.

3 Ibid., 14.

4 Ibid., 15.

I: LIKE LIONS

1 Chester Wilmot, *The Struggle for Europe* (London: Collins, 1952), 292.

2 Gordon A. Harrison, *Cross Channel Attack* (Washington: Center of Military History, 1951), 304.

3 Max Hastings, *Overlord: D-Day and the Battle for Normandy* (New York: Simon and Schuster, 1984), 87–88.

4 Col. C.P. Stacey, *The Victory Campaign: The Operations in North-West Europe, 1944–1945*, vol. 3 (Ottawa: Queen's Printer, 1960), 650.

5 Hastings, 88.

6 Carlo D'Este, *Decision in Normandy: The Unwritten Story of Montgomery and the Allied Campaign* (London: Penguin Books, 2001), 114.

7 Wilmot, 292.

8 Stacey, 116.

9 Ibid., 650–52.

10 Wilmot, 293.

11 Ibid.

12 John Man, *The D-Day Atlas: The Definitive Account of the Allied Invasion of Normandy* (New York: Facts on File, 1994), 64.

13 Reginald Roy, *1944: The Canadians in Normandy* (Toronto: Macmillan of Canada, 1984), 23.

14 Stacey, 650–52.

15 Alex McKee, *Caen: Anvil of Victory* (London: Souvenir Press, 1964), 70.

16 Bernard Law, Viscount Montgomery of Alamein, *The Memoirs of Field Marshal The Viscount Montgomery of Alamein, K.G.* (London: Collins, 1958), 254.

17 Ibid.

18 Ibid., 222–23.
19 North Nova Scotia Highlanders War Diary, June 1944, RG24, Library and Archives Canada, n.p.
20 Will Bird, *No Retreating Footsteps: The Story of the North Nova Scotia Highlanders* (Hantsport, NS: Lancelot Press, 1983), 68–69.
21 Ibid., 69–70.
22 Jean E. Portugal, *We Were There: The Navy, the Army and the RCAF—A Record for Canada,* vol. 5 (Shelburne, ON: The Battered Silicon Dispatch Box, 1998), 2448.
23 North Nova Scotia War Diary, n.p.
24 Jacques Castonguay and Armand Ross, *Le Régiment de la Chaudière* (Lévis, PQ: n.p., 1983), 245–46.
25 Ibid., 245.
26 Bird, 70–71.
27 Sherbrooke Fusiliers War Diary, June 1944, RG24, Library and Archives Canada, 4.
28 Ibid., 4.
29 Bird, 71.
30 Bill McAndrew, Donald E. Graves, and Michael Whitby, *Normandy 1944: The Canadian Summer* (Montreal: Éditions Art Global, 1994), 47–48.

2: THROW THEM INTO THE SEA

1 Walter Warlimont, "The Invasion," in *Fighting the Invasion: The German Army at D-Day,* David C. Isby, ed. (London: Greenhill Books, 2000), 88.
2 Tony Foster, *Meeting of Generals* (Agincourt, ON: Methuen, 1986), 306.
3 Chester Wilmot, *The Struggle for Europe* (London: Collins, 1952), 190.
4 Hans Speidel, "Ideas and Views of Genfldm Rommell, Commander of Army Group B, on Defense and Operations in the West in 1944," in *Fighting the Invasion,* David C. Isby, ed., 41–42.
5 Wilmot, 191–92.
6 Ibid., 192.
7 Freiherr Geyr von Schweppenburg, "Preparations by Panzer Gruppe West," in *Fighting the Invasion,* David C. Isby, ed., 74–75.
8 Ibid., 75. ·
9 Wilmot, 193.
10 Hans von Luck, *Panzer Grenadier: The Memoirs of Colonel Hans von Luck* (Westport, CT: Praeger Publications, 1989), 138.
11 B.H. Liddell Hart, *History of the Second World War* (New York: G.P. Putnam's Sons, 1970), 575.
12 Col. C.P. Stacey, *The Victory Campaign: The Operations in North-West Europe, 1944–1945,* vol. 3 (Ottawa: Queen's Printer, 1960), 122.

13 "Campaign in France, 1944: Answers by Gen. Blumentritt to questions submitted by Chester Wilmot," University of Victoria Special Collections, 3.

14 Hubert Meyer, *The History of the 12. ss-Panzerdivision "Hitlerjugend"* (Winnipeg: J.J. Fedorowicz Publishing, 1994), 40.

15 Michael Reynolds, *Steel Inferno: 1 ss Panzer Corps in Normandy* (New York: Dell Publishing, 1997), 16–17.

16 Meyer, 40.

17 Kurt Meyer, *Grenadier* (Winnipeg: J.J. Fedorowicz, 1994), 117–20.

18 Reynolds, 79.

19 Hubert Meyer, 41.

20 Arnold Warren, *Wait For The Waggon: The Story of the Royal Canadian Army Service Corps* (Toronto: McClelland and Stewart, 1961), 280.

21 Bill McAndrew, Donald E. Graves, and Michael Whitby, *Normandy 1944: The Canadian Summer* (Montreal: Éditions Art Global, 1994), 46.

22 Cameron Highlanders of Ottawa (M.G.) War Diary, June 1944, Appendix 10 (D(2) Coy), RG24, Library and Archives Canada, 1.

23 Cameron Highlanders of Ottawa (M.G.) War Diary, June 1944, Appendix 15 Diary of Lt.-Col. P.C. Klaehn, RG24, Library and Archives Canada, 1.

24 Dave McIntosh, *High Blue Battle: The War Diary of No. 1 (401) Fighter Squadron, RCAF* (Toronto: Stoddart Publishing, 1990), 147–48.

25 Jean E. Portugal, *We Were There: The Navy, the Army and the RCAF—A Record for Canada*, vol. 7 (Shelburne, ON: The Battered Silicon Dispatch Box, 1998), 3284–85.

26 McIntosh, 13.

27 B.B. Schofield, *Operation Neptune* (London: Ian Allen, 1974), 106–11.

28 Brereton Greenhous, Stephen Harris, et. al., *The Crucible of War, 1939–1945: The Official History of The Royal Canadian Air Force*, vol. 3 (Toronto: University of Toronto Press, 1995), 409.

29 Schofield, 106–11.

3: GOING INTO THE ATTACK

1 Ken Moore, interview by author, Esquimalt, BC, 15 May 2004.

2 Christopher Grant, *An Illustrated Data Guide to World War 11 Bombers* (St. Catharines, ON: Vanwell Books, 1997), 49–60.

3 Moore interview.

4 Ibid.

5 N.a., *Listen to Us: Aircrew Memories* (Victoria, BC: The Victoria Publishing Co., 1997), 265–66.

6 Ibid., 266–67.

7 Moore interview.

8 Ibid.

9 N.a., "The Royal Canadian Navy's Part in the Invasion," Directorate of History, Department of National Defence, 219.

10 C. Anthony Law, *White Plumes Astern: The Short, Daring Life of Canada's MTB Flotilla* (Halifax: Nimbus Publishing, 1989), 69–74.

11 Ibid., 14–15.

12 "The Royal Canadian Navy's Part in the Invasion," 51.

13 Ibid.

14 Law, 37.

15 Ibid.

16 Ibid., 74–75.

17 Robert Gardiner, ed., *Conway's All the World's Fighting Ships: 1922–1944* (London: Conway Maritime Press, 1980), 250–51.

18 "The Royal Canadian Navy's Part in the Invasion," 210.

19 Law, 75–76.

20 "The Royal Canadian Navy's Part in the Invasion," 220.

21 Ibid.

22 Law, 76.

23 "The Royal Canadian Navy's Part in the Invasion," 210.

24 Law, 76.

25 Ibid., 78.

4: A PICNIC

1 Don Mingay, interview by Michael Boire, Collingwood, ON, November 2003.

2 Maj. Michael Boire, "Notes on RMC Graduates," correspondence with author, October 2004.

3 D.G. Cunningham, "Royal Military College Club of Canada Report," n.d., copy in possession of author.

4 Boire correspondence.

5 Ibid.

6 Ibid.

7 "Department of National Defence (Army) Public Relations–Promoted Brigadier," Bulletin, Directorate of History, n.p.

8 David O'Keefe, "Notes on Kenneth Gault Blackader," Black Watch Regimental Museum and Archives.

9 Eric Luxton, ed. *1st Battalion, The Regina Rifles Regiment, 1939–1946* (Regina: The Regiment, 1946), 38.

10 Col. C.P. Stacey, *The Victory Campaign: The Operations in North-West Europe, 1944–1945,* vol. 3 (Ottawa: Queen's Printer, 1960), 125.

11 Gordon Brown and Terry Copp, *Look to Your Front... Regina Rifles: A Regiment at War, 1944–45* (Waterloo, ON: Laurier Centre Military Strategic Disarmament Studies, 2001), 58.

12 Lt. Col. F.N. Cabeldu, "Battle Narrative of the Normandy Assault and First Counter-Attack," 145.2C4013(D2), Directorate of History, Department of National Defence, 3.

13 Maj. D.G. Crofton, "'C' Company—Landing on D-Day," 145.2C4013(D4), Directorate of History, Department of National Defence, 3.

14 N.a., "Memorandum of Interview with Lt. Col. F.M. Matheson, OC, Regina Rif. by Historical Offr, 24 Jun. 44," 145.2R11011(4), Directorate of History, Department of National Defence, 3.

15 Royal Winnipeg Rifles War Diary, June 1944, RG24, Library and Archives Canada, 5.

16 Lochie Fulton, interview by Ken MacLeod, Victoria, BC, 9 February 1998.

17 Gordon Maxwell, "Battles," Perspectives, Alex Kuppers, ed. (Royal Winnipeg Rifles Assoc. British Columbia Branch, 2003), 101.

18 Gordon Maxwell, group interview of Royal Winnipeg Rifle members by Ken MacLeod, Vancouver, BC, September 1997.

19 Royal Winnipeg Rifles War Diary, 5.

20 Fulton interview.

21 Bruce Tascona and Eric Wells, *Little Black Devils: A History of the Royal Winnipeg Rifles* (Winnipeg: Frye Publishing, 1983), 148.

22 Cabeldu, "Battle Narrative of the Normandy Assault and First Counter-Attack," 3.

23 Sherbrooke Fusiliers War Diary, June 1944, Appendix 27 Canadian Armoured Regt Operation Overlord Account of Action D Day to D+6 Inclusive, RG24, Library and Archives Canada, 1.

24 N.a., "Memorandum of Interview with Brig. D.G. Cunningham, Comd 9 Cdn Inf Bde by Historical Officer, 26 Jun 44," RG24, Library and Archives Canada, 1.

25 Capt. P.F. Ramsay, "Battle Narrative: 'B' Coy, 1 C Scot R," 145.2C4(D6), Directorate of History, Department of National Defence, 3.

26 3rd Canadian Infantry Division GS War Diary, June 1944, Appendix Jacket No. 1 Message Log, RG24, Library and Archives Canada.

27 Ibid.

28 Fulton interview.

29 Tascona and Wells, 149.

30 Stacey, 126.

31 Luxton, 39.

32 1st Hussars War Diary, June 1944, RG24, Library and Archives Canada, n.p.

33 "Memorandum of Interview with Lt. Col. Matheson," 3.

34 Brown and Copp, 74.

35 Ibid., 65.

36 Stacey, 126.

37 Cabeldu, "Battle Narrative of the Normandy Assault and First Counter-Attack," 3.
38 Ramsay, "Battle Narrative: 'B' Coy, 1 C Scot R," 3.
39 13th Canadian Field Regiment, RCA War Diary, June 1944, RG24, Library and Archives Canada, 3.
40 Ibid.

5: PERFORMANCE MOST CREDITABLE
1 Col. C.P. Stacey, *The Victory Campaign: The Operations in North-West Europe, 1944–1945*, vol. 3 (Ottawa: Queen's Printer, 1960), 70.
2 Maj. J.R. Martin, "Report No. 147 Historical Section Canadian Military Headquarters: Part One: The Assault and Subsequent Operations of 3 Cdn Inf Div and 2 Cdn Armd Bde, 6–30 June 44—N.W. Europe," 3 December 1945, Directorate of History, Department of National Defence, para. 230.
3 Cameron Highlanders of Ottawa (MG) War Diary, June 1944, Appendix 7 'B' Coy ChofO(MG), RG24, Library and Archives Canada, n.p.
4 Will R. Bird, *North Shore (New Brunswick) Regiment* (Fredericton, NB: Brunswick Press, 1963), 234.
5 N.a., "Memorandum of Interview With Brig K.G. Blackader, Comd 8 Cdn Inf Bde by Historical Officer, 24 Jun 44," 018(D13), Directorate of History, Department of National Defence, 2.
6 North Shore (New Brunswick) Regiment War Diary, June 1944, RG24, Library and Archives Canada, 2.
7 Bird, *North Shore (New Brunswick) Regiment*, 234.
8 Ibid.
9 Cameron Highlanders of Ottawa (MG) War Diary, Appendix 7, n.p.
10 Joe Ryan, interview by John Gregory Thompson, Cobourg, ON, 6 November 2003.
11 Bird, 235.
12 Charles Richardson, interview by John Gregory Thompson, London, ON, 10 March 2003.
13 Bird, 235.
14 Stacey, 134.
15 Bird, 236.
16 Ibid., 236–37.
17 Ibid., 238.
18 R.M. Hickey, *The Scarlet Dawn* (Campbelltown, NB: Tribune Publishing Limited, 1949), 204.
19 "Memorandum of Interview with Brig K.G. Blackader," 2.
20 Stacey, 127–28.
21 Don Learment, interview by John Gregory Thompson, Guelph, ON, 21 November 2003.

22 Ibid.

23 North Nova Scotia Highlanders War Diary, June 1944, RG24, Library and Archives Canada, n.p.

24 Will Bird, *No Retreating Footsteps: The Story of the North Nova Scotia Highlanders* (Hantsport, NS: Lancelot Press, 1983), 74.

25 Ibid., 75.

26 Ibid., 74.

27 Ibid.

28 Don Learment, "Soldier, POW, Partisan: My Experiences During the Battle of France, June–September 1944," *Canadian Military History*, Spring 2000, 94.

29 Bird, *No Retreating Footsteps*, 75.

30 Ibid.

31 North Nova Scotia Highlanders War Diary, n.p.

32 Bird, *No Retreating Footsteps*, 76.

33 Learment, 94.

34 North Nova Scotia Highlanders War Diary, n.p.

35 Ibid.

36 N.a., "Memorandum of Interviews with Capt (A/Maj) A.J. Wilson, Nth NS Highrs, 18 Jun 44 and Capt (A/Maj) E.S. Gray, Nth NS Highrs, 29 Jun 44 by Historical Offr: The Engagement at Buron and Authie, 7 Jun 44," 145.2N2011(D3), Directorate of History, Department of National Defence, 2.

37 Will Bird, *The Two Jacks: The Amazing Adventures of Major Jack M. Veness and Major Jack L. Fairweather* (Toronto: The Ryerson Press, 1954), 10.

38 "Memorandum of Interviews with Wilson and Gray," 2.

39 Bird, *No Retreating Footsteps*, 80.

40 "Memorandum of Interviews with Wilson and Gray," 2.

41 Sherbrooke Fusiliers War Diary, June 1944, RG24, Library and Archives Canada, 5.

42 "Memorandum of Interviews with Wilson and Gray," 2.

43 Learment, 94–95.

44 "Memorandum of Interviews with Wilson and Gray," 2.

6: BAPTISM AT AUTHIE

1 Gordon Brown and Terry Copp, *Look to Your Front... Regina Rifles: A Regiment at War, 1944–45* (Waterloo, ON: Laurier Centre Military Strategic Disarmament Studies, 2001), 62.

2 Kurt Meyer, *Grenadier* (Winnipeg: J.J. Fedorowicz, 1994), 121.

3 Michael Reynolds, *Steel Inferno: I SS Panzer Corps in Normandy* (New York: Dell Publishing, 1997), 22.

4 N.a., "Special Interrogation Report: Brigadeführer Kurt Meyer, Comd 12 SS Pz Div 'Hitler Jugend' (6 June 1944–25 Aug 1944)," Reginald Roy Collection, University of Victoria Special Collections, 2.

5 Reynolds, 24.
6 Ibid., 23.
7 Ibid., 21–24.
8 Ibid., 23.
9 Hubert Meyer, *The History of the 12. SS-Panzerdivision "Hitlerjugend"* (Winnipeg: J.J. Fedorowicz Publishing, 1994), 204.
10 Reynolds, 37–41 and Appendices IV and V.
11 Terry Copp, *Fields of Fire: The Canadians in Normandy* (Toronto: University of Toronto Press, 2003), 18–19.
12 George Forty, *British Army Handbook: 1939–1945* (Phoenix Mill, England: Sutton Publishing, 1998), 67.
13 Reynolds, 34–41.
14 Hubert Meyer, 40–41.
15 Kurt Meyer, 121.
16 Ibid., 122.
17 Ibid.
18 Ibid.
19 H.M. Jackson, *The Sherbrooke Regiment (27th Armoured Regiment)* (n.p., 1958), 125.
20 Merritt Hayes Bateman, interview by Tom Torrie, 28 May 1987, University of Victoria Special Collections.
21 George Mahon, "Letter to Lt. Col. Gordon, June 25 1944," Melville Burgoyne Kennedy Gordon fonds, MG 30–E367, Vol. I, Personal Correspondence, Library and Archives Canada.
22 Jean E. Portugal, *We Were There: The Navy, the Army and the RCAF—A Record for Canada*, vol. 5 (Shelburne, ON: The Battered Silicon Dispatch Box, 1998), 2451.
23 George Mahon letter.
24 Bateman interview.
25 Sherbrooke Fusiliers Regiment War Diary, June 1944, RG24, Library and Archives Canada, Appendix: "B Squadron, 27 CAR (SFR)—Summarized by Lieut. L.N. Davies," 3.
26 Ibid.
27 Sherbrooke Fusiliers Regiment War Diary, Appendix: "27 Canadian Armoured Regiment—Diary of Events of 'D' Day and D plus I by Sgt. T.C. Reid, No. 2 Troop, 'C' Sqn," 2–3.
28 Hubert Meyer, 42.
29 Don Learment, interview by John Gregory Thompson, Guelph, ON, 21 November 2003.
30 N.a., "Descriptive Record," Melville Burgoyne Kennedy Gordon fonds, Library and Archives Canada, n.p.

31 Don Learment, "Soldier, POW, Partisan: My Experiences During the Battle of France, June–September 1944," *Canadian Military History,* Spring 2000, 95.

32 Will Bird, *The Two Jacks: The Amazing Adventures of Major Jack M. Veness and Major Jack L. Fairweather* (Toronto: The Ryerson Press, 1954), 11–12.

33 Ibid., 12.

34 Ibid., 12–13.

35 Ibid., 13.

36 Will Bird, *No Retreating Footsteps: The Story of the North Nova Scotia Highlanders* (Hantsport, NS: Lancelot Press, 1983), 90.

37 Ibid., 91.

38 Bird, *The Two Jacks,* 13.

39 Bird, *No Retreating Footsteps,* 91.

40 Ibid., 93.

41 Kurt Meyer, 122.

7: DON'T DO ANYTHING CRAZY

1 Will Bird, *The Two Jacks: The Amazing Adventures of Major Jack M. Veness and Major Jack L. Fairweather* (Toronto: The Ryerson Press, 1954), 13.

2 Ibid., 14.

3 N.a., "Combat Lessons—7 CDN INF BDE," RG24, Library and Archives Canada, 5.

4 Bird, 15–16.

5 Ibid., 16–17.

6 Jack Byrne, interview by John Gregory Thompson, St. Joseph, ON, 10 October 2003.

7 N.a., "Memorandum of Interviews with Capt (A/Maj) A.J. Wilson, Nth NS Highrs, 18 Jun 44 and Capt (A/Maj) E.S. Gray, Nth NS Highrs, 29 Jun 44 by Historical Offr: The Engagement at Buron and Authie, 7 Jun 44," 145.2N2011(D3), Directorate of History, Department of National Defence, 3.

8 Jean E. Portugal, *We Were There: The Navy, the Army and the RCAF—A Record for Canada,* vol. 5 (Shelburne, ON: The Battered Silicon Dispatch Box, 1998), 2469.

9 Col. C.P. Stacey, *The Victory Campaign: The Operations in North-West Europe, 1944–1945,* vol. 3 (Ottawa: Queen's Printer, 1960), 128.

10 Will Bird, *No Retreating Footsteps: The Story of the North Nova Scotia Highlanders* (Hantsport, NS: Lancelot Press, 1983), 98.

11 Ibid., 100.

12 Don Learment, "Soldier, POW, Partisan: My Experiences During the Battle of France, June–September 1944," *Canadian Military History,* Spring 2000, 95.

13 Ibid., 96.
14 Don Learment, interview by John Gregory Thompson, Guelph, ON, 21 November 2003.
15 Learment, "Soldier, POW, Partisan," 96.
16 Ibid.
17 Learment interview.
18 Howard Margolian, *Conduct Unbecoming: The Story of the Murder of Canadian Prisoners of War in Normandy* (Toronto: University of Toronto Press, 1998), 60.
19 Ibid., 44–45.
20 Hubert Meyer, *The History of the 12. SS-Panzerdivision "Hitlerjugend"* (Winnipeg: J.J. Fedorowicz Publishing Inc., 1994), 45.
21 Margolian, 58–60.
22 Richard M. Ross, *The History of the 1st Battalion Cameron Highlanders of Ottawa* (M G) (n.p., n.d.), 42.
23 "Memorandum of Interviews with Capt (A/Maj) A.J. Wilson," 3.
24 William Boss, *Up the Glens: Stormont, Dundas and Glengarry Highlanders, 1783–1994* (Cornwall, ON: Old Book Store, 1995), 186–87.
25 Bird, *No Retreating Footsteps*, 100.
26 North Nova Scotia Highlanders War Diary, RG24, Library and Archives Canada, n.p.
27 Portugal, *We Were There*, vol. 5, 2469–70.
28 Sherbrooke Fusiliers Regiment War Diary, Appendix: "27 Canadian Armoured Regiment (SFR) #4 Troop," RG24, Library and Archives Canada, 3.
29 North Nova Scotia Highlanders War Diary, n.p.
30 Stormont, Dundas and Glengarry Highlanders War Diary, June 1944, RG24, Library and Archives Canada, n.p.
31 Sherbrooke Fusiliers Regiment War Diary, 3–4.
32 Stacey, 132.
33 Sherbrooke Fusiliers Regiment War Diary, 5.
34 Stacey, 132.
35 Byrne interview.
36 Boss, 187.
37 Stormont, Dundas and Glengarry Highlanders War Diary, n.p.
38 3rd Canadian Infantry Division GS War Diary, June 1944, Appendix Jacket No. 1 Message Log, RG24, Library and Archives Canada.
39 Kurt Meyer, *Grenadier* (Winnipeg: J.J. Fedorowicz, 1994), 122–23.
40 Ibid., 124.
41 Hubert Meyer, 45.
42 Margolian, 62–63.
43 Bird, *No Retreating Footsteps*, 97.

44 Margolian, 63.
45 Ian J. Campbell, *Murder at the Abbaye: The Story of Twenty Canadian Soldiers Murdered in the Abbaye d'Ardenne* (Don Mills, ON: Oxford University Press, 1996), 77.
46 Margolian, 64.
47 Learment interview.
48 Learment, "Soldier, POW, Partisan," 96.
49 Margolian, 63.
50 Learment, "Soldier, POW, Partisan, 96.
51 Margolian, 69–70.
52 Hubert Meyer, 48–54.

8: THE DEVIL DANCED
1 Dan Hartigan, *A Rising of Courage: Canada's Paratroops in the Liberation of Normandy* (Calgary: Drop Zone Publishers, 2000), 170.
2 Ibid., 153–54.
3 Ibid., 167.
4 Ibid., 156–60.
5 Col. C.P. Stacey, "Report No. 139 Historical Section Canadian Military Headquartersr: The 1st Canadian Parachute Battalion in France (6 June– 6 September 1944), 11–12.
6 Ibid., 12.
7 Chester Wilmot, *The Struggle for Europe* (London: Collins, 1952), 294.
8 John A. Willes, *Out of the Clouds: The History of the 1st Canadian Parachute Battalion* (Perry, ON: Port Perry Printing, 1995), 91.
9 Brian Nolan, *Airborne: The Heroic Story of the 1st Canadian Parachute Battalion in the Second World War* (Toronto: Lester Publishing, 1995), 105.
10 Hartigan, 162.
11 Ibid., 169.
12 Ibid., 169.
13 1st Canadian Parachute Battalion War Diary, June 1944, RG24, Library and Archives Canada, 10.
14 Hartigan, 174.
15 Napier Crookenden, *Dropzone Normandy: The Story of the American and British Airborne Assault on D-Day 1944* (New York: Charles Scribner's Sons, 1976), 31.
16 Hartigan, 173–75.
17 Ibid., 175–76.
18 Ibid., 176.
19 Ibid., 176–77.
20 Ibid., 177–80.

9: GREEN AS GRASS

1 Bernard Law, Viscount Montgomery of Alamein, *The Memoirs of Field Marshal The Viscount Montgomery of Alamein, K.G.* (London: Collins, 1958), 251.

2 Carlo D'Este, *Decision in Normandy: The Unwritten Story of Montgomery and the Allied Campaign* (London: Penguin Books, 2001), 163.

3 Montgomery, 252.

4 Col. C.P. Stacey, *The Victory Campaign: The Operations in North-West Europe, 1944–1945*, vol. 3 (Ottawa: Queen's Printer, 1960), 141–42.

5 D'Este, 73.

6 Ibid., 161.

7 Chester Wilmot, *The Struggle for Europe* (London: Collins, 1952), 297.

8 Stacey, 80.

9 Wilmot, 299.

10 Hubert Meyer, *The History of the 12. ss-Panzerdivision "Hitlerjugend"* (Winnipeg: J.J. Fedorowicz Publishing, 1994), 49–50.

11 N.p., "Combat Lessons–7 CDN INF BDE," RG24, Library and Archives Canada, 1.

12 Gordon Brown and Terry Copp, *Look to Your Front... Regina Rifles: A Regiment at War, 1944–45* (Waterloo: Laurier Centre Military Strategic Disarmament Studies, 2001), 58.

13 Stewart A.G. Mein, *Up the Johns! The Story of the Royal Regina Rifles* (North Battleford, SK: Turner-Warwick Publications, 1992), 113.

14 Jean E. Portugal, *We Were There: The Navy, the Army and the RCAF—A Record for Canada*, vol. 6 (Shelburne, ON: The Battered Silicon Dispatch Box, 1998), 2917–18.

15 Tony Foulds, "In Support of the Canadians: A British Anti-Tank Regiment's First Five Weeks in Normandy," *Canadian Military History*, Spring 1998, vol. 7, 73.

16 Portugal, *We Were There*, vol. 6, 2917–18.

17 Royal Winnipeg Rifles War Diary, June 1944, RG24, Library and Archives Canada, 6.

18 Portugal, *We Were There*, vol. 6, 3015.

19 N.a., "Memorandum of Interview with Brig H.W. Foster, Comd 7 Cdn Inf Bde 22 Jun 44: 7 Cdn Inf Bde in the Assault and the Achievement of its Objective," 018(D13), Directorate of History, Department of National Defence, 1.

20 Brigadier H.W. Foster, "7 CIB—Combat Lessons," RG24, vol. 10986, Library and Archives Canada, 2.

21 Portugal, *We Were There*, vol. 6, 3015.

22 Ibid., 2981–82.

23 13th Field Regiment, RCA War Diary, June 1944, RG24, Library and Archives Canada, 3.

24 Portugal, *We Were There*, vol. 2, 912.

25 Ibid.

26 Meyer, 50.

27 Regina Rifles War Diary, June 1944, RG24, Library and Archives Canada, n.p.

28 Reginald Roy, *Ready for the Fray: The History of the Canadian Scottish Regiment (Princess Mary's) 1920 to 1955* (Vancouver: Evergreen Press, 1958), 231–32.

29 13th Field Regiment, RCA War Diary, 3.

30 1st Hussars Armoured Regiment War Diary, June 1944, RG24, Library and Archives Canada, 4.

31 Ibid.

32 A. Brandon Conron, *A History of the First Hussars Regiment, 1856–1980* (n.p., 1981), 65–66.

33 Harold Bertrand Gonder, interview by Mark C. Hill, 23 July and 7, 8, 9 August 1985, University of Victoria Special Collections.

34 Ibid.

35 Mein, 113.

36 Portugal, *We Were There*, vol. 2, 912.

37 Ibid., 833–34.

38 Ibid., 834–35.

39 Ibid., 835.

10: NOW YOU DIE

1 Hubert Meyer, *The History of the 12. SS-Panzerdivision "Hitlerjugend"* (Winnipeg: J.J. Fedorowicz Publishing, 1994), 50.

2 Bruce Tascona and Eric Wells, *Little Black Devils: A History of the Royal Winnipeg Rifles* (Winnipeg: Frye Publishing, 1983), 151.

3 Meyer, 50.

4 Ibid.

5 Tony Foulds, "In Support of the Canadians: A British Anti-Tank Regiment's First Five Weeks in Normandy," *Canadian Military History*, Spring 1998, vol. 7, 74.

6 Harold Bertrand Gonder, interview by Mark C. Hill, 23 July and 7, 8, 9 August 1985, University of Victoria Special Collections.

7 Ibid.

8 Richard M. Ross, *The History of the 1st Battalion Cameron Highlanders of Ottawa (M G)*, (n.p., n.d.), 44.

9 Maj. G.T. MacEwan, "Battle Narrative: D-Day and the Counter-Attack on Putot-en-Bessin," 145.2C4013(D3), Directorate of History, Department of National Defence, 5.

10 Foulds, 74.

11 MacEwan, "Battle Narrative," 5.

12 Lochie Fulton, interview by Ken MacLeod, Victoria, BC, 9 February 1998.

13 Jean E. Portugal, *We Were There: The Navy, the Army and the RCAF—A Record for Canada,* vol. 6 (Shelburne, ON: The Battered Silicon Dispatch Box, 1998), 2918–19.

14 Royal Winnipeg Rifles War Diary, June 1944, RG24, Library and Archives Canada, 7.

15 Ibid.

16 Col. C.P. Stacey, *The Victory Campaign: The Operations in North-West Europe, 1944–1945,* vol. 3 (Ottawa: Queen's Printer, 1960), 135.

17 Portugal, *We Were There,* vol. 6, 2982.

18 Meyer, 52.

19 Royal Winnipeg Rifles War Diary, 7.

20 Portugal, *We Were There,* vol. 6, 2985.

21 Ibid., 2983.

22 Ibid.

23 Ibid., 3044.

24 Ibid., 3017.

25 Ibid., 3045.

26 N.a., "Memorandum of Interview with CSM Belton, B Coy, R Wpg Rif, 14 Jun 44," 145.2R20011(1), Directorate of History, Department of National Defence, n.p.

27 Portugal, *We Were There,* vol. 6, 3045.

28 Ibid.

29 Ibid., 3015–18.

30 Stacey, 136.

31 Howard Margolian, *Conduct Unbecoming: The Story of the Murder of Canadian Prisoners of War in Normandy* (Toronto: University of Toronto Press, 1998), 80–81.

32 Ibid., 82–87.

33 Ibid., 90–93.

34 Ibid., 96–99.

II: ONE HELL OF A GOOD SCRAP

1 Jim Parks, interview by Ken MacLeod, Vancouver, BC, November 1997.

2 Ibid.

3 Lt. Col. F.N. Cabeldu, "Battle Narrative of the Normandy Assault and First Counterattack," 145.2C4013(D2), Directorate of History, Department of National Defence, 3.

4 Tony Foulds, "In Support of the Canadians: A British Anti-Tank Regiment's first five weeks in Normandy," *Canadian Military History,* Spring 1998, vol. 7, 74.

5 Lt. Col. C.M. Wightman, "Battle Narrative: Putot en Bessin Counter Attack–June 8th, 1944 and the move to Rots," 145.2C(D4), Directorate of History, Department of National Defence, 2.

6 Reginald Roy, *Ready for the Fray: The History of the Canadian Scottish Regiment (Princess Mary's), 1920 to 1955* (Vancouver: Evergreen Press, 1958), 233.

7 Major C.M. Wightman, "Personal Diary," Reginald Roy Collection, University of Victoria Special Collections, 3.

8 Roy, 234.

9 W. Berry, "Personal Accounts of Counter Attack on Putot," Appendix to Canadian Scottish Regiment War Diary, June 1944, Library and Archives Canada, n.p.

10 Geoffrey D. Corry, interview by Tom Torrie, 12 August 1987, University of Victoria Special Collections.

11 Thomas William Lowell Butters, interview by Tom Torrie, 19 August 1987, University of Victoria Special Collections.

12 Cabeldu, 4.

13 Maj. G.T. MacEwan, "Battle Narrative: D Day and the Counter-Attack on Putot-en-Bessin," 145.2C4013(D3), Directorate of History, Department of National Defence, 6.

14 Ibid.

15 Cabeldu, 4.

16 MacEwan, 6.

17 Pte. R.H. Tutte, "The Advance, Occupation and Holding of the Bridge at Putot-en-Bessen As I Saw It," Appendix to Canadian Scottish War Diary, June 1944, Library and Archives Canada, n.p.

18 Pte. W.A.P. Campbell, "Personal Narrative in Personal Notes of Assault by C Scot R Personnel," 145.2C4013(D1), Directorate of History, Department of National Defence, 1.

19 MacEwan, 6.

20 Roy, 236.

21 Lt. Thos. W.H. Butters, "Counter Attack on Putot-en-Besson on 9th [sic] June 44 and the Subsequent 24 hrs at the bridge: Collective Report by 17 Pl. 'D' Coy. 1 C.Scot.R," Appendix to Canadian Scottish Regiment War Diary, June 1944, Library and Archives Canada, n.p.

22 Butters interview.

23 Tutte, n.p.

24 Ibid.

25 Campbell, 1.

26 N.a., "War Diary 'A' Coy. 1 C. Scot R.," Appendix to Canadian Scottish Regiment War Diary, June 1944, Library and Archives Canada, 2.

27 Ibid.
28 Jack Daubs, interview by John Gregory Thompson, London, ON, 9 October 2003.
29 Roy, 237–38.
30 "War Diary 'A' Coy. 1 C. Scot R.," 2.
31 Roy, 238.
32 "War Diary 'A' Coy. 1 C. Scot R.," 2.
33 Roy, 238.
34 Campbell, 1.
35 "War Diary 'A' Coy. 1 C. Scot R.," 2.
36 Corry interview.
37 Wightman, "Battle Narrative," 3.

12: FIGHT TO THE DEATH
1 Michael Reynolds, *Steel Inferno: 1 ss Panzer Corps in Normandy* (New York: Dell Publishing, 1997), 95.
2 Howard Margolian, *Conduct Unbecoming: The Story of the Murder of Canadian Prisoners of War in Normandy* (Toronto: University of Toronto Press, 1998), 71–73.
3 Terry Copp, *Fields of Fire: The Canadians in Normandy* (Toronto: University of Toronto Press, 2003), 72.
4 Kurt Meyer, *Grenadier* (Winnipeg: J.J. Fedorowicz, 1994), 125.
5 Ibid., 126.
6 Ibid.
7 Ibid.
8 Jean E. Portugal, *We Were There: The Navy, the Army and the RCAF—A Record for Canada*, vol. 2 (Shelburne, ON: The Battered Silicon Dispatch Box, 1998), 912.
9 Hubert Meyer, *The History of the 12. ss-Panzerdivision "Hitlerjugend"* (Winnipeg: J.J. Fedorowicz Publishing, 1994), 55.
10 G.W.L. Nicholson, *The Gunners of Canada*, vol. 2 (Toronto: McClelland & Stewart, 1972), 282.
11 Hubert Meyer, 55.
12 Ibid., 55.
13 Ibid.
14 Portugal, *We Were There*, vol. 2, 836–839.
15 Richard M. Ross, *The History of the 1st Battalion Cameron Highlanders of Ottawa (M G)*, (n.p., n.d.), 45.
16 N.a., "Memorandum of Interview with Lt. Col. F.M. Matheson, OC, Regina Rif. by Historical Offr, 24 Jun. 44," 145.2R11011(4), Directorate of History, Department of National Defence, 3.

17 Ibid.
18 Portugal, *We Were There*, vol. 2, 881.
19 "Memorandum of Interview with Lt. Col. Matheson," 3.
20 Portugal, *We Were There*, vol. 2, 839–43.
21 Kurt Meyer, 126–27.
22 Portugal, 843–55.
23 Hubert Meyer, 57.
24 "Memorandum of Interview with Lt. Col. Matheson," 4.
25 Stewart A.G. Mein, *Up the Johns! The Story of the Royal Regina Rifles* (North Battleford, SK: Turner-Warwick Publications, 1992), 115.
26 Ross, 45.
27 3rd Canadian Anti-Tank Regiment War Diary, June 1944, RG24, Library and Archives Canada, 3.

13: POTENTIAL MENACE REMOVED

1 N.a., "The Royal Canadian Navy's Part in the Invasion," Directorate of History, Department of National Defence, 220.
2 C. Anthony Law, *White Plumes Astern: The Short, Daring Life of Canada's MTB Flotilla* (Halifax: Nimbus Publishing, 1989), 80–81.
3 "The Royal Canadian Navy's Part in the Invasion," 221.
4 Law, 85.
5 "The Royal Canadian Navy's Part in the Invasion," 221.
6 Ibid., 157.
7 Joseph Schull, *Far Distant Ships: An Official Account of Canadian Naval Operations in World War II* (Toronto: Stoddart Publishing, 1991), 296.
8 Ibid.
9 "The Royal Canadian Navy's Part in the Invasion," 196–97.
10 Ibid., 198.
11 Michael Whitby, "Masters of the Channel Night: The 10th Destroyer Flotilla's Victory Off Ile De Batz, 9 June 1944," *Canadian Military History*, vol. 2, no. 1, 1993, 7–8.
12 Ibid., 9.
13 "The Royal Canadian Navy's Part in the Invasion," 162.
14 Ibid., 163.
15 Whitby, 5.
16 Schull, 287–88.
17 "The Royal Canadian Navy's Part in the Invasion," 164.
18 Whitby, 8.
19 "The Royal Canadian Navy's Part in the Invasion," 164–66.
20 Ibid., 169.
21 Whitby, 13.

22 "The Royal Canadian Navy's Part in the Invasion," 172.

23 Whitby, 13.

24 Don Cheney, interview by Glen Cook, 16 November 2000, Ottawa, Canadian War Museum Oral History Project Collection.

14: WITH RAGE AND SORROW

1 Carlo D'Este, *Decision in Normandy: The Unwritten Story of Montgomery and the Allied Campaign* (London: Penguin Books, 2001), 164.

2 Michael Reynolds, *Steel Inferno: 1 ss Panzer Corps in Normandy* (New York: Dell Publishing, 1997), 104.

3 D'Este, 166.

4 Ibid.

5 Hubert Meyer, *The History of the 12. ss-Panzerdivision "Hitlerjugend"* (Winnipeg: J.J. Fedorowicz Publishing, 1994), 58.

6 Reynolds, 103.

7 Ibid.

8 Meyer, 58.

9 A. Brandon Conron, *A History of the First Hussars Regiment, 1856–1980* (n.p., 1981), 66.

10 Meyer, 58–59.

11 Reynolds, 102.

12 Meyer, 59.

13 Alex McKee, *Caen: Anvil of Victory* (London: Souvenir Press, 1964), 84–85.

14 Lt. Col. F.N. Cabeldu, "Battle Narrative of the Normandy Assault and First Counter-Attack," 145.2C4013(D2), Directorate of History, Department of National Defence, 4.

15 Reginald Roy, *Ready for the Fray: The History of the Canadian Scottish Regiment (Princess Mary's) 1920 to 1955* (Vancouver: Evergreen Press, 1958), 239.

16 Pte. R.H. Tutte, "The Advance, Occupation and Holding of the Bridge at Putot-en-Bessen As I Saw It," Appendix to Canadian Scottish War Diary, June 1944, Library and Archives Canada, n.p.

17 Ibid.

18 N.a., "War Diary 'A' Coy. 1 C. Scot R.," Appendix to Canadian Scottish Regiment War Diary, June 1944, Library and Archives Canada, 2.

19 Tutte, n.p.

20 "War Diary 'A' Coy. 1 C. Scot R.," 3.

21 Tutte, n.p.

22 "War Diary 'A' Coy. 1 C. Scot R.," 3.

23 Ibid.

24 Roy, 239–40.

25 Tutte, n.p.

26 Ibid.

27 Capt. P.F. Ramsay, "Battle Narrative: 'B' Coy, 1 C Scot R," 145.2C4(D6), Directorate of History, Department of National Defence, 5.

28 Maj. L.J. Henderson, "'D' Coy Activities at Putot-en-Besson Bridge, 9 June 44," 1 C.Scot.R, Appendix to Canadian Scottish Regiment War Diary, June 1944, Library and Archives Canada, n.p.

29 Roy, 239–40.

30 "War Diary 'A' Coy. 1 C. Scot R.," 3.

31 Cabeldu, 4.

32 Robert Lowder Seaborn, interview by Cameron Falconer, 23 February 1983, University of Victoria Special Collections.

33 "Letter written by Fred to Cousin Arne in Canada," Robert Lowder Seaborn and Family Papers, Library and Archives Canada, n.p.

34 Seaborn interview.

35 Ibid.

15: TOO GREAT A RISK

1 W.R. Freasby, ed., *Official History of the Canadian Medical Services, 1939–1945, Vol. 1: Organization and Campaigns* (Ottawa: Queen's Printer, 1956), 221–23.

2 Bill McAndrew and Terry Copp, *Battle Exhaustion: Soldiers and Psychiatrists in the Canadian Army, 1939–1945* (Montreal: McGill-Queen's University, 1990), 111.

3 Ibid., 112.

4 Ibid., 113.

5 Freasby, 223–24.

6 Bill McAndrew, Donald E. Graves, and Michael Whitby, *Normandy 1944: The Canadian Summer* (Montreal: Éditions Art Global, 1994), 58.

7 Joseph Greenblatt Correspondence, June 10, 1944, Archival Collection CN: 19990209–002, DOCS MANU 58A 1 155.3-6, Canadian War Museum.

8 Freasby, 225–26.

9 Kurt Meyer, *Grenadier* (Winnipeg: J.J. Fedorowicz, 1994), 128.

10 Roger Chevalier, interview by author, Courseulles-sur-Mer, 23 May 2003.

11 Le Régiment de la Chaudière War Diary, June 1944 (trans. Tony Poulin from RG24, Library and Archives Canada), in possession of the author, n.p.

12 3rd Canadian Infantry Division GS War Diary, June 1944, Appendix Jacket No. 1 Message Log, RG24, Library and Archives Canada.

13 Le Régiment de la Chaudière War Diary.

14 George V. Eckenfelder, interview by Tom Torrie, 7 August 1987, University of Victoria Special Collections.

15 Ibid.

16 Alex McKee, *Caen: Anvil of Victory* (London: Souvenir Press, 1964), 85.

17 3rd Canadian Infantry Division, message log.

18 2nd Canadian Armoured Brigade War Diary, June 1944, RG24, Library and Archives Canada, n.p.

19 Sherbrooke Fusiliers Regiment War Diary, June 1944, RG24, Library and Archives Canada, 8.

20 Jean E. Portugal, *We Were There: The Navy, the Army and the RCAF—A Record for Canada*, vol. 2 (Shelburne, ON: The Battered Silicon Dispatch Box, 1998), 913.

21 13th Field Regiment War Diary, June 1944, RG24, Library and Archives Canada, 4.

22 Col. C.P. Stacey, *The Victory Campaign: The Operations in North-West Europe, 1944–1945*, vol. 3 (Ottawa: Queen's Printer, 1960), 138.

23 3rd Canadian Infantry Division War Diary, message logs.

24 Stormont, Dundas and Glengarry Highlanders War Diary, June 1944, RG24, Library and Archives Canada, n.p.

25 Highland Light Infantry War Diary, June 1944, RG24, Library and Archives Canada, n.p.

26 Ibid.

27 Ibid.

28 Ibid.

16: FIX BAYONETS

1 Stormont, Dundas and Glengarry Highlanders War Diary, June 1944, RG24, Library and Archives Canada, n.p.

2 William Boss, *Up the Glens: Stormont, Dundas and Glengarry Highlanders, 1783–1994* (Cornwall, ON: Old Book Store, 1995), 187.

3 Jean E. Portugal, *We Were There: The Navy, the Army and the RCAF—A Record for Canada*, vol. 3 (Shelburne, ON: The Battered Silicon Dispatch Box, 1998), 1460.

4 Boss, 188.

5 Portugal, *We Were There*, vol. 3, 1312.

6 Ibid., 1311.

7 Boss, 188.

8 Portugal, *We Were There*, vol. 3, 1383.

9 Alex McKee, *Caen: Anvil of Victory* (London: Souvenir Press, 1964), 85.

10 Walter Warlimont, *Inside Hitler's Headquarters, 1939–45* (New York: Frederick A. Praeger, 1964), 427–29.

11 Michael Reynolds, *Steel Inferno: 1 SS Panzer Corps in Normandy* (New York: Dell Publishing, 1997), 103.

12 Hans von Luck, *Panzer Grenadier: The Memoirs of Colonel Hans von Luck* (Westport, CT: Praeger Publishers, 1989), 145.

13 Ibid., 145–46.
14 John A. Willes, *Out of the Clouds: The History of the 1st Canadian Parachute Battalion* (Perry, ON: Port Perry Printing, 1995), 85.
15 Maj. John P. Hanson, "Canadian Para Bn Corres re Ops 1st Cdn Para Bn from various officers," 145.4013(D5), Directorate of History, Department of National Defence, 3.
16 Willes, 86.
17 Brian Nolan, *Airborne: The Heroic Story of the 1st Canadian Parachute Battalion in the Second World War* (Toronto: Lester Publishing, 1995), 106.
18 Ibid., 106–107.
19 John R. Madden, recorded recollections, 1987, University of Victoria Special Collections.
20 Ibid.
21 Willes, 86–87.
22 Dan Hartigan, *A Rising of Courage: Canada's Paratroops in the Liberation of Normandy* (Calgary: Drop Zone Publishers, 2000), 220.

17: GETTING NOWHERE
1 Col. C.P. Stacey, *The Victory Campaign: The Operations in North-West Europe, 1944–1945,* vol. 3 (Ottawa: Queen's Printer, 1960), 138.
2 Chris Vokes, *Vokes: My Story* (Ottawa: Gallery, 1985), 147.
3 Ernest Côté, interview by Michael Boire, Ottawa, 14 November 2003.
4 2nd Canadian Armoured Brigade War Diary, June 1944, RG24, Library and Archives Canada, n.p.
5 Ibid., n.p.
6 Ibid.
7 Ibid.
8 Ibid.
9 Ibid.
10 Dan Hartigan, *A Rising of Courage: Canada's Paratroops in the Liberation of Normandy* (Calgary: Drop Zone Publishers, 2000), 219–22.
11 Napier Crookenden, *Dropzone Normandy: The Story of the American and British Airborne Assaults on D-Day, 1944* (New York: Charles Scribner's Sons, 1976), 263.
12 North Nova Scotia Highlanders War Diary, June 1944, RG24, Library and Archives Canada, n.p.
13 Ibid.
14 Harold Bertrand Gonder, interview by Mark C. Hill, 23 July and 7, 8, 9 August 1985, University of Victoria Special Collections.
15 Reginald Roy, *Ready for the Fray: The History of the Canadian Scottish Regiment (Princess Mary's) 1920 to 1955* (Vancouver: Evergreen Press, 1958), 241–42.

16 Ibid.

17 Hubert Meyer, *The History of the 12. ss-Panzerdivision "Hitlerjugend"* (Winnipeg: J.J. Fedorowicz Publishing, 1994), 61.

18 Michael Reynolds, *Steel Inferno: 1 ss Panzer Corps in Normandy* (New York: Dell Publishing, 1997), 106.

19 Regina Rifles War Diary, June 1944, RG24, Library and Archives Canada, n.p.

20 Dave McIntosh, *High Blue Battle: The War Diary of No. 1 (401) Fighter Squadron, RCA F*(Toronto: Stoddart Publishing, 1990), 148.

21 Jean E. Portugal, *We Were There: The Navy, the Army and the RCAF—A Record for Canada*, vol. 7 (Shelburne, ON: The Battered Silicon Dispatch Box, 1998), 3277–78.

22 Ralph Bennett, *Ultra in the West: The Normandy Campaign, 1944–45* (London: Hutchinson & Co., 1979), 74.

23 Clarence R. Dunlap, interview by Chris Bell, 1, 10, 17 March and 21 April 1983, University of Victoria Special Collections.

24 Max Hastings, *Overlord: D-Day and the Battle For Normandy* (New York: Simon and Schuster, 1984), 174.

25 Bennett, 75.

26 Reynolds, 106–108.

18: ATTACK AT ONCE

1 Michael Reynolds, *Steel Inferno: 1 ss Panzer Corps in Normandy* (New York: Dell Publishing, 1997), 108.

2 Ibid.

3 Stormont, Dundas and Glengarry Highlanders War Diary, June 1944, RG24, Library and Archives Canada, n.p.

4 3rd Canadian Infantry Division GS War Diary, June 1944, Appendix Jacket No. 1 Message Log, RG24, Library and Archives Canada.

5 Ibid.

6 J. Allan Snowie, *Bloody Buron: The Battles of Buron Normandy—08 July 1944* (Erin, ON: The Boston Mills Press, 1984), 38.

7 Ibid.

8 Ibid., 39.

9 3rd Canadian Infantry Division GS War Diary, Message Log.

10 Snowie, 39.

11 Highland Light Infantry War Diary, June 1944, RG24, Library and Archives Canada, 15.

12 Michael R. McNorgan, "Black Sabbath for the First Hussars: Action at Le Mesnil Patry, 11 June 1944," *Fighting for Canada: Seven Battles, 1758–1945*, ed. Donald E. Graves (Toronto: Robin Brass Studio, 2000), 282.

13 2nd Canadian Armoured Brigade War Diary, June 1944, RG24, Library and Archives Canada, n.p.

14 3rd Canadian Infantry Division GS War Diary, Message Log.

15 2nd Canadian Armoured Brigade War Diary, n.p.

16 1st Hussars War Diary, June 1944, RG24, Library and Archives Canada, 6.

17 A. Brandon Conron, *A History of the First Hussars Regiment, 1856–1980* (n.p., 1981), 67.

18 Michael R. McNorgan, "Black Sabbath for the First Hussars: Action at Le Mesnil Patry, 11 June 1944," *Fighting for Canada: Seven Battles, 1758–1945,* ed. Donald E. Graves (Toronto: Robin Brass Studio, 2000), 281–282.

19 Jean E. Portugal, *We Were There: The Navy, the Army and the RCAF—A Record for Canada,* vol. 3 (Shelburne, ON: The Battered Silicon Dispatch Box, 1998), 1447.

20 2nd Canadian Armoured Brigade War Diary, n.p.

21 1st Hussars War Diary, 6.

22 Queen's Own Rifles War Diary, June 1944, RG24, Library and Archives Canada, n.p.

23 W.T. Barnard, *The Queen's Own Rifles of Canada, 1860–1960: One Hundred Years of Canada* (Don Mills, ON: The Ontario Publishing Company Limited, 1960), 201.

24 N.a., "Interview with Major J.H. Gordon, Queen's Own Rifles," Directorate of History, Department of National Defence, 2.

25 Portugal, *We Were There,* vol. 3, 1473.

26 N.a., *Vanguard: The Fort Garry Horse in the Second World War* (Doetincham, Holland: Uitgevers-Maatschappij, D. Misset, NV, n.d), 138.

27 Hubert Meyer, *The History of the 12. SS-Panzerdivision "Hitlerjugend"* (Winnipeg: J.J. Fedorowicz Publishing, 1994), 69.

28 Ibid.

29 N.a., "46th Royal Marine Commandos, 6–12 June 1944," PRO DEFE2/977 Public Records Office, London, n.p.

30 *Vanguard,* 139.

31 Fort Garry Horse War Diary, June 1944, RG24, Appendix No. 1, Library and Archives Canada, 6.

32 Portugal, *We Were There,* vol. 3, 1474.

33 *Vanguard,* 139.

34 Portugal, *We Were There,* vol. 3, 1747.

35 *Vanguard,* 139.

36 Portugal, *We Were There,* vol. 3, 1474–75.

37 *Vanguard,* 139–40.

38 Portugal, *We Were There,* vol. 3, 1475–76.

39 *Vanguard,* 140.

40 Meyer, 70.

41 *Vanguard,* 140.

42 *Vanguard,* 24.

43 Portugal, *We Were There*, vol. 3, 1476.
44 *Vanguard*, 24.
45 Portugal, *We Were There*, vol. 3, 1475.
46 *Vanguard*, 158.
47 "46th Royal Marine Commandos," n.p.
48 Meyer, 71.

19: WE'VE BEEN SUCKED IN

1 2nd Canadian Armoured Brigade War Diary, June 1944, RG24, Library and Archives Canada, n.p.
2 Michael R. McNorgan, "Black Sabbath for the First Hussars: Action at Le Mesnil Patry, 11 June 1944," *Fighting for Canada: Seven Battles, 1758–1945*, ed. Donald E. Graves (Toronto: Robin Brass Studio, 2000), 288.
3 2nd Canadian Armoured Brigade War Diary, n.p.
4 Ibid.
5 McNorgan, 288–89.
6 North Shore (New Brunswick) Regiment War Diary, June 1944, RG24, Appendix 6, Library and Archives Canada, n.p.
7 12th Field Regiment, RCA War Diary, June 1944, RG24, Library and Archives Canada, n.p.
8 1st Hussars War Diary, June 1944, RG24, Appendix 10: "Account of Personal Experiences in Action on Sun Jun 11-44 by Trooper I.O. Dodds," Library and Archives Canada, 1.
9 McNorgan, 294.
10 Hubert Meyer, *The History of the 12. SS-Panzerdivision "Hitlerjugend"* (Winnipeg: J.J. Fedorowicz Publishing, 1994), 67.
11 Bill McAndrew, Donald E. Graves, and Michael Whitby, *Normandy 1944: The Canadian Summer* (Montreal: Éditions Art Global, 1994), 62.
12 1st Hussars War Diary, June 1944, RG24, Library and Archives Canada, 6.
13 Jean E. Portugal, *We Were There: The Navy, the Army and the RCAF—A Record for Canada*, vol. 2 (Shelburne, ON: The Battered Silicon Dispatch Box, 1998), 655–58.
14 N.a., "Interview with Major J.H. Gordon, Queen's Own Rifles," Directorate of History, Department of National Defence, 2.
15 Roy Whitsed, *Canadians: A Battalion at War* (Mississauga, ON: Burlington Books, 1996), 202.
16 Ibid.
17 McNorgan, 295.
18 1st Hussars War Diary, "Account of Personal Experiences in Action on Sun Jun 11-44 by Trooper I.O. Dodds," 1.
19 Alex McKee, *Caen: Anvil of Victory* (London: Souvenir Press, 1964), 89.

20 Jim Simpson, interview by John Gregory Thompson, Windsor, ON, 13 September 2003.
21 Bill McCormick, interview by John Gregory Thompson, Galt, ON, 3 October 2003.
22 1st Hussars War Diary, "Account of Personal Experiences in Action on Sun Jun 11-44 by Trooper I.O. Dodds," 1.
23 McKee, 90.
24 McNorgan, 293.
25 A. Brandon Conron, *A History of the First Hussars Regiment, 1856–1980* (n.p., 1981), 68.
26 "Interview with Major J.H. Gordon," 2.
27 Conron, 69.
28 1st Hussars War Diary, "Account of Personal Experiences in Action on Sun Jun 11-44 by Trooper I.O. Dodds," 1.
29 McNorgan, 276.
30 Ibid.
31 Conron, 69.
32 Jack Martin, interview by John Gregory Thompson, Scarborough, ON, 1 October 2003.
33 Portugal, *We Were There*, vol. 2, 641–42.
34 McKee, 90.
35 Simpson interview.
36 Ibid.
37 Lieutenant R. Rae, "Special Report: Action at le Mesnil-Patry–11 June 44, Mortar Officer's Story," 145.2Q2011(4), Directorate of History, Department of National Defence, n.p.
38 Martin interview.
39 Whitsed, 203.
40 Rae, "Special Report, Action at le Mesnil-Patry–11 June 44, Results," n.p.
41 Portugal, *We Were There*, vol. 2, 658–59.
42 1st Hussars War Diary, "Account of Personal Experiences in Action on Sun Jun 11-44 by Trooper I.O. Dodds," 1–2.

20: GUESS WE GO

1 Hubert Meyer, *The History of the 12. ss-Panzerdivision "Hitlerjugend"* (Winnipeg: J.J. Fedorowicz Publishing, 1994), 67–68.
2 Ibid.
3 Michael R. McNorgan, "Black Sabbath for the First Hussars: Action at Le Mesnil Patry, 11 June 1944," *Fighting for Canada: Seven Battles, 1758–1945*, ed. Donald E. Graves (Toronto: Robin Brass Studio, 2000), 301.
4 Meyer, 68.

398 / HOLDING JUNO

5 Art Boyle, interview by John Gregory Thompson, London, ON, 30 September 2003.

6 Lieutenant R. Rae, "Special Report: Action at le Mesnil-Patry–11 June 44, Results," 145.2Q2011(4), Directorate of History, Department of National Defence, n.p.

7 Jean E. Portugal, *We Were There: The Navy, the Army and the RCAF—A Record for Canada*, vol. 2 (Shelburne, ON: The Battered Silicon Dispatch Box, 1998), 678.

8 Ibid., 679.

9 Ibid.

10 McNorgan, 304.

11 Ibid., 305.

12 Bill McCormick, interview by John Gregory Thompson, Galt, ON, 3 October 2003.

13 Ibid.

14 2nd Canadian Armoured Brigade War Diary, June 1944, RG24, Library and Archives Canada, n.p.

15 1st Hussars War Diary, June 1944, RG24, Library and Archives Canada, 7.

16 2nd Canadian Armoured Brigade War Diary, n.p.

17 1st Hussars War Diary, 7.

18 "1st Hussars Drive Into Ambush, Save Caen Hinge, in Saga of Sacrifice at Caen," *London Evening Free Press*, 9 September 1944, p. 1.

19 McNorgan, 305–306.

20 Portugal, *We Were There*, vol. 2, 641–42.

21 1st Hussars War Diary, 7.

22 Portugal, *We Were There*, vol. 3, 1448.

23 Jim Simpson, interview by John Gregory Thompson, Windsor, ON, 13 September 2003.

24 Alex McKee, *Caen: Anvil of Victory* (London: Souvenir Press, 1964), 92.

25 A. Brandon Conron, *A History of the First Hussars Regiment, 1856–1980* (n.p., 1981), 73.

26 Larry Allen, "WWII Diary of L. Allen—The Story of a D-Day Soldier," 1st Hussars Regimental Museum.

27 McCormick interview.

28 Jack Martin, interview by John Gregory Thompson, Scarborough, ON, 1 October 2003.

29 McNorgan, 307–308.

30 Ibid., 308.

31 Jack Martin interview.

32 Portugal, *We Were There*, vol. 2, 683.

33 John Marteinson and Michael R. McNorgan, *The Royal Canadian*

Armoured Corps: An Illustrated History (Toronto: Robin Brass Studio, 2000), 247.

34 Simpson interview.

21: VIVE LE CANADA!

1 1st Hussars War Diary, June 1944, RG24, Appendix 10: "Account of Personal Experiences in Action on Sun Jun 11-44 by Trooper I.O. Dodds," Library and Archives Canada, 2–3.

2 Larry Allen, "WWII Diary of L. Allen—The Story of a D-Day Soldier," 1st Hussars Regimental Museum.

3 Roy Whitsed, *Canadians: A Battalion at War* (Mississauga, ON: Burlington Books, 1996), 203–205.

4 Howard Margolian, *Conduct Unbecoming: The Story of the Murder of Canadian Prisoners of War in Normandy* (Toronto: University of Toronto Press, 1998), 112–16.

5 Jean E. Portugal, *We Were There: The Navy, the Army and the RCAF—A Record for Canada*, vol. 2 (Shelburne, ON: The Battered Silicon Dispatch Box, 1998), 1024–25.

6 Col. C.P. Stacey, *The Victory Campaign: The Operations in North-West Europe, 1944–1945*, vol. 3 (Ottawa: Queen's Printer, 1960), 140.

7 W.T. Barnard, *The Queen's Own Rifles of Canada, 1860–1960: One Hundred Years of Canada* (Don Mills, ON: The Ontario Publishing Co., 1960), 202–203.

8 Hubert Meyer, *The History of the 12. SS-Panzerdivision "Hitlerjugend"* (Winnipeg: J.J. Fedorowicz Publishing, 1994), 69.

9 1st Hussars War Diary, n.p.

10 Meyer, 69.

11 Portugal, *We Were There*, vol. 2, 683.

12 A. Brandon Conron, *A History of the First Hussars Regiment, 1856–1980* (n.p., 1981), 74.

13 Barnard, 203.

14 Michael Reynolds, *Steel Inferno: 1 SS Panzer Corps in Normandy* (New York: Dell Publishing, 1997), 106.

15 Dave Kingston, interview by John Gregory Thompson, Mississauga, ON, 10 September 2003.

16 Charles Martin, *Battle Diary: From D-Day and Normandy to the Zuider Zee* (Toronto: Dundurn Press, 1994), 22–23.

17 Jim McCullough, interview by John Gregory Thompson, Loretto, ON, 9 September 2003.

18 Jim Simpson, interview by John Gregory Thompson, Windsor, ON, 13 September 2003.

19 Martin, 23.
20 Portugal, *We Were There*, vol. 5, 2318–19.
21 Ibid., 2318.
22 Jacques Henry, *La Normandie en flammes: journal de guerre du capitaine Gérard Leroux, officier d'intelligence au Régiment de la Chaudière*, trans. Alex McQuarrie (Conde-sur-Noireau: C. Corlet, 1984), 397–98.
23 Le Régiment de la Chaudière War Diary, June 1944, RG24, Library and Archives Canada, 378.
24 Max Hastings, *Overlord: D-Day and the Battle For Normandy* (New York: Simon and Schuster, 1984), 130.
25 Napier Crookenden, *Dropzone Normandy: The Story of the American and British Airborne Assault on D-Day 1944* (New York: Charles Scribner's Sons, 1976), 267.
26 John R. Madden, recorded recollections, 1987, University of Victoria Special Collections.
27 Dan Hartigan, *A Rising of Courage: Canada's Paratroops in the Liberation of Normandy* (Calgary: Drop Zone Publishers, 2000), 232.
28 Madden recorded recollections.
29 Ibid.
30 Hartigan, 234.
31 Ibid., 234–35.
32 Ibid., 235–37.
33 Ibid., 239.
34 Madden recorded recollections.
35 Portugal, *We Were There*, vol. 5, 857–59.
36 Ibid.
37 Stacey, 140.
38 Ibid.

BOOKS

Barnard, W.T. *The Queen's Own Rifles of Canada, 1860–1960: One Hundred Years of Canada*. Don Mills: Ontario Publishing Co., 1960.

Battledress Ballads: 3 Canadian Infantry Division. N.p., n.d.

Bennett, Ralph. *Ultra in the West: The Normandy Campaign*. London: Hutchinson & Co., 1979.

Bird, Will R. *North Shore (New Brunswick) Regiment*. Fredericton: Brunswick Press, 1963.

———*No Retreating Footsteps: The Story of the North Nova Scotia Highlanders*. Hantsport, NS: Lancelot Press, 1983.

———*The Two Jacks: The Amazing Adventures of Major Jack M. Veness and Major Jack L. Fairweather*. Toronto: The Ryerson Press, 1954.

Boss, William. *Up the Glens: Stormont, Dundas and Glengarry Highlanders, 1783–1994*. 2nd ed. Cornwall, ON: Old Book Store, 1995.

Brown, Gordon and Terry Copp. *Look to Your Front... Regina Rifles: A Regiment at War, 1944–45*. Waterloo, ON: Laurier Centre Military Strategic Disarmament Studies, 2001.

Campbell, Ian J. *Murder at the Abbaye: The Story of Twenty Canadian Soldiers Murdered in the Abbaye d'Ardenne*. Don Mills, ON: Oxford University Press, 1996.

Castonguay, Jacques and Armand Ross. *Le Régiment de la Chaudière*. Lévis, PQ: n.p., 1983.

Conron, A. Brandon. *A History of the First Hussars Regiment, 1856–1980*. N.p., 1981.

Copp, Terry. *Fields of Fire: The Canadians in Normandy*. Toronto: University of Toronto Press, 2003.

Copp, Terry and William McAndrew. *Battle Exhaustion*. Montreal: McGill-Queen's University Press, 1990.

Copp, Terry and Robert Vogel. *Maple Leaf Route: Caen*. Alma, ON: Maple Leaf Route, 1983.

Crookenden, Napier. *Dropzone Normandy: The Story of the American and British Airborne Assault on D-Day 1944*. New York: Charles Scribner's Sons, 1976.

D'Este, Carlo. *Decision in Normandy: The Unwritten Story of Montgomery and the Allied Campaign*. London: Penguin Books, 1994.

1st Battalion, The Highland Light Infantry of Canada: 1940–1945. Galt, ON: Highland Light Infantry of Canada Assoc., 1951.

Forty, George. *British Army Handbook: 1939–1945.* Phoenix Mill, England: Sutton Publishing, 1998.

Foster, Tony. *Meeting of Generals.* Agincourt, ON: Methuen, 1986.

Freasby, W.R., ed., *Official History of the Canadian Medical Services, 1939–1945, Vol. 1: Organization and Campaigns.* Ottawa: Queen's Printer, 1956.

——. *Official History of the Canadian Medical Services, 1939–1945, Vol. 2: Clinical Subjects.* Ottawa: Queen's Printer, 1953.

Gardiner, Robert, ed. *Conway's All the World's Fighting Ships: 1922–1944.* London: Conway Marine Press, 1980.

Grant, Christopher. *An Illustrated Data Guide to World War II Bombers.* St. Catharines, ON: Vanwell Books, 1997.

Graves, Donald E., ed. *Fighting for Canada: Seven Battles, 1758–1945.* Toronto: Robin Brass Studio, 2000.

Greenhous, Brereton and Stephen Harris, et. al. *The Crucible of War, 1939–1945: The Official History of the Royal Canadian Air Force, Vol. 3.* Toronto: University of Toronto Press, 1995.

Harrison, Gordon A. *Cross Channel Attack.* Washington: Center of Military History, 1951.

Hartigan, Dan. *A Rising of Courage: Canada's Paratroops in the Liberation of Normandy.* Calgary: Drop Zone Publishers, 2000.

Hastings, Max. *Overlord: D-Day and the Battle of Normandy.* New York: Simon & Schuster, 1984.

Hickey, R.M. *The Scarlet Dawn.* Campbellton, NB: Tribune Publishers, 1949.

Henry, Jacques. *La Normandie en flammes: journal de guerre du capitaine Gérard Leroux, officier d'intelligence au Régiment de la Chaudière.* Conde-sur-Noireau: C. Corlet, 1984.

Isby, David C., ed. *Fighting the Invasion: The German Army at D-Day.* London: Greenhill Books, 2000.

Jackson, H.M. *The Sherbrooke Regiment (12th Armoured Regiment).* N.p., 1958.

Kuppers, Alex, ed. *Perspectives.* Royal Winnipeg Rifles Assoc., British Columbia Branch, 2003.

Law, C. Anthony. *White Plumes Astern: The Short, Daring Life of Canada's MTB Flotilla.* Halifax: Nimbus Publishing, 1989.

Liddell Hart, B.H. *History of the Second World War.* New York: G.P. Putnam's Sons, 1970.

Listen to Us: Aircrew Memories. Victoria, BC: The Victoria Publishing Co., 1997.

Luck, Hans von. *Panzer Grenadier: The Memoirs of Colonel Hans von Luck.* Westport, CT: Praeger Publishers, 1989.

Luxton, Eric, ed. *1st Battalion, The Regina Rifles Regiment, 1939–1946.* Regina: The Regiment, 1946.

McAndrew, Bill, Donald Graves, and Michael Whitby. *Normandy 1944: The Canadian Summer*. Montreal: Éditions Art Global, 1994.

McIntosh, Dave. *High Blue Battle: The War Diary of No. 1 (401) Fighter Squadron, RCAF*. Toronto: McClelland and Stewart, 1961.

McKee, Alex. *Caen: Anvil of Victory*. London: Souvenir Press, 1964.

Man, John. *The D-Day Atlas: The Definitive Account of the Allied Invasion of Normandy*. New York: Facts on File, 1994.

Margolian, Howard. *Conduct Unbecoming: The Story of the Murder of Canadian Prisoners of War in Normandy*. Toronto: University of Toronto Press, 1998.

Marteinson, John and Michael R. McNorgan. *The Royal Canadian Armoured Corps: An Illustrated History*. Toronto: Robin Brass Studio, 2000.

Martin, Charles Cromwell. *Battle Diary: From D-Day and Normandy to the Zuider Zee*. Toronto: Dundurn Press, 1994.

Mein, Stewart A.G. *Up the Johns! The Story of the Royal Regina Rifles*. North Battleford, SK: Turner-Warwick Publications, 1992.

Meyer, Hubert. *The History of the 12. SS-Panzerdivision "Hilterjugend."* Winnipeg: J.J. Fedorowicz Publishing, 1994.

Meyer, Kurt. *Grenadier*. Winnipeg: J.J. Fedorowicz, 1994.

Montgomery, Bernard Law. *The Memoirs of Field Marshal The Viscount Montgomery of Alamein, K.G.* London: Collins, 1958.

Nicholson, G.W.L. *The Gunners of Canada, Vol. 2*. Toronto: McClelland & Stewart, 1972.

Nolan, Brian. *Airborne: The Heroic Story of the 1st Canadian Parachute Battalion in the Second World War*. Toronto: Lester Publishing, 1995.

Portugal, Jean E. *We Were There: The Navy, the Army and the RCAF—A Record for Canada. Vol. 1–7*. Shelburne, ON: The Battered Silicon Dispatch Box, 1998.

Reynolds, Michael. *Steel Inferno: I SS Panzer Corps in Normandy*. New York: Dell Publishing, 1997.

Ross, Richard M. *The History of the 1st Battalion Cameron Highlanders of Ottawa (M G)*. N.p, n.d.

Roy, Reginald H. *1944: The Canadians in Normandy*. Toronto: MacMillan of Canada, 1984.

——*Ready for the Fray: The History of the Canadian Scottish Regiment (Princess Mary's), 1920 to 1955*. Vancouver: Evergreen Press, 1958.

Ruffee, G.E.M. *The History of the 14 Field Regiment Royal Canadian Artillery, 1940–1945*. Amsterdam: Wereldbibliotheek, NV, 1945.

Schofield, B.B. *Operation Neptune*. London: Ian Allan, 1974.

Schull, Joseph. *Far Distant Ships: An Official Account of Canadian Naval Operations in World War II*. Toronto: Stoddart Publishing, 1991.

Service, G.T. *The Gate: A History of the Fort Garry Horse*. Calgary: n.p., 1971.

Snowie, J. Allan. *Bloody Buron: The Battles of Buron Normandy—08 July 1944*. Erin, ON: The Boston Mills Press, 1984.

Stacey, C.P. *The Victory Campaign: The Operations in North-West Europe, 1944–1945*. Vol. 2. Ottawa: Queen's Printer, 1960.

Tascona, Bruce and Eric Wells. *Little Black Devils: A History of the Royal Winnipeg Rifles*. Winnipeg: Frye Publishing, 1983.

Vanguard: The Fort Garry Horse in the Second World War. Doetincham, Holland: Uitgevers-Maatschappij, C. Misset, NV, n.d.

Vokes, Chris. *Vokes: My Story*. Ottawa: Gallery, 1985.

Warlimont, Walter. *Inside Hitler's Headquarters, 1939–45*. New York: Frederick A. Praeger, 1964.

Warren, Arnold. *Wait for the Waggon: The Story of the Royal Canadian Army Service Corps*. Toronto: McClelland and Stewart, 1961.

Whitsed, Roy. *Canadians: A Battalion at War*. Mississauga, ON: Burlington Books, 1996.

Willes, John A. *Out of the Clouds: The History of the 1st Canadian Parachute Battalion*. Port Perry, ON: Port Perry Printing, 1995.

Wilmot, Chester. *The Struggle for Europe*. London: Collins, 1952.

MAGAZINES, NEWSPAPERS, ARTICLES

"1st Hussars Drive Into Ambush, Save Caen Hinge, in Saga of Sacrifice at Caen." *London Evening Free Press* 9 September 1944: 1.

Foulds, Tony. "In Support of the Canadians: A British Anti-Tank Regiment's First Five Weeks in Normandy." *Canadian Military History* Spring 1998: 71–78.

Haller, Oliver. "The Defeat of the 12th ss, 7–10 June 1944." *Canadian Military History* Spring 1996: 8–25.

Learment, Don. "Soldier, POW, Partisan: My Experiences During the Battle of France, June–September 1944." *Canadian Military History* Spring 2000: 91–104.

Whitby, Michael. "Masters of the Channel Night: The 10th Destroyer Flotilla's Victory Off Ile De Batz, 9 June 1944." *Canadian Military History* vol. 2, no. 1: 5–14.

UNPUBLISHED MATERIALS

Allen, L. "WWII Diary of L. Allen—The Story of a D-Day Soldier," 1st Hussars Regimental Museum.

Andrews, J.J. (Major). "Battle Narrative–D Day and the Counter Attack at Putot-en-Bessin." 145.2C4(D5), Directorate of History, Department of National Defence.

Boire, Michael (Major). "Notes on RMC Graduates." Correspondence with author. October 2004.

Cabeldu, F.N. (Lieutenant Colonel). "Battle Narrative of the Normandy Assault and First Counter-Attack." 145.2C4013(D2), Directorate of History, Department of National Defence.

———. "Narrative of Normandy Assault." 145.2C4013(D1), Directorate of History, Department of National Defence.

Cameron Highlanders of Ottawa (MG) War Diary, June 1944. RG24, Library and Archives Canada.

"Campaign in France, 1944: Answers by General Blumentritt to questions submitted by Chester Wilmot," Reginald Roy Collection, University of Victoria Special Collections.

"Canadian Operations in North-West Europe, August 1944, Extracts from Memoranda (Series 7)," Reginald Roy Collection, University of Victoria Special Collections.

"Canadian Operations in North-West Europe, June 1944, Extracts from Memoranda (Series 1)." 018(D13), Directorate of History, Department of National Defence.

"Canadian Parachute Battalion Correspondence re: Ops 1st Cdn. Para. Bn. from various officers (Cunningham, Hanson, Bradbrooke)." 145.4013(D5), Directorate of History, Department of National Defence.

Canadian Scottish Regiment, 1st Battalion War Diary, June 1944. RG24, Library and Archives Canada.

"Combat Lessons—7 CDN INF BDE." RG24, Library and Archives Canada.

Crerar Papers, "Appointment and Promotions-Officers, Period Feb 1942 to Jan. 1943." MG30 E157 Vol.5, Library and Archives Canada.

Crofton, D.G. (Major). "'C' Company–Landing on 'D' Day." 145.2C4013(D4), Directorate of History, Department of National Defence.

"Department of National Defence (Army) Public Relations–Promoted Brigadier," Bulletin. Directorate of History, n.p.

"Descriptive Record," Melville Burgoyne Kennedy Gordon fonds. MG30-E367, Library and Archives Canada.

8th Canadian Infantry Brigade War Diary, June 1944. RG24, Library and Archives Canada.

5th Canadian Field Company, Royal Canadian Engineers War Diary, June 1944. RG24, Library and Archives Canada.

1st Canadian Parachute Battalion War Diary, June 1944. RG24, Library and Archives Canada.

1st Hussars (6th Canadian Armoured Regiment) War Diary, June 1944. RG24, Library and Archives Canada.

Fort Garry Horse (10th Canadian Armoured Regiment) War Diary, June 1944. RG24, Library and Archives Canada.

Foster, H.W. (Brigadier), "7 CIB—Combat Lessons." RG24, Library and Archives Canada.

46th Royal Marine Commandos, 6–12 June 1944. PRO DEFE2/977, Public Records Office, London.

14th Field Regiment, Royal Canadian Artillery War Diary, June 1944. RG24, Library and Archives Canada.

Granatstein Papers. York University Archives and Special Collections, Scott Library.

Greenblatt, Joseph. "Correspondence." Archival Collection CN: 19990209–002, DOCS MNU 58A I 155.3-6, Canadian War Museum.

Highland Light Infantry of Canada War Diary, June 1944. RG24, Library and Archives Canada.

"Interview with Major J.H. Gordon, Queen's Own Rifles 8Bde 3 Canadian Division." Directorate of History, Department of National Defence.

Le Régiment de la Chaudière War Diary, June 1944. RG24, Library and Archives Canada.

MacEwan, G.T. (Major), "Battle Narrative: D-Day and the Counter-Attack on Putot-en-Bessin." 145.2C4013(D3), Directorate of History, Department of National Defence.

Mahon, George. "Letter to Lt. Col. Gordon, June 25 1944." Melville Burgoyne Kennedy Gordon fonds. MG30-E367, vol. I, Personal Correspondence, Library and Archives Canada.

Martin, J.R. (Major). "Report No. 147 Historical Section Canadian Military Headquarters: Part One: The Assault and Subsequent Operations of 3 Cdn Inf Div and 2 Cdn Armd Bde, 6–30 Jun 44–N.W. Europe." 3 December 1945. Directorate of History, Department of National Defence.

"Memorandum of Interview with CSM Belton, B Coy, R Wpg Rif, 14 Jun 44." 145.2R20011(1), Directorate of History, Department of National Defence.

"Memorandum of Interview with Brig. K.G. Blackader, Comd 8 Cdn Inf Bde by Historical Officer, 24 Jun 44." 018(D13), Directorate of History, Department of National Defence.

"Memorandum of Interview with Brig. D.G. Cunningham, Comd 9 Cdn Inf Bde by Historical Officer, 26 Jun 44." RG24, Library and Archives Canada.

"Memorandum of Interview with Brig. H.W. Foster, Comd 7 Cdn Inf Bde 22 Jun 44: 7 Cdn Inf Bde in the Assault and the Achievement of its Objective." 018(D13), Directorate of History, Department of National Defence.

"Memorandum of Interview with Lt. Col. F.M. Matheson, OC, Regina Rifles by Historical Officer, 24 Jun 44." 145.2R11011(4), Directorate of History, Department of National Defence.

"Memorandum of Interviews with Capt (A/Maj) A.J. Wilson, Nth NS Highrs, 18 Jun 44 and Capt (A/Maj) E.S. Gray, Nth NS Highrs, 29 Jun 44 by Historical Officer: The Engagement at Buron and Authie, 7 Jun 44." 145.2N20011(D3), Directorate of History, Department of National Defence.

Nicholson, G.W.L. (Major). "Report No. 139 Historical Section Canadian
    Military Headquarters: The 1st Canadian Parachute Battalion in France,
    6 June–6 September 1944." 7 July 1945. Directorate of History,
    Department of National Defence.
19th Field Regiment, Royal Canadian Artillery War Diary, June 1944. RG24,
    Library and Archives Canada.
9th Canadian Infantry Brigade War Diary, June 1944. RG24, Library and
    Archives Canada.
North Nova Scotia Highlanders War Diary, June 1944. RG24, Library and
    Archives Canada.
North Shore (New Brunswick) Regiment War Diary, June 1944. RG24, Library
    and Archives Canada.
O'Keefe, David. "Notes on Kenneth Gault Blackader," Black Watch Regimental
    Museum and Archives. In possession of author.
Rae, R. (Lieutenant). "Special Report: Action at le Mesnil-Patry–11 June 44,
    Mortar Officer's Story." 145.2Q2011(4), Directorate of History, Department
    of National Defence.
Ramsay, P.F. (Captain). "Battle Narrative, 'B' Coy, 1 C. Scot R." 145.2C4(D6),
    Directorate of History, Department of National Defence.
The Recollections of the Regina Rifles: N.W. Europe World War 2, June 6,
    1944–May 8, 1945. Looseleaf folder in possession of author.
Roy, Reginald (Lieutenant). "1 Canadian Parachute Battalion in Normandy:
    Historical Sketch." 25 September 1952. 145 4.013(D4), Directorate of
    History, Department of National Defence.
"The Royal Canadian Navy's Part in the Invasion." Directorate of History,
    Department of National Defence.
"The Royal Canadian Navy's Part in the Invasion of Northern
    France–Operation 'Overlord' (A first narrative prepared by the RCN
    Historical Section–London)," Draft 'A', Narrative 'B', vol. 1. D779G7W3 v.5,
    Directorate of History, Department of National Defence.
"Royal Military College Club of Canada Report–D.G. Cunningham." In
    possession of author.
Royal Regina Rifles Regiment, 1st Battalion War Diary, June 1944. RG24, vol.
    15198, Library and Archives Canada.
Royal Winnipeg Rifles War Diary, June 1944. RG24, Library and Archives
    Canada.
Seaborn, Robert Lowder. Diary, Robert Lowder Seaborn and family. MG31 F 18,
    vols. 2–6, Library and Archives Canada.
"Second Canadian Armoured Brigade: Operation Overlord–The Assault on
    the Beaches of Normandy, 6–11 June 1944–Sequence of Events and
    Lessons Arising Therefrom," vol. 10455. RG24, Library and Archives
    Canada.

2nd Canadian Armoured Brigade War Diary, June 1944. RG24, Library and Archives Canada.

7th Canadian Infantry Brigade War Diary, June 1944. RG24, Library and Archives Canada.

The Sherbrooke Fusiliers Regiment (27th Canadian Armoured Regiment) War Diary, June 1944. RG24, Library and Archives Canada.

"Special Interrogation Report, Brigadefuhrer Kurt Meyer, Comd 12 SS PZ DIV 'Hitler Jugend' (6 June 1944–25 Aug 1944)." Reginald Roy Collection, University of Victoria Special Collections.

Stormont, Dundas and Glengarry Highlanders War Diary, June 1944. RG24, Library and Archives Canada.

3rd Canadian Anti-Tank Regiment War Diary, June 1944. RG24, Library and Archives Canada.

3rd Canadian Infantry Division GS War Diary, June 1944. RG24, Library and Archives Canada.

13th Field Regiment, Royal Canadian Artillery War Diary, June 1944. RG24, Library and Archives Canada.

12th Field Regiment, Royal Canadian Artillery War Diary, June 1944. RG24, Library and Archives Canada.

"War Diary Extracts, Vol. 19: HQ RCE 3 Cdn Inf Div, War Diary–Jun 44." Reginald Roy Collection, University of Victoria Special Collections.

Whitby, Michael. "RCAF Strength and Casualties During Normandy Campaign," 8 April 1994. Directorate of History, Department of National Defence.

Wightman, Major C.M. (Lieutenant Colonel). "Battle Narrative: Putot En Bessin Counter Attack–June 8, 1944 and the Move to Rots." 145.2C(D4), Directorate of History, Department of National Defence.

———"Personal Diary." Reginald Roy Collection, University of Victoria Special Collections.

INTERVIEWS AND CORRESPONDENCE

Andrews, Joseph James. Interview by Cameron Falconer. Victoria, BC. 8 March 1983. University of Victoria Special Collections.

Bateman, Merritt Hayes. Interview by Tom Torrie. Sidney, BC. 28 May 1987. University of Victoria Special Collections.

Bettridge, Bill. Interview by John G. Thompson. Brampton, ON. 14 October 2003.

Boyle, Art. Interview by John G. Thompson. London, ON. 30 September 2003.

Butters, Thomas William Lowell. Interview by Tom Torrie. Victoria, BC. 19 August 1987. University of Victoria Special Collections.

Byrne, Jack. Interview by John G. Thompson. St. Joseph, ON. 10 October 2003.

Cheney, Don. Canadian War Museum Archives.

Chevalier, Roger. Interview by author. Courseulles-sur-Mer. 23 May 2003.

Corry, Geoffrey D. Interview by Tom Torrie. Victoria, BC. 12 August 1987. University of Victoria Special Collections.

Côté, Ernest. Interview by Michael Boire. Ottawa. 14 November 2003.

Daubs, Jack. Interview by John G. Thompson. London, ON. 9 October 2003.

Dunlap, Clarence. Interview by Chris Bell. Victoria, BC. 1, 10, 17 March and 21 April 1983. University of Victoria Special Collections.

Eckenfelder, George V. Interview by Tom Torrie. Victoria, BC. 7 August 1987. University of Victoria Special Collections.

Fulton, Lochie. Interview by Ken MacLeod. Victoria, BC. 9 February 1988.

Gonder, Harold Bertram. Interview by Mark C. Hill. Victoria, BC. 23 July and 7, 8, 9 August 1985. University of Victoria Special Collections.

Hall, A.C. Vassar. Interview by Chris D. Main. Victoria, BC. 7, 11, 15 May 1979. University of Victoria Special Collections.

Jackson, Rolph. Interview by John G. Thompson. Toronto. 2 September 2003.

Kingston, Dave. Interview by John G. Thompson. Mississauga, ON. 10 September 2003.

Learment, Don. Interview by John G. Thompson. Guelph, ON. 21 November 2003.

McCormick, Bill. Interview by John G. Thompson. Galt, ON. 3 October 2003.

McCormick, Bill. Telephone interview by John G. Thompson. Galt, ON. 14 February 2004.

McCullough, Jim. Interview by John G. Thompson. Loretto, ON. 9 September 2003.

Madden, John R. 1987. Recorded recollections. University of Victoria Special Collections.

Martin, Jack. Interview by John G. Thompson. Scarborough, ON. 1 October 2003.

Maxwell, Gordon. Interview by Ken MacLeod. Vancouver, BC. September 1997.

Mingay, Donald. Interview by Michael Boire. Collingwood, ON. November 2003.

Moore, Ken. Interview by author. Esquimalt, BC. 15 May 2004.

Parks, Jim. Interview by Ken MacLeod. Vancouver, BC. November 1997.

Plows, Arthur Howard. Interview by Chris D. Main. Victoria, BC. 18, 31 August 1978. University of Victoria Special Collections.

Ryan, Joe. Interview by John G. Thompson. Cobourg, ON. 6 November 2003.

Seaborn, Robert Lowder. Interview by Cameron Falconer. Victoria, BC. 23 February 1983. University of Victoria Special Collections.

Simpson, Jim. Interview by John G. Thompson. Windsor, ON. 13 September 2003.

Wightman, Cyrill Merrott. Interview by Cameron Falconer. Victoria, BC. 8 February 1983. University of Victoria Special Collections.

GENERAL INDEX

Ranks given for individuals are highest attained as of June 12, 1944

INDEX OF FORMATIONS, UNITS, AND CORPS

ABOUT THE AUTHOR

MARK ZUEHLKE'S critically acclaimed *Juno Beach: Canada's D-Day Victory: June 6, 1944,* and trilogy about Canada's World War II Italian Campaign—*Ortona: Canada's Epic World War II Battle, The Liri Valley: Canada's World War II Breakthrough to Rome,* and *The Gothic Line: Canada's Month of Hell in World War II Italy*—have established him as the nation's leading writer of popular military history. He is also the author of *The Canadian Military Atlas: The Nation's Battlefields from the French and Indian Wars to Kosovo, The Gallant Cause: Canadians in the Spanish Civil War, 1936–1939,* and *Scoundrels, Dreamers, and Second Sons: British Remittance Men in the Canadian West. Juno Beach* and *Holding Juno* are the first two volumes in a series that will trace the Canadian role throughout the Normandy Campaign.

Also a novelist, he is the author of the popular Elias McCann series, which follows the misadventures and investigations of a community coroner in Tofino, British Columbia. The first in this series, *Hands Like Clouds,* won the Crime Writers of Canada Arthur Ellis Award for Best First Novel. It was followed by *Carry Tiger to Mountain* and, most recently, *Sweep Lotus.*

Zuehlke lives in Victoria, British Columbia, where, when not writing, he enjoys backpacking, cycling, kayaking, cooking Italian food, and gardening.